THE "HOW TO" GRANTS MANUAL

THE "HOW TO" GRANTS MANUAL

Successful Grantseeking Techniques for Obtaining Public and Private Grants

Eighth Edition

David G. Bauer

ROWMAN & LITTLEFIELD
Lanham • Boulder • New York • London

Published by Rowman & Littlefield
A wholly owned subsidiary of The Rowman & Littlefield Publishing Group, Inc.
4501 Forbes Boulevard, Suite 200, Lanham, Maryland 20706
www.rowman.com

Unit A, Whitacre Mews, 26-34 Stannary Street, London SE11 4AB

British Library Cataloguing in Publication Information Available

Library of Congress Cataloging-in-Publication Data

Bauer, David G.
  The "how to" grants manual : successful grantseeking techniques for obtaining
public and private grants / David G. Bauer. - Eighth edition.
     pages cm
  Includes bibliographical references and index.
  ISBN 978-1-4758-1010-3 (hardcover) — ISBN 978-1-4758-1011-0 (e-book)
1. Fund raising. 2. Grants-in-aid. 3. Nonprofit organizations. I. Title.
  HG177.B38 2015
  658.15'224—dc23

                                                                    2014046455

Contents

Part 2: Public/Government Funding Opportunities

Part 3: Private/Foundation Funding Opportunities

Part 4: Private/Corporate Funding Opportunities

Exhibits, Figures, and Tables

Exhibits

Figures

Tables

Introduction

MUCH HAS CHANGED IN THE GRANTS MARKETPLACE since the last edition of *The "How To" Grants Manual* and yet much has remained the same. For example, over the span of my career I have surveyed over forty thousand of my seminar participants and found that the main factors that predisposed proposal rejection forty-five years ago are still at work today. These include:

- initiating the proposal development process at the last minute
- lacking knowledge about the prospective grantor
- focusing on what the proposal developer or the prospective grantee wants as opposed to the grantor's agenda

In my effort to understand how grantseekers view my proactive grantseeking system, I have augmented my seminars with one-on-one hourly consultations every ninety days for one year with staff and faculty members from various institutions. The purpose of these meetings is to help these individuals develop and implement grants strategies aimed at improving their grants success and coaching them toward their personal career goals. These consultations have grown into intensive fellowship programs at colleges and universities throughout the United States.

The opportunity to work intensively with these fellows has afforded me a unique perspective. Most importantly, I have learned more about the world that you, the grantseeker, operate within and how difficult it is to incorporate proactive grantseeking into your proposal development behavior. Secondly, the experience has provided me with an exceptional learning opportunity that spans the majority of federal granting agencies and hundreds of granting programs from both the public and private grants marketplaces. Having to individualize grants' strategies for hundreds of fellows from many different disciplines has provided me with more experience than I would have ever gained if I had to rely solely on my limited experience in my own research field.

While most of this intensive work with fellows has occurred in the university setting, my fellows have had to partner on proposals with many nonprofit groups to obtain access to subjects, implement model projects, and evaluate effectiveness. The results of this new experience has had a transformative effect on me, how I teach, and the way in which I created this eighth edition of *The "How To" Grants Manual*.

The genesis of the first edition of *The "How To" Grants Manual* was based on my experience with grant-funded programs for primary and secondary education and drug and alcohol abuse prevention. Then, as director of a university research office, my experience was broadened to include higher education and diverse grant- and research-related projects. I was also fortunate enough to have the opportunity to develop and conduct grant training programs for major nonprofit organizations such as Girl Scouts of the USA, 4-H, Camp Fire, Boys & Girls Clubs of America, and the YMCA. While working with these organizations, I brainstormed problem areas to expand their grants quest and this certainly helped me to develop a wider grants perspective. Even though these experiences were rewarding, they paled by comparison to what I learned through my grants fellowship programs. Instead of being in front of the room and telling participants to do it this way in a one- or two-day grants seminar, the fellowship programs forced me to sit down with my fellows week in and week out and live through each of the prescriptive steps and techniques contained in this book.

What I realized quickly is that the one constant that has remained the dominant theme in my forty-five-year career in this field is the pressure of proposal deadlines and the need to make time to prepare a grant-winning proposal. While technology has provided for faster and better databases and grant searches, electronic proposal submittal, e-mail, and Skype, it seems as though the world turns even faster now and that we are more time handicapped by our texting and Facebooking. Trying to be a proactive rather than a reactive grantseeker is getting even more difficult. Toward dealing with this problem, I have expanded the chapter on time management and also encourage you throughout the book to develop and adhere to a grants plan for success.

Effective grantseekers must stay focused, have priorities, and make difficult decisions concerning their time allocation. What's difficult for most grantseekers is that to be successful they must proactively anticipate a stressful situation (a grant proposal deadline) and approach it early. They have to find a way to take time away from today's pressing problems and employ deferred gratification. The fact of the matter is that the prize of a funded proposal and what it can do for your career and organization is more important than many of the things you will do today that depletes all of your time. Unfortunately, we are all programmed and reinforced to seek instant gratification. But to be successful in grantseeking, you must think about the grant strategies you can do today, ten months prior to the deadline!

The most rewarding part of my grants coaching has been watching how a funded proposal impacts one's career. Fellows have thanked me and clients have given me plaques in appreciation of how this intensive one-on-one consulting has reaped benefits to their organization such as increased indirect costs and enhanced prestige. In reality, I really did not do much more than help them keep their eyes on the prize and follow the proactive grant strategies contained in this book.

I am still convinced that even without a grants coach of your own, you can develop a proactive grants plan and make these strategies work for you. Procuring a funded grant does not take luck. It takes fortitude and allocating time to your career priorities. May your proactive grantseeking pay off for you and your organization.

Part 1

GETTING READY TO SEEK GRANT SUPPORT FOR YOU AND YOUR ORGANIZATION

1

Grantseeking Pitfalls and Potential Hazards

T HE FAST PACE OF OUR PROFESSIONAL LIVES and, not so coincidentally, advances in electronic technology have helped sustain two critical issues that continue to impact the grants marketplace. These include:

- deceitful grant schemes that employ the Internet to lure the uninitiated grantseeker to fall for unproductive or just plain false promises for fast and efficient grants success
- hiring a grant writer because we are short of time and think we can pay a consultant to embrace our idea, find a grantor, and create a proposal that we can take over once the money comes in

I have always maintained the utmost respect for the theoretical basis for the creation of the grants mechanism. Whether it is a wealthy individual who creates a foundation, a corporation that wants to further research in the marketplace, or a government granting agency that announces a funding opportunity, you cannot top the collective genius and creativity of mankind to propose solutions, initiate research, and implement model or demonstration projects that will increase our knowledge and impact a problem.

This book is dedicated to the grants process that has brought about great innovations in research and social advances in health, education, and society as a whole. But when there is $500 billion available in federal grants and another $66.84 billion in foundation and corporate grants, there will always be a small percentage of individuals who want to subvert the grants mechanism for their own selfish purposes. Unfortunately, fraud is alive and flourishing in the grants marketplace. We must be aware of it and be willing to alert authorities when we see it. We cannot allow the benefits that have been realized through the appropriate use of the grants mechanism to be discredited or overshadowed by those who abuse it for their ill-gotten gains.

Deceitful Grant Schemes

Over the last few years I have been retained by prosecuting attorneys at the Federal Trade Commission to provide research and expert testimony in their efforts to shut down several grant schemes. One of my cases was an operation that scammed over $100 million. It did so through a website that promised to provide subscribers with access to federal, state, and private grant opportunities to pay off their mortgage and credit card debt and provide them with free money. As part of my expert witness testimony I had to research hundreds of these claims. Of course, they proved to be false. Many of them used wording that preyed on *individuals* who believed there were federal grants available to pay for their personal needs. Of course, the scammer attempted to escape from any prosecution through the caveat that individuals are listed as eligible to apply for billions of dollars in government grants. But anyone who is familiar with the federal grants marketplace knows that few, if any individuals, will ever succeed in personally attracting a federal grant or showing up on a list of grantees.

You may have even seen or heard of grant scammers that encourage individuals to buy their products and services by leading potential customers to believe they are eligible to apply for billions in federal grants for a host of personal needs, including grants for European travel. Actually, one of my seminar participants brought one of the books in question to my seminar and I looked up the European travel opportunity. It turns out it was a Fulbright fellowship—an opportunity that is not available to anyone except truly outstanding scholars.

Unfortunately, these schemes discredit the real grants process. For example, one fraudulent website instructed its subscribers to submit a mass produced, one-size-fits-all proposal to numerous foundations and government programs rather than a tailored proposal to a carefully researched and selected grant program.

Irrespective of what these fraudulent websites state, developing a quality proposal still entails:

- initiating the grantseeking process early to avoid the deadly mistake of submitting hastily prepared proposals at the last minute

- researching each prospective grantor
- obtaining proposal review criteria
- using all of the procured information to create and tailor a quality, compelling proposal that meets the grantor's agenda

Foremost, if you really want to assess or evaluate your chances of success with a particular grant program before you invest too much time in the process, look at the list of successful grantees to see what they proposed to do with the grant funding and how you compare. (All federal grantors must provide a list of successful grantees under the Freedom of Information Act.) On the foundation side, a few minutes reviewing the foundation's 990 IRS tax return, which is available by law, will tell you who and what they fund. And so far, I have not found any private or public grantors that pay off home mortgages or credit card debts or provide free money! (See chapters 14 and 22 for an explanation of how to acquire a list of past grantees and 990 IRS tax returns.)

Determining Whether, When, and How to Use a Grant Writer or Consultant

Thousands of legitimate and expert consultants market their services to nonprofits to help them create grant proposals. Most are honest and, in some cases, their services can be very helpful. But even my consultant colleagues are concerned about individuals who have little knowledge of grantseeking and the proposal process, and hire grant writers without realizing how much the grant writer has to do or how much time it takes to develop a successful proposal.

Hiring a grant writer/consultant to create a proposal may seem like a viable alternative to many grantseekers because they do not believe they have the time to invest in proposal development. And there are some situations where hiring a grant writer/consultant may be appropriate. However, the conditions must be right. Before hiring a grant writer/consultant, ask yourself the following questions:

- Is this a grant you probably will not compete for again? If so, then using a grant writer may be okay. If you plan to reapply or seek spin-off proposals, you will pay over and over again for the consultant's skills instead of developing them yourself.
- Will hiring a grant writer/consultant to develop this particular proposal have an adverse long-term effect on the rest of your staff or faculty? For

instance, will they question why they should use their spare time to write any grants in the future? Will they always ask for a grant writer?

- What is the grant writer's/consultant's success rate with this particular grant program? Who has the consultant worked for? Can the consultant provide you with references?
- How will the time and effort of the grant writer/consultant be paid? How have past contractors reimbursed the consultant?

Avoid grant writers/consultants who request a percentage of the award or state that you do not have to pay them unless you get awarded the grant. The federal Office of Management and Budget (OMB) has rules concerning this that are quite clear. No payment can be made for any services that occurred before the award date. These are referred to as *nonreimbursable costs* and include those related to preparing the proposal. The grantor is paying for what you will do with their funding now that you have it, and not what you did to get it. Do not allow grant writers/consultants to write themselves into a proposal for funding that does not require their services after the award date. (See chapter 18 on OMB circulars.)

In addition, while it is not illegal to pay for services involved in creating a proposal to a foundation or corporation that occurred before the award date and start of the proposal, it is unethical. Simply put, the grantor should be paying for the project or research and not for the efforts of creating the proposal.

There are several more important issues to be dealt with when contemplating the use of a grant writer/consultant:

- Positioning with Grantors: Using a grant writer/consultant creates confusion for granting program personnel. Who is really responsible for the idea and creation of the proposed project? The grantor may wonder if the prospective grantee can implement the project if he or she cannot even write the proposal. Who does the grantor call if there is a problem? Who will be around to write subsequent proposals in the case of a multiple-year grant?
- Relationship Building: Building a relationship with a grantor is essential for continued success. This starts right from the beginning of the process with preproposal contact. It is important that the researcher, project director, or principal investigator build this relationship and not the grant writer/consultant. In fact, using a grant writer/consultant may actually subvert the relationships critical to continued grant success. This is particularly true if you or someone on your team is not present when calling or meeting with a grantor.

- Development and Maintenance of Your Grants Program: Like other things in life, success in the grants marketplace is based on teaching people to fish and not on fishing for them. Both federal and private grantors respect even novice grantseekers who are trying to learn and employ the basics of successful, proactive grantseeking.

If you must use a grant writer/consultant, require him or her to record what he or she does by completing the figures and exhibits found throughout this book. For example, you could use Exhibit 14.1, the Federal Grants Research Form, to establish the minimum steps a grants consultant must take to increase the likelihood of winning a federal grant. By requiring the consultant to complete the actions outlined in the figures and exhibits, you will know what he or she did, when it occurred, and what resulted. In other words, you will know what you are paying for.

I encourage you to read the book to know what grantseeking entails before you hire a grant writer/consultant. Once you know what grantseeking requires, you will be better able to determine if, when, and how to contract with a consultant.

While my experience has demonstrated that preparing your own proposal has many advantages, I am not dissuading you from using consultants in your proposal for *specific* activities. For example, consultants are frequently used effectively for evaluation and software design. But the same rules apply. Do not pay for work before the award date and make sure to develop a detailed spreadsheet outlining the consultant's scope of work.

By avoiding fraudulent grant schemes and understanding the pros and cons of using grant writers/consultants, you are starting off on the right foot and are now ready to embark on your path to grant success.

2

Your Plan for Grants Success and How to Get There

M ANY GRANTSEEKERS START THE PROPOSAL development process before they have a clear idea of what they want to use grant funding to accomplish. They see peers going after a grant and feel they should jump right in before they consider where a funded proposal will take them and how it will impact their career or their organization's mission. Whether you are a new grantseeker at a nonprofit organization (NPO) or a new faculty member at a college or university, you may think that any grant you get will be good for your career and your organization. It cannot hurt to bring in money, right? Well, consider the possible outcomes:

- When you receive a grant, it has a dramatic effect on how you are perceived in your field. You use your time to do what is required in the grant. You publish the results, speak at conferences, and establish a track record. These actions position you in your field. Many of my fellows regret that they did not think about how grant funding could steer their career in a particular area before they pursued a specific grant. While the grant opportunity may have seemed too good to pass by, it ended up not representing their true interests or passions and what they wanted from their career.

- While a specific grant-funded project may seem timely, procuring the grant funds and conducting the project or research may be detrimental to your organization. Most, if not all, NPOs have a mission or case statement that governs their activities, and a funded project may move the organization off course from pursuing their stated purpose. (See chapter 8, Elements of a Case/Mission Statement.)

In a few chapters you will be moving through the maze to grants success. Each successful grants quest leads to more knowledge, but also to more questions and additional grant opportunities. Success gathers momentum. But beware that if securing grant money is your only goal, you may be propelled down a pathway that leads to areas in which you have little professional interest, or may not want to spend a lifetime pursuing. Being forewarned is being fore-armed.

Developing Your Career Grants Plan

Securing grant funds should be well thought out and viewed as a predetermined effort that moves you toward your career goals and your organization toward its mission. To accomplish this you must first determine what your vision of success is in your field.

In a survey of my grants seminar participants, less than 2 percent reported that they left graduate school with a five-year career plan. Planning to find a job and pay off student loans is not a career plan. None had considered how grantseeking could fit into their career plan or had a long-term vision of what they would call success in their field. Unfortunately, they were unaware of the fact that possessing a well-developed vision of what you personally call success in your career acts like a rudder on a ship. It steers you where you want to go.

I have found that implementing the visioning process outlined in Denis Waitley's classic book *The Psychology of Winning*[1] is one of the keys to my success. He states that to *achieve* something you must first *conceive* it and then *believe* it. Therefore, your first step is to conceive your vision, articulate it into your grants plan, and believe in it.

Waitley goes on to explain that you move in the direction of your dominant thought every waking moment of your life and that focusing on your dominant thought will inevitably lead you to victory in all of your challenges. Waitley's work concerning dominant thoughts is reinforced by Earl Nightingale's famous 1957 recording, "The Strangest Secret."[2] The late writer, speaker, and broadcaster discussed the Law of Dominant Thought in his recording and called it the key to success by proclaiming, "We become what we think about." The one thought that drives you and your grants quest must be clearly identified, and this thought plus your vision must be incorporated into your career grants plan.

It is important that you alone create a definition of success for both your-self and your career. If you are an academic or a nonprofit program manager, state your vision of success and define it. How much time will you devote to grants? To research? To teaching? To program management? To administra-tion? Quantify each part of your vision and determine how it can be advanced by external grant funding.

Exhibit 2.1 helps you determine your personal vision and what role grant-seeking will play in that vision. It starts with a long-term vision of success in your field and then moves on to where you want to be in five years. Clarify your vision by asking what resources you think you will need. For example, will you need special reassigned time or time specifically allocated to your grant as opposed to your regular workload or schedule? If so, how much time will you need to achieve success? Do you require partial reassigned time for your grant-funded project or full-time release time? Remember, you cannot perform your current workload plus your grant workload unless you want to risk working 200 percent of your time and violating the laws that define pay-ment under grants. For example, if you make $80,000 and release 50 percent of your time to accomplish the task outlined in your project, you will need to get $40,000 in salary from your funded grant.

Continue to answer the questions regarding your five-year vision. What personnel will you require? Project coordinators? Lab assistants? Work-study

EXHIBIT 2.1
Your Personal Grants Plan

1. Vision
   - What is your vision of success in your field?
   - What part of that vision will you have achieved in five years?
   - What projects, programs, and research will you be performing?
   - How do these projects, programs, and research fit into your vision of success?
   - What part of these will be grant supported?

2. Reassigned Time: What percent of your time each year will be devoted to these projects/programs/research as opposed to your current job responsibilities?
   Year 1 _____   Year 2 _____   Year 3 _____   Year 4 _____   Year 5 _____

   Based on the percent of time you will be devoting to projects/programs/research, what is the estimated cost of your grant-related salary/wages, including fringe benefits, each year?
   Year 1 _____   Year 2 _____   Year 3 _____   Year 4 _____   Year 5 _____

(continued)

EXHIBIT 2.1
(Continued)

3. What personnel will be required to assist you in performing the tasks you would like to accomplish each year of your vision, and what is the estimated cost?

Project Coordinator(s)

Number: Year 1 _____ Year 2 _____ Year 3 _____ Year 4 _____ Year 5 _____

Cost: Year 1 _____ Year 2 _____ Year 3 _____ Year 4 _____ Year 5 _____

Laboratory Assistant(s)

Number: Year 1 _____ Year 2 _____ Year 3 _____ Year 4 _____ Year 5 _____

Cost: Year 1 _____ Year 2 _____ Year 3 _____ Year 4 _____ Year 5 _____

Graduate Assistant(s)

Number: Year 1 _____ Year 2 _____ Year 3 _____ Year 4 _____ Year 5 _____

Cost: Year 1 _____ Year 2 _____ Year 3 _____ Year 4 _____ Year 5 _____

Work-Study Student(s)

Number: Year 1 _____ Year 2 _____ Year 3 _____ Year 4 _____ Year 5 _____

Cost: Year 1 _____ Year 2 _____ Year 3 _____ Year 4 _____ Year 5 _____

Other (list):

Number: Year 1 _____ Year 2 _____ Year 3 _____ Year 4 _____ Year 5 _____

Cost: Year 1 _____ Year 2 _____ Year 3 _____ Year 4 _____ Year 5 _____

4. What facilities will be required to house these individuals each year? In-house, off-campus, etc. What do you estimate the required square footage to be each year?

Facility	Square Footage
Year 1: _____	_____
Year 2: _____	_____
Year 3: _____	_____
Year 4: _____	_____
Year 5: _____	_____

5. What new equipment (computers, software, machines, vehicles, etc.) will you and your staff need each to accomplish the projected tasks and what will the estimated cost be?

New Equipment	Estimated Cost
Year 1: _____	_____
Year 2: _____	_____
Year 3: _____	_____
Year 4: _____	_____
Year 5: _____	_____

(continued)

EXHIBIT 2.1
(Continued)

6. How many publications will you submit each year and in what journals?

        #   Journal

Year 1: _____   _____

Year 2: _____   _____

Year 3: _____   _____

Year 4: _____   _____

Year 5: _____   _____

Books or chapters for publication? If yes, how many and under what titles?

        #   Title

Year 1: _____   _____

Year 2: _____   _____

Year 3: _____   _____

Year 4: _____   _____

Year 5: _____   _____

Presentations at conferences/meetings? If yes, how many and at what conferences/meetings?

        #   Conference/Meeting

Year 1: _____   _____

Year 2: _____   _____

Year 3: _____   _____

Year 4: _____   _____

Year 5: _____   _____

7. Based on salary/wages, personnel, and equipment, what is the total amount of resources needed each year? Of this total how much will be requested each year from your organization/institution? How much will be needed in grants each year?

	Total	From Organization/ Institution	From Grants
Year 1:	_____	_____	_____
Year 2:	_____	_____	_____
Year 3:	_____	_____	_____
Year 4:	_____	_____	_____
Year 5:	_____	_____	_____

students? Graduate assistants? And so on. By estimating the cost of the components you need to fulfill your five-year plan, you can come up with a total cost and then determine if any of the cost may be covered by your normal budget process. If so, subtract this amount from the total so that you can arrive at an estimate of the amount you must procure through grants.

When developing your vision, it is important to include how you will disseminate the results of your work. Question 6 in Exhibit 2.1 requires special attention. Will you publish the results of your work? If so, how many articles will you publish and in what journals? Will you create a website to make your findings available to others in your field? Will you present your findings at a meeting or conference? If so, which one? For your vision to provide you with guidance and direction, you must outline specific tasks that are indicative of your accomplishment of success. In *The Psychology of Winning*, Waitley insists that you give a number or a quantifier to everything on your five-year plan. You cannot merely say you will publish *several* articles. You must be explicit in terms of the number of articles and the time frame in which they will be published. For example, one article in twenty-four months, three articles in the next thirty-six months, and so on.

This visioning process is critical in that it will help you develop benchmarks to keep your five-year plan in focus as you start out toward your first-year goals. Your five-year plan will provide you with a guide for success as defined by you, and it should be reviewed, updated, and changed on a yearly basis. A sample five-year personal grants plan (see Exhibit 2.2) is included for your review.

EXHIBIT 2.2
Sample Personal Grants Plan

---

1. Vision

- What is your vision of success in your field?
    - Internationally recognized researcher, name recognition, young graduates wanting to work in my group, to be generally considered an authority in the field
    - Achieved via publications, invitations for talks
    - Elected fellowship and/or research awards from Electrochemical Society (such as Uhlig Award), International Society of Electrochemistry, American Chemical Society, and Materials Research Society

- What part of that vision will you have achieved in five years?
    - Should be on the trajectory; at least known in smaller cities
    - Widely published
    - Premium publications

(continued)

EXHIBIT 2.2
(Continued)

- What projects, programs, and research will you be performing?
  - Electrochemical Applications in Materials and Biological research
  - Advanced Nuclear Materials
  - Microbial Electrochemistry for Environment and Energy

- How do these projects, programs, and research fit into your vision of success?
  - My interests and are directly aligned.

- What part of these will be grant supported?
  - 100% ideally

2. Reassigned Time: What percent of your time each year will be devoted to these projects/programs/research as opposed to your current job responsibilities?

   Year 1 <u>40%</u>   Year 2 <u>40%</u>   Year 3 <u>50%</u>   Year 4 <u>50%</u>   Year 5 <u>60%</u>

   Based on the percent of time you will be devoting to projects/programs/research, what is the estimated cost of your grant-related salary/wages including fringe benefits each year?

   Year 1 <u>$55K</u>   Year 2 <u>$55K</u>   Year 3 <u>$80K</u>   Year 4 <u>$80K</u>   Year 5 <u>$110K</u>

3. What personnel will be required to assist you in performing the tasks you would like to accomplish each year of your vision and what is the estimated cost?

   Graduate Student (GS)/Project Director (PD)

   Number: Year 1 <u>4GS</u>   Year 2 <u>5GS</u>   Year 3 <u>5GS & 1PD</u>   Year 4 <u>6GS & 1PD</u>
              Year 5 6GS & 2PD

   Cost: Year 1 <u>$140K</u>   Year 2 <u>$175K</u>   Year 3 <u>$250K</u>   Year 4 <u>$300K</u>
              Year 5 $405K

   Laboratory Assistant(s)

   Number: Year 1 ____   Year 2 ____   Year 3 ____   Year 4 ____   Year 5 ____
   Cost: Year 1 ____   Year 2 ____   Year 3 ____   Year 4 ____   Year 5 ____

   Graduate Assistant(s)

   Number: Year 1 ____   Year 2 ____   Year 3 ____   Year 4 ____   Year 5 ____
   Cost: Year 1 ____   Year 2 ____   Year 3 ____   Year 4 ____
   Year 5 ____

   Work-Study Student(s)

   Number: Year 1 ____   Year 2 ____   Year 3 ____   Year 4 ____   Year 5 ____
   Cost: Year 1 ____   Year 2 ____   Year 3 ____   Year 4 ____   Year 5 ____

(continued)

EXHIBIT 2.2
(Continued)

Other (list): Undergraduate Student (US)

Number: Year 1 <u>1</u>   Year 2 <u>2</u>   Year 3 <u>2</u>   Year 4 <u>3</u>   Year 5 <u>4</u>

Cost: Year 1 <u>$5K</u> Year 2 <u>$10K</u> Year 3 <u>$10K</u> Year 4 <u>$15K</u> Year 5 <u>$20K</u>

4. What facilities will be required to house these individuals each year? In-house, off-campus, etc. What do you estimate the required square footage to be each year?

	Facility	Square Footage
Year 1:	Existing Facility	
Year 2:	Existing Facility	
Year 3:	Existing Facility	
Year 4:	Need new office space	100 sq ft
Year 5:	Need new office space	100 sq ft

5. What new equipment (computers, software, machines, vehicles, etc.) will you and your staff need each to accomplish the projected tasks and what will the estimated cost be?

	New Equipment	Estimated Cost
Year 1:		
Year 2:		
Year 3:		
Year 4:	Raman Spectroscopy	$100K
Year 5:	FTIR microscopy	$100K

6. How many publications will you submit each year and in what journals?

	#	Journal
Year 1:	2	JECS, ES&T
Year 2:	2	ES&T. E&F, EA
Year 3:	5	ES&T, E&F, EA
Year 4:	7	ES&T, E&F, EA
Year 5:	10	ES&T, E&F, EA, PNAS

Books or chapters for publication? If yes, how many and under what titles?

	#	Title
Year 1:		
Year 2:		
Year 3:		
Year 4:		
Year 5:		

(continued)

EXHIBIT 2.2
(Continued)

Presentations at conferences/meetings? If yes, how many and at what conferences/meetings?

#	Conference/Meeting
Year 1: 1	ECS
Year 2: 1	ECS/ANS
Year 3: 3	ECS/ANS/ACS
Year 4: 3	ECS/ANS/ACS
Year 5: 3	ECS/ANS/ACS

7. Based on salary/wages, personnel, and equipment, what is the total amount of resources needed each year? Of this total how much will be requested each year from your organization/institution? How much will be need in grants each year?

	Total	From Organization/ Institution	From Grants
Year 1:	$200K	$35K	$165K
Year 2:	$240K	$45K	$195K
Year 3:	$340K	$50K	$290K
Year 4:	$395K	$35K	$360K
Year 5:	$535K	$35K	$500K

Exhibit 2.3 will help you break your five-year plan down into a one-year plan and assist you in determining the immediate resources you will need. First, review your five-year plan and indicate what initial steps are critical to begin movement toward your vision. What smaller steps must you take now to begin the process? What components will require grant funding? Second, determine who might be able to help you achieve the initial steps. Consider putting together a small group of individuals and organizations that are interested in your project or research area and have had experience working with you. Potential group members could include individuals from your undergraduate, graduate, and postgraduate work. Consider advisors, mentors, and colleagues as potential project consultants, coinvestigators, or consortium partners.

Review the yearly plan annually. Hold your own feet to the flame. What did you accomplish? Where did you meet your goals? Where did you exceed them?

EXHIBIT 2.3
Setting Your Goals and Enlisting Support

1. What steps can you take in the next 12 months to move you toward your five-year vision? (These steps could include procuring smaller start-up or initiation grants, needs assessment grants, grants to develop preliminary data, or grants for a minimal amount of essential equipment or software.)

2. What resources do you need to help you initiate these first steps? (These resources should include a list of potential advisors, mentors, colleagues, etc., with whom you can brainstorm your topic, enlist support, or develop a consortia approach.)

3. Whom will you contact and when?

   Who   When

   _____   _____
   _____   _____
   _____   _____
   _____   _____

Rewrite your second-year goals to incorporate what was not accomplished in the previous plan. Eliminate those goals that are inappropriate and add new ones. For example, year two may contain work on your newly funded grant, or on a reapplication if your original grant was rejected. In either case, year two's plan is still all about achieving your vision and dominant thought.

Now your task is to continually add another year to your five-year plan. Yes, year six and so on. This way you will always have an active five-year plan.

Keep a record of each year's plan and accomplishments. This record will prove to be invaluable when you have a performance review for a raise or a tenure package at a college or university. No matter when you are reviewed, you will have five years of future tasks and proposals that your employer can see and will not get if your contract is not renewed.

Once you have identified your dominant thought, defined your vision, and written your five-year plan, you will come to your first major grantseeking crossroads. Yogi Berra once said, "When you come to a fork in the road, take it,"[3] and you will. I have always preferred having a plan and have told my students that if you do not have a plan, any road will get you there. The only problem is that you will not know when you are there. I hope you understand the necessity of having a plan and are ready to move into the next phase of successful grantseeking. The projects, programs, and research you propose are important to you, your career, your organization, and the fields you will impact.

Notes

1. Denis Waitley, *The Psychology of Winning* (New York: Berkeley Books, 1984).
2. Earl Nightingale, "The Strangest Secret for Succeeding in the World Today" (CD-Unabridged) (Simon & Schuster Audio/Nightingale-Conant, 2011).
3. Yogi Berra, *The Yogi Book* (New York: Workman Publishing, 1999), 48.

3

Creating a Success-Based Proactive Grants System

FOLLOWING A PROACTIVE GRANTS SYSTEM and staying focused on one's grantseeking goals sounds simple. However, time constraints can make the process difficult. Whether grantseeking is your full-time job or a part-time pursuit you probably have a hard time accomplishing everything you need in the time you have available.

If you are a teacher or a faculty member, you are trying to integrate grantseeking with teaching, advising, doing research, publishing, and attending department and committee meetings. If you are a nonprofit manager, you are trying to integrate grantseeking with board meetings, staff meetings, and other multitasking duties. And if you are a nonprofit staff member or volunteer, finding the time to allocate to grantseeking might seem impossible. Therein lies the dilemma we all must face. What can we accomplish today and what can we put off until tomorrow?

When faced with a task that comes with a future deadline, many people choose to put the task off until tomorrow or as long as possible. Unfortunately, grantseeking is one of those tasks usually perceived as deadline driven. Let's face it: The fact that proposals must be submitted by a certain date is the absolute bane of the grantseeker's existence. The meetings we have, the students we need to advise, and the classes we must teach today cannot be put off. But our grantseeking tasks can be put off until some time in the future, closer to the deadline. (Or at least we think it can.)

Lack of time isn't the only thing that keeps prospective grantseekers from accomplishing their goals. Many grantseekers mistakenly believe that the proactive steps needed to ensure grants success are difficult or unpleasant.

Some even feel that they require them to act outside of their comfort zones. This became apparent to me in my consulting. In my grantseeking fellows program I require the participants to develop a contract that lists the grant-seeking steps they will carry out over the next ninety days. Every ninety days they must meet with me and report on their success. What I have discovered is that they frequently do not like to make the various forms of preproposal contact with their prospective grantors that I suggest. They will go to great lengths to avoid making face-to-face, telephone, and even e-mail contact with funders, especially federal program officers. They will wait until right before I am back on campus to complete as many of the tasks as possible on their contracts. Unfortunately, while this procrastination may be normal and even understandable, in the long run it will sabotage their grant success.

Creating a winning proposal is not just about writing faster or staying up later the night before the proposal is due. Several critical steps in proactive grantseeking need to be integrated into your busy life months before the deadline.

This book provides a systematic approach filled with proactive steps to help you cope with the time issues and other hurdles that accompany grant-seeking. The system has been implemented at large and small nonprofit or-ganizations throughout the United States, including hundreds of schools and universities, and is applicable whether one grant proposal is produced per year or twenty. The proposal development sequence you choose to imple-ment from this book is designed to foster grants success immediately and be the basis for your grantseeking well into the future. I am convinced of the success of this system and know for a fact that its use yields grant success rates of over 50 percent.

Hundreds of billions of dollars will be granted this year. In fact, these funds must be awarded; otherwise grantors will either lose the money, or in the case of foundations, be penalized by the Internal Revenue Service if 5 percent of their assets are not awarded each year. The question is, are you motivated *enough* to learn and practice the relatively simple, proactive steps outlined in this book to successfully access these funds? My background in psychology reminds me that all behavior is motivated. Even last-minute, reactive grant-seeking is evidence of grantee motivation. What you need to do is ask yourself if you are sufficiently inspired to put into practice the proactive steps that will increase your grant success and ensure that the time you invest in grantseek-ing is well spent. Some of my clients have mistakenly praised me for motivat-ing their faculty and staff to get interested in pursuing grants. The truth is that I cannot motivate anyone. Only you can motivate yourself. The question is whether you are ready to make a concerted effort to apply a proactive, timely approach to grantseeking.

Chapter 2, particularly Exhibit 2.1, has asked you to focus on your vision and five-year plan. But before your dancing digits hit the keyboard or you put pen to paper, spend a little time asking yourself the following questions and reviewing the corresponding principles that are integral to a proactive, successful grants system.

- First, how do the grants funds you are seeking fit with your predetermined goals and those of your institution or organization?
- Second, what does the prospective grantor want and how does this correlate with what you want?
- Third, what problem will these grant funds solve or impact?

Obviously, we have our work cut out for us. So let's start with the first principle.

Principle 1: All proposals you create should take your organization or institution toward its predetermined goals. To refresh yourself with these goals, review your organization's or institution's mission statement and identify its stated purpose and objectives. To be more specific, apply this concept to your particular division, department, program, or center rather than your entire organization or institution. One large foundation I encountered had a stated rule that they would entertain only one proposal per institution or nonprofit organization. In this case, the university I was working with interpreted this to mean each college within the institution could send in one proposal. Therefore, they sent in eight proposals to the same foundation. The foundation returned all eight proposals and instructed the university to review its priorities and submit the one proposal that had the potential to move the institution toward its main concern. The foundation added that it was not its job to pick one of the eight because that action could actually move the university away from its mission.

Principle 2: The grantor is concerned about meeting its program's goals and objectives, not yours. Grantors do not care what you want. They are concerned about what they want. They fund projects for their reasons, not yours. Therefore, to create a compelling proposal that motivates the grantor to send you money, you must follow a basic writing rule. Always write from the reader's point of view.

Principle 3: Grantors want to know that their grant will solve or impact a problem. They want to believe that their funding will hasten an action that was going to happen anyway, but probably at a slower pace and over a prolonged period. They view their funding as a catalyst in an equation, and they want to be assured that the program or project initiated with their grant funds is the correct course of action to take for themselves (the grantor) as well as the grantee. In fact, I have even expressed to a grantor that my organization was prepared to do the project even without the grantor's support but that it would take years to be able to put it in place. The grantor wants assurance that it is not just the opportunity to apply for their grant funds that motivates the prospective grantee. The grantor wants to feel confident that the grantee was headed in that direction anyway.

Grantors want to believe that your organization or institution is the right one to fund and that you will work to continue the project or research after their support ends. They want to feel they have made a gift that will keep on giving. By following principles 1, 2, and 3, you set up a logical framework for some type of continuation.

Your consideration of a career-enhancing grants strategy does not begin with a specific grantor and a looming deadline. If you are reading this chapter with perspiration dripping from your forehead because of a rapidly approaching deadline, stop! My first suggestion is to forgo the application and read on since pursuing this grant will most likely result in rejection. You simply do not have enough time to take advantage of the proactive grants system suggested in this book. However, if this is impossible (because your supervisor, manager, or administrator is forcing you to apply, or for some other reason), skip part 1 of this book and move on to those chapters dedicated to proposal development. When your proposal is rejected, you can then read part 1 to determine how best to approach a resubmittal.

The grants strategies in this book require you to use the same system each time you approach the grants marketplace for a project or program. The key to success is recognizing that you do not inherently know how to approach grantors or to write your proposals. The grants marketplace is based on *change*. The very fact that grantors (be they federal, foundation, or corporate) solicit requests is based on their desire to fund *new* approaches, protocols, and solutions to problems.

This represents a planning dilemma. The strategy or approach that worked in the last proposal may not work in the next one. Even the proactive grant-seeking techniques we employed may need to be changed. To be successful we must constantly question the way we like or prefer to approach grantseeking and force ourselves to determine with each and every application or proposal if the field has changed and, therefore, whether our approach must change.

Grantseeking should be thought of as the successful negotiation of a maze. We must be open to looking at various avenues and hope that we do not ultimately choose the wrong one, or a dead end. You may find the book *Who Moved My Cheese* as helpful as I have in this respect.[1] The book is short and easy to read, and while the lessons are universal, they are particularly insightful with respect to negotiating the grants maze. Just the names of the characters should entice you into reading it. Two characters in the book are mice named Sniff and Scurry. (How many grantseekers have you seen sniffing the money and scurrying after it?) The book's other two characters are little people named Hem and Haw. They successfully navigate the maze and find the cheese (grant money) but refuse to believe that their previously successful strategies are not working to find more cheese (grant money). They try nonproductive strategies over and over again hoping for different results. The book's main tenant is that you must be ready to change again and again because the cheese (a metaphor for what you want) is always being moved.

I understand now why I sometimes fail at getting grantseekers to employ my suggested proactive strategies. It is tough to manage one's time effectively and to act proactively when surrounded by constant change. However, this book will show you that by collecting grantor research before scurrying off to write a proposal, you will be able to uncover changes that have occurred and then be able to take these changes into account when developing your ever-evolving grants strategy.

The purpose of this chapter is to provide a compelling basis for moving you from submitting a last-minute, self-focused proposal to a proactive, planned approach based on the grantor's needs and wants. So far you have looked at how the grantor's needs and those of your organization complement each other. Now it is time to learn how to develop a proactive system.

Developing a Proactive System

Many well-intentioned grantseekers begin the process by creating a proposal and searching for a grantor, or they learn of grants with a rapidly approaching deadline and try to get a proposal completed quickly. However, this is called *reactive grantseeking* and results in high rates of rejection (90 to 100 percent).

By contrast, in proactive grantseeking you spend time researching a prospective grantor before writing and submitting a proposal. As a proactive grantseeker you will uncover information that will help you increase your chances of acceptance by:

- determining what the grantor is really looking for (the grantor's hidden agenda)
- predicting your likelihood of success before investing additional time
- tailoring your proposal to the funding source's needs

The difference between reactive and proactive grantseekers is *when* and *how* they invest their time and how these variables influence their success rate.

Proactive grantseekers put in small amounts of time *throughout* the grant-seeking process. The reactive grantseeker invests a lot of time just prior to the deadline. This approach often results in last-minute, general proposals that are designed to fit almost any possible grantor's guidelines, lack specificity, and are not targeted or tailored to the needs of the grantor. In addition, they are usually easily recognizable because of a preponderance of statements beginning with "We want," "We need," and "We propose to do," and contain little reference to why the grantor would want to fund the proposal.

Unfortunately, this self-focus has been aided by the use of computers for researching grantors. In many cases, overzealous and self-focused grantseekers secure printouts of all the grantors who have funded projects even remotely related to theirs and then send the same proposal to every grantor on the list. What these grantseekers overlook is that this shotgun approach results in high rates of rejection and negative positioning with funding sources.

Whenever your proposals (or those of your nonprofit organization) result in failure, you risk positioning your organization in a negative manner. Of course, grantseeking always results in a certain percentage of rejection. This is bound to happen. But how much rejection can you, the grantseeker, and your organization afford before the very appearance of your name on a proposal elicits a negative reaction from grantors? What is the success rate you need to achieve to avoid negative positioning? Anything less than a 50 percent success rate results in negative positioning. An 80 or 90 percent failure rate could not possibly create a positive image for your organization with the grantor's staff or reviewers.

Embracing a proactive approach to grantseeking means starting the process early. This enables the grantseeker to employ quality assurance techniques to increase his or her chances of success and avoid negative positioning. A proactive grantseeker has enough time to conduct a quality circle exercise or mock review of his or her proposal before submittal, using the same review system that is to be used by the grantor. This technique helps to ensure that the submitted proposal represents the grantseeker's best effort. By starting early and finishing your proposal three to four weeks before the grantor's deadline, you will be able to have your proposal read and scored by friendly role players who can pick up any errors before your proposal is submitted for its real review. While chapters 16 and 25 provide details on how to use a grants quality circle to improve a proposal, the simple fact is that you will not have enough time to use this invaluable technique unless you become a proactive grantseeker!

Exhibit 3.1 shows what kinds of reviewer comments are likely to be received when proactive grantseeking is abandoned. Last-minute submissions that are quickly put together often contain spelling, grammar, and punctua-

EXHIBIT 3.1
Sample Reviewer's Comments

APPLICATION NUMBER

Technology Innovation Challenge Grant Program
Individual Technical Review Form—Tier 1

SUMMARY ASSESSMENT

Please summarize your overall thoughts about the application in light of your previous comments on "significance" and "feasibility," and mention any important points on which the application is unclear so that these points can be raised with the applicant.

> The conversational style was welcome and easy reading. For once there was an absence of educational "buzz words." However, watch out for too much informal style (e.g., the phrase "parents don't have a clue").
>
> Don't forget to identify acronyms: GSAMS was identified only in a letterhead in the appendix.
>
> It is extremely important to proofread your application. There were no less than nineteen grammar and punctuation errors. If simple details like these are not corrected as a matter of professionalism, can one reasonably be expected to properly manage several million dollars?

OVERALL GRADE: <u>B</u>

A = high, B = medium, C = low

---

tion errors, especially when they are submitted electronically, since grantor websites do not provide tools such as spelling and grammar check. You can be sure the staff and the reviewers will remember poor-quality submissions like this, but for all the wrong reasons!

I quickly learned that the best strategy for winning grants was to tailor each and every proposal to the perspective of the potential grantor. After a reactive grantseeking failure, I remembered a theory I learned as a psychology major and I applied it to grantseeking. Forty-five years later, I can unequivocally say that this theory has helped me to develop millions of dollars in successful projects and research for nonprofit organizations. I share this theory with you to help you approach grantseeking from the grantor's perspective and to provide you with the basis for developing a tailored proposal to each grantor.

Festinger's Theory of Cognitive Dissonance

Dr. Leon Festinger developed the theory of cognitive dissonance while performing research on cognitive development and the assimilation of new information.[2] In summary, Festinger found that preconceived ideas and constructs have a filtering effect on newly presented information. If the new information does not support preexisting concepts, students react negatively to learning and to assimilating the new data. Festinger labeled this resistance to new information as "dissonance." According to his theory, individuals do not view new data with an open mind, and that which does not match their preexisting constructs creates static or dissonance. In essence, we want to maintain homeostasis, and we tend to see and hear that which reinforces our existing beliefs and omit that which does not.

In my next attempt to write a proposal, I remembered Festinger's work and wanted to be sure my proposal would be "seen" by the reviewers. In fact, I concluded that to truly be read and understood, I needed to know more about the way the grantor viewed the world. The first grants seminar I attended dedicated hours on how to write clearly. And while I believe that writing clearly is very important, I was more intrigued by the idea of creating consonance rather than dissonance. At that point I remember my high school English teacher's mantra: Write from the point of view of the reader. That is when I realized how important it was that I understood how my prospective grantor saw the world and the way in which his or her grant funding impacted and changed it. That is also when I realized how important it was for me to do my grantor homework.

Values-Based Grantseeking

By expanding Festinger's theory, I developed the values glasses theory and the concepts of values-based grantseeking. A common mistake of grantseekers is to write their proposals based on their own values. They mistakenly assume that the prospective grantor has similar values and that grantors will read their proposals from their (the grantseeker's) point of view. Another mistake is to attempt to use the proposal to try to influence or change the values of a grantor. Do not try to show that the funding source's granting pattern is unenlightened or misguided as this will result in dissonance and rejection. Some grantseekers also make the mistake of using their own vocabulary in proposals, forgetting that grantors will read and react to proposals based on their own (the grantor's) vocabulary.

Figure 3.1 illustrates the grantseeker's predicament. As a proactive, values-based grantseeker, he or she must strive to get the facts through the lenses (filters) of the grantor over to the brain of the grantor who controls the hand, arm, and money (check) the grantseeker wants.

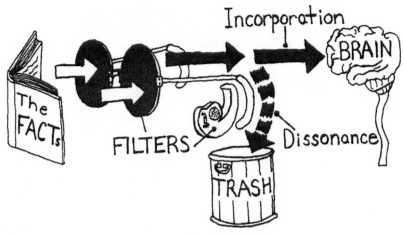

FIGURE 3.1
Values-Based Grantseeking

The ensuing chapters are all based on uncovering the information you need to understand the values of the grantor so that your proposal can be written and presented in such a way that it reinforces your prospective grantor's values. Values-based grantseeking entails uncovering information about the grantor that will help you develop an appreciation and understanding of the grantor's values glasses. Once you have this information, you can use it as a guide to your approach, helping you select the right needs data and vocabulary to include in your proposal and ensuring that you present a compelling case for funding.

Successful grantseekers avoid jeopardizing their chances at being funded by remaining sensitive to the values of the grantor. They do not pander to the grantor, or wrap a wolf in sheep's clothing, but their approach to proposal preparation does reflect their knowledge of the grantor and, ultimately, respect for the grantor's values.

If you follow this theory through, it will be obvious to your prospective grantor that you know what the grantor values and that rejecting your proposal would be a repudiation of his or her (the grantor's) own values. In fact, not funding you would be unpleasant, create internal static, and produce dissonance!

This theory does not apply just to private funding sources (foundations and corporations). Proposals to federal and state grantors are read by staff and peer reviewers who are also likely to give the best scores to proposals tailored to their beliefs. In fact, reviewers selected by government bureaucrats are likely to be professionals who have perspectives and values similar to those of the government bureaucrats.

To be truly successful, your proactive grants system should be based on a triple win: meeting the needs of the grantor, your organization, and you (the proposal developer). You need not invest more time in the process than the reactive grantseeker; you just need to invest your time earlier and more wisely. Instead of a seventy-two-hour, last-minute, Herculean proposal effort, invest ten hours per month for seven months. This will give you plenty of time to research the grantor, make preproposal contact, and construct a tailored proposal—all without the stress of a last-minute effort!

Completing the proactive steps in this book is essential to the development of each of your grant-winning proposals so that you have an understanding of the grantor and what the funding source needs to get for awarding this grant to you and your organization. The more you know of the grantor's past funded proposals and where the funding source is moving in the future, the better able you will be to tailor your proposal. In addition, your writing style will become more positive as you are convinced that you will meet the grantor's needs as well as your needs and the needs of your organization.

If there is one lesson that grantseeking has taught me in the millions of dollars of grant-funded projects I have completed in my forty-five year career, it is that you can make a living doing a lot of things, but what is truly important is making a living while making a difference. If the strategies outlined in the following chapters help you move toward achieving and living your vision, then I have reached my goal in writing this book.

Notes

1. Spencer Johnson, *Who Moved My Cheese?* (New York: G. P. Putman's Sons, 2002).

2. Leon Festinger, *A Theory of Cognitive Dissonance* (Stanford, CA: Stanford University Press, 1962).

4

Integrating Time Management into a Successful Grants Career

WHEN DISCUSSING TIME MANAGEMENT, I like to begin with a quote from Michael Altshuler: "The bad news is time flies. The good news is you're the pilot."[1]

From the previous chapters, you have already figured out that a reactive, last-minute, hastily prepared proposal is a formula for rejection and a waste of valuable time. The remaining chapters of this book focus on the techniques and proactive steps to grants success. Your task is to organize the steps into an effective time management system that works for you. I know that these steps and strategies have provided my personal grants career with a success rate of more than 50 percent. In my grants coach consulting, I have witnessed success rates over 80 percent. One of my fellows turned a failure rate of zero grants for eight proposals to seven grants out of eight proposals for a total of $900,000 over an eighteen-month period. He credits his success to the proactive steps outlined in this book. I credit him for adapting his proactive grantseeking into an efficient time management system that allowed him to take advantage of these strategies. He did this adapting and integrating while maintaining the demanding roles of faculty member, researcher, parent, spouse, and dedicated church member.

What I have learned from my grants coaching is that managing one's time is extremely difficult and that changing the way it is allocated is even harder. Faculty member, nonprofit manager, or staff person, your everyday duties and personal obligations force you to distribute your time to those tasks that are the "do it now" type like reports, budgets, meetings, and the student that requires immediate attention. Since your potential grant might have a deadline that is six or more months away it is no wonder that you push the proactive steps to grants success off. Most of you barely have time to read this book, let alone implement the suggested steps.

I sometimes feel bad that, as a grants coach, the proactive steps I promote can be viewed in the same vein as your six-month dental checkup and cleaning. The appointment every six months is a good oral hygiene practice but you may repress the possibility of short-term pain or discomfort and just plain forget it. Besides, you have more pressing needs. This is why you get a phone call or e-mail to remind you of your dental appointment. The benefits of routine oral checkups and cleanings are in the future, as are the benefits of implementing a proactive grants system.

In most cases, proposal developers are expected or encouraged to perform grantseeking activities in addition to their normal job responsibilities and in their *spare* time. In the college and university setting, grantseeking is done after preparing course work, teaching, advising, and participating in committee assignments. Seldom are faculty members or staff given release time to write their proposals. The goal, they are told, is to work extra hard to prepare a proposal and get it funded. Then they can get reassigned time from their normal duties to carry it out. While carrying it out, the successful grantseeker is expected to find the time to create yet another proposal. There is precious little time left for anything else—like having a life!

Rarely are there personnel at nonprofit organizations, including colleges and universities, whose main job responsibility is to write grants for other staff members or faculty. While there are some job descriptions that include proposal preparation as a job responsibility, these are usually jobs in state or regional government agencies, where federal grant moneys are passed through to local grantseekers. And the fact of the matter is that even individuals hired solely as grant writers do not have enough time to fulfill their duties. In addition, the hired grant writer rarely has the expertise needed to create a funded proposal. A hired grant writer can help in the process, but in the long run, only the content expert can create a winning proposal (see chapter 1).

Many grantseekers are overwhelmed by the *total* amount of work involved in proposal preparation. Because of this, they procrastinate and avoid approaching proposal development until it is too late to do an adequate job. Yet they still create last-minute, hurried proposals and hope they will do the trick. This reminds me of a quote from Baltasar Gracian: "A wise person does at once, what a fool does at last. Both do the same thing; only at different times."[2]

Over the past forty-five years, I have researched and experimented with many time-management efficiency systems. My goal was to see which techniques could be successfully applied to this proactive grantseeker's dilemma. My background in psychology, particularly in the field of personal motivation, has provided me with a unique framework to consider why people engage in the proposal creation process and why proactive grantseeking is embraced by some grantseekers and not by others.

Nonprofit managers and university administrators frequently remark that my seminars and materials have motivated their staff or faculty to get involved in grantseeking. I remind them that I cannot motivate anyone and that all human behavior is motivated by the individual. It has always been difficult for me to observe the wasted time grantseekers spend on a reactive grants process that ultimately ends in rejection. But I am reminded that I am dealing with a reward process that is similar to delayed gratification. Complete the proactive steps now, and in six months you will be ready and able to prepare the grant-winning proposal; a year from now you will be spending the grantor's money to make your grants plan a reality. Now that is deferred gratification!

This chapter presents a two-step process for developing your grants strategy. First is a system for organizing the proactive grantseeking strategies that help you achieve grants success. The second is using time management techniques to implement proactive grantseeking strategies.

System for Organizing Proactive Grantseeking Strategies—The Swiss Cheese Book

Alan Lakein, an early leader in time management, suggests in his book *How to Get Control of Your Time and Life*[3] that when you face a large, complex task that cannot be accomplished in an uninterrupted time span, divide it into smaller, less overwhelming parts. In his book a mouse is faced with its dream: a huge piece of cheese. However, the mouse must move this large, heavy chunk of cheese. Instead of putting off the task or forgoing the cheese altogether because it feels overwhelmed, the mouse decides to turn the solid block of cheese into Swiss cheese by eating holes into it. By doing so, the mouse is essentially dividing the chore of moving the hunk of cheese into manageable parts so the final task of carrying the cheese away is less onerous (Figure 4.1)

Lakein's example of a mouse confronted by the job of carrying away a huge piece of cheese is analogous to a grantseeker presented with the prospect of creating a grant proposal. While preparing and getting your proposal funded may seem like an overwhelming, crushing task, you can eat holes through the process and break it into smaller, controllable parts by strategically employing a number of logical steps (the scope) in a particular order (the sequence). The secret is not to dwell on the *whole* proposal preparation process. By accomplishing the smaller steps that lead up to the desired end, you can maintain a sense of control, or as I often refer to it, a sense of order in the universe.

FIGURE 4.1
Swiss Cheese Concept

I have applied Lakein's concept to grantseeking and developed what I call a "Swiss cheese book." The Swiss cheese book consists of a set of tabs placed in a three-ring binder dedicated to a problem that you, the proposal developer, have selected to seek grants to impact. I have divided the task of developing a proposal into steps, with each corresponding to one tab in the Swiss cheese book. This book is arranged so that the worksheets, letters, e-mails, forms, and tables in each chapter can be completed and placed behind the corresponding tabbed sections. Please note that all of these materials can also be found in an interactive electronic version of the publisher's website by going to https://rowman.com/ISBN/9781475810110 and requesting the supplementary materials for *The "How To" Grants Manual.*

It is simple to construct a Swiss cheese book. Purchase an inexpensive set of tabbed index dividers that comes with precut, blank tab inserts and place the appropriate title on each tab. Or you may print out the Swiss cheese tab titles listed in Exhibit 4.1 and insert them into the precut tabs. Then print or download the exhibits, figures, and tables from this book, three-hole punch them, and file them behind the appropriate tabbed sections in your three-ring binder.

As a case in point, if you in your literature search came across a research study particularly relevant to your problem, you could make a copy of the

EXHIBIT 4.1
Swiss Cheese Book Tab Titles

Introduction & Documenting Need	Researching Private/ Foundation Grantors	Submission & Follow-Up Private/Corporate Proposals
Developing Solutions & Redefining Ideas	Contacting Private/ Foundation Grantors	
Credibility & Partners	Creating Private/ Foundation Proposals	
Researching Public/ Gov't Grantors	Submission & Follow-Up Private/Found. Proposals	
Contacting Public/ Gov't Grantors	Researching Private/ Corporate Grantors	
Creating Public/ Gov't Proposal	Contacting Private/ Corporate Grantors	
Submission & Follow-Up Public/ Gov't Proposals	Creating Private/ Corporate Proposals	

article and place it under the tab for "Documenting Need" (see chapter 5). Or you could place a copy of just the article's summary or abstract under the tab, but include with it a complete article citation and a reference to where you have the whole article archived. The Swiss cheese book system will also work for filing and retaining possible solutions, advisory committee notes, grantor research, preproposal contact results, and so forth.

The same techniques employed in a hardcopy version of the Swiss cheese book could also be employed electronically. You could create a folder for each of your tabs, scan pertinent information like relevant literature into your computer, and place the information under the appropriate automated folder. A computer-based version of the Swiss cheese book has many advantages. For instance, you can scan in material or save links to online material such as journal articles and videos of your brainstorming session, work with advisory groups, and speakers at conferences and meetings for use in later proposal development.

Review the following list of suggested Swiss cheese tabs.

- Tab 1: Personal Grants Plan
  Chapter 2: Your Plan for Grants Success and How to Get There
- Tab 2: Documenting Need
  Chapter 5: Searching the Literature to Document Your Statement of Need: Creating an Urgent and Compelling Case

- Tab 3: Developing Solutions and Redefining Ideas
  Chapter 6: Developing and Evaluating Alternative Solutions
  Chapter 7: Creating Key Search Terms to Identify the Best Grantor(s): Redefining Your Project and Improving Your Research/Grants Profile
- Tab 4: Credibility and Partners
  Chapter 8: Capitalizing on Your Capabilities
  Chapter 9: Forming Grant-Winning Teams and Consortia: Recruiting Volunteers for Advisory Groups
- Tab 5: Researching Public/Gov't Grantors
  Chapter 13: Researching the Federal Government Marketplace
- Tab 6: Contacting Public/Gov't Grantors
  Chapter 14: Completing Your Research and Contacting Government Grantors, Past Grantees, and Past Reviewers to Increase your Success Rate
- Tab 7: Creating Public/Gov't Proposals
  Chapter 15: Planning the Successful Federal Proposal
  Chapter 16: Improving Your Federal Proposal: The Grants Quality Circle
- Tab 8: Submission and Follow-Up Public/Gov't Proposals
  Chapter 17: Submission: What to Do and What Not to Do
- Tab 9: Researching Private/Foundation Grantors
  Chapter 22: Researching Potential Private Foundation Grantors: How to Find the Foundation That Is Best Suited to Fund Your Project
- Tab 10: Contacting Private/Foundation Grantors
  Chapter 23: Contacting a Private Foundation Before Submission
- Tab 11: Creating Private/Foundation Proposals
  Chapter 24: Applying for Private Foundation Funds: Letter of Inquiry and Letter Proposal
- Tab 12: Submission and Follow-Up Private/Foundation Proposals
  Chapter 25: Quality Circles, Proposal Submission, the Decision, and Follow-Up: Private Foundation Funding Sources
- Tab 13: Researching Private/Corporate Grantors
  Chapter 27: Researching Corporate Grantors: How to Find the Corporate Funding Source Best Suited to Fund Your Project
- Tab 14: Contacting Private/Corporate Grantors
  Chapter 28: Preproposal Contact with Corporate Grantors
- Tab 15: Creating Private/Corporate Proposals
  Chapter 29: Applying for Corporate Funds
- Tab 16: Submission and Follow-Up Private/Corporate Proposals
  Chapter 30: Corporate Proposal Submission, the Decision, and Follow-Up

You will find that the Swiss cheese concept and the creation of Swiss cheese books will provide you with an organized approach to proposal preparation and the development and use of effective proactive grantseeking strategies that will result in a more effective use of your time. In addition, this approach will help you improve your organization's image with funding sources by enabling you to present your project as well planned and thought out. Grantors are favorably impressed during preproposal contact with an organized grantseeker who can reference and substantiate the important points he or she may explore in an interview. They want to fund a project director or principal investigator who will be as organized in carrying out the proposal as he or she is introducing and discussing it with them.

Using Time Management Techniques to Implement Proactive Grantseeking Strategies

This section focuses on how time management techniques can help you implement the steps in a proactive grants system and how to avoid last-minute, flawed proposal preparation.

The techniques presented here include the latest, most useful, technology-driven methods as well as those older approaches that have worked for my grants fellows. Briefly consider how a technique could be applied to your busy life and focus on the ones that could work. Do not waste time on those time management techniques that look good but that cannot, for one reason or another, become a committed tool in your work style. I suggest you review all of them and then put into practice a combination of those that you think will work best for you on your road to grants success.

David Allen, in his book *Getting Things Done: The Art of Stress-Free Productivity,*[4] provides several useful strategies that my grants fellows have applied to proactive grantseeking. One basic tenet is that to-do lists do not work effectively when you try to apply them to proactive grantseeking. I agree with Allen in his observation that a project list is of minimal use because you cannot do a project. You can only do the action steps that the project requires.[5] The proactive grantseeking process does not translate well to a to-do list since you cannot do a grant proposal. But you can do the proactive steps required in creating a winning proposal.

Allen's book and his organizational system may work for you in rearranging all of your work and, indeed, your life. However, keep in mind that his focus is not on the nonprofit or university workplace. It is on the corporate level. I personally gravitated to the nonprofit world to avoid focusing totally on corporate productivity. While I enjoy an intellectual atmosphere, it would be way too much for me to be as organized as David Allen. However, I still found several of his concepts useful in implementing proactive grants success.

One of Allen's techniques that can be adapted and easily applied to time management related grantseeking is the development of a tickler file. David Allen suggests you label twelve manila folders with the months of the year and thirty-one daily files labeled 1 through 31 to represent the days of the month.[6] While Allen uses these files to do everything, you can just use them just for grantseeking if you choose. The purpose of these files is to keep you on task when projects take multiple steps and the integration of time to collect data, recontact collaborators, and so on. Basically, the tickler system will help you keep the necessary proactive grant steps in front of you at all times.

For example, you select the file folder for the current month and place the appropriate day file folder behind it. On March 1 you remove any tasks left undone in February's folder and reinsert them in March's thirty-one daily folders. The interactive exhibits that go with this book (which can be found at https://rowman.com/ISBN/9781475810110) will help you determine the tasks to put in the files and collect the data needed for your winning grants approach.

For instance, if you were going to contact a colleague to discuss his or her role as an advisor to your proposal effort or possible interest as a collaborator, you put that action step in a folder. But wait, maybe you want to e-mail him or her a one-page concept paper first. Okay, then you must place that action step earlier in March. Pick a date (a folder) and place a note in it to write the concept paper and send it to your colleague in preparation for you contacting him or her. Then contact your colleague on the date selected for follow-up. The rest of this book comprises the actions you should take each month until the *deadline*. Once you determine the program and the deadline, you back up from that date to the present and write your daily prescription for success—the proactive steps in the monthly folders that will ultimately be placed in the daily folders.

If you cannot complete all of the proactive steps before the deadline, recalibrate and look at the next deadline date. Many federal programs rely on two or more deadlines in their yearly grants cycle. Above all, be realistic. Can you get the necessary steps done in view of your time constraints, academic calendar, holidays, vacations, and those other things you *must* do?

Many of the critical proactive steps can be accomplished while at a professional meeting or conference if you practice advanced planning. Preproposal contact with a grantor at a conference is often achievable if it is set up months in advance. In other words, put a note in your March tickler file to contact the granting official to arrange a meeting at the July conference you both will be attending. What day will you phone, e-mail, and follow up with the granting official?

One of my grants fellows successfully integrated the Swiss cheese book concept with David Allen's tickler file system. The necessary data is stored in the three-ring Swiss cheese binder but the tickler files keep him on track each month. Other fellows have successfully used other systems for making sure that the proactive grants steps are accomplished when they need to be. Several have set up tickler files to automatically e-mail them on preselected dates to notify them that they need to make appointments, write one-page concept papers, and so forth. Whatever the case, the necessity to incorporate whatever means you choose to keep you on track will be more evident as the rest of the steps in the proactive, winning grants system unfold.

Why is it so difficult to allocate the time necessary to complete the grants steps? For one thing there are many unknowns. For example, setting up that discussion with your potential advisory committee member may take several e-mails or phone calls and therefore much more time than you had anticipated.

I challenge my fellows in the following way. I ask them if their grant acquisition and all it entails is worth one hour per week (fifty-two hours per year) to their field, their students, and their career. Of course they answer yes. Then I ask them to find the hour. Some say they will use a lunch hour. Others choose to go to work one hour earlier one day per week. Some will carve the hour out of their at-home office time. The important thing is to force yourself to set aside sixty minutes a week. Do whatever it takes. You are worth it and the results will astound you.

Several of my fellows have found that going into work thirty minutes early two times a week works for them. While they may have tried to set aside a half or whole day for their grant proposal development they quickly found out that their most imaginative and energized work was created in shorter time frames. They were right. In fact, studies have shown that in the classroom, students retain 80 percent of the material in the first thirty minutes and 20 percent for the next thirty minutes.

Therefore, use a short, uninterrupted time frame and preferably not during office hours since they are often plagued by unscheduled disruptions. Go into your office or lab early. Leave the lights off if possible and the door locked. Don't make coffee. Don't talk with your colleagues. Turn off your cell phone. Don't answer your text messages. Guard your time and focus on sticking to your plan.

A lot can be accomplished in an hour. You can use the time to update your literature search or to develop a concept paper to discuss with a potential advisory committee member or collaborator. You can also use it to do one of the other proactive steps we have not yet discussed. Since we have just begun describing the proactive steps necessary in a successful grants system you will soon have many more steps to consider adding to your files and accomplishing in the hour you have set aside weekly.

One secret to success is writing down the steps you must accomplish and then prioritizing them. Start each day by taking fifteen minutes to organize your time blocks. You can use "A priority, B priority, and C priority" or "must do, should do, and nice to do." Then look at your list and determine which ones will have the greatest impact on your career.

It is inevitable that some tasks will get moved to "should do" and "nice to do," but the point is that a "must do" on your list of proactive steps to grants success should not be forgotten. If you can't complete it as originally scheduled, it should be moved to tomorrow or designated for a specific day next week.

If you are integrating your proactive grants steps into your other career-related tasks such as publishing, teaching, meetings, and so on, it is easy to see why actions related to a deadline eight months from now do not take precedence. Remember, however, they could be catalytic to moving your career ahead by accomplishing your five-year plan and catapulting you toward your vision of success.

In the article "The Best Time Management Techniques," Maggie McCormick suggests that the best use of time is to set what she calls SMART goals.[7] These goals are specific, measurable, attainable, realistic, and timely. The proactive grant steps in this book fit the SMART concept, especially when you add the "timely" part to your planning.

The hard part is developing and adhering to a time management system. If the one you currently use will allow for the proactive steps outlined in this book, then that's great. If you think you are ready to try something that may be better, here are the top ten books on time management according to amazon.com[8] at the time this book was written:

- *The Skinny on Time Management: How to Maximize Your 24-Hour Gift* by Jim Randel
- *Eat That Frog: 21 Great Ways to Stop Procrastinating and Get More Done in Less Time* by Brian Tracy
- *Getting Things Done: The Art of Stress-Free Productivity* by David Allen
- *Time Power: A Proven System for Getting Done in Less Time Than You Ever Thought Possible* by Brian Tracy
- *Work Less, Do More: The 14-Day Productivity Makeover* by Jan Yager
- *The Time Trap: The Classic Book on Time Management* by R. Alec Mackenzie
- *Autobiography of Benjamin Franklin* by Benjamin Franklin

- *The 25 Best Time Management Tools & Techniques: How to Get More Done Without Driving Yourself Crazy* by Pamela Dodd
- *Remember Everything You Read: The Evelyn Wood 7-Day Speed Reading & Learning Program* by Stanley D. Frank
- *Future Shock* by Alvin Toffler

If you think apps for time management could work for you, check out Amelia Gray's article, "Top 50 Apps for Time Management."[9] Many of them can be used with an iPhone, iPod touch, iPad, or Droid, and all are designed to maximize your time and simplify your life.

If you would rather not spend your money on apps, several time management tools allow free access to basic features, including:

- Desktop iCalendar Lite
- VueMinder Calendar Lite
- Efficient PIM Free
- TimeTo Light

At this point, I have encouraged you to develop a proactive grants system and to consider adapting a time management strategy to integrate the necessary steps into your monthly and, ultimately, daily to-do lists. You are now beginning to recognize the need for and the benefits of a twelve- to eighteen-month approach to each grantor and its deadline. Once you embrace this proactive grants system, you will select multiple grantors (both public and private), each one requiring its own tailored plan. This may seem complex. However, remember that the grants process in itself is simple and it works. You just repeat the process for each grantor and, since you have more than one area of interest, for each of your distinct projects.

To avoid being overwhelmed and losing sight of your five-year goal, I suggest you consider using a simple computer program or software tool to help you envision the *whole* five-year process. You may already have a program that you use for outlining projects. Or you may have access to one that your organization has purchased the rights to use. For the purpose of organizing this book and for demonstrating how to keep your proactive grants system integrated into your five-year vision, I have chosen to use the SmartDraw software program (www.smartdraw.com, 800-768-3729).

You can use a Gantt chart or a program evaluation review technique (PERT) chart software program. For simplicity's sake, and to keep your vision alive, SmartDraw's basic PERT chart software works just fine. The key to this visualization is that there is a scope and sequence to the steps you take for each grant opportunity you pursue. Some steps or activities can be done

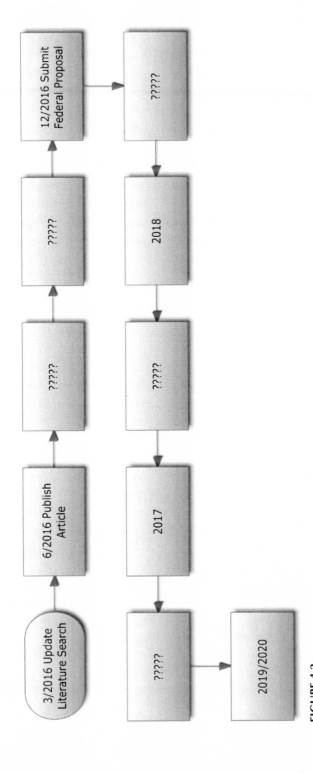

FIGURE 4.2
Action Steps Chart: Sample Five-Year Plan

simultaneously. Others can only be accomplished after a previous task is successfully completed.

Figure 4.2 provides a visual representation of what I refer to as an *action steps chart* throughout many of the chapters in this book. This particular chart depicts a sample five-year plan. The start date is March 2016 and the first action step is updating your literature search. As you can see from the chart, proposal #1 has a submission deadline date of December 2016. The question marks in the boxes represent the other steps that must be integrated into a five-year plan. The rest of the proactive grants system steps that must be placed on the one-year 2016 chart follow starting in chapter 6.

Notes

1. Time Management and Goal-Setting Quotes. Retrieved from www.time-management-guide.com/goal-time-quotes.html.

2. Time Management and Goal-Setting Quotes. Retrieved from www.brainyquote.com/quotes/authors/b/b.

3. Alan Lakein, *How to Get Control of Your Time and Life* (New York: American Library, 1974).

4. David Allen, *Getting Things Done: The Art of Stress-Free Productivity* (New York: Penguin Group, 2001).

5. Allen, *Getting Things Done,* 38.

6. Allen, *Getting Things Done,* 174.

7. Maggie McCormick, "The Best Time Management Techniques," *eHow.* Retrieved from www.ehow.com/way_5581081_time-management-techniques.html.

8. www.amazon.com/TOP-TEN-BOOKS-TIME-MANAGEMENT/1m/R34QKG 0QTE.

9. Amelia Gray, "Top 50 Apps for Time Management," *WorldWideLearn.* Retrieved from worldwidelearn.com/education-articles/top-50-apps-for-time-management.html.

5

Searching the Literature to Document Your Project's Statement of Need: Creating an Urgent and Compelling Case

WHENEVER I AM AFFORDED the chance to interact with government or private grant personnel, I ask, "What are the most common mistakes that grantseekers make in their proposals?" It turns out that the most common mistake is not following instructions. The second most common mistake is not developing a clear and credible statement of the need to be addressed or the problem they are proposing to solve.

In their zeal and enthusiasm to get money to get started, proposal writers often begin with what they want to do (project methods and protocols) before establishing the need for this or any solution. While this rush to action is understandable—grantseekers are, after all, action-oriented "doers"—this jump to the solution assumes that both you and the grantor know the importance of addressing the need or problem. By making this assumption, you forfeit your opportunity to:

- Demonstrate your command of the latest research in the field.
- Reinforce your credibility as an expert in the field.
- Show confidence in a thorough knowledge of the need or problem that will reinforce an exemplary solution.

Focus on the need or problem that your project seeks to impact. Develop a three- or four-sentence description that describes the need or problem that your proposal (and the grantor's money) will address. Review your problem statement to be sure that it does not contain or present a solution. The proposal component will come later. Start with the problem, not your solution.

To ensure that the description of your need or problem is clear and con- cise, present it to a colleague whose level of expertise is similar to that of your prospective grantor (its reviewers, board members, or staff members). If your test elicits a response that indicates that he or she sees the problem, you are on the right track. Too much jargon or the use of vocabulary that requires an advanced understanding of your field is not good. Trying to be too com- plex to impress your reader will introduce confusion. Remember, even the National Science Foundation cautions you to write for a scientifically literate lay reader.

Many grantseekers make a fatal error when attempting to provide evidence of the need or the problem by documenting the *means* to an end, rather than the end. For example, a prospective grantee who desires a building might mistakenly show evidence of need by providing architecture plans and the documentation of a leaky roof and the presence of asbestos in the existing building. These are not reasons enough for a grantor to fund a building. What the grantseeker should document is the difference between what can be done in the existing facility and what more a new facility would enable the organization to do. In other words, the grantseeker should let the prospective grantor know how a new building would facilitate increased research, pro- grams, and services, or better solve the problems of the organization's clients. The building (or lack of it) is not the problem. It is the means to an end, and the end is what needs to be documented.

Researchers are faced with a similar dilemma. The need is not the research protocol they propose to carry out but rather the benefits of their research and the problems it will be used to solve. Even pure bench research must seek to close a gap of knowledge in the field. The documentation of the need must include a cohesive explanation of how current research has driven the researcher to ask additional questions, seek to test other relationships, and advance the field so that new and even more poignant questions can be asked and answered in the future.

When you are seeking funding for a model or demonstration project, you must first document that there is a problem. Beware: The problem cannot be that your solution does not yet exist. Even though you may believe that your project is a huge improvement over what exists in the field, you must docu- ment the problem and that the current solutions are inadequate. The need is not that your solution or program is not in place. It's that the problem is not being addressed adequately and, as a result, is growing. Your solution is a means to the end. The end is reducing or solving the problem.

After you are satisfied with the quality and appropriateness of your de- scription of the need or problem, place it under question 1 on the Needs As- sessment Worksheet (Exhibit 5.1).

EXHIBIT 5.1
Needs Assessment Worksheet

1. What is the problem?

2. What data do we have to document the problem? (What exists now?)

3. What information do we need to create a compelling and accurate assessment of the problem?

4. What information do we have to provide a clear picture of the desired state of affairs that should or could exist? (What ought to be in the future?)

5. What will happen in the field if the problem is not addressed in a timely manner (the urgency and motivation)?

Documenting the Need or Problem

The way to demonstrate that the need or problem *really* exists, and is not just your opinion, is to collect and organize a search of the most relevant literature in the field. This literature search is a *must* for every type of grant, be it research, demonstration, or project. How do you know that there is a need? How do you know this is a problem? What has been explored to date? Who has done work on solving the problem, and what has that work left unanswered?

At this point you should collect all the information you can on the need or problem. This includes information on past attempts that have failed to solve the problem, and successful attempts that have reduced or affected the problem somewhat, and moved the field ahead to its current position. Use the Internet in your search. Using your favorite search engine, put in the descriptor terms associated with your problem area. To reduce the number of hits, look at what journals or other publications have reported on the problem. Journals are one of the best sources for reviewed and, hence, credible research. Make note of any references to how the research was supported (government funding source, private grantor, etc.) This information may prove valuable to you later when you begin to research the grants marketplace. Collect international, national, regional, and local data. This way you will be prepared to make the case for the problem irrespective of your potential grantor's geographic focus. Enter several of your most significant examples of data that document the problem under question 2 on the Needs Assessment Worksheet (see Exhibit 5.1).

As you consider the existing literature and studies, you will begin to make observations about the data you wish you had to make a more thorough case.

List the information you need to create a more gripping and accurate assessment of the problem under question 3 in Exhibit 5.1. If your completion of Exhibit 5.1 demonstrates that you are weak in the area of needs documentation, or if it becomes difficult to locate studies, literature, or data to document the problem you seek funds to solve, you may find that you need to attract a small foundation or corporate needs assessment grant to help you. For example, if data or studies exist on a national level only, you may decide to prepare a proposal to develop knowledge on a regional or local problem. Yes, it may be possible to locate a local or regional grantor that will value the fact that its modest investment may help you document the problem where it "lives" and ultimately make it possible for you to attract larger grants from other funding sources for conducting your project. A needs assessment grant also can help to position you as the resident expert in your field and provide you with an improved tool to use in the measurement of the need or later in evaluation.

Remember that eventually you must deal with how to measure the extent of the problem to prove that your solution actually works. Therefore, when conducting your literature search, make note of how others in the field have used metrics to define the problem. You may find that the measurement indicators you uncover are not appropriate to use on your solution and that there is no established method to measure the problem. In this situation, you could make the case for a grant to develop accurate and reliable measurement and assessment tools to determine how well your intervention reduces the problem. And making this assessment tool available to others who develop differing approaches to reducing the problem could make your assessment grant even more fundable.

See chapter 22 for information on how to locate potential private funding sources for small needs assessment grants as well as grants to develop reliable measurement and assessment tools.

Creating a Gap between What Exists Now in the Field and What Could or Should Be

Being selected as a grant recipient is based on several variables, many of which are addressed in this book. The most important variable is how well you provide a clear and documented statement of the problem. Grantors are motivated by a desire to alter or impact a problem. Their motivation is enhanced when proposal developers reinforce the importance of their (the grantors') commitment for changing and improving the current condition. Grantseekers can do this by creating a discernable gap between what exists now (based on their search of the literature) and what could or should be (Figure 5.1).

```
┌─────────────────────────────────────────────────────────────────────┐
│                              THE GAP                                  │
│                                                                       │
│   What exists now. What is real.              What could be. The goal. │
│   What the present situation is.  _____ The desired state of    │
│                                               affairs, level of achievement. │
└─────────────────────────────────────────────────────────────────────┘
```

FIGURE 5.1
The Gap Diagram

As you search the literature, be on the lookout for statements or quotes from influential granting officials, corporate executives, foundation directors, or field experts concerning the importance or relevance of solving or reducing the problem. These types of statements or quotes can serve as documentation of the gap between what we know now and what would, could, should, or ought to be. What or who can you quote that documents the value of knowing, proving, or reducing the problem and what ought to be in the future? Record information you gather on the desired state of affairs on the Needs Assessment Worksheet (see Exhibit 5.1, question 4).

The first edition of this book over twenty-five years ago warned the proposal writer to avoid suggesting the *value* of the results of his or her proposal. At that time, this was seen as researcher bias and suggested that the researcher had previous knowledge of the results of the research, and thus the outcomes of testing his or her hypothesis. Much has changed since then as corporations and government agencies have moved from viewing research as a way of expanding knowledge to viewing it for application possibilities and what it can be worth. Even basic researchers must document how their research will move the field forward, save time and money, and expand knowledge that another scientist will use to apply to unique solutions. While grantors refer to these changes or advances in the field as *significant* or *broader impacts,* the focus is on the potential application of the advances to the field.

In addition, all proposal developers, including researchers, need to identify the possible impact of not addressing the problem immediately. It is imperative that they provide grantors with a futuristic reference to why the problem needs to be addressed now. Since your proposal will be evaluated against hundreds of others, and grantors will often have to address multiple gaps in one field, your needs documentation must be compelling. What will continue to happen that is counterproductive in your field, or cannot happen, if this question is not answered? How is time and money wasted if we do not "know"? Use Exhibit 5.1, question 5, to record your thoughts on this question.

Types of Needs Assessment

The two basic grants marketplaces—public (federal, state, and local government agencies) and private (foundations and corporations)—rely on very different forms of need assessment. However, at this point in the grants process you may not know for certain which marketplace you are pursuing, or which specific grantor or grant program you will be approaching. Therefore, as you collect studies, reports, and statistics that document the problem or gap, be especially aware of how it is measured or described.

Since you do not yet know which type of grantor you will be pursuing, you might be wise to search for and record needs documentation data that you might normally overlook because it is not scientifically valid. (Remember, many grantseekers who assume they will be approaching only federal grant sources discover that they could benefit from a small needs assessment grant from a local foundation or corporate grantor to strengthen their larger federal proposal.)

Most researchers and innovative program and project developers seeking government (federal and state) grants and sizable grants from larger foundations will search for and record information derived from three sources outlined in the Statistically Based Needs Documentation Table (Table 5.1): statistical analysis, survey, and studies. These types of grantors have professional staffs, use a peer-review process that is based on their knowledge of the major contributors in the field and their work, and prefer needs statements based on facts and studies. Use the information outlined in Table 5.1 to categorize and evaluate the data you have collected. Are there problems with the data or the approach? Are there gaps or conflicting results?

Researchers should be wary of becoming so impassioned in the documentation of their project that they run the risk of being perceived as arrogant or disrespectful of their fellow scientists. Imagine you are writing a proposal for a research project, and you have decided to document the need by citing relevant research in the field. Besides making sure that your references document both the urgency of the problem and your command of the current knowledge in the field, be certain not to include statements about the citations that minimize the work of other researchers, or make them appear ignorant because they did not understand the importance of reducing or eliminating the problem the way that you do. Remember that the researchers quoted in your citations, or one of their graduate students, doctoral students, or friends, may be on your prospective grantor's review committee. Keep sight of the fact that the last thing you want to do is cause dissonance in the reviewers.

TABLE 5.1
Statistically Based Needs Documentation Table

METHOD	*POSITIVES*	*NEGATIVES*
Statistical Analysis: Most funders like to see a few well-chosen statistics. With this approach you use existing data to develop a statistical picture of the needs population: • Census data/records • Government studies/ reports • Reports and research articles	• Abundance of studies and data • Little cost to access data • Allows for flexibility in drawing and developing conclusions • Analysis of data is catalytic in producing more projects and proposals as staff "sees" the need	• Can be very time consuming • Bias of staff shows up in studies quoted • Belief on funder's part that anything can be proven with statistics • If original data have questionable validity, your extrapolation will be inaccurate
Survey: Very commonly used approach to gathering data on the needs population. This approach is useful even when the survey is carried out with volunteers and has limited statistical validity. Accurate surveys may entail control groups, random samples, computers, and statistical analysis. However, acknowledging that the results of your survey cannot be extrapolated beyond the sample group will prove more than adequate in most situations.	• High credibility with funders • Excellent flexibility in design of survey to get at problem areas and document exactly what you want to document • Demonstrates local need • Provides proof of your concern for the problem well in advance of proposal preparation • Small sample size and identified needs population provide for an inexpensive means of assessment	• Takes time to conduct survey properly • Small sample size and nonrandom sample make it impossible to extrapolate to the entire needs population
Studies: Citation of relevant research in the field or area of need. Common approach to document the gap between what is and what ought to be for research and model projects. The search should focus on literature that resulted from a controlled study or use of a scientific approach.	• Citing studies demonstrates the proposal developer's thoroughness and expertise in the area and command of the subject data • Studies provide an unbiased approach to documentation of need	• Unless properly organized, the literature search may seem disjointed and overwhelming to the reader • Time consuming

Be aware also that you could cause dissonance by citing references, researchers, or data that the reviewers do not favor. While the reviewers' reactions to specific information are not totally in your control, the more you know about the values and background of the reviewers and decision makers, the better able you will be to avoid this problem.

TABLE 5.2
Needs Assessment Table

METHOD	POSITIVES	NEGATIVES
Key Informant: Solicit information from individuals whose testimony or description of what exists for the client population or state of affairs is credible because of their experience and expertise. This includes elected officials, agency heads, police chiefs, delinquency case workers, parole officers, etc. Funders may value their opinions and insights.	• Easy to design. • Costs very little. • You control input by what you ask and whom. • Excellent way to position your organization with important people (shows you're working on common problems and concerns).	• Most funding sources recognize that you have selected and included comments from those individuals sympathetic to your cause, and that you may be leaving out parts of the population who feel differently.
Community Forum: Host or sponsor public meetings. You publicize the opportunity to present views of the populace and invite key individuals to speak.	• Easy to arrange. • Costs very little. • Increases your visibility in the community. • Promotes active involvement of the populace. • Funder may like the grassroots image it creates.	• Site of forum has profound effect on amount and type of representation. • You can lose control of the group and have a small vocal minority slant that turns the meeting into a forum for complaints.
Case Studies: An excellent way to assist the funder in appreciating what representative members of the client population are up against. Select individuals from the needs population or client group, and provide an analytical, realistic description of their problem or situation, need for services, etc.	• Easy to arrange. • Costs very little. • Increases sensitivity to the client's "real world." • Very moving and motivating.	• Your selection of a "typical" client may be biased and represent a minority of cases. • You must describe one "real" person, not a composite of several. The anonymity of the person must be ensured.

Most foundations and corporations do not have professional staff. Nor do they use outside reviewers or formal scoring systems to evaluate proposals. They are generally interested in seeing a few references concerning the current research in the field, but they are more concerned with the local or regional impact of the proposed work. In fact, the use of a statistically driven needs assessment may prove counterproductive in helping these types of grantors visualize the need. Corporate and foundation grantors usually respond well to case studies or examples of the human side of the need. Review the Needs Assessment Table (Table 5.2) for some ideas on how you might collect some less statistically based but motivating data. While the strategies outlined in Table 5.2 do not hold up well under scientific review, they do help at getting the grantor to *see* the problem.

After reviewing Exhibit 5.1 and Tables 5.1 and 5.2, you may be thinking of what additional needs assessment tools might be required to make a compelling case to the grantor, or how you can combine the different techniques to have the greatest impact. I have seen a federal review group react positively to the placement of a case study in a very statistically and scientifically based proposal. The fact that the project initiators took the time to interview clients put a real human side to their proposal. Whatever the case may be, by having a variety of needs assessment techniques at your disposal, you will enhance your ability to tailor your proposal to your specific grantor.

After you, the grantseeker, document a need, ask yourself the following question: Would you dedicate your own money to closing this gap between what we know now and what we could know or do? Many grantseekers say no to this question, but they are happy to take someone else's money. Compelling and motivating proposals come from grantseekers who truly believe that their project is critical to closing the gap and would use their own money if they had it.

Many proposals contain very innovative and creative solutions that could result in a great impact in its field. But because the proposal developer has failed to document the gap and problem accurately and definitively, the grantor is left doubting whether the grantee will be able to prove that a change has occurred. The current grants marketplace emphasizes accountability and wants to fund scientifically valid, reproducible studies. Government and private grantors want you to demonstrate that the gap or problem will be reduced. Only by a comprehensive search of what has been done and how it has been measured and documented can you prove to the grantor that you know the problem thoroughly and will be accountable for measuring the impact they (the grantor) can take credit for.

6

Developing and Evaluating Alternative Solutions

FROM THE PRECEDING CHAPTERS, you can already deduce that the grant-winning solution is not based on which approach *you* favor. It is based on the one that the grantor or the reviewer thinks is the best. Since *best* is a values-based term, the strategy suggested in this chapter is to review the problem and to develop at least two or three approaches that could be used to solve it without introducing your own biases or values. Since you have not identified all of your prospective grantors at this point and researched what they want, keep an open mind and generate a variety of solutions that could appeal to that unknown but perfect grantor.

The purpose here is to create several possible alternative solutions or protocols that work to solve the identified problem. These alternatives will be used to uncover potential grantors and in discussions with grantors during preproposal contact. By developing several approaches, you demonstrate that you are flexible and that you are willing to eventually settle on a solution that fits both you and the grantor. However, it is important to be clear that your final proposal will embrace only one approach. You will not be sending the prospective grantor three ways to solve the problem and asking them to pick one. Your final proposal will be very focused. But you are not there yet.

Using a scientific method would require that you review the literature first, develop solutions, and then evaluate them to identify the best choices. The truth is that most grantseekers display their own biases by deciding on an approach, intervention, or solution first and then identifying data that reinforces it. Essentially, their values glasses use selective discrimination to view only the data that validate their selected approach.

I urge you not to succumb to this very natural tendency because it may keep you from uncovering unique and sometimes novel grant-winning solutions. Try as best you can to be impartial and to explore at least several of the possible solutions. In my seminars I like to remind myself, as well as my participants, of Joyce Cary's (1888–1957) quote: "It is the tragedy of the world that no one knows what he doesn't know—and the less a man knows, the more sure he is that he knows everything."[1]

In addition to appearing open-minded, this approach will generate many possible solutions that can be used with grantors in preproposal discussions to elicit their feedback and to uncover the criteria they may be using to select their grant recipients. The grantseeker who approaches a potential grantor in preproposal contact with only one solution to the problem not only demonstrates a myopic viewpoint, but also has little to fall back on if the grantor is not interested in that particular approach or indicates that that approach has already been tried with poor results. Your project or research is important enough that in these cases you will be sure to have "backup" solutions, protocols, or approaches to present.

Also, it is crucial to recognize that granting agencies, their staffs, and their reviewers all have their own values glasses that they use to view and evaluate ideas and approaches. By having several solutions ready, you will have a much better chance of hitting the grantor's hot spot. To develop and present the approach that you believe will be the grant winner, you must uncover the variables that the grantor will consider in making its selections. Will it see the *best* approach as the one that:

- Is the most cost efficient?
- Is the most reliable and valid?
- Will have the greatest impact in the field?
- Is likely to be applied in the field?

The strategies for gathering grantor research presented in chapters 13, 22, and 29 will help you determine the variables considered by your prospective grantor. But at this point you need to come up with at least two solutions and develop a system you will eventually employ to evaluate them.

Brainstorming More Fundable Ideas

One of the most productive techniques for developing a variety of alternative solutions to problems is to organize a brainstorming session. Ask a small group of colleagues who have some related knowledge or interest in your problem area to join you in exploring unique and creative approaches to solving or reducing the problem you have identified. Whether this exercise is accomplished in a small, face-to-face group setting; through a conference call; or over the Internet; inviting others to share in idea generation taps the collective genius of the group and builds support for your proposal. In fact, the brainstorming process can even promote the concept that your project includes the input of others. This way colleagues and volunteers will be more willing and eager to work at night and on weekends in an effort to promote a proactive approach that exceeds the deadline. This initial group may even form the nucleus of a project team, advisory group, or consortia (more on this in chapter 9).

Care should be taken to state the purpose of the brainstorming session to the group. At this point, you will just be exploring possible alternative solutions to the problem. However, many researchers are reluctant to share their ideas and creative solutions because they fear that they will be stolen by colleagues. In the majority of cases, this fear is unwarranted. Most colleagues can be trusted and discussing proposal ideas and solutions with them will help eliminate the development of narrow, self-focused grant ideas. In addition, more and more grantors are interested in sponsoring consortium grants, and brainstorming ideas can provide an ideal way to foster the development of a

EXHIBIT 6.1
Rules to Successful Brainstorming

1. Break your participants into groups of five to eight.
2. Ask for a volunteer to act as a neutral group leader to facilitate the process (encouraging and prodding other members, checking the time, etc.). Appoint one if necessary.
3. Ask for a volunteer to act as a recorder. Appoint one if necessary. You may even want to use a recording device.
4. Set a time limit. Ten minutes will be plenty.
5. State one question or research problem (e.g., reducing the number of high school dropouts, nutritional needs of pregnant adolescents, increasing awareness of wildlife preservation, the role of genes in obesity).
6. Ask the group members to generate and present as many possible solutions to the problem as they can within the time limit.
7. Encourage the group members to piggyback on each other's ideas (suggesting a new idea that adds to the one already given).
8. Record all answers, combining those that are similar. Actual electronic recording of the session is optimal if everyone agrees to it.
9. Avoid any evaluation or discussion of the ideas until the process is over. This rule is critical for productive brainstorming. The recorder can ask to have an idea repeated but should allow no comments, negative or positive from others (e.g., "We can't do that!" "That's stupid!" or "I love your thinking!").

consortium. Since you may be employing this technique as a vehicle to create partners and consortia, it is critical that you share ideas in a noncompetitive forum. However, if any concerns should arise related to the ownership of the ideas as intellectual property or as part of a noncompetitive agreement, they should be addressed immediately. Universities can provide intellectual property agreements, noncompetitive agreements, and patent or copyright forms, and are usually willing to share these forms with nonprofit organizations.

Brainstorming is a simple technique for quickly generating a list of creative ideas. To obtain maximum benefit from the process, provide your group participants with Rules to Successful Brainstorming (Exhibit 6.1). While most individuals will say they know how to brainstorm, many frequently stop the creative brainstorming process too soon and start evaluating approaches before they should. Reviewing the rules in Exhibit 6.1 will help avoid this.

Cost-Benefit Analysis

An important aspect of any fundable idea is its economic feasibility. Funding sources want to know that you have chosen methods that will produce the best results for the least amount of money. The following Cost-Benefit Analysis Worksheets (Exhibits 6.2 and 6.3) will help you demonstrate fiscal accountability. If your problem area involves solutions that will be part of a demonstration project or program, use Exhibit 6.2 to help grantors compare and evaluate the approaches you present to them. If your problem is clearly related to a solution that would commonly be called a *research protocol*, then Exhibit 6.3 will be more useful.

Take a few minutes to complete the exhibit you find most appropriate for your situation. Select two or three solutions that present different approaches. Some variables to consider are differing cost estimates and expected benefits, and the inclusion of consortia or large-scale solutions.

Instructions for Completing Exhibit 6.2

Column 1. Place brief descriptions of two or three approaches you are considering in column 1. For example, a project to feed senior citizens could range from a meals-on-wheels program to group meals to a food cooperative for the elderly. The approaches you present should meet the goals of the project from your brainstormed list of ideas.

Column 2. Record the estimated total cost of each idea and methodology in column 2. This figure can be taken from your Preproposal Summary and Approval Form (see Exhibit 10.1 in chapter 10) and is intended to be an estimate

EXHIBIT 6.2
Cost-Benefit Analysis Worksheet for Projects/Programs

Summary of Idea and Methodology	Total Cost for Each Idea and Methodology	Total Number of Persons Served for Each Idea and Methodology	Total Cost per Person Served for Each Idea and Methodology	Positive Points of Each Idea and Methodology	Negative Points of Each Idea and Methodology

of the cost of the approach, not a final budget. One way to ensure variety in the approaches and in the amount of funds required is to select the approach you favor and determine how you would have to alter it if you could have only one-half of the amount requested.

Column 3. Use column 3 to estimate the total number of people who will be affected by each approach. Remember to roll out the benefits over several years and, if applicable, over the life of the equipment to be used.

Column 4. Enter the estimated cost per person or client served for each approach. This is essential since funding sources are apprehensive about sponsoring projects that possess an unrealistic cost per individual served. Projects with a high cost per person are considered a waste of money by many funders because grantseekers may have great difficulty securing continued or follow-up funding for such projects. If one of the proposed outcomes is replication of the project, the high cost per person may be a serious limitation.

Column 5. Summarize the positive points of each idea and methodology in this column. By having this information on hand, some funders may actually consider supporting a more costly approach because they can see how the outlined advantages outweigh the expense.

Column 6. In this column, outline the disadvantages or drawbacks to each approach. This demonstrates your honesty, which will increase both your credibility with funders and their confidence in you. Funders know that each approach has pitfalls or variables that must be controlled, so be forthright and point them out. While this may appear to be highlighting your Achilles heel, you garner the grantor's confidence when you show that you will not forget the problems and will deal with them in your proposal.

Instructions for Completing Exhibit 6.3

Column 1. In this column, place a brief synopsis of the protocol or approach you are suggesting to prove or disprove your research question.

Column 2. Estimate the total cost for each protocol and approach.

Column 3. For each protocol and approach listed, briefly state the broader impacts or significance to the field.

Column 4. List the limitations or extraneous variables that make each protocol or approach difficult. Be sure to include any variables that may restrict its usefulness or its possibility for extrapolation.

Use these worksheets each time you refine your project ideas or research protocols and bring completed Cost-Benefit Analysis Worksheets to preliminary meetings with funding officials. They will be impressed that you considered their financial interest while designing your project or research.

EXHIBIT 6.3
Cost-Benefit Analysis Worksheet for Research Protocols/Approaches

Summary of Research Protocol/Approach	Total Cost for Each Research Protocol/Approach	Broad Impacts in Field for Each Research Protocol/Approach	Variables that Present a Challenge for Each Research Protocol/Approach

Executives of profit-making companies are very sensitive about maintaining cost efficiency in all of the investments they make. They carry over their corporate values glasses to their work with nonprofits. By taking costs into account when refining your project ideas or research protocols, you will win more grants. By brainstorming more approaches to solving problems, you will not only appear to be open to considering more solutions, you will also initiate a process that can lead to uncovering more potential grantors.

Figure 6.1 illustrates the next step to place on your action steps chart. So far you have done or are doing the following tasks.

1. You have clearly identified a problem, a need, or a gap that must be closed and have updated your search of relevant literature in your field.
2. You are developing ideas, methodologies, solutions, innovative protocols, projects, and research to increase knowledge and practices to impact the problem.

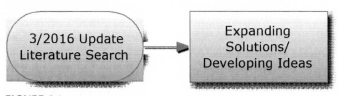

FIGURE 6.1
Action Steps Chart: Expanding Solutions

Note

1. http://izquotes.com/quote/325934.

7

Creating Key Search Terms to Identify the Best Grantor(s): Redefining Your Project and Improving Your Research/Grants Profile

<hr>

THE SECRET TO TAPPING INTO THE $566.84 BILLION in federal, foundation, and corporate grant funds is to find the right grantor for your research or project. The first step to finding the right grantor is to determine the best key words or terms to use in your funding source database searches. Grants databases allow you to enter key search terms into their systems, which they then match to similar words in their database, and then to funding sources with interest in that area. The key search words contained in the databases are either selected by the grantors represented in the database or by the best efforts of data input personnel. A match between a key word and a grantor is frequently referred to as a *hit*.

Online databases are improving every day. They are faster and contain more helpful information than ever to assist you in matching your proposal to the most appropriate grantor or grantors. But your success still relies on your development and use of the *right* key words for your search. Grantors and database managers look at the world through their own values glasses and unique lenses. The key words they select to describe the grantor's interests may be quite different than the key search terms you would use to define your research or project. That is why it is so important when developing key search terms to think about your project from a grantor's perspective and how others might describe it and its benefits. Unfortunately, the more zealous you are as a grantseeker, the harder it sometimes is to look at your project and its benefits with flexibility and an open mind. For example, when I was working with an organization assisting the blind, the grantseekers initially did not want to use the term *blind* as a search term. They felt it was an old and somewhat discriminatory term. I suggested using *visually impaired, visually challenged,* or *visually handicapped.* They preferred *people without sight* as their key search term, but they did not get any hits. When they used *blind* and *visually impaired,* they uncovered many granting opportunities. They decided that the use of these words was not so bad after all as long as it helped them find the money and right grantor for their project. The moral of the story is to be wary of how your own values glasses and specialized jargon may keep you from recognizing and using the most productive key search words or terms. Also be aware of the fact that databases don't always use the newest and most politically correct terms. They often use more outdated terms that were used for cataloguing previously granted awards. For example, you might think it's a good idea to search for grant opportunities supporting research or projects related to mentally retarded individuals by using the newest term, *intellectually and developmentally disabled (IDD).* However, it may take several years for this search term or phrase to make it into databases and you may get more hits under *mentally impaired, mentally challenged,* or *mentally disadvantaged.*

Before you begin the process of determining your key words, review the literature in the field. What are the terms used in the literature, and what is their frequency of use? What are the terms commonly used in related news releases and presentations? Are related terms consistently used throughout these sources? Are the terms changing and evolving? What terms from your literature search resulted in hits?

Many of the grants databases let you review the terms they use to categorize grants interests. Many of the grants databases discussed in this book use a thesaurus of key terms to help you develop a more productive list of search words. The secret is to use several terms and see which combination meets with what appears to be the most interested grantors. Also take into consideration that most of the electronic databases allow you to place quotation marks around phrases to perform a more precise search. For example, if you search using *higher education* without quotation marks, the database's use of Boolean logic would search under *higher* and under *education* and then both *higher education* and *education higher.* But by placing quotation marks around the two-word phrase, it would search only for grantors whose interest area was *higher education.* Obviously, the same holds true for the previously mentioned search terms (visually impaired, mentally challenged, etc.).

Redefining Your Research or Project to Develop More Key Search Terms

The more key words you can use to define your research or project and its benefits, the more grantors you may be able to uncover who could see how your project relates to their needs. By redefining your project you can develop more search terms and thus increase the likelihood of relating your project to new and different grantors. However, project redefinition calls for more flexibility than just identifying different terms. Redefinition requires that you look carefully at your project and ask how you could change it slightly to make it and its contributions valuable to other constituency groups, causes, or interest areas, thereby expanding the universe of your potential grantors.

For example, a project aimed at developing the writing skills of fourth-grade students was cleverly redefined to look at how the Internet could be used to increase reading and writing skills. In fact, the grantseeker (teacher) used the Internet to connect fourth graders to elderly individuals at a senior citizens center who became their adopted grandparents and communicated with them via e-mail. Through e-mail, the students strengthened their reading and writing skills and actually got writing tips from their adopted grand-mothers and grandfathers. The high school computer club also got involved by training the students and the elderly on how to use e-mail to connect with one another, thereby making a community service project out of it. This example of redefinition moved the project from benefiting the fourth grade to a much larger world and allowed the grantseeker to expand her search words to include several relevant fields such as seniors and elderly. It also eventually led her to the key word that worked. Ultimately, the grantor selected was interested in techniques to engage the senior brain in mentally stimulating activities and thereby reduce the risk of developing dementia; learning new skills like e-mailing just happened to be one of these techniques!

Research grant ideas can also be redefined by extrapolating to other areas and fields. The focus of the research could be slightly changed, or others involved in similar projects with a slightly different approach could be invited to participate in a consortium grant. As with the generation of project grant ideas, you are limited only by your own level of creativeness. For example, if you use *basic science* in your field as your key search term, the National Science Foundation (NSF) will appear as a potential grantor. If in your quest to understand the basic science you could also impact a major health problem, you could use the potential extrapolation of your research to attract funding from the National Institutes of Health (NIH) as well. Both grantors could potentially fund you to set up your research to complete your protocol—but for two entirely different reasons. NIH might fund you because your research may create a new drug or procedure related to a specific disease. NSF might fund you because your research may demonstrate why and how molecules bond together to form a new and unique substance.

While the goal of this process is to uncover the less than obvious grantors, the process of redefinition is not intended to take you off track from your grants plan or to turn you into a grants mercenary who will do anything for money regardless of where it takes you or your organization. If you do not like the direction redefinition takes you, do not go there. But if redefinition allows you to locate even partial funding for a related project that keeps you, your career, and your grants plan operational, you may want to pursue it rather than to be a purist with no funding.

To uncover your most operant terms, complete the Redefinition/Key Search Terms Worksheet (Exhibit 7.1). This worksheet should be used to help develop key search terms for identifying potential government funding sources, as well as foundation grantors. However, I suggest you use a different worksheet (Exhibit 7.2) to help you develop corporate key search terms.

EXHIBIT 7.1
Redefinition/Key Search Terms Worksheet

---

1. *Values:* What words would grantors use to describe the value of their program to the field?

2. *Subject Area Terms:* Subject areas such as employment, environment, mental health, and child development are used as key search terms in many of the electronic grantor databases. List the subject areas that your project can be related to or impacts.

3. *Other Potentially Relevant Fields:* How could you change the focus of your project so that it could be potentially related to more subject areas or fields, and what would these areas or fields be?

4. *Constituency Groups:* Many government and private funding sources focus their grant priorities by the constituency groups they want to impact, such as children, at-risk youth, elderly, economically disadvantaged, and so on. What constituency group(s) would a funding source have to care about to support your project?

5. *Project Location:* What is the geographic location for your project, and how could you redefine it to better appeal to a grantor's geographic perspective?

   City/Community   County/Borough/Parish   State
   Regional   National   International

6. *Type of Grant:* What type of grant support are you looking for, and how could you redefine your project to attract grantors interested in different types of support?

   Model/Demonstration Project   Research Project   Needs Assessment Grant
   Planning Grant   Training Grant   Discretionary
   Unsolicited Proposal   Contract   Other

7. *Consortia Partners:* What potential partners or collaborators could you involve to assist in redefining your project and enhancing your funding perspective? What are the advantages of including them?

Searching for corporate grantors requires a special focus because of the unique way corporate grantors view the grants process and its benefits. When searching for corporate grantors, you must take into consideration that corporations usually prefer to support projects where they "live" and like to fund projects that can be related to their profits, products, and workers. Use the Corporate Redefinition Worksheet (see Exhibit 7.2) to develop search terms associated with the following:

- hiring, retaining, educating, or training today's workforce as well as the future's
- employee benefits and resulting corporate benefits
- positioning of the corporation as a concerned partner in the field and in your geographic area

In addition, consider whether there is or could be a direct benefit between your project and increasing corporate profits through:

- possible patents or new product development
- product enhancement, redesign, or reengineering
- product position or sales

EXHIBIT 7.2
Corporate Redefinition Worksheet

1. How does your intended project or research relate to the concerns of corporate (for-profit) grantors? What are your shared values?

2. Does or can your project or research provide benefits to corporations in the areas of:
   - Employee development or skill enhancement? If so, how?
   - Employee benefits (including health, quality of life, low costs or risks)?
   - If so, how?
   - Public relations (promotion of a concerned and responsible image in the community)?
   - If so, how?

3. Can you redefine your project so that it increases corporate profits by:
   - Promoting a lead to new product development (possible patents, etc.)? If so, explain.
   - Enhancing current products through new applications, redesign, etc.? If so, explain.
   - Increasing sales through product positioning with clients, students, etc.? If so, explain.

Developing Your Research/Grants Profile

Many of the databases you encounter will encourage you to provide them with a profile consisting of your search terms so that a constant search for new potential grantors can be carried out automatically and sent to you by e-mail. This search component is available on several free, as well as sub-scription-only, electronic funding databases. These databases are discussed in greater detail in Chapters 13 and 22.

The success of all of these systems relies on your development of key words. The time to develop and redefine your project for the key words is when the need and the innovative solutions are fresh in your mind. After you have read this chapter and completed the accompanying exhibits, you will increase your understanding of how you could conduct a database search for grantors that could be so specific as to determine which grantors funded projects related to these key search terms in certain zip codes!

To help you visualize the process thus far, you have done or are doing the following tasks:

1. You have clearly identified a problem, a need, or a gap that must be closed and have updated your search of relevant literature in your field as it relates to the identified problem.
2. You have developed ideas, methodologies, solutions, innovative pro-tocols, projects, and research to increase knowledge and practices to impact the problem.
3. You are developing key terms to use in database searches to locate the most appropriate grantors.

A diagram of this effort to date might look like the one shown in Figure 7.1. Each chapter discusses another step in the proactive funding process. How will you work them into your plan and when?

FIGURE 7.1
Action Steps Chart: Developing Search Terms

8

Capitalizing on Your Capabilities

W HY WOULD A FUNDING SOURCE SELECT your organization and you, as the project director or principal investigator, to grant funds to? If your response is, "Because we thought up a fabulous project," you are not looking at your proposal from the grantor's perspective. Even if your approach to solving the problem is creative and dynamic, the grantor's ultimate decision is based on who it believes can best carry out the project. While grantors expect creativity and superior ideas, they make their final decision based on the grantee's ability to complete the project.

While the criteria used to evaluate federal applications vary from department to department, office to office, and program to program, most government grant applications include review criteria that specifically address the capabilities of the project's key personnel and the extent to which the grantee's own resources can support the proposed project. For example, the Department of Education commonly refers to these selection criteria as "Quality of Personnel" and "Adequacy of Resources." In terms of quality of the project personnel, the Department of Education wants to know the qualifications, including relevant training and experiences, of the project director or principal investigator and other key personnel. Often, they are also interested in knowing the extent to which the applicant encourages applications for employment from persons who are members of groups that have been traditionally underrepresented based on race, color, national origin, gender, age, or disability.

The National Science Foundation (NSF) evaluates these two variables under its general review criteria titled "Intellectual Merit of the Proposed Activity." Proposals to the NSF will be evaluated in part on how well qualified the proposer (individual or team) is to conduct the project, the quality of the proposer's prior work (when applicable), and if there is sufficient access to resources at the grantee's organization to support the project.

Many federal agencies and departments allocate points to each of the review criteria they select. Others rank them on a scale. While the scoring method used to evaluate the quality of key personnel and the adequacy of resources will vary with each program, you will be asked repeatedly to document why your organization's resources and you and your partners' skills and background make you the perfect choice to carry out the proposal. You will also be asked how you plan to address any areas of weakness.

While your proposed project or research is still in the idea stage and not fully fleshed out, it is appropriate to begin to think about the quality of your key staff and your institutional resources. As you think through personnel and resource requirements, you can begin to identify those areas where you may come up short compared to your competition. By beginning to think about the following questions you will ultimately be better able to identify possible collaborators, co-principal investigators, and consortia partners who will improve your funding chances. (Chapter 9 specifically deals with developing teams and partners.) Although you are not expected to be able to fully address these issues at this stage in the process, taking a few minutes to think about them now will help you in the long run and prepare you for what you will need in the future.

- Do you have job descriptions that reflect the skills needed to carry out your proposed work effectively?
- Are the duties of personnel clearly defined?
- What relevant qualifications do the proposed personnel possess, especially the project director? (Focus on their experience and training in fields related to the objectives of the project, though other information may be considered.)
- Will proposed personnel need to be trained for the project?
- How much time will the proposed personnel actually devote to the project?
- To what extent do you encourage employment applications from and hire members of traditionally underrepresented groups?

When evaluating your adequacy of resources, determine if your facilities and equipment are adequate for your project purposes and what special sources of experience or expertise will be required.

The importance of this documentation is even more evident when you compete for government contracts. In this very competitive process of bidding on the completion of a well-defined deliverable, you must actually include a capability statement that documents your capacity, resources, and related experience in producing the desired end. Even if you are the lowest bidder for the contract, you can be passed over for a higher, but more capable, bidder.

In many instances, making a grantor's first cut means that you are now on a short list of potential grantees, which includes hundreds as opposed to thousands of applications. What can you do to enhance your proposal in such a way that it makes the final award list? Be ready with the facts about your capability and capacity to do an excellent job.

Because they are fearful of appearing arrogant or boastful, many well-intended grantseekers are hesitant to enhance their proposals by emphasizing their unique qualifications. This is unfortunate. While you should not create falsehoods or downgrade your competition, you do need to analyze your institution's capabilities and the characteristics that differentiate you from the other applicants. Your prospective grantor needs to know that your proposal has a greater likelihood of success because of your and your collaborators' personal capabilities and your institution's distinct advantages. These advantages are not hypothetical but rather the actual resources involved in the successful completion of the activities and methods that your project or research will use.

Every funding source will want to know why you are its best choice for funding, and developing a list of your organization's special qualities for uniquenesses will go a long way toward convincing a grantor that yours is the right organization to fund.

When to Use Similarity as a Uniqueness

In model or demonstration grants, as opposed to research proposals, you may need to consider varying the uniqueness approach slightly. If one of the desired outcomes of the grant is to develop a model that can be applied to other client populations, organizations, institutions, or colleges, then you need to demonstrate your similarity to others in your field that face the same problem. You do not want to highlight the *unique* qualities of your institution because they limit extrapolation to similar groups and would weaken your case for the model's ability to be replicated. Instead, you want to identify the variables you share with others and focus on the uniquenesses that allow you and your organization or institution to develop, test, and produce materials that will be useful to those who will follow the results of your work or copy your model. For example, other groups may not have the ability to produce a training program and transmit it via satellites. However, they can still receive and use the training and then replicate the programs.

Uniqueness Exercise

Most foundations and corporations do not have a review process that is as well defined or documented as do public funding sources. But they still have the same question in mind: "Why should we fund you and your organization to do this project?" Later, in parts 2, 3, and 4 of this book, you will learn where to include these important credibility builders (uniquenesses) in your proposal. But why wait to identify them until you are filling out your application? Consider developing a list you can use with many grant opportunities. Start now and be one step ahead of the game.

Use the following brainstorming exercise to develop a data bank of your organization's unique features. This exercise will add a little excitement and flavor to meetings and can be done with a variety of groups such as staff, volunteers, clients, board members, and grants advisory committee members. Keep the information you develop in your Swiss cheese book, where it will be ready for use in proposals, endorsement letters, and preproposal contact. This material can also be placed on your organization's website and made available to others who might be able to use it in their proposal development.

Please note that you may encounter some initial reluctance to this exercise because some individuals think it promotes bragging. However, these same individuals probably believe that humility and occasional begging will move grantors to take pity on your organization and fund your proposals. They are wrong! From the grantor's point of view, the humble, woe-are-we approach does not highlight the reasons a prospective grantee should be funded and may actually do the opposite.

To combat this problem, remind all those participating in the exercise of its positive results. After the exercise, you will have a list of factors that make your organization a strong contender from which you will be able to select those uniquenesses that may appeal to a particular funding source. Also, the exercise will refocus those participating in the activity on the positive attributes of your organization and away from the negative.

1. Distribute the Uniqueness Worksheet (Exhibit 8.1) to the group, remind the group of the rules for brainstorming (outlined in chapter 6), and set a time limit for brainstorming.
2. Record the group's answers to questions 1 and 2.
3. Ask the group to rank the order of the responses to the questions from a potential grantor's perspective with rank number 1 being the most positive uniqueness or qualification.
4. Have the group select the top three answers for both questions and combine them to develop a list of your organization's most positive

uniquenesses or qualifications with respect to the adequacy of your institutional resources and the quality of your project personnel.

EXHIBIT 8.1
Uniqueness Worksheet

Federal and state proposal applications require information on your
organization's ability to perform the tasks you outline in your proposal. Your
unique qualities or attributes are what enable you to perform these tasks. The
sections of government applications that require this information are sometimes
referred to as *Adequacy of Institutional Resources and Quality of Project
Personnel.*

On government applications, these sections may be assigned a point value.
While these components may not be mandatory on foundation and corporate
proposals, the information they contain is equally important in convincing
private funding sources that your organization is the right grantee for them.

What makes your organization uniquely suited to carry out the work outlined
in your proposal? How will you provide the grantor with the assurance it will
receive a job well done?

1. *Adequacy of Institutional Resources:* Please list the positive qualities and
   uniquenesses that your organization or institution possesses that will ensure
   a grantor that you are the best place to do the job. When applicable, include
   factors such as:

   • relevance of purpose and mission
   • geographic location
   • relationship and availability to subject population
   • presence of animal laboratories
   • data analysis capabilities
   • _____
   • _____
   • _____
   • _____

2. *Quality of Project Personnel:* Please list the unique qualifications of your
   project personnel. Take into consideration factors such as:

   • years of related experience
   • number of publications and presentations
   • awards and special recognition
   • number and dollar amounts of grants and contracts successfully carried out
   • _____
   • _____
   • _____
   • _____

If your institution has a computer or decision lab, have the group meet there so you are in close proximity to the hardware and software necessary to produce instant rank ordering and frequency distributions.

Use the final list to select uniquenesses that will convince funders that their money will go further with you than with any other prospective grantee. For example, a particular funding source may be impressed with your total number of years of staff experience, central location of buildings, special equipment, and broad needs populations and geographic coverage.

Your uniquenesses list will also prove valuable in:

- selecting consortia partners or additional team members who can fill personnel voids or improve your capabilities
- recruiting and training staff, board members, and volunteers
- developing case statements
- using other fund-raising techniques such as direct mail and wills and bequests

Do not forget to include yourself, the proposal initiator, project director, or principle investigator, as a uniqueness. Your previous work, publications, collaborative efforts, awards, and recognition are important components of your organization's overall uniqueness.

One culminating activity is to have half of your group role-play a grantor and the other half role-play a prospective grantee. Review one of the problems or needs your organization is planning to address and your organization's proposed solution. Then have the individuals playing the grantor ask those playing the prospective grantee why the grantseeker's organization should be the one selected to implement the proposed solution. Have the grantee group start by saying, "Our organization is particularly suited to implement this solution because. . . ."

Using Your Organization's Case/Mission Statement to Support Your Proposal

Your case or mission statement is another key ingredient in convincing the grantor that your organization should be selected for funding. When you submit your application for funding, your approach should be based on the following three important factors:

1. There is a compelling need for the project.
2. Your organization is uniquely suited to carry out the project.

3. The project supports your organization's stated purpose or mission and fits with what you are currently doing or planning to do.

The third factor is especially important. Your case or mission statement should demonstrate your organization's predetermined concern for the project area. If yours is a joint or consortia proposal, the mission or case statement of all the participating organizations should provide a documentable concern for the problem you will address. In short, this statement should give the funding source written documentation that the purpose of your organization (its reason for existing), your project, and the grantor's values and concerns are a perfect match.

Using Your Existing Case or Mission Statement

Most nonprofit organizations have an existing case or mission statement. Educational organizations use it to provide the foundation for accreditation and in faculty and staff recruitment. While an institution's case or mission statement can provide the framework for a college, division, department, institute, or center, even the lowest level of the organization should be able to state its case for existence and inclusion in the future of the organization.

Grantors do not want their grant funding to influence what your organization becomes. Instead, they want you to tell them where your organization wants to go and how your proposal will help move it toward that goal.

If you have a case or mission statement, use it to convince the grantor of your purpose. If you do not have a case or mission statement, or if the one you have is no longer appropriate or too long, consider updating it, editing it to one concise page, or developing a new one tailored to the grants marketplace.

Elements of a Case/Mission Statement

Your case or mission statement should consist of how and why your organization got started, what your organization is doing today, and where your organization is going in the future. Use the Case/Mission Statement Worksheet (see Exhibit 8.2) to determine what should be included in your case statement.

How and Why Your Organization Got Started

Explain the original societal problems or needs that resulted in the formation of your organization. Most funding sources will find societal need today more

EXHIBIT 8.2
Case/Mission Statement Worksheet

This worksheet can be completed based on the broad definition of your organization, college, or university, or on a smaller subunit such as your center, institute, school, department, or program.

1. *How and Why Your Organization Got Started:* _____

_____

_____

_____

Year: _____ Primary Movers/Founders: _____
Original Mission: _____

_____

2. *Today—Where Your Organization is Now:* _____

_____

Changes from the Original Mission: _____

_____

Societal Need—Changes in Clients/Students: _____

_____

Current Priorities: _____

_____

Clients: _____
Staff: _____
Buildings: _____

3. *Future—Where Your Organization Will Be Five Years from Now:* _____

_____

Anticipated Changes in Mission: _____

_____

Anticipated Changes in Need: _____

_____

Resulting Changes in Facilities and Staff: _____

_____

4. *Existing or New Opportunities That Will Be Present to Move Your Organization Toward Its Plans/Goals:* _____

_____

important than the number of years your organization has been in existence. In fact, some funding sources actually have the greatest doubts about those nonprofit organizations that have been around the longest. These funders believe that such organizations generally are bureaucratic, have a tendency to lose sight of their mission, and have more so-called deadwood on their payrolls than younger nonprofit organizations.

What Your Organization Is Doing Today

Describe your organization's activities. What are its current priorities, programs, resources, and uniquenesses? Who are its clients? How has the passage of time affected its original mission and reason for being?

Where Your Organization Is Going in the Future

Because funding sources look at their support as an investment, they want to be sure they invest in organizations that will be around when their funding runs out. In other words, they want the organizations they invest in to have a five-year, ten-year, or even longer plan for operation. By demonstrating to funding sources that your organization has a long-range plan and the ability to secure future funding, you will show grantors that you are worthy of their funding and that the project they invest in will continue to benefit people for many years to come.

Remember, potential grantors are most interested in how funding your proposal will move both of your organizations (theirs and yours) toward each of your missions. Funding sources consistently work to separate applicants who sought them out simply as a source of money from applicants who can demonstrate that the direction outlined in their proposal is predetermined and an important component of their organization's overall mission.

In a funded proposal to the BellSouth Foundation for over $250,000, the successful grantee told BellSouth that it was that organization's goal and priority to approach the very same problem that BellSouth funding was designed to impact. In fact, the successful grantee told BellSouth it could show over five years' worth of meeting minutes and budget expenditures that demonstrated its commitment to dealing with the problem. The grantee also went so far as to suggest that it would be committed to the same course of action even without BellSouth's grant. Yes, the grantee told BellSouth that this course of action was so much a part of its goals, stated priorities, and mission that the organization would move ahead with the project anyway! Naturally the grantee also let BellSouth know the project would take ten years without Bell-South's money instead of three years with it. The BellSouth money would be the catalyst in the equation for change. It would hasten the result. BellSouth wanted to be part of the project and funded it.

The importance of relating your proposal to your organization's mission cannot be overemphasized. Before soliciting a potential grantor, be sure to ask yourself whether you are going to the funder just because you heard it had money and you want some or because your proposal can serve the missions you both value.

Review the components of this chapter. You should have identified your strengths such has having the correct resources and personnel to complete the grant successfully. More importantly, your efforts thus far should have elucidated those areas where you may fall short and need to bolster your team.

Remember, identifying your uniquenesses and the elements of your case or mission statement will help you develop a successful proposal. In fact, this is one more proactive step the successful grantseeker will integrate into his or her grants plan. Will you add it to yours?

Figure 8.1 summarizes what your proactive system should look like at this point. When do you plan on brainstorming your capabilities and those of your organization and your consortia partners?

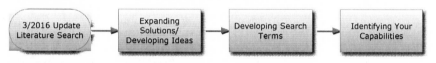

FIGURE 8.1
Action Steps Chart: Identifying Your Capabilities

9

Forming Grant-Winning Teams and Consortia: Recruiting Volunteers for Advisory Groups

M UCH HAS CHANGED IN THE GRANTS MARKETPLACE relative to the acceptance of proposals that call for consortia agreements between nonprofit organizations, for-profit companies, school districts, and institutions of higher education. When the first edition of this manual was written, it was rare to find co-directors or co-principal investigators. It was almost as if federal program officers thought a grant with two directors would be difficult to monitor and that it would be hard to hold co-directors accountable. Due to the complexities of research and model projects, a new paradigm has been raised that values the advantages of sharing expertise, expensive equipment, multiple sites, recruitment of subjects, and the like. There are new funded projects with four and five principal investigators or project directors at sites in different states and even countries.

This change is generally positive and from the grantor's point of view works to ensure excellence, efficacy, and reduced costs. This trend makes your job harder. You must reach across organizations, disciplines, and experts in the field to create the most convincing team to get your grant awarded. But getting funded is just the start. Your consortia or team must work together effectively to implement the project you created. Through all the expectations, deliverables, expenditures, and problems, you must keep your consortia or team together and still talking to each other over the span of a project that may last two years, three years, or longer.

Once I was asked to investigate a failed attempt by a university to set up an interdisciplinary, innovative team that had expended over $1 million in internal start-up funding and did not produce one proposal. I met with the group and asked each member about his or her experience working in groups as a team member. (I could not even call this particular group a team. In fact, it was so dysfunctional that it should have been referred to as a committee.) Despite all of the advanced degrees they had, only one had any instruction on how to be an effective team member, and the instruction was minimal. Follow-up work with major national and international nonprofit groups revealed the same results. Profit-making companies expend millions of dollars on team training while the nonprofit world spends very little. Nevertheless, grant proposal development and the formation of an effective team are critical to your grants success.

As I continued to conduct surveys on team building with my seminar participants, I began to reflect on how much of my success in grantseeking was really related to my ability to get groups to focus on the outcomes of our work and to develop respect for each other's contributions to our goals. Even with a major in psychology with a focus on motivation, advanced degrees in educational administration, and a school superintendent certification, I only had one formal course that even came close to providing team-building training: Psychology 402, Group Dynamics. I remember the class quite clearly. It was taught in a seminar hall with 150 students. There was no lab and we never met in any setting other than a large auditorium, and I certainly did not learn how I impacted a group or team. With that in mind, what formal and informal experiences have developed your insight in how you impact a group or team?

- Where did you learn your team skills?
- Where did you obtain feedback about the impact you have on group process and functioning?
- If in your education you were the curve breaker and had the best scores, how are you now sharing and taking pride in the collective group accomplishment of the team?

If you were able to answer these questions easily and have positive team experience, you will still find the concepts presented in this chapter interesting. Even if the concepts are already familiar to you, are they practiced by your other team members? Probably not, since *team work* and *feedback* are words that are not often heard in colleges, universities, and nonprofit organizations. But wouldn't it be great to operate in an environment where feedback and improved team functioning is a priority and a shared responsibility?

The success of a proposal and the completion of a project rely on the incorporation of a complex mixture of supporting partners and expertise. How this combined effort is created and maintained is fast becoming one of the most critical elements in attracting grant and contract support from government sources, as well as private foundations and corporations. In most cases, the creation of these critically important relationships has been left to chance and luck. However, by employing the science of group dynamics and team interaction, you can move your grant-related groups away from relying on chance and toward increased efficiency and accountability.

The following suggestions for improving your grants success by increasing the effectiveness of your grant-related groups comes from my work and experience with grants professionals who have taken part in my effective grant team-building workshop. Participants of this workshop have been eager to improve how they function in teams and to work on developing more productive approaches to increase their group's effectiveness. I believe their positive responses to increasing personal and group effectiveness is a function of the difficulties they have encountered when attempting to work on proposal development with experts from their interdisciplinary fields—something they are asked to do more and more frequently.

In today's grants marketplace, it is rare to find a project director or principal investigator who possesses *all* of the expertise needed to complete a grant-funded project in any area, and research projects frequently depend on expertise in several disciplines that may have previously been thought to be unrelated. These interdisciplinary projects may now be completed by cooperating professionals who think about and approach problems from radically different viewpoints. Even demonstration grants and model projects require community integration and support from partners who just a few years ago would not have been approached but now must provide board resolutions, letters of support and endorsement, matching contributions, or in-kind support.

Consider the following suggestions for evaluating and improving your own personal group skills and the team skills of your grant-related groups such as advisory committees, advocacy groups, proposal development teams, centers of excellence, multidisciplinary groups, consortia partners, and so on.

Recognizing the Roles That Make an Effective Team

There are many theories and much research on effective team formation and development in the corporate world. Applying successful techniques to the nonprofit world and colleges and universities has just begun. However, after helping several universities develop more effective grant-related volunteer groups and development teams, I believe the basic element to group success and team building is the role that individuals take in a group and how well the varying roles interact with one another to maximize strengths.

As you select the members of your grant-related groups or analyze the composition of your existing group or development team, take into consideration the roles that must be assumed to ensure effective group functioning. While a variety of techniques and materials can be used to assist team members in developing awareness of the roles involved in a productive team, one simple and easy-to-use system is the *Team Dimension Profile* by Inscape Publishing (order through David G. Bauer Associates, Inc.). This profile or survey helps individuals understand and value the contribution they make to successful innovation teams or groups by allowing them to determine their personal approach to thinking and behavior (conceptual, spontaneous, normative, or methodical) and their role on the team or group (creator, advancer, facilitator, refiner, or executor) without going into great detail. The process uses common sense.

Review the following four basic approaches to thinking and behavior. Consider which one best describes the approach you use in the team innovation process and the approaches taken by those with whom you work. Keep in mind that many individuals use more than one approach and, in essence, develop their own unique team and task orientation.

- *Conceptual Approach:* The individual who takes a conceptual approach is the idea developer who like to brainstorm alternatives, focus on the future, and develop new theories. These are the innovative, big-idea generators. You need them on your team to ensure that the approach to the problem is fresh and new. However, having several of these types on your team can be problematic. While they can come up with multiple approaches when presented with a problem, they do not always think things through. In the aforementioned dysfunctional group that spent $1 million with nothing to show for it, four out of the seven team members had this orientation. When I asked why they had never written any of their solutions (grant ideas) down, they said, "Why bother? At our next meeting we will brainstorm even better ones."
- *Spontaneous Approach:* Those who take a spontaneous approach are freethinkers with little respect for traditions or rules. They move from one subject to another, focus on many things at once, and are sometimes impatient. Freethinkers are great at thinking outside of the box. They will come up with wildly creative projects. Three of my seven dysfunctional team members were high in this characteristic. As you might imagine, this turned out to be the formula for a group process disaster. Because the team essentially operated without any rules, members continually skipped meetings, which meant that the majority of each meeting was spent on updating the members who had missed the previous meeting.

- *Normative Approach:* The individuals who take this approach want to see consequences before acting, prefer the norm or the familiar, and rely on past experiences and expectations. They question all proposed plans and find holes in them before a reviewer or grantor does. Individuals with this perspective are critical thinkers. If a team is unbalanced and has numerous members with this orientation, proposed approaches can be overanalyzed and one may never be selected and put into a grant proposal because, in their view, it is not perfect yet.
- *Methodical Approach:* Those who take a methodical approach like order in the universe. They are rational, follow scientific methods and step-by-step processes, and prefer to focus on details that make everything fit together. Your team needs to have this perspective represented not only to get the proposal and budget completed, but also to keep everyone on task in carrying out the funded project. The failed million-dollar team I mentioned actually had one of these types of individuals. This person ended up dropping out of the group. In reality, she was driven out because she slowed up the pace of the conceptual and spontaneous members by writing down their ideas.

These four approaches to innovation focus on how the individual approaches work together in a group and how the various combinations of these approaches affect the completion of the work inherent in successful group or team projects. Research by Allen N. Fahden and Srinivsa Namakkal[1] resulted in their identification of five roles that must be present in a team or group to achieve project success: the creator, the advancer, the facilitator, the refiner, and the executor.

The theory is that in a well-functioning team, all of the five roles are present and the individual team members can hand tasks back and forth, utilizing the strengths that each role provides. Subgroups are developed when the team has more than one member who can function in each role and, therefore, can share tasks.

- *Creator:* Grant-winning solutions must be innovative and fresh and often require team members to think creatively. The creator does just that. This individual helps generate new and unusual concepts, ideas, and solutions to the problem and then passes them on to the advancer. Creators become bored discussing and explaining their ideas (which to them are getting old) and can upset the group by coming up with newer and greater ideas before the team has completed working through the previous task. Creators will create grant proposal idea number 2 before number 1 is written. If not thoughtfully enjoined with the challenges and creativity of making idea number 1 work, they have a tendency to lose interest and skip group meetings.

- *Advancer:* In this role, the individual sees great ideas, solutions, or approaches and develops new ways to promote them. The advancer develops objectives and plans by the most direct and efficient means. On grants teams, advancers talk others through a new idea or concept, get the other team members on board, and keep them excited about the project. In addition, they are usually good at making preproposal contact with potential grantors.
- *Facilitator:* This is the group manager's role. This person monitors the proposal development process and work task distribution. This is a critical role for efficient proposal preparation and group productivity. When problems occur with the proposed protocol or solution, the facilitator hands tasks back to the responsible parties for their input and clarification.
- *Refiner:* This is the group's "devil's advocate." Refiners challenge, analyze, and follow a methodical process to detect process flaws or leaps in logic or process that creators sometimes make in brainstorming new approaches. They pass ideas and plans back to the facilitator to take to the creator and advancer.
- *Executor:* Executors are the workhorses of the group. They may not enjoy the more visible leadership roles. Their fun is in making the process an orderly and efficient one. Not only are they critical for developing the solution and proposal implementation plan, they are also essential in carrying out the proposal after it is funded. They pay attention to details and insist on quality.

On a successful team, the facilitator ensures that tasks are handed off from the creator to the advancer, from the advancer to the refiner, and from the refiner to the executor. You can probably see yourself in one or more of these roles and now understand why some of your group efforts have failed: One or more of the five team roles—creator, advancer, refiner, executor, or facilitator—were missing and no one recognized this or was willing to assume the missing roles.

Poor team performance results when there is an excess of team members assuming similar roles or coming from comparable orientations. A solid, functioning group or team identifies the approaches and roles of its members, defines tasks, and hands them off from one role to another, allowing group members to focus on their strengths in the process. It also recognizes what roles are missing from the group. With awareness, the group can either add additional team members with the necessary orientation and skills, or the existing members can consciously take on the roles that are lacking and assume the subsequent tasks.

Higher education and nonprofit organizations are plagued by poorly functioning groups. From the dreaded committee assignments to proposal development teams, we have witnessed legendary failures.

The for-profit world has assumed the lead in developing highly successful teams at all levels, from the shop floor to top management. In his book *Teamwork Is an Individual Skill: Getting Your Work Done When Sharing Responsibility,*[2] Christopher Avery suggests that the first step to developing successful teams is to rid ourselves of the misconceptions we have about teamwork. One misconception we need to discard is that team members need to like each other. Believe it not, we do not necessarily need to like each other's personality to operate successfully. What we need to do is appreciate each group member's specific approach and to understand how it helps to get the job done. The second misconception we must eliminate is that our personalities and individual orientations are paramount. We should leave our personal needs and ego at the door of each group meeting. In actuality, being a team player does not mean you cannot be yourself or that you cannot expect something back from the group for your time. The key to group success is to be yourself, act normally but responsibly, and recognize and appreciate what each group member naturally brings to the table. This knowledge will help you develop teams comprising individuals with the mix of approaches and orientations necessary to achieve success. Finally, we have to realize that it is okay to *use* each other in a positive fashion by comparing our skill set to the tasks that proactive grantseeking requires and allocate those tasks to the team member who can accomplish them with proficiency and ease because they suit his or her skill set. Even though *use* is not a positive term in the nonprofit world, we need to rethink how we each have a responsibility to know our skills and to inform others how to use our skills to the team's advantage.

The purpose of this chapter is not to make you a master guru of team building. Rather, it is to convince you of the importance of this concept in relationship to your grants quest. Hopefully, you will begin think about how you can use it and want to learn more about it. If you're interested, you might add to your to-do list a little reading in the area, including the works of Patrick Lencioni, author of the New York Times best-seller *The Five Dysfunctions of a Team*[3] and *Overcoming the Five Dysfunctions of a Team: A Field Guide.*[4] (While I enjoyed his book *Death by Meeting,*[5] I will confine my comments to his team-related series.) In his books, Lencioni refers to five dysfunctions that affect teams:

- absence of trust
- fear of conflict
- lack of commitment

- avoidance of accountability
- inattention to results

I have found that briefly discussing these concepts with my grant fellows seems to create the right atmosphere in team meetings and helps to avoid the blockages caused by personality problems.

Developing a winning grants team requires that the members have skills unique to not only creating a proposal, but carrying out the project successfully. Select your team members by interest and skills. Develop agreed-on rules (attendance, meeting time, recordings, feedback, etc.). Identify the most appropriate approaches for the following grants tasks and which team role would best accomplish them: creator, advancer, facilitator, refiner, or executor. (While these tasks will be explained in greater detail in subsequent chapters, they are listed here to consider in relationship to team or consortia building.)

- *Brainstorm Interventions:* This is a task role for the creator. Your innovative approach to the problem will come from one who by nature generates unusual concepts and ideas to solve problems. However, teams must be balanced. The $1 million internal grant that failed to develop any external proposals had five creators. They created new ideas and at each monthly meeting spent the $1 million but never wrote any ideas down because they were sure that at the next meeting they would generate new, better ones.
- *Research Grantors:* An advancer would be the best person for this task. He or she would take the most direct and efficient means to uncover who might fund the project by taking your list of key words and searching the databases.
- *Contact Grantees, Obtain Information on Reviewers and the Review Process, and Make Preproposal Contact with Potential Grantors:* This individual must be willing to contact past grantees to learn how and what they did to get funding to advance their cause. This team member must also identify the scoring rubric that will be used to evaluate the proposal and get background information on the reviewers. Once a prospective grantor has been identified, this person should also be responsible for all preproposal contact. The best person to accomplish these tasks is the advancer.
- *Perform and Update the Literature Search:* This task requires a refiner and an executor to be sure that no study or citation is missed and that they are correct.
- *Refine the Intervention/Evaluation Design:* This task requires the skill of the creator, advancer, and refiner. The creator comes up with ways to overcome problems that arise when the refiner does his or her devil's

advocate process and finds faults while the advancer keeps the other excited about the new changes in the project.

- *Develop a Detailed Spreadsheet:* A spreadsheet needs to be developed that lays out all the tasks, when they must be accomplished, who must accomplish them, the supplies, equipment, and consultants needed, and the milestones for each task. The spreadsheet results in a budget and requires an executor and a refiner.
- *Coordinate and Carry Out a Quality Circle:* A mock review of the draft proposal must be conducted. This is a perfect job for the facilitator.
- *Manage the Grant-Funded Project:* The executor prefers implementation and needs to keep the creator from changing the proposal. Let the executor organize and carry out the grant. If a problem arises, the refiner can help out and the facilitator can handle the problem.

This provides you with an idea of how the effective team uses each others' natural way of approaching the grants process. Often individuals enjoy playing a blend of roles. I suggest identifying the tasks and asking who would like to perform which functions. Any function or task not selected by the team must be covered by an added, additional team member or by a current member who is flexible enough to jump in and do it.

Legal Guidance for Those Involved in Your Project/Research

While I do not want to raise your concern to a level of paranoia over individuals who may steal your ideas and projects, you must consider how to protect yourself and your collaborators from this type of problem. To keep your professional and personal relationships on a positive, trustworthy basis, it is necessary to discuss the professional expectations and ethical standards you expect from each other.

Consortia partners, team members, and advisory group members should be briefed concerning your expectations related to the following:

- *Conflicts of interest:* Does working with your group conflict with their own research or grant-related projects or other groups in which they are an active member?
- *Nondisclosure agreements:* It is not uncommon to be asked to sign an agreement that assures the group (project initiators) that you will not inform other people or groups about the project, its protocols, or the ideas that are brainstormed and discussed.

- *Noncompetition agreements:* This upfront agreement acknowledges that all parties will work together and that one partner will not split from the consortia or group and submit a proposal that competes with the team's proposal.
- *Patent or copyright agreement:* If the project in question could result in a project, approach, article, book, or theory, it is recommended that the grounds for ownership and the sharing of any of these be spelled out in advance.

For readers who are part of a college or university, the vice president for research will usually have an Office of Intellectual Property that will supply forms, agreements, and guidance on how to approach your partners and retain the necessary records. In some instances this office will even apply for copyrights and patents for you. For those of you in a nonprofit organization, I suggest that you recruit an individual from higher education to be on your advisory committee and ask him or her to get any agreements or forms you may need from his or her university. Then you can tailor these agreements or forms to fit your needs. (More on advisory committees later in this chapter.)

Involving Volunteers

One of the most important resources in a successful grants effort is the involvement of volunteers. When grantors are faced with volunteers who believe so strongly in a project they are willing to work to further its ends with no personal benefit, the credibility of your project and the lead applicant's organization is greatly enhanced.

Involving others to increase your potential to attract funding suggests that who you know may be more valuable that what you know and how you write your proposal. But a poorly developed idea and proposal will need much more than just friends and the suggestions presented here. If you have a great idea or proposal, however, you owe it to yourself and to your team to take advantage of every possible edge in your quest for funding. This includes involving individuals who can help ensure that your proposal receives the attention it deserves. One foundation director told me that approximately one-third of her foundation's grants went to the board members' favorite projects; one-third to the board members' friends' favorite projects; and the remaining one-third to the most skilled grantseekers who created a motivating, organized proposal based on the foundation's values.

While this may sound like politics, hold your condemnations just one more minute. The politics of grantseeking is a fascinating area that spells *m-o-n-e-y* for those who master the art. Do not be frightened or disgusted by the word *politics*. The politics of grantseeking is a very understandable process that enables individuals to become advocates for what they value and believe in.

Those people who know your organization and identify with your cause or mission deserve to know how they can be of service to you and the cause or field you represent. When asked to become advocates for your project, individuals are free to say no or that they are too busy, but you should not make this decision for them by assuming that they would not want to be involved. There is no harm in asking, and you will be surprised by how many individuals welcome your invitation.

Consider exploring the area of advocacy and how you can help others help you. The worksheets in this chapter will assist you in certifying who your advocates are and how they can best serve you. You will probably discover that there are more supporters for your project than you realized.

Grants Advisory Committees

One highly effective method for involving volunteers in your grants quest is to develop an advisory committee focused on the need or problem your grant proposal will address. For example, while working for a university-affiliated hospital, I initiated one advisory committee on health promotion and wellness for children and another on research for children's diseases with different individuals on each committee. Even though you should think of your advisory committee as an informal affiliation of individuals you invite to take part in attracting grants to the problem area you have chosen, you may be able to recruit more members and support if you leave the word *grant* out of the committee's title. Include the problem instead. For example, I called one of the groups I initiated the Committee for Promoting Research on Children's Diseases instead of the Grants Committee for Promoting Research on Children's Diseases.

Invite fellow professionals, individuals from other organizations and the community, and corporate members who are interested in the area you have identified. By inviting a cross-section of individuals to join your committee, you develop a wider base from which to draw support. Ask yourself who would care if you developed grants resources to solve a particular problem. The one common denominator for all the committee members should be their concern for positive change in the identified area of need. Develop a list of individuals, groups, and organizations you think would volunteer a little of their time to be instrumental in making progress in the problem area. Be sure to include:

- individuals who might know foundation, government, or corporate grantors
- colleagues who may have previously prepared a proposal for the grantor you will be approaching or who may have acted as grant reviewers

Also consider current and past employees, board of trustee members, and former clients.

Grant Resources

After you have identified individuals or groups that would be interested in seeing change in the area identified, make a list of skills and resources that would be helpful in developing your proposal. Match these with the types of individuals who might possess them. Your list of skills and resources may give you some ideas about whom you should recruit for your grants advisory committee. Consider the skills and resources and the types of individuals that could be useful in:

- preparing your proposal (writers, experts in evaluation design or statistics, and individuals with computer programming skills)
- making preproposal contact (individuals with sales and marketing skills and people who travel frequently—especially to Washington, D.C.)
- developing consortia or cooperative relationships and subcontracts (individuals who belong to other nonprofit groups with similar concerns)

All volunteers, including your advisory committee members should be asked to review the Grant Resources Inventory (Exhibit 9.1) and to indicate those resources they are willing to contribute. Tailor the list to include only what you need, and if you know of specific assets possessed by your volunteers, do not be afraid to ask.

How to Incorporate Advocates to Increase Grants Success

While teams and consortia are formal, organized components of proactive grantseeking, advisory groups and volunteers are more informal. In fact in an advisory capacity they may never be told they are a part of your list of advisors. You may seldom have a meeting of your select advisors and certainly no rules and by-laws. The following suggestions on how to use these groups and individuals follow a basic hierarchical system based on their willingness to perform specific activities:

EXHIBIT 9.1
Grant Resources Inventory

Please indicate the resource areas you would be willing to help with. At the end of list, provide more detailed information. In addition, if you are willing to meet with funding sources please list the geographic areas you travel to frequently.

___ Evaluation of Projects
___ Computer Equipment
___ Computer Programming
___ Spreadsheets on Methods and Protocols
___ Objectives, Hypothesis, Specific Aims
___ Budgeting, Accounting, Developing Cash Flow Forecasts, Auditing
___ Audiovisual Assistance (Equipment, DVDs, etc.)
___ Website Development
___ Travel to Make Contact with Grantors
___ Writing, Editing, Submission
___ Searching for Funding Sources
___ Equipment/Materials
___ Space for Program/Research
___ Other:

Description of Resources:

Areas Frequently Visited:

- Level D—Lowest Level of Involvement: Brainstorm and critique ideas
- Level C—Middle Level of Involvement: Write letters of endorsement, provide names of possible linkages to grantors
- Level B—Higher Level of Involvement: Will work on the proposal and funded grant as a consultant
- Level A—Highest Level of Involvement: Will act as a team member and possible a co-investigator

Other specific activities to consider in relation to advocacy roles of individuals on your list are:

- contacting funding sources for you and setting up appointments or conference calls
- providing expertise in particular areas (finance, marketing, and so on)
- accompanying you to meetings with potential funders or even visiting a funding source for you

Use the Advocacy Planning Sheet (Exhibit 9.2) to organize your approach.

EXHIBIT 9.2
Advocacy Planning Sheet

Project Title:

Project Director:

Select from the following list of techniques those you can suggest your advocates employ to advance your project.

- Endorsement letters
- Testimonials
- Letters of introduction to grantors
- Set appointments with granting officials
- Accompany you to see funding sources
- Go to see grantors for you

Techniques for This Project	Advocates to Be Used	Who Will Contact Advocate & When	Desired Outcome	Date Completed

Endorsement Letters

One very effective way to use advocates is to request that they write endorsement letters related to your organization's credibility and accomplishments. Without guidance, however, many advocates will develop endorsement letters that focus on inappropriate aspects of your project or organization. To prevent this, spell out what you are looking for. Provide advocates with a draft endorsement letter that suggests what you would like them to consider including in their letters, such as:

- pertinent facts or statistics that you may then quote or use in your proposal
- the length of time they have worked with you or your organization (for example, number of hours, consortia, or cooperative work relationships)
- a summary of their committee work and their major accomplishments

Advocates should almost be able to scan your draft, print it on their stationary, and sign it. If the grantor has any special requirements concerning endorsement letters, make sure they are followed.

Contacts

Another way to involve your advocates is to present them with the names of potential grantors and their board members and to ask whether they know any of the grantors' key individuals. This approach is particularly useful if your advocates are reluctant to reveal all of their contacts and are holding back to see how serious you are in researching potential grantors.

If your advocates are trusting, you can ask them outright for a comprehensive list of their contacts. This includes asking your grants advisory committee members to reflect on their ability to contact a variety of potential grantors that may be helpful in your grants effort. To take this proactive approach, follow these steps:

1. Explain the advocacy concept to the individuals you have identified and how the information they provide will be used. Ask each participant to complete an Advocacy Webbing Worksheet (Exhibit 9.3) and return it to you. Some organizations find they have better results in introducing the advocacy concept when they relate the concept to a major project of the organization that has widespread support.

EXHIBIT 9.3
Advocacy Webbing Worksheet

Our organization's ability to attract grant funds is increased substantially if we can talk informally with a funding official (or board member) before we submit our formal proposal. However, it is sometimes difficult to make preproposal contact without having a link to the funding source. We need your help. By completing this worksheet, you will identify any links that you may have with potential grantors and increase our grants success dramatically.

If you have a link with a funding source that our research indicates may be interested in supporting one of our projects, we will contact you to explain the project and discuss possible ways you could help us. For example, you could write an endorsement letter, arrange an appointment, or accompany us to see the funding source. Even a simple phone call could result in our proposal actually being read and not just left in a pile. No matter what the case may be, you can rest assured that we will obtain your complete approval before any action is taken and that we will never use your name or link without your consent.

Links to foundations, corporations, and government funding sources are worth hundreds of thousands of dollars per year, and your assistance can ultimately help us continue our vital mission. Thank you for your corporation.

Your Name:
Your Phone No.
Your Email:
Your Address:

1. What foundations or corporate boards are you, your spouse, or close friends on?

2. Do you know anyone who is on a foundation or corporate board? If so, who and what board?

3. Does your spouse know anyone on a foundation or corporate board? If so, who and what board?

4. Have you served on any government committees? If so, please list.

5. Do you know any government funding contacts? If so, please list.

2. Distribute the Advocacy Webbing Worksheet to the individuals you have identified as possible advocates. This may be done in a group or individually.
3. Input the advocacy information you collect from the completed worksheets in your computer, or file it.
4. When a match between a potential funder and an advocate is made, call your advocate and discuss the possibility of having him or her arrange a meeting for you with the funding source. Ask the advocate to attend the meeting with you to add credibility to your presentation.

Keep all completed Advocacy Webbing Worksheets on file and update them periodically. This is a good activity for volunteers. Be aware, however, that care should be taken to safeguard advocacy data. Advocacy data should be considered personal information that is privileged; you must not allow open access to the data or you will be violating your advocate's trust. Store the information on your personal computer, and keep a copy of your program or file in a safe place. This approach will ensure the privacy of this confidential information. When a potential funding source is identified, search your advocacy database to determine whether any of your advocates have relationship to the potential funding source.

You may have an advocate who:

- is a member of both your organization and the funding source's board
- can arrange an appointment to get you in to talk to the funder
- can write a letter to a "friend" on the funding source's board
- has worked for the grantor or been a reviewer for the funder's grant program

Community Support

Advocacy can also play a valuable role in developing and documenting community support for your project. Some funding sources require that you demonstrate community support in the form of advisory committee resolutions and copies of the minutes of meetings, and more grantors are encouraging the development of consortia when applying for funding. Whether you are looking at a joint submittal for your proposal or just endorsement and support, it is important to start the process of applying for a grant early so that deadlines do not interfere with your ability to document your advisory committee's involvement and valuable work. To deal creatively with the area of community support:

- Put together a Swiss cheese book (see chapter 4) to focus on your problem area.
- Organize an advisory committee to examine the problem area.
- Involve the advisory committee in brainstorming project ideas, examining needs assessment techniques, writing letters of endorsement, and providing links to funders.

Review the worksheet on Developing Community Support (Exhibit 9.4) to help you determine how to use community support to increase your fundability. Organize your supporters and maximize your chances for success by working through and with your volunteers, involving those individuals who can be of service to your cause from enhancing your resources to helping identify links to funders.

EXHIBIT 9.4
Developing Community Support Worksheet

#	Techniques	Applicability of the Techniques to This Project	Who Will Call Meeting	Members of Committee	Date
1	Use advisory committee to brainstorm uniquenesses of your organization.				
2	Use advisory committee to work on setting up needs assessment.				
3	Use advisory committee to brainstorm project ideas.				
4	Use advisory committee to develop a public relations package and to produce it (printing, etc.), including newspaper coverage for your organization (press releases, interviews) and television coverage (public service announcements, talk shows).				
5	Have an artist perform or have an open house for key people in the community.				
6	Other				

Involving Existing Boards, Advisory Groups, Volunteers, and Staff

Do not overlook the advantages of using linkages that your organization's existing groups, volunteers, and staff may already have. These individuals and groups have already demonstrated an affinity for your organization and your programs. Participation in this opportunity should be voluntary, and while some administrators may express concern over asking paid staff to contribute names of friends and relatives who have connections to funding sources, they will be surprised at the voluntary response they receive. Involve your employee associations and unions, and initiate the idea by relating it to strong needs and well-accepted programs and projects that many people want to see developed or expanded.

Many nonprofit organizations already have boards and standing committees that can be invited to become involved in this webbing and linkage process. Most corporate people will be happy that they have been asked to participate in a game that the corporate world plays all the time. From my experience at universities, I have also found that department chairs, deans, and members of boards of institutes and centers usually respond favorably to the concept.

The key to acceptance of the webbing and linkage process is to assure those participating that linkages will not be contacted without their knowledge or approval and, in most cases, their assistance.

How to Use Webbing and Linkage Information

To get the most out of your newly discovered linkages, list them by linkage type (for example, foundation, corporate, federal, state, and so forth). Then use the funding source research tools described in chapters 13, 22, and 27 to look up the interest areas of the grantors to which you have a link. Review your organization's needs and projects and look for potential matches with the grantors. When a match is found, make preproposal contact through your linkage.

How to Enlist Support from Membership Groups/Organizations

Add the major membership organization in your field to your advisory list. Many of these groups are also potential grantors. Even though their award amounts are usually small, any support from the major organization in your field demonstrates that what you are doing is deemed valuable by your peers.

Another way to enhance your proposal's fundability is to consider applying the involvement hierarchy here as well. Would the organization endorse the importance of projects or research like yours for the benefit of the field of interest? Would they help with linkages to grantors, or with setting up meetings? Or would they go right to the top and consider partnering in a consortia proposal? On one occasion I asked a national organization to endorse a research project. I included a copy of their mission statement to demonstrate how we were aligned in purpose. I then presented them with a list of last year's grantees to show them how a consortia approach would fit them and the grantor. We actually submitted my organization's proposal through the national organization because this enhanced our fundability. We became the main contractor and a win-win relationship evolved.

Where You Are

Once you have completed the proactive step of team and consortia building, you are faced with how to integrate the concept of webbing and linkages into your plan. First you must ask yourself if this concept fits with your plans for success. If it does, you must then determine where to insert it. Can you suggest it at a conference or meeting where your team or consortia members are in attendance? Can you add it to the agenda of one of your regularly scheduled meetings? Could the concept be the basis for a special retreat?

Your next step is to consider incorporating a grants advisory committee in your proactive planning. Consider the benefits of having such a committee and look at the roles the committee members could play in providing:

- letters of endorsement
- contact with funding officials
- community support
- linkages to grantors

Your job is to decide if you want to take advantage of the valuable strategies in this chapter and when. Figure 9.1 depicts the suggested system thus far.

FIGURE 9.1
Action Steps Chart: Creating Grant-Winning Teams

Notes

1. Allen N. Fahden and Srinivasa Namakkal, *Team Dimension Profiles* (Minneapolis, MN: Inscape Publishing, Inc., 1995).

2. Christopher M. Avery, with Meri Aaron Walker and Erin O'Toole Murphy, *Teamwork Is an Individual Skill: Getting Your Work Done When Sharing Responsibility* (San Francisco: Berrett-Koehler Publishers, Inc., 2001).

3. Patrick Lencioni, *The Five Dysfunctions of a Team* (San Franciso: Jossey-Bass, 2002).

4. Patrick Lencioni, *Overcoming the Five Dysfunctions of a Team: A Field Guide* (San Francisco: Jossey-Bass, 2005).

5. Patrick Lencioni, *Death by Meeting* (San Francisco: Jossey-Bass, 2006).

10

Documenting Organizational Support for Your Proposal: Preproposal Approval

B<small>EFORE YOU LAUNCH INTO YOUR GRANTOR SEARCH</small>, you need to consider whether your application will be supported and approved by your sponsoring organization. While almost all colleges, universities, and other nonprofit organizations have a sign-off procedure for proposals, few have a sign-on requirement. The Preproposal Summary and Approval Form (Exhibit 10.1) has been designed to help you with this issue. Exhibit 10.1 could be subtitled "The Grantseeker's Insurance Policy." When you have ideas you would like to seek funding for, fill out this form before writing your full-scale proposal. Then have the form reviewed by your grants or research office, proposal review committee, staff, or administrators, and have it returned to you with their criticisms and suggestions. Many organizations find it useful to make the preproposal summary and approval form available electronically to the appropriate individuals as an e-mail attachment.

The purpose of the preproposal summary and approval form is to elicit comments from your organization's leaders and to have them endorse your solution. The form actually provides a vehicle to test the acceptance of your idea or project with your superiors. This is important because they should agree on the use of institutional resources before you invest hours of your time on proposal development.

There are many benefits to using the preproposal summary and approval form at this point in the process. Since proposal developers have not yet invested a great deal of time writing their proposals, they are less defensive when their project summary is criticized, suggested improvements are easier to make, and, if necessary, plans to deal with a lack of support can be developed.

Using this form can also be beneficial when proposals must be approved before they are submitted. Make sure the form is reviewed by those people who will be signing the final proposal. This way these individuals will know in advance that the proposed project is coming. Have these key people comment on the areas they question or have a problem supporting. If they have no problems, they can endorse by signing at number 10 of the exhibit. If they

EXHIBIT 10.1
Preproposal Summary and Approval Form

---

1. Proposed Proposal Director/Project Director:

2. Statement of the Problem:

3. Brief Statement of the Solution:

4. How the Project Relates to Our Mission/Goals:

5. Suggested Grantor:
   Special Grantor Requirements:
   _____ Matching Funds
   _____ Other

6. Estimated Cost of Project:

7. Proposed Project Personnel   Reassigned Time/New Employee

   _____   _____

   _____   _____

   _____   _____

8. Facilities Required:
   Square Feet: _____   Desired Location: _____

9. Equipment Needed for Project (Note if equipment is on hand or is to be provided by grant, and if any special maintenance will be required):

10. Signature/Approval (Your signature represents approval of any institutional support outlined above): _____

11. Conditional Signature/Approval: _____
    Approval to proceed with full proposal development as long as the proposal developer meets the following conditions:

Attach a brief summary/concept paper to this approval form and a list of potential/probable funding sources. If your have consortia partners/collaborators involved in your project, also attach the Preproposal Summary and Approval Form for Consortia Partners.

have a condition that must be met first, they can list the condition under number 11 of the exhibit and provide their conditional signature. This ensures that the time, money, and resources spent in your proposal preparation process will not be met with a negative response internally and result in failure to have your proposal signed when ready for submittal.

This preproposal summary and review process also enables decision makers to be made aware of important issues and the potential grantor's specific requirements, and gives them an opportunity to comment on them. This includes, but is not limited to, the following:

- reassigned time for project director or principal investigator to work on the grant when funded
- matching funds commitment
- space, equipment, support personnel, and other resource allocations

Because the form is generic and allows for the inclusion of the suggested grantor's specific requirements, it can be used with all of the grants marketplaces and with any grantor you uncover in the next three sections of this book.

Your grantseeking efforts are more likely to receive support and to provide a basis for matching funds and other resource allocations when you appraise your administration of your entrepreneurial grant effort and see its endorsement in advance of submittal. This will reduce the chances of getting a grantor excited about your project and then you not being able to submit your proposal because of internal problems and a refusal to sign off by your administration later.

When you have consortia partners or collaborators involved in your grant proposal, it is equally important to make sure they are on board. Many partners may not realize that they need approval because this is just a proposal and not a funded grant. However, your research office will require that your partners, subcontractors, or consultants have their organization's complete backing.

The Preproposal Summary and Approval Form for Consortia Partners (Exhibit 10.2) can be used to ensure that your partners have their institution's approval. Your research or sponsored project's office may actually have its own forms that you must have completed by your partners to create and submit the budget. Even in these situations, I recommend that reassigned time and the support services that are required to complete the tasks outlined in your agreement are committed to by your partner's institution.

EXHIBIT 10.2
Preproposal Summary and Approval Form for Consortia Partners

---

1. Title of Project/Research:

2. Projected Grant Source/Program:

3. Lead Organization:

4. Project Personnel   % of Time on Grant   Costs Donated or Charged
                                                                        to Grant

   Co-PIs/Partners   _____   _____
   Consultants   _____   _____
   Other   _____   _____

5. Equipment/Software/Lab and Other Support Dedicated to this Project:

6. Signature/Approval of Collaborative Authorized Agent: _____

Review your action steps chart to see where and when preproposal approval fits into your proactive grants plan (Figure 10.1).

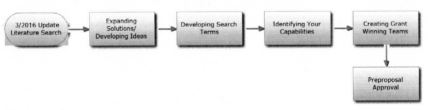

FIGURE 10.1
Action Steps Chart: Preproposal Approval

11

Where the Money Is: Selecting the Right Marketplace for Your Project

THE TWO MAIN SOURCES OF SUPPORT for universities and nonprofit organizations and their grant requests are public (government) and private philanthropy. Each marketplace and its subcategories are very different from one another in whom they fund, the amount of support they provide, and what they will require of you and your organization.

Not only are there vast differences between the various types of grantors in each of the marketplaces, there are also differences in how the marketplaces are viewed in terms of prestige and credibility. When determining which grants marketplace is right for you and your project or research, you must take into consideration how both your career plan and your organization may be affected by the grants marketplace hierarchy.

Whether you are using research grant funding to build your rationale for gaining tenure at a university or for a promotion in a nonprofit organization, peer-reviewed grant awards are viewed as the most prestigious and credible. Except for earmarked pork grants, most competitive federal grants (research and model projects) are peer reviewed and carry the highest regard in the grants world. Other peer-reviewed grants from state agencies, counties, and cities follow in a descending order.

Foundation grant awards are usually considered less prestigious than peer-reviewed government grant awards because most are decided by internal staff and board members who may not be experts in the field. Some private grantor decision makers may be knowledgeable in the field, but true peer review is used by only a select few. The few that use peer review are considered more prestigious, but the system is much less refined than federal peer-reviewed grants. Being able to say you were funded by a foundation like the Robert Wood Johnson Foundation is more noteworthy than saying you were funded by a community foundation.

Grants made by nonprofit organizations, professional societies, service clubs, membership associations, and national and international groups in your field are viewed by many as the next most prestigious because they are reviewed and selected for funding by your peers. While these awards are usually for small amounts, they are credibility builders.

Corporate grantors are the lowest on the scale since they are viewed by many as pay or remuneration for services, research, or knowledge wanted by the grantor. With more and more university–corporate alliances, this formerly clear demarcation has become blurred. How a corporate grant is viewed in terms of credibility and prestige is linked to the project's objectivity and whether the research conducted was free from bias.

So, as you look at the major marketplaces, you must consider your career, your organization, your research or project, and your position in the field. Breaking through the glass ceiling to get a highly coveted federal grant may mean starting with a grant from a less prestigious marketplace sector, such as a foundation. This funding will allow you to gather preliminary data, test hypotheses, publish in journals, and build a track record that improves your image as well as that of your organization. Remember, where you work and the letterhead on your stationery *will* make a difference with each grantor segment.

Now that you have reviewed in a broad sense how the different grant marketplaces must be integrated into your career plan, it is time to get down to specifics. Start by reviewing the distinct characteristics of each marketplace, where the money is, and who your competition is.

General Grants Marketplace Information

I have administered a grants marketplace quiz as a pretest assessment instrument to over forty-five thousand grantseekers since 1975. These grantseekers attended one of my training seminars and, therefore, were not randomly selected and may not represent all grantseekers. However, they do vary widely in grants expertise and background. What is interesting and surprising is that more incorrect answers are given to the quiz today than ever before. Why is this, when today's grantseekers are exposed to an abundance of information about grants and funding sources through the general media, professional journals, newsletters, conferences, grant databases, and e-mail alerts? I believe that improved grants information may, in fact, contribute to current misconceptions about the grants marketplace and, consequently, to faulty grant strategies.

Grantseekers, and the administration they work for, read announcements about universities and nonprofit groups that attract large, million-dollar grant awards. These awards that make the news are usually exceptions to the rule. These awards unfortunately are often interpreted by well-meaning, motivated grantseekers and their administrators as the norm or average. Nonprofit leaders use these larger awards to shape their view of the marketplace. Judging the marketplace by these extremely high awards that make headlines thus creates and reinforces misconceptions about grant making and influences unrealistic expectations about the level of grant support from each sector of the marketplace. As a result, many grantseekers end up basing their strategic grants decision making on fantasy or wishful thinking rather than on fact.

Both the private and public marketplaces reflect the global financial markets. While the most current recession and its impact on the stock market and unemployment was dramatic and caused distress to people all around the world, it was not the first or the last turmoil that the grants marketplace has had or will have to endure.

The 1980s experienced a recession that directly impacted the grants marketplace. While the federal government tried to stimulate the economic recovery in a number of ways, there was a concerted effort to reduce grants and hold programs at no growth. In addition, there were no increases in salaries and wages paid under federal grants. This included research and medical research. There was an effort to eliminate entire departments such as the Department of Education. Grantseekers generally overreacted to these cuts and no-growth policies and often did not even apply. The result in some programs was a small reduction in funding (e.g., 5 percent) but a dramatic reduction in applications. The grants herd mentality scared off a lot of applicants. Because of this, grantseekers who applied to certain programs actually had an increased chance for funding. Eventually the budget was balanced and there were raises in pay ceilings on grants and actual increases in grant appropriations.

By extrapolating this phenomenon to the current situation, it is easy to understand the importance of looking beyond the news clips related to the government grant reductions to how these cutbacks will affect the applicant pool and the percentage of awards made.

Now we face another recession. In this instance, the federal government has not created a new bureaucracy to stimulate the economy as it did in the past with the Comprehensive Employment Training Act. Instead, the Economic Stimulus Act placed additional funds into existing grant programs in an attempt to avoid waste and duplication. In 2009 and 2010, many of the existing government granting agencies had special grants deadlines and extra review panels. This resulted in billions of dollars in new funded proposals. While some question the value of the stimulus funds, I believe that history will show that these funds and grants not only added to the employment of graduate students and researchers but also resulted in valuable research and projects that will benefit our society for decades. In addition, the Obama administration should get credit for not starting an entirely new system to distribute the grants related to stimulus funds. The use of existing programs and the peer review of grant funds, rather than the earmarking and pork process, will result in more good.

Under President Obama there were several additional grant deadlines for existing programs and funding of billions of dollars in stimulus funds for research and demonstration grants. Unfortunately, these increases have now been followed by reductions in grant funds as a result of the political deadlock in Washington. The shutdown of the federal government, the resulting budget cuts due to sequestration, and bartering over raising the debt ceiling limit have had a dramatic effect on the research enterprise in the United States.

For example, like the other nondefense spending federal agencies, the National Institutes of Health (NIH) had to cut 5 percent of its budget for FY 2013 to comply with sequestration. Because NIH funnels about 85 percent of its budget to researchers, it had to scale back some grants. And, according to an analysis by United for Research (a coalition of research institutes and patient advocates), the NIH cuts could result in the elimination of as many as 20,500 U.S. research jobs. Meanwhile, the National Science Foundation, facing similar cuts estimated it would give out one thousand fewer research grants and awards in 2013, affecting as many as three thousand researchers.[1] Obviously the budgets of other major scientific research funders like the Department of Agriculture, the National Endowment of Humanities, the Department of Energy, and the Department of Education have also been dramatically impacted by sequestration and have had to reduce research grants in both number and size.

A survey conducted by the Association of Public and Land-Grant Universities, the Association of American Universities, and the Science of Coalition has shown that sequestration has already started to diminish the United States's research capabilities. The survey examines sequestration's impact on campuses and the results suggest that the automatic federal spending cuts have resulted in fewer federal grants, canceled and delayed research projects, staff reductions, and reduced learning opportunities.[2] What is clear is that if Congress does not reverse its course soon, university research will be negatively impacted far into the future.

The success rates of funded proposals versus applications is at an all-time low and the increased competition to get a proposal funded will continue until the federal deficit and budget picture clears. I encourage you to continue developing, submitting, and resubmitting proposals regardless of Congress's current appropriations. The federal agencies you will be applying to use the number of applications they receive to gage the interest in the field. So do not overreact to funding reductions. Keep the pressure on. When increased funding does occur, federal program officers may remember who went to bat for their programs.

According to the official federal grants portal at Grants.gov, there are one thousand different grant programs across all twenty-six federal grant-making agencies awarding more than $500 billion annually. This figure of $500 billion is slightly misleading. Due to the definition of what a grant is and who is eligible to receive one, the actual amount for competitive grantseeking is less. However, this is only one part of the grants marketplace and, while federal monies may be reduced, other sectors of the marketplace may increase.

Private grantors (foundations and corporate) will continue to award billions in grant funds as well as equipment to nonprofits. However, keep in mind that this marketplace is heavily influenced by the economic situation in the United States as well as the global markets. Its growth depends on profits, sales, and stock markets. Since many foundations make their grants from the dividends in their stock portfolios, most grants experts base the growth or constriction of this marketplace on the Standard & Poor's 500 Index. Many foundations and corporate foundations saw their assets decline at extraordinary rates. This has impacted their grant making, but market increases have helped to improve the situation.

Considering the varying opinions on the pace of the economic recovery and the fluctuations in employment rates, this marketplace is likely to make retreats and advances for some time to come, but in general, I expect some growth unless there is a catastrophic economic event. What do you think? Remember, your perception of the grants marketplace has a tremendous impact on how you will conduct your grantseeking.

Take a minute to answer the following questions. This will help you develop insight into who your competition is and where the money is—two critical areas to assist you in choosing the correct marketplace.

1. In the United States, approximately how many nonprofit organizations are eligible to receive gift and grants?
   a. 50,239
   b. 511,485
   c. 1,052,495
   d. 853,428

2. What was the total amount of private money (nongovernment) donated to these nonprofit organizations (see question 1) as tax-deductible gifts in 2012?
   a. $10 billion
   b. $26 billion
   c. $133 billion
   d. $335 billion

3. The total amount of private money donated to nonprofit organizations came from the following four basic sources. Indicate the percentage attributed to each source.
   a. Foundation grants _____%
   b. Corporate grants _____%
   c. Bequests _____%
   d. Individual giving _____%

4. How much grant funding came from the federal marketplace in 2013?
   a. $75 billion
   b. $100 billion
   c. $200 billion
   d. $500 billion

Turn to end of this chapter for the correct answers.

If taking this quiz reaffirmed what you already knew to be true, that is great. If your answers were incorrect, be thankful that you now know the correct answers and can avoid approaching the wrong marketplace and experiencing unnecessary rejection.

Most of my seminar participants guess that foundation grants account for 40 to 50 percent of the $335 billion donated in private money, with corporate grants at 30 to 35 percent, and bequests and individuals representing the balance of 15 to 30 percent.

I wish these misconceptions were correct. That would mean that foundation and corporations would have significantly more grant funding. However, wishful thinking will not get you a grant. Knowledge and sound grants strategy will pay off in the end with a funded project.

The fact is that the foundation and corporate marketplace provides over $66 billion in grants, and their funding of projects can provide a catalyst in attracting the more plentiful government grant funds. However, these private grantors complain about the wild ideas and inappropriate monetary requests presented to them by grantseekers who have not done their homework and know little about the grants marketplace. To avoid this, I suggest you approach the marketplace in the following manner.

First, research the sector of the grants marketplace with the greatest amount of funds: the government marketplace (federal, state, county, and city). To approach these potentially valuable partners with knowledge and conviction, read through the government funding section (part 2) that follows. Take time to log on to the appropriate websites and do a search. Talking to a federal program official will often provide you with valuable insights into what you need to do to make you and your project more competitive and fundable.

Federal grantors fund great projects and research that have considerable preliminary data that promises results that work. They want data to take the guesswork out of grants. Once when I presented a dynamic grant idea, one federal grant program officer told me she thought my project was fantastic and that her program liked to fund fantastic projects built on great ideas that had the potential to transform the field. However, she needed to see preliminary data to guarantee some degree of success. I asked her how I could get the data without grant money and she told me to get a foundation grant. Then she set me up with a private foundation director to discuss the project. The foundation funded us and turned a $175,000 feasibility study into a four-year multimillion-dollar federal grant. The foundation even applauded my effort to contact the larger federal granting source first to ascertain its interest because it knew that the federal grants program had more money than it did.

Approach the smaller marketplace after you can demonstrate that you have searched the government grants area and can show why the private marketplace (foundations, corporations, nonprofit organizations, membership groups, professional societies, and service clubs) provides your best opportunity. Keep in mind that foundations and corporations may provide valuable start-up funding to develop preliminary data, test hypotheses, and develop your consortia that will eventually result in larger grants from the government. See Parts 3 and 4 of this book for a more detailed discussion of private funding opportunities.

Remember, if you can recognize when you have identified an inappropriate grantor for your proposal and you are requesting an inordinate amount of funding, by choosing not to apply, you avoid positioning your institution and yourself negatively, and you keep your grants success rate up. Leaning about each of the marketplaces and developing your strategies from the information provided in this book is bound to pay off for you.

Question	Correct Answer
1. In the United States, approximately how many non-profit organizations are eligible to receive gifts and grants?	c. 1,052,495
2. What was the total amount of private money (nongovernment) donated to these nonprofit organizations (see question 1) as tax-deductible gifts in 2012?	d. $335 billion
3. The total amount of private money donated to non-profit organizations came from the following four basic sources. Indicate the percentage attributed to each source.	
Foundation grants	15% ($48.96 B)
Corporate grants	5% ($17.88 B)
Bequests	8% ($27.73 B)
Individual giving	72% ($240.60 B)
4. How much grant funding came from the federal marketplace in 2013?	d. $500 billion

Notes

1. Jim Malewitz, "Sequestration Cuts into Scientific Research," *Governing.* Retrieved from www.governing.com/news/state/sl-sequestration-cuts-into-scientific-research.html.

2. "Seven Months of Sequestration Already Eroding America's Research Capabilities," *Association of Public and Land-Grant Universities.* Retrieved from www.phys.org/wire-news/145641438/seven-months-of-sequestration-already-eroding-americas-research.html.

Part 2

PUBLIC/GOVERNMENT FUNDING OPPORTUNITIES

12

Understanding the Government Grants Marketplace

The History of Federal and State Grants

THE CONCEPT OF TRANSFERRING LARGE TRACTS OF LAND by making a grant predates our U.S. Constitution. Our founding fathers granted land to states to set up systems of public higher education. The colleges and universities set-up within these systems were referred to as *land-grant institutions.* The early colonial governments realized there was an educational void or problem in that the few private colleges were able to develop the educated citizens the nation required. The economy was also agrarian based and few private colleges focused on agriculture. In an effort to fill that void, land-grant colleges and universities were formed. This began the concept of focusing on a specific problem that federal and state government wanted to impact. The public works projects from the Great Depression era used federal grants for funding. Educating farmers to end the dust bowl through the use of modern farming techniques was largely accomplished through a Department of Agriculture grant program to states to initiate a youth education program known as 4-H. The original purpose of the program was to have youth teach their parents new farming techniques.

While the use of a government grants mechanism was established early in our country's history, the mechanism we twenty-first-century grantseekers know really took off in the 1940s, particularly during World War II. During the war the government stepped up grants primarily to deal with medical and scientific problems created by the war. These grants resulted in many advances, including the discovery of penicillin.

The 1950s witnessed the creation of the National Science Foundation and grants to close the gap in science created by the Soviet launching of *Sputnik*. The federal government expanded the use of the grants mechanism from health and science to education. Presidents began to utilize the grants mechanism to push for changes in their chosen areas of interest, and in many ways these grant programs became synonymous with their legacies. For example, President John F. Kennedy's New Frontier Initiative and President Lyndon B. Johnson's Great Society Initiative were both driven through a grants mechanism to improve education, health, and social programs. Historically, when there is a national problem the grants mechanism has been used to come up with a solution. For instance, the 1970s' recession gave birth to the Comprehensive Employment Training Act, a grant program to retrain and upgrade worker skills and increase employment.

Both Republican and Democratic administrations and Congress have used grant-related initiatives to create change and make a direct and often immediate impact on our cultural, social, health, education, and scientific and research infrastructure. An example is the Faith-Based Initiative, started under the George W. Bush administration, which allows religious-based organizations to apply for federal grants. The former separation of church and state requirements were lifted and in some government grant programs religiously affiliated groups actually got preferential treatment when competing with other nonprofit organizations. This was a dramatic departure from previous administrations' use of the grants mechanism. The Obama administration has kept the Office of Faith-Based Initiatives, but there are issues concerning the office's ability to restrict which faiths are eligible to apply for these grants.

While both Democrats and Republicans have used the grants mechanism, there are underlying philosophical differences as to the type of mechanisms that each group prefers. Republicans tend to favor local, regional, and state distribution of federal government grant dollars. Democrats tend to prefer national programs directed from Washington.

In the 1970s, a growing trend developed on how to allocate federal grant dollars. The trend was based on federalism or the belief that the federal government should give funds back to state and local governments for them to distribute. The notion was that states should have the right to set their own agendas.

President Ronald Reagan used this new federalism or revenue sharing to cut and eliminate funding for programs that were previously controlled by federal agencies. Federal funds for categorical grants aimed at specific problems or areas were reduced, eliminated, or combined in an effort to support the administration's philosophy of "the government governs best which governs the least." It will be interesting to observe how the Tea Party and other conservative movements affect the use of the federal grants mechanism.

The idea of allowing states to grant funding to their priorities still has a lot of support. However, the concept is not tenable in the areas of research and model or demonstration grants. Even staunch conservatives agree that we must have a federal controlling management system for these types of grants or a wasteful duplication of efforts will occur.

The next section of this chapter describes the various mechanisms for distributing grants in more detail. It is important that you, the grantseeker, are familiar with these different types of mechanisms so that you can develop your grant strategies accordingly and recognize when to shift your grants research away from federal agencies and to state or local government agencies that control the moneys you desire.

When reviewing the various mechanisms, keep in mind that the current lack of agreement on how to handle the mandatory budget cuts that are a part of the last-minute agreement on raising the federal debt ceiling has been very problematic to the grants marketplace. Initially, across-the-board cuts were required of all federal programs. Since there was no authority given to the agencies to use their discretion in what programs to reduce, this across-the-board reduction caused a great deal of harm. Some programs could have been cut and others deemed more important could have been kept at the original budgeted level. But that permission was withheld on the original reduction. Later these agencies were given more decision-making authority over where and how to arrive at the budgeted levels. However, the grants marketplace has still suffered serious setbacks.

Categorical Grants

As previously mentioned, categorical grants are designed to promote proposals within very specific, well-defined areas of interest. These grant opportunities address a specific area with which a federal program is concerned, such as arts, humanities, drug abuse, dropout prevention, nutrition for the elderly, or research on certain diseases and scientific advances. The House of Representatives and the Senate, using a system of committee hearings, select the problems to be addressed, provide for debate, vote on appropriations, and encourage prospective grantees to design approaches to solve or reduce the problem, or to increase knowledge in the area through research.

Project and research grants are awarded by various agencies under these congressionally authorized programs. Ideally, grants are awarded to the organizations (and individuals) whose proposals most clearly match the announced program guidelines. Most federal grant programs use nongovernmental review panels (often referred to as peer-review panels) to evaluate the projects. Peer review helps ensure that the best proposals are selected for funding. Because project design is left to the grantseekers, there is room for a wide variety of creative solutions, making the project and research grant approach very popular among grantseekers.

Government granting agencies require grantseekers to complete detailed applications. As categorical grants have increased, each federal agency that controls funds has developed its own grants system. Grant applications and the administration of grants differ in format from agency to agency, and sometimes from program to program within the same agency. Even with the use of online submittal through Grants.gov, the applications are tedious, complicated, and time consuming to complete. It is a challenge to tailor your proposal content to meet the requirements of the granting agency as well as your own needs. There is usually a three- to six-month review process, which may include an internal staff review by federal agency personnel, and a peer review. Successful grantees are required to submit frequent reports, maintain accurate project records, follow Office of Management and Budget guidelines, and agree to federal audits and site visits by government staff.

To be successful in research and project grants, grantseekers must be mindful of the constant changes in emphasis and appropriations. Hidden agendas and shifts in focus result from the funding agency's prerogative to interpret and be sensitive to the changes in the field of interest, and to what Congress appropriates each year. Be mindful that while presidents may set priorities, Congress appropriates the funds. The federal budget changes dramatically from what the president presents, and generally, Congress likes the control that categorical grants provide.

The recent budget cuts are particularly problematic to the categorical grants area because the majority of the federal budget is for entitlement benefits which are difficult to expurgate. Categorical grants are discretionary programs and are normally the first to absorb reductions in federal spending. The fall 2014 election resulted in Republicans gaining control of the House and Senate. What remains to be seen is how conservative and Tea Party influences will affect the grants marketplace. This shift could result in a concerted effort to balance the budget and reduce the federal deficit by cutting federal agencies' grant expenditures. For example, the National Science Foundation has recently come under scrutiny for funding research that conservative Republicans believe is wasteful and unnecessary. In fact, requests for reductions in NSF's budget have been made due to conservative Republicans definition of science. Retiring baby boomers facing degenerative diseases may be the best hope for categorical funded grants since they may support increased research in those areas affecting their lives.

Earmarked Grants

In grants earmarking, more commonly referred to as *pork legislation,* a project bypasses federal agency oversight and is placed in a bill that Congress is likely to pass. Bills that are popular or necessary to our country may have a number of very specific projects attached to them that have little or nothing to do with the bills themselves. When passed, these specific projects do not have to go through an internal (agency) or peer-review process. In cases where a mandated review is required, the reviewers' comments, recommendations, and scores are irrelevant since the grant must be funded anyway. Once approved, the project must be handled by a federal agency (usually the most logical categorical program) that cannot question or alter the approved, funded project.

This process has become so widespread that most colleges, universities, local governments, and major nonprofit organizations spend millions each year to retain special lobbyists in Washington, D.C., to assist them in getting senators and congress people to insert earmarks for them in federal legislation. The practice is so pervasive that while working with a college to assist in getting federal funding for a researcher, I had to wait for permission from the university's earmarking consultant before I could contact a program officer to pursue competitive, peer-reviewed grant sources.

If not curtailed, the earmarking mechanism could eliminate entire categorical federal grants programs, especially since earmarked funding is frequently taken from the budgets of categorical programs. For example, one year the Fund for the Improvement of Postsecondary Education had *all* its appropriate funds earmarked for special projects.

Under earmarking, there is no internal staff or peer review to evaluate and select the highest quality projects and research. The only ones to be funded are those with the ability to push the other pigs out of their way at the federal grants trough. It is easy to see how this practice could be used to fund inferior research as well as poor model and demonstration grants, and devastate the peer-reviewed grants system. It is also easy to see why it is publicly criticized for funding wasteful projects such as the "bridge to nowhere" in Alaska.

The use of earmarking has increased so significantly that Congress has considered legislation to eliminate the practice, or shed so much public scrutiny on it that it is drastically reduced. Even with this new emphasis on reducing earmarking and promoting transparency by requiring the sponsor's name, it will be difficult to stop the pork process now that it has reached the current level. While earmarking appears at first to be very inviting and an easy way for your organization to get needed resources, there is a disadvantage to consider. Many of the federal officers whose jobs entail administering grant programs, ensuring that their programs accomplish their goals, and organizing peer reviews, see earmarking as a threat. Earmarking threatens their agency's credibility since they are the ones who will get blamed when these often ill-conceived projects are publicized. This is particularly frustrating since they have nothing to do with the choice of the grantee or the funding of the grant, but still have to administer it and send out the funds. Interviews with some program officers have revealed a lot of irritation with grantees who are subverting the grants system through earmarking. As a result, earmarked grantees can experience great difficulty in moving from a pork grant back to a peer-reviewed grant within the same agency and program.

Due to budget battles and issues related to the debt ceiling, earmarking has been in the spotlight and was supposed to be reduced. So far, this has not been the case. Like the other types of grants mechanisms, you need to understand earmarking so that you can determine the ramifications involved in using it.

Formula Grants

The term *formula grants* refers to granting programs under which funds are allocated according to a set of criteria (or a formula). The criteria for allocation of these grant funds may be census data, unemployment figures, number of individuals below the poverty level, number of people with disabilities, and the like, for a state, city, or region. Formula grant programs are generally specific to a problem area or geographic region and historically have been used to support training programs in the fields of health, criminal justice, and employment. They are rarely encountered in research areas but have been used to distribute funds for research equipment.

The formula grant funds must pass through an intermediary, such as a state, city, or county government, or a commission, before reaching the grantee. The formula grants mechanism is another example of the new federalism that started developing in the early 1970s. While the general guidelines for formula grants are developed at the federal level, the rules are open to interpretation, and local input can significantly alter the intent of the original federal program. To encourage local control and input into how federal funds are spent, the formula grants mechanism requires a mandated review by local officials but usually very little accountability or evaluation of the actual impact of the funds. Because of this, it is difficult to substantiate the results of these programs at subsequent congressional appropriations hearings, which means that the programs placed in formula grant formats are often easy targets for elimination.

Block Grants

The block grant concept was founded on the premise that it is not the purview of the federal government to force the states to follow categorical grant program priorities. Similar categorical grant programs were blocked, or synthesized into groups of related programs, and federal funds were sent directly to the states. The states could set their priorities and grant the federal funds to the high-priority areas and projects they saw fit.

The block grant mechanism allowed the federal government to reduce staff formerly used to administer categorical grant programs. Decreases in staff were limited, however, because the federal government still had to direct the research component of categorical programs to avoid duplication and to coordinate research efforts.

Because of the federal government's continued involvement in the administration of grants (especially research grants), and Congress's desire to deal with problems in health research, education, employment, and crime, the late 1980s marked the decline of the block grant mechanism of the early Reagan years, and the use of categorical funding mechanisms increased. Virtually all of the new grant programs introduced from the 1990s to 2014 have been categorical grant programs designed to impact existing and new problems. Between the federal income tax cuts, the recession, the bank bailouts, the ongoing wars, and the growing federal deficits, new categorical grant areas will not be likely unless a major threat or new problem appears. As efforts are made to balance future budgets, categorical grant programs will probably be the first to be cut or condensed into block grants.

Contracts

No discussion of federal support would be complete without a discussion of government contracts. In recent years, the differences between a grant and a contract have become harder to discern. Indeed, after hours of negotiation with a federal agency on your grant, you may end up having to finalize your budget with a contract officer.

While there are several types of contracts, including fixed-cost and cost-reimbursable contracts, as well as those that allow the contractor to add additional costs incurred during the contract, the basic difference between a grant and a contract is that a contract outlines precisely what the government wants done. You are supplied with detailed specifications, you propose a procedure to produce what the government agency has specified, and the contract is usually awarded on a lowest-bid basis. With a contract, there is decidedly less flexibility in creating the approach to the problem. To be successful in this arena, you must be able to convince the federal contracting agency that you can perform the contract at an acceptable level of competency and at the lowest bid. Contracts are also published or advertised in different ways than grants. Grant opportunities can be found in the *Catalog of Federal Domestic Assistance* and on Grants.gov while contracts are advertised in Federal Business Opportunities (FedBizOpps.gov). These resources are explained in chapter 13.

The $500 billion in federal grants quoted in question 4 of the quiz in chapter 11 does *not* include government contract moneys. One reason that contract moneys are not included in federal grant statistics has to do with rollovers. Grant funds are appropriated and awarded in the federal budget year, which runs from October 1 to September 30. Grants awarded on a one-year time frame from award date may allow for a short, no-cost extension, but even multiyear grants contain a caveat that future funding is dependent on yearly budget allocations. While grantees can usually obtain an extension on expending their awarded grant funds beyond the end of their grant period, rollovers of unexpended federal agency funds are prohibited. Unexpended grant funds revert back to the federal treasury, except for federal contracts. For example, the Department of Defense may accrue rollover funds in certain contract areas for several years. The rollover variable makes it virtually impossible to estimate how much total contract funding is available from all of the federal agencies in any one year. However, it is safe to say that the variety, number, and dollar value of government grant contracts are staggering and go far beyond the $500 billion in government grants cited in chapter 11, and could be in the trillions of dollars.

Contracts have been increasingly pursued by nonprofit groups in recent years. For example, shifts away from domestic grant program funds have led some nonprofit organizations to look at Department of Defense contract opportunities for implementation of their programs and research. However, the contracts game requires a successful track record and documentable expertise. The best way to break into this marketplace is to identify a successful bidder and inquire as to whether you can work with that bidder as a subcontractor.

Many nonprofit groups have found that they can reduce the problems they routinely encounter in bidding contracts by developing separate profit and nonprofit entities for dealing with such issues as security agreements, academic freedom, patents, and copyrights. In addition, changes in the contracts area have been made to simplify government purchasing and to reduce paperwork. These changes, brought on by scandals over inflated prices for parts, have alleviated some of the problems associated with the administration of contract bids. Still, bidding on government contracts is a task for experienced grantseekers only.

State Government Grants

As a grantseeker, you will frequently discover a federal grant opportunity in which the eligible recipient must be a state agency. In these cases, federal funds are passed on for dissemination to the state agency that the state designates as best suited to do so. The federal program officers will know where the funds were directed in each state. States may also allocate their own funds into state grant programs. In some instances they may be required to put matching funds into the federal program as a requirement to receive the federal funds. Information on all federal funding must be accessible to the public and, therefore, are listed in the public grants resource Grants.gov (to be explained in chapter 13). Most states do not have a similar public database. To discover state grant opportunities, you will need to look at state agency websites and talk to state officials. Many states appropriate grant funds to programs and projects their elected officials value. For example, states that have secured funding from the tobacco company settlement use these funds as their legislature and executives see fit. One state used the funds for grant opportunities related to the expansion of opportunities and employment in the technology sector, while a number of other states have used the funds to develop antismoking programs.

It is difficult to estimate how many grant dollars are awarded through individual state program initiatives. Many states develop their own initiatives in the social welfare and health areas, while few states deal in research funding. In most states, the majority of state grant funds are federal funds that must pass through the states to you, the grantseeker.

There are some grantseeker advantages to state control of grants. State-controlled grants funded by the federal government are easier to access than federal grants. They require less long-distance travel and allow you to use state and local politicians to make your case heard. These advantages are counterbalanced, however, by the fact that some states develop their own priorities for these pass-through federal funds. States may add additional restrictions and use a review system made up of state bureaucrats and political appointees. Although states have their own moneys, granting programs, and rules, if they distribute grant moneys obtained from the federal government, they must guarantee that the eventual recipient of those funds will follow all federal rules and circulars.

Many of the federal government grantseeking techniques found in the preceding chapters of this book also apply to accessing state grant funds. However, to determine which of the government sectors (federal or state) is best for your proposal you must first learn how to research the government marketplace.

13

Researching the Federal Government Marketplace

F EDERAL GRANT PROGRAMS ARE CREATED BY CONGRESS and federal funding is appropriated each fiscal year. Many federal grant programs are initiated as acts of Congress (for example, the Higher Education Act). While the
acts may create programs that legally exist for a set number of years before
they are reviewed, the funding for all federal government grant agencies and
their programs is currently limited to one federal budget year (from October
1 to the following September 30).

At the time of this book's publication, the current federal grants calendar
is the 2014–2015 budget year (October 1, 2014, through September 30, 2015).
The president submits his preferred budget to Congress in the spring for the
new fall budget year. For years, the Congress and the president have not been
able to agree on the budget. When the budget does not get passed before the
beginning of the new fiscal year (October 1), Congress passes a continuing
resolution to keep the federal government operating while the parties work out
their differences on what to cut and what to add. Continuing resolutions usually maintain the current level of funding for existing programs. Most recent
federal budgets have had to operate on continuing resolutions from October 1
until January or February. During this four-month period there are deadline
dates to deal with and peer reviews to conduct. Hence, federal program officers
must operate as if they had the same budget as the previous year.

The key for you to remember is that a multiyear funded grant award is
not guaranteed. Each year of that award is subject to changes based on the
agency's appropriation by Congress. Each yearly award is guaranteed for that
year only.

To make matters more confusing, you may receive your grant award notice in June for a one-year grant. In this case, even though the federal fiscal year in which you were awarded will end on September 30, you are in essence given an extension from October to the following May to complete your research or project. It all depends on the federal fiscal budget year that your funding is awarded under.

Federal Research Tools

How do you research and track federal grant opportunities? Federal law requires the availability of public knowledge and opportunity for input regarding government grants. As such, there are several tools to help you find federal funding sources for your projects and research.

Table 13.1 provides a quick reference to these tools; some are free and others are subscription or membership based. Many of these tools listed are linked to key words that describe the federal program and its purposes. In these cases, you should use the key words that describe your project or research to search each resource to uncover potential matches with federal grant programs. As you start out, you may cast a wide net to capture as many prospects as possible and then reduce the number by refining your key search terms. Remember that each resource has its own vocabulary and that a grantor may be linked to a term in one resource and not in another.

The remainder of this chapter provides an in depth description of each tool listed in Table 13.1. However, in general, you should look for federal programs that align with:

- the problem you are interested in
- the general types of solutions your want to get funded
- the amount of money you are looking for
- the number of years of support you want
- your organization's eligibility to apply

You should also look at the program's current and future appropriations as well as its assistance considerations such as matching funds.

Exhibit 13.1 can be used to record your research on those programs that at first glance appear to warrant more investigation. You can use this worksheet to compare your project or research with the funding source's profile. In chapter 14 you will learn how to complete and analyze your research to determine your best choices for funding.

TABLE 13.1
Federal Research Tools

Name	Description	Where to Get It
Grants.gov	Central storehouse for information on over 1,000 federal grant programs and access to $500 billion in annual awards (see sample entry)	Free online access at http://www.grants.gov
Catalog of Federal Domestic Assistance (CFDA)	A database of all federal programs created by law (see sample entry)	Free online access at http://www.cfda.gov If you wish to purchase a hard copy, call the U.S. Government Printing Office (GPO) at (202) 512-1800 in the DC metro area or toll-free at (866) 512-1800, or order from GPO's online bookstore at http://bookstore.gpo.gov. A hard copy can also be found at Federal depository libraries throughout the United States (see this table).
Federal Register	Official news publication for the federal government; makes public all meetings, announcements of granting programs, regulations, and deadlines (see sample entry)	Free online access at http://www.federalregister.gov A hard copy can found at federal depository libraries throughout the United State (see this table).
FedBizOpps (Federal Business Opportunities)	This government database lists notices of proposed government procurement actions, contract awards, sales of government property, and other procurement information.	Free online access at http://www.fbo.gov or www.fedbizopps.gov.
Federal Depository Libraries	Public and university libraries that allow free access to government publications like the *CFDA, Federal Register,* and the Congressional Record.	To locate a library near you, visit http://www.gpo.gov/libraries.

(continued)

TABLE 13.1
(Continued)

Name	Description	Where to Get It
Agency newsletters, publications, requests for proposals, and guidelines	Many federal agencies publish newsletters to inform you about the availability of funds and program accomplishments. You may also request application materials, guidelines, and so on.	Usually free online availability from agency. See "Regulations, Guidelines, and Literature" in the *CFDA* section of this chapter.
GrantSelect	Fee-based subscription database providing information on more than 14,000 funding opportunities.	Order online via *GrantSelect's* web form or offline by downloading the appropriate forms and sending or faxing the subscription order to: Schoolhouse Partners, LLC 1281 Win Hentschel Blvd. West Lafayette, IN 47906 (765) 237-3390 Fax: (765) 463-3501 info@grantselect.com
Sponsored Programs Information Network (SPIN)	Fee-based membership database that tracks over 6,000 government, private, and nonprofit funding sources.	You can find more information about SPIN memberships by calling (800) 727-6427 or visiting www.infoedglobal.com 5 Washington Square, Suite 2 Albany, NY 12205-5512
Pivot (Community of Science)	Community of Science grant search-engine that provides information on funding opportunities and provides tools to support collaboration in the field of research development.	To make use of *Pivot* your university of college must buy a subscription. Contact sales at sales@refworks-cos.com or 789 E. Eisenhower Parkway P.O. Box 1346 Ann Arbor, MI 48106-1346 (734) 761-4700
GrantSearch from the Grants Resource Center (GRC) of the American Association of State Colleges and Universities	*GrantSearch* is a funding database providing federal and foundation grant information.	GrantSearch is designed exclusively for GRC member campuses. GRC membership is open to public and private higher education institutions. For information on GRC membership, contact Executive Director Rich Dunfee at (202) 478-4697

EXHIBIT 13.1
Preliminary Investigation of Potential Federal Funding Opportunity

> Federal Funding Opportunity: _____
>
> How does your project or research compare with the funding source's profile in the following areas?
>
> - Problems/Interests
> - Uses and Restrictions (Solutions)
> - Grant Size ($)
> - Duration of Funding (Year, Multiyear)
> - Eligibility
> - Current Appropriations
> - Future Appropriations
> - Assistance Considerations

Grants.gov

Grants.gov is a central storehouse for free information on over one thousand grant programs and access to approximately $500 billion in annual awards. By registering once on this site, your organization can apply for grants from twenty-six federal grant-making agencies.

Grants.gov allows you to electronically find and apply for grant opportunities as well as track your application. The website also offers free subscriptions for e-mail notifications of new grant postings.

You do not have to register with Grants.gov if you want only to find grant opportunities. However, if you want to apply for a grant, you and your organization must complete the Grants.gov registration process, which takes three to five business days to complete. Most colleges, universities, and large nonprofit organizations are registered on Grant.gov and have an authorized organization representative (AOR). There may be more than one AOR for an organization. Check with your institution's grants office before beginning the registration process.

Once you have gained access to Grant.gov's home page (www.grants.gov) click "Search Grants" to perform a search. Then follow the instructions on the screen. A basic search can be conducted using keywords or key phrases, the funding opportunity number, or the *Catalog of Federal Domestic Assistance* (CFDA) number. You can refine your search by also selecting the opportunity status (open, closed, archived), the funding instrument type (all, cooperative

EXHIBIT 13.2
Sample Search Results Grants.gov

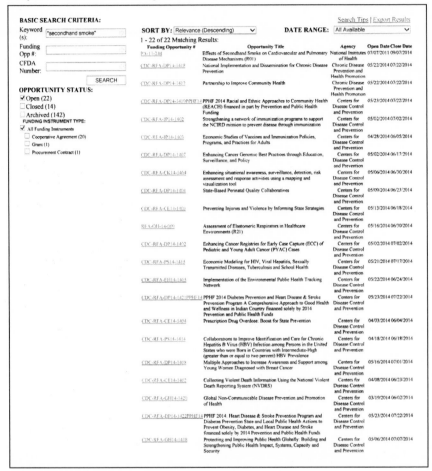

agreement, grant, procurement contract, other), eligibility (all, city government, county government, nonprofit, private institution of higher education,
public institution of higher education, etc.), the category (all, arts, business,
community development, etc.), and the agency (all, Department of Education
[DOE], Department of Energy, Department of Defense, etc.).

In the sample search (Exhibit 13.2), the grantseeker performed a basic
search for programs using *secondhand smoke* as the key phrase. The opportunity status was *open* and the funding instrument type, eligibility, category,
and agency were *all*. Search results are shown on the search page (see Exhibit
13.2). The matching results showed that there were twenty-two funding opportunities that used the phrase *secondhand smoke*.

When using phrases to search for funding opportunities, the phrases may or may not be surrounded by double quotation marks. Putting quotes around *secondhand smoke* searches for opportunities that contain the exact phrase *secondhand smoke* in that exact order. Using *secondhand smoke* without quotation marks would search for opportunities that contain *secondhand, smoke,* and both in any order.

By clicking one of the programs listed on the search results, the grantseeker can retrieve a synopsis of the grant opportunity, as well as:

- links to the full announcement contained in either the *Federal Register* (another free federal resource to be explained later) or one of the grant-making agency's publications.
- application instructions

The first funding opportunity listed in Exhibit 13.2 was selected: PA-11-244 Effects of Secondhand Smoke on Cardiovascular and Pulmonary Disease Mechanisms (R01), with the National Institutes of Health (NIH) as the funding agency. By clicking on the program, the grantseeker obtained the synopsis for this grant opportunity (Exhibit 13.3). In this case, the program title for PA-11-244 is "Effects of Secondhand Smoke on Cardiovascular and Pulmonary Disease Mechanisms (R01)." Clicking on "Full Announcement" in the synopsis did not bring the grantseeker to the *Federal Register* as it does with opportunities funded from other agencies such as the DOE. Instead the grantseeker had to scroll through the synopsis to the section entitled "Additional Information" to find the link to the full announcement. In this case the full announcement can be found in the grant-making agency's publication (http://grants.nih.gov/grants/guide/pa-files/PA-11-244.html).

Often, the information provided in the full announcement will begin to provide you with the information necessary to determine how well this grant opportunity matches with your project or research. For example, you should be able to uncover the eligibility requirements, the cost sharing or matching requirements, the expected number of awards, the total funds available, the maximum and minimum award amounts (the award ceiling and floor), and the award project period. Both the synopsis and the full announcement also provide you with a five-digit CFDA number, which can be used for searching the CFDA.

Catalog of Federal Domestic Assistance

The CFDA is another free valuable resource for searching through the available competitive and discretionary grant opportunities. The primary purpose of the CFDA is to assist users in identifying programs that meet specific

EXHIBIT 13.3
Opportunity Synopsis Grants.gov

‹ Back | Link

PA-11-244
Effects of Secondhand Smoke on Cardiovascular and Pulmonary Disease
Mechanisms (R01)
National Institutes of Health — Department of Health and Human Services

SYNOPSIS DETAILS
VERSION HISTORY
FULL ANNOUNCEMENT
APPLICATION PACKAGE

The synopsis for this grant opportunity is detailed below, following this paragraph. This synopsis contains all of the updates to this document that have been posted as of 7/7/2011. If updates have been made to the opportunity synopsis, update information is provided below the synopsis.

If you would like to receive notifications of changes to the grant opportunity click send me change notification emails. The only thing you need to provide for this service is your email address. No other information is requested.

Any inconsistency between the original printed document and the disk or electronic document shall be resolved by giving precedence to the printed document.

General Information

Document Type:	Grants Notice	Posted Date:	Jul 7, 2011
Funding Opportunity Number:	PA-11-244	Creation Date:	Jul 7, 2011
Funding Opportunity Title:	Effects of Secondhand Smoke on Cardiovascular and Pulmonary Disease Mechanisms (R01)	Original Closing Date for Applications:	Sep 7, 2014
		Current Closing Date for Applications:	Sep 7, 2014
		Archive Date:	Oct 8, 2014
Opportunity Category:	Discretionary	Estimated Total Program Funding:	
Funding Instrument Type:	Grant	Award Ceiling:	
Category of Funding Activity:	Environment Health	Award Floor:	
Category Explanation:			
Expected Number of Awards:			
CFDA Number(s):	93.113 -- Environmental Health 93.837 -- Cardiovascular Diseases Research 93.838 -- Lung Diseases Research		
Cost Sharing or Matching Requirement:	No		

Eligibility

Eligible Applicants:	City or township governments
	Independent school districts
	Native American tribal governments (Federally recognized)
	Nonprofits having a 501(c)(3) status with the IRS, other than institutions of higher education
	Small businesses
	Nonprofits that do not have a 501(c)(3) status with the IRS, other than institutions of higher education
	For profit organizations other than small businesses
	County governments
	Others (see text field entitled "Additional Information on Eligibility" for clarification)
	Public and State controlled institutions of higher education
	State governments
	Public housing authorities/Indian housing authorities
	Special district governments
	Native American tribal organizations (other than Federally recognized tribal governments)
	Private institutions of higher education
Additional Information on Eligibility:	Other Eligible Applicants include the following: Alaska Native and Native Hawaiian Serving Institutions; Eligible Agencies of the Federal Government; Faith-based or Community-based Organizations; Hispanic-serving Institutions; Historically Black Colleges and Universities (HBCUs); Indian/Native American Tribal Governments (Other than Federally Recognized); Non-domestic (non-U.S.) Entities (Foreign Organizations); Regional Organizations; Tribally Controlled

(continued)

EXHIBIT 13.3
(Continued)

Colleges and Universities (TCCUs) ; U.S. Territory or Possession; Foreign (non-U.S.) components of U.S. Organizations are allowed.

Additional Information

Agency Name: National Institutes of Health

Description: This Funding Opportunity Announcement (FOA) issued by the National Heart, Lung, and Blood Institute and National Institute of Environmental Health Sciences National Institutes of Health, invites applications that propose to better characterize the dose-response relationship between secondhand smoke (SHS) exposure and the cardiovascular and pulmonary diseases by improving our understanding of the mechanisms by which SHS contributes to these diseases. The recent Institute of Medicine (IOM) report on Secondhand Smoke Exposure and Cardiovascular Effects: Making Sense of the Evidence serves as the basis for this initiative. A wide range of research including animal and human laboratory studies, cohort and case control studies, and natural experiments resulting from home, workplace, and/or community changes in SHS exposure are consistent with this initiative.

Link to Additional Information: http://grants.nih.gov/grants/guide/pa-files/PA-11-244.html

Contact Information: If you have difficulty accessing the full announcement electronically, please contact:

NIH OER Webmaster FBOWebmaster@OD.NIH.GOV
If you have any problems linking to this funding announcement, please contact the NIH OER Webmaster

Synopsis Version History

The following files represent the modifications to this synopsis with the changes noted within the documents. The list of files is arranged from newest to oldest with the newest file representing the current synopsis. Changed sections from the previous document are shown in a light grey background.

Synopsis Version Name	Modification Description	Date Modified
Current Version		Jul 7, 2011

DISPLAYING: Current Version

General Information

Document Type:	Grants Notice	Posted Date:	Jul 7, 2011
Funding Opportunity Number:	PA-11-244	Creation Date:	Jul 7, 2011
Funding Opportunity Title:	Effects of Secondhand Smoke on Cardiovascular and Pulmonary Disease Mechanisms (R01)	Original Closing Date for Applications:	Sep 7, 2014
		Current Closing Date for Applications:	Sep 7, 2014
		Archive Date:	Oct 8, 2014
Opportunity Category:	Discretionary	Estimated Total Program Funding:	
Funding Instrument Type:	Grant	Award Ceiling:	
Category of Funding Activity:	Environment Health	Award Floor:	
Category Explanation:			
Expected Number of Awards:			
CFDA Number(s):	93.113 -- Environmental Health 93.837 -- Cardiovascular Diseases Research 93.838 -- Lung Diseases Research		

Cost Sharing or Matching Requirement: No

Eligibility

Eligible Applicants: City or township governments
Independent school districts
Native American tribal governments (Federally recognized)
Nonprofits having a 501(c)(3) status with the IRS, other than institutions of higher education
Small businesses
Nonprofits that do not have a 501(c)(3) status with the IRS, other than institutions of higher education
For profit organizations other than small businesses

(continued)

EXHIBIT 13.3
(Continued)

County governments
Others (see text field entitled "Additional Information on Eligibility" for clarification)
Public and State controlled institutions of higher education
State governments
Public housing authorities/Indian housing authorities
Special district governments
Native American tribal organizations (other than Federally recognized tribal governments)
Private institutions of higher education

Additional Information on Eligibility:	Other Eligible Applicants include the following: Alaska Native and Native Hawaiian Serving Institutions; Eligible Agencies of the Federal Government; Faith-based or Community-based Organizations; Hispanic-serving Institutions; Historically Black Colleges and Universities (HBCUs); Indian/Native American Tribal Governments (Other than Federally Recognized); Non-domestic (non-U.S.) Entities (Foreign Organizations); Regional Organizations; Tribally Controlled Colleges and Universities (TCCUs) ; U.S. Territory or Possession; Foreign (non-U.S.) components of U.S. Organizations are allowed.

Additional Information:

Agency Name:	National Institutes of Health
Description:	This Funding Opportunity Announcement (FOA) issued by the National Heart, Lung, and Blood Institute and National Institute of Environmental Health Sciences National Institutes of Health, invites applications that propose to better characterize the dose-response relationship between secondhand smoke (SHS) exposure and the cardiovascular and pulmonary diseases by improving our understanding of the mechanisms by which SHS contributes to these diseases. The recent Institute of Medicine (IOM) report on Secondhand Smoke Exposure and Cardiovascular Effects: Making Sense of the Evidence serves as the basis for this initiative. A wide range of research including animal and human laboratory studies, cohort and case control studies, and natural experiments resulting from home, workplace, and/or community changes in SHS exposure are consistent with this initiative.
Link to Additional Information:	http://grants.nih.gov/grants/guide/pa-files/PA-11-244.html
Contact Information:	If you have difficulty accessing the full announcement electronically, please contact:

NIH OER Webmaster FBOWebmaster@OD.NIH.GOV
If you have any problems linking to this funding announcement, please contact the NIH OER Webmaster

There are no attached files.

Selected Grant Applications for Download

Download the application and its instructions by selecting the corresponding download link. Save these files to your computer for future reference and use. You do not need Internet access to read the instructions or to complete the application once you save them to your computer.

READ BELOW BEFORE YOU APPLY FOR THIS GRANT!
Before you can view and complete an application package, you MUST have Adobe Reader installed. Application packages are posted in Adobe Reader format. You may receive a validation error using incompatible versions of Adobe Reader. To prevent a validation error, it is now recommended you uninstall any earlier versions of Adobe Reader and install the latest compatible version of Adobe Reader. If more than one person is working on the application package, ALL applicants must be using the same software version. Click to download the required Adobe Reader if you do not have it installed already.

Please click the support tab for additional resources.

Below is a list of the application(s) currently available for the Funding Opportunity.

To download the application instructions or package, click the corresponding download link. You will then be able to save the files on your computer for future reference and use.

CFDA	Opportunity Number	Competition ID	Competition Title	Agency	Instructions and Application
	PA-11-244	FORMS-C	Use for due dates after 9/24/2013	National Institutes of Health	Download

objectives of the potential applicant and to obtain general information on federal assistance programs. As of June 1, 2014, the CFDA contained detailed program descriptions for 2,271 federal assistance programs. The top five issuing agencies by number of programs are the Department of Health and Human Services (39%), the Department of the Interior (21%), the Department of Agriculture (20%), the Department of Justice (10%), and the Department of Housing and Urban Development (10%).

The website www.cfda.gov is the primary means of disseminating the CFDA. However, the Government Printing Office continues to print and sell hardcopies of the CFDA to interested buyers. For ordering and access information see Table 13.1, Federal Research Tools.

The CFDA is divided into three basic sections: the indices, the program descriptions, and the appendices. The print edition of the CFDA contains seven indexes that can be used to help you identify your specific areas of program interest more efficiently. They are as follows:

- *Agency Index Summary:* Provides a description of the functions and activities of federal agencies responsible for administering programs in the CFDA.
- *Agency Program Index:* Lists all programs in the CFDA in numerical order by the five-digit program identification number, the program title, the federal agency responsible for administering the program, and whether the program offers financial assistance, no financial assistance, or a combination of both.
- *Functional Index Summary:* Lists the basic functional categories and the subcategories that further identify specific areas of interest. Following the Summary is the Functional Index listing each program number and title under the appropriate basic category and subcategory.
- *Subject Index:* The most commonly used index that provides a detailed listing of programs by various topics, popular name, general functional terms, categories of services, and selected beneficiaries, and is followed by the applicable program numbers.
- *American Recovery and Reinvestment Act Index:* Lists CFDA programs that are funded in whole or part by the American Recovery and Reinvestment Act (ARRA) of 2009, Public Law 111.5.
- *Applicant Eligibility Index:* Allows you to look up a program to see whether you are eligible to apply. Because you must already know of the program to use this index, it is not a great help in identifying sources.
- *Deadlines Index:* Enables you to look up the deadline dates for programs to see whether the programs have a single or multiple deadline system.

Users should also be aware of the other sections of the CFDA that provide valuable information, such as:

- the archived program listings, which identifies programs that have been archived since the previous edition
- the added program listings, which identify programs that have been added since the previous edition
- the cross-listing of changes to program numbers and titles, which lists programs that have undergone a title change, or a program number change due to restructuring of programs, or reorganization of a federal agency

The center section of the printed CFDA and the listings available on the CFDA website contain descriptions of federal programs listed by program number in the same numerical sequence as in the Agency Program Index. Detailed information concerning programs is contained under the description of each CFDA program.

Once you have gained access to CFDA's website, enter a key word or CFDA program number in the section to the right of CFDA's home page. Then click "SEARCH." In the sample search (Exhibit 13.4), the grantseeker is again interested in secondhand smoke but instead of searching via this key phrase, the grantseeker searched by the CFDA program number, which was obtained from the Grants.gov synopsis and the NIH's full announcement previously procured. In the example's funding opportunity (PA-11-244), three different CFDA numbers were listed: one under Environmental Health, one under Cardiovascular Diseases Research, and one under Lung Diseases Research. This may be due to the fact that the NIH is listed as the participating organization on the full announcement with the National Heart, Lung, and Blood Institute and the National Institute of Environmental Health Sciences listed as components of the participating organization. For the purpose of this example, the number under Cardiovascular Diseases Research, CFDA 93.837, was selected.

EXHIBIT 13.4
Sample Search *Catalog of Federal Domestic Assistance* **(CFDA)**

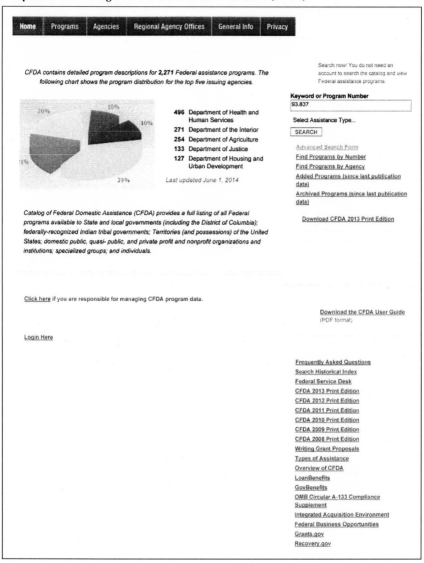

| Home | Programs | Agencies | Regional Agency Offices | General Info | Privacy |

CFDA contains detailed program descriptions for **2,271** *Federal assistance programs. The following chart shows the program distribution for the top five issuing agencies.*

496 Department of Health and Human Services
271 Department of the Interior
254 Department of Agriculture
133 Department of Justice
127 Department of Housing and Urban Development

Last updated June 1, 2014

Catalog of Federal Domestic Assistance (CFDA) provides a full listing of all Federal programs available to State and local governments (including the District of Columbia); federally-recognized Indian tribal governments; Territories (and possessions) of the United States; domestic public, quasi- public, and private profit and nonprofit organizations and institutions; specialized groups; and individuals.

Click here if you are responsible for managing CFDA program data.

Login Here

Search now! You do not need an account to search the catalog and view Federal assistance programs.

Keyword or Program Number
93.837

Select Assistance Type...

SEARCH

Advanced Search Form
Find Programs by Number
Find Programs by Agency
Added Programs (since last publication date)
Archived Programs (since last publication date)

Download CFDA 2013 Print Edition

Download the CFDA User Guide
(PDF format)

Frequently Asked Questions
Search Historical Index
Federal Service Desk
CFDA 2013 Print Edition
CFDA 2012 Print Edition
CFDA 2011 Print Edition
CFDA 2010 Print Edition
CFDA 2009 Print Edition
CFDA 2008 Print Edition
Writing Grant Proposals
Types of Assistance
Overview of CFDA
LoanBenefits
GovBenefits
OMB Circular A-133 Compliance Supplement
Integrated Acquisition Environment
Federal Business Opportunities
Grants.gov
Recovery.gov

Search results are shown in Exhibit 13.5. By clicking on the program of interest, the grantseeker can retrieve a CFDA entry describing the program. The CFDA entry provides different information than the Grants.gov synopsis and the full program announcement. Therefore, it is wise to review all three to get a complete picture of your program of interest.

EXHIBIT 13.5
CFDA Search Results

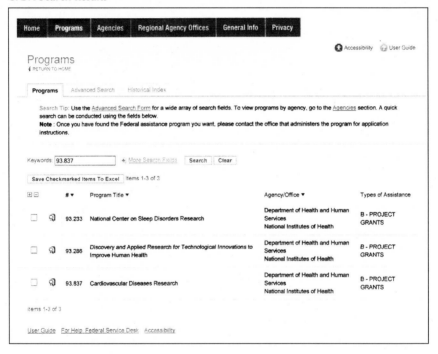

The sample CFDA entry (Exhibit 13.6) has been included to show the information provided in this valuable resource. All program description entries contain the following basic information:

- *Program Number and Title:* Each program in the CFDA is preceded by a five-digit program identification number. The first two digits identify the federal department or agency that administers the program, and the last three numbers identify the agency's program. The numbers are assigned in a numerical sequence. The program title is the descriptive name given to a program. The popular name is the less descriptive name by which programs are commonly known.
- *Agency:* This is the branch of government administering the program. Please note that in our example the agency is listed as the Department of Health and Human Services and the NIH is listed as the office.
- *Authorization:* You need this information to fill out some program applications or to look up the testimony and laws creating the funding (for the hard-core researcher and grantseeker only).
- *Objectives:* Compare these general program objectives to your project. Do not give up if you are off the mark slightly; contact with the funding source may uncover new programs, changes, or hidden agendas.
- *Types of Assistance:* Review the general type of support from this source, and then compare the information to your project definition. Currently, programs in the CFDA are classified into fifteen types of assistance, with formula and project grants being the most popular.
- *Uses and Use Restrictions:* Compare your project to this description of the potential uses for the assistance provided to meet stated objectives, and the specific restrictions placed on the use of the funds.
- *Eligibility Requirements:* Be sure your organization is designated as a legal recipient (applicant eligibility). If it is not, find an organization of the type designated and apply as a consortium or under a cooperative agreement. Determine whether your project can benefit those that the program is intended to benefit (beneficiary eligibility). Make sure you have the credentials or documentation required prior to, or along with, your application for assistance (credentials/documentation).
- *Application and Award Process:* This section includes information on preapplication coordination, application procedures, award procedure, deadlines, range of approval and disapproval time, appeals, and renewals. Do not let the deadline data bother you. If the award cycle has passed, you should still contact the agency and position yourself for the following year by requesting copies of old applications and a list of current grantees and by asking to be a reviewer.

- *Assistance Considerations:* This includes information on formula and matching requirements. It also includes a section describing the period during which the assistance is normally available, whether there are many restrictions placed on the time permitted to use the funds awarded, and the time of disbursements of the assistance, for example, lump sum, annually, quarterly, or as required. Make note of any match you are required to provide. This will be useful in evaluating funding sources. Matching requirements may eliminate some funding sources from your consideration because your organization may not have any resources available for this purpose. In addition, assistance considerations will help you develop your project planner (see chapter 15). When you know about matching requirements in advance, you can identify what resources your organization will be required to provide. Watch for confusing comments such as this: "a match is not required, but is advised." You must find out from past grantees if this suggested match was actually a prerequisite.
- *Postassistance Requirements:* This section provides you with reports, audits, and records requirements.
- *Financial Information:* This section includes account identification, obligations, range and average of financial assistance, and program accomplishments. It gives you an idea of what funds the agency program may have received, but do not take the information here as the last word. One entry I reviewed said the funding agency had $3 million for research. When contacted, the agency had over $30 million to disseminate under the program described and similar ones in CFDA. Refer to the entry, but investigate it further.
- *Regulations, Guidelines, and Literature:* Download any materials that appear useful.
- *Information Contacts:* This section includes information on the contact at the regional or local office as well as the headquarters office and the website address. Store and use this information to begin contacting funders as outlined later in this book. If provided, note the name, address, phone number, and e-mail address of the contact. While the contact person, address, phone number, or e-mail address may have changed, you will at least have a place to start.
- *Related Programs:* Some CFDA entries include suggestions of other programs that are similar or related to your area of interest. This is like a free redefinition. While these suggestions are usually obvious, you may not have already uncovered the programs in your research. Therefore, review this section for leads.

EXHIBIT 13.6
Sample CFDA Entry

Cardiovascular Diseases Research

Number: 93.837

Agency: Department of Health and Human Services

Office: National Institutes of Health

PROGRAM INFORMATION

Authorization (040):

Public Health Service Act, Section 301, 422 and 487, as amended, Public Laws 78-410 and 99-158, 42 U.S.C. 241, 42 U.S.C. 285, and 42 U.S.C. 288, as amended; Small Business Reauthorization Act of 2000, Public Law 106-554.

Objectives (050):

To foster research and prevention, education, and control activities related to heart and vascular diseases and to develop young scientist investigators in these areas. Small Business Innovation Research (SBIR) program: To increase private sector commercialization of innovations derived from Federal research and development; to increase small business participation in Federal research and development; and to foster and encourage participation of socially and economically disadvantaged small business concerns and women-owned small business concerns in technological innovation. Small Business Technology Transfer (STTR) program: To stimulate and foster scientific and technological innovation through cooperative research and development carried out between small business concerns and research institutions; to foster technology transfer between small business concerns and research institutions; to increase private sector commercialization of innovations derived from Federal research and development; and to foster and encourage participation of socially and economically disadvantaged small business concerns and women-owned small business concerns in technological innovation.

Types of Assistance (060):

PROJECT GRANTS

Uses and Use Restrictions (070):

Grants may support stipends, research expenses, supplies, travel, and research training tuition as required to perform the research effort. Restrictions or limitations are imposed against the use of funds for entertainment, foreign travel, general-purpose equipment, alterations and renovations, and other items not regularly required for the performance of research. Individual Predoctoral and Postdoctoral National Research Service Awards (NRSAs) are made directly to individuals for research training in specified biomedical shortage areas. Institutional NRSA awards may be made to eligible institutions to enable them to appoint individuals selected by the institution for research training. Certain service and payback provisions may apply to postdoctoral individuals upon termination of the award or termination of the appointment. SBIR Phase I grants (of approximately 6-months' duration) are to establish the technical merit and feasibility of a proposed research effort that may lead to a commercial product or process. Phase II grants are for the continuation of research initiated in Phase I that is likely to result in commercial products or processes. Only Phase I awardees are eligible to apply for Phase II support. STTR Phase I grants (normally of 1-year duration) are to determine the scientific, technical, and commercial merit and feasibility of the proposed cooperative effort that has potential for commercial application. These awards are made to small

(continued)

EXHIBIT 13.6
(Continued)

businesses working in collaboration with academic institutions. Phase II funding is based on results of research initiated in Phase I and scientific and technical merit and commercial potential of Phase II application. Fast-Track is an option whereby Phase I and Phase II SBIR or STTR projects are submitted and reviewed concurrently with the aim of reducing or eliminating the funding gap between Phase I and Phase II. While the intent of the SBIR/STTR programs is commercialization (Phase III), no SBIR/STTR funds are allowed for commercialization activities such as patents; market and sales; market research; business development/product development/market plans; legal fees, travel and other costs including labor relating to license agreements and partnerships.

Eligibility Requirements (080)

Applicant Eligibility (081):
Any nonprofit organization engaged in biomedical research and institutions or companies organized for profit may apply for almost any kind of grant. Only domestic, non-profit, private or public institutions may apply for NRSA Institutional Research Training Grants. An individual may apply for an NRSA or, in some cases, for a research grant if adequate facilities to perform the research are available. SBIR grants can be awarded only to United States small business concerns (entities that are independently owned and operated for profit, or owned by another small business that itself is independently owned and operated for profit, are not dominant in the field in which research is proposed, and have no more than 500 employees including affiliates). Primary employment (more than one-half time) of the principal investigator must be with the small business at the time of award and during the conduct of the proposed project. In both Phase I and Phase II, the research must be performed in the U.S. or its possessions. To be eligible for funding, a grant application must be approved for scientific merit and program relevance by a scientific review group and a national advisory council. SBIR projects must be performed at least 67% by the applicant small business in Phase I and at least 50% of the Project in Phase II. STTR grants can be awarded only to United States small business concerns (entities that are independently owned and operated for profit and have no more than 500 employees) that formally collaborate with a university or other non-profit research institution in cooperative research and development. The principle investigator may be employed with the small business concern or collaborating non-profit research institution as long as s/he has a formal appointment with or commitment to the applicant small business concern. At least 40% of the project is to be performed by the small business concern and at least 30% by the non-profit research institution. In both Phase I and Phase II, the research must be performed in the U.S. and its possessions.

Beneficiary Eligibility (082):
Any nonprofit or for-profit organization, company or institution engaged in biomedical research. Only domestic for-profit small business firms may apply for SBIR and STTR programs.

Credentials/Documentation (083):
Individual NRSA awardees and Institutional NRSA trainees must be citizens or noncitizen nationals of the United States, or have been admitted for permanent residency. Two levels of training are available: graduate level predoctoral training and postdoctoral training. All potential trainees must possess a desire for training in one of the health or health-related areas specified by the National Institutes of Health. Each applicant must be sponsored by an accredited public or private nonprofit institution engaged in such training. Costs will be determined in accordance with OMB Circular No. A-87 for State and local governments. For-profit organization costs are determined in accordance with Subpart 31.2 of the Federal Acquisition Regulations. For other grantees, costs will be determined in accordance with DHHS Regulations 45 CFR, Part 74, Subpart Q. For SBIR and STTR grants, applicant organization (small business concern) must present a research plan that has potential for commercialization and furnish evidence that scientific competence, experimental methods, facilities, equipment, and funds requested are appropriate to carry out the plan. SBIR and STTR applicants must use the SF424 Research and Related (R&R) application for electronic submission through grants.gov. Electronic submission of

(continued)

EXHIBIT 13.6
(Continued)

NIH Research Performance Progress Reports (RPPR) apply for non-competing continuations (e.g., second year of Phase II). OMB Circular No. A-87 applies to this program. OMB Circular No. A-87 applies to this program.

Application and Award Process (090)

Preapplication Coordination (091):
Preapplication coordination is not applicable. Environmental impact information is not required for this program. This program is excluded from coverage under E.O. 12372.

Application Procedures (092):
This program is excluded from coverage under OMB Circular No. A-102. OMB Circular No. A-110 applies to this program. This program is excluded from coverage under OMB Circular No. A-102. OMB Circular No. A-110 applies to this program. Grant applications are submitted electronically. Visit the following link to obtain application information and instructions (http://grants1.nih.gov/grants/funding/424/index.htm)

Award Procedure (093):
All accepted applications are evaluated by an appropriate initial review group (study section). All grant applications receive a final secondary review by the National Heart, Lung, and Blood Advisory Council. Staff inform applicants of the results of the review. If support is contemplated, staff initiate preparation of awards for grants. All accepted SBIR/STTR applications are evaluated for scientific and technical merit by an appropriate scientific peer review panel and by a national advisory council or board. All applications receiving a priority score compete for available SBIR/STTR set-aside funds on the basis of scientific and technical merit and commercial potential of the proposed research, program relevance, and program balance among the areas of research.

Deadlines (094):
Contact the headquarters or regional office, as appropriate, for application deadlines.

Range of Approval/Disapproval Time (095):
> 180 Days. Regular Grants: From 7 to 9 months. SBIR/STTR Grants: About 7-1/2 to 9 months.

Appeals (096):
A principal investigator (P.I.) may question the substantive or procedural aspects of the review of his/her application by communicating with the staff of the Institute. A description of the NIH Peer Review Appeal procedures is available in the NIH Guide at the following URL http://grants.nih.gov/grants/guide/notice-files/NOT-OD-11-064.html.

Renewals (097):
> 180 Days. Renewal applications are reviewed in the same manner as new applications.

Assistance Consideration (100)

Formula and Matching Requirements (101):
This program has no statutory formula.
This program has no matching requirements. This program has no matching requirements.
This program does not have MOE requirements. This program has no matching requirements.

Length and Time Phasing of Assistance (102):
The National Heart, Lung, and Blood Advisory Council may recommend funding for periods ranging from 1 to 5 years. Funding commitments are made annually. The National Heart, Lung, and Blood Advisory Council may

---

(continued)

EXHIBIT 13.6
(Continued)

recommend funding for periods ranging from 1 to 5 years. Funding commitments are made annually. SBIR: Normally, Phase I awards are for 6 months; normally, Phase II awards are for 2 years. STTR: Normally, Phase I awards are for 1 year; normally, Phase II awards are for 2 years. Award length may vary depending on the recommendation of the scientific review group, the national advisory council, successful annual performance, and availability of funds. A formal notification in the form of a Notice of Award (NoA) will be provided to the applicant organization. See the following for information on how assistance is awarded/released: Award length may vary depending on the recommendation of the scientific review group, the national advisory council, successful annual performance, and availability of funds. See the following for information on how assistance is awarded/released: A formal notification in the form of a Notice of Award (NoA) will be provided to the applicant organization.

Post Assistance Requirements (110)

Reports (111):
No program reports are required. No cash reports are required. Annual reports on progress and expenditures are required. Final reports are required within 120 days of termination. Reports are required after termination of NRSAs to ascertain compliance with the service and payback provisions. Annual reports on progress and expenditures are required. Final reports are required within 120 days of termination. Reports are required after termination of NRSAs to ascertain compliance with the service and payback provisions. No performance monitoring is required.

Audits (112):
In accordance with the provisions of OMB Circular No. A-133 (Revised, June 27, 2003), "Audits of States, Local Governments, and Non-Profit Organizations," nonfederal entities that expend financial assistance of $500,000 or more in Federal awards will have a single or a program-specific audit conducted for that year. Nonfederal entities that expend less than $500,000 a year in Federal awards are exempt from Federal audit requirements for that year, except as noted in Circular No. A-133.

Records (113):
Grantees generally must retain financial and programmatic records, supporting documents, statistical records, and all other records that are required by the terms of a grant, or may reasonably be considered pertinent to a grant, for a period of 3 years from the date the annual FSR is submitted. For awards under SNAP (other than those to foreign organizations and Federal institutions), the 3-year retention period will be calculated from the date the FSR for the entire competitive segment is submitted. Those grantees must retain the records pertinent to the entire competitive segment for 3 years from the date the FSR is submitted to NIH. Foreign organizations and Federal institutions must retain records for 3 years from the date of submission of the annual FSR to NIH. See 45 CFR 74.53 and 92.42 for exceptions and qualifications to the 3-year retention requirement (e.g., if any litigation, claim, financial management review, or audit is started before the expiration of the 3-year period, the records must be retained until all litigation, claims, or audit findings involving the records have been resolved and final action taken). Those sections also specify the retention period for other types of grant-related records, including F&A cost proposals and property records. See 45 CFR 74.48 and 92.36 for record retention and access requirements for contracts under grants.
In accordance with 45 Code of Federal Regulations, Part 74.53(e), the HHS Inspector General, the U.S. Comptroller General, or any of their duly authorized representatives have the right of timely and unrestricted access to any books, documents, papers, or other records of recipients that are pertinent to awards in order to make audits, examinations, excerpts, transcripts, and copies of such documents. This right also includes timely and reasonable access to a recipient's personnel for the purpose of interview and discussion related to such documents. The rights of access are not limited to the required retention period, but shall last as long as records are retained.

(continued)

EXHIBIT 13.6
(Continued)

Financial Information (120)

Account Identification (121):
75-0872-0-1-552.

Obligations (122):
(Project Grants) FY 12 $1,426,764,627; FY 13 est $1,426,764,627; and FY 14 est $1,426,764,627 - In fiscal year 2012, 2,979 research grants and National Research Service Awards were made. The estimates of fiscal year 2013 are 2,689 research grants and 290 National Research Service awards. The estimates for fiscal year 2014 are 2,689 research grants and 290 National Research Service Awards. In fiscal year 2012, for new and competing renewal awards: 4,337 grant applications were received, and of these, 606 were awarded; 258 National Research Service Award applications were received, and of these, 61 were awarded. Small Business innovation Research Awards/Small Technology Transfer Research Awards: In fiscal year 2012, 45 Phase I awards, and 48 Phase II awards were made.

Range and Average of Financial Assistance (123):
Grants: $5,000 to $11,262,237; $479,063. SBIR Phase I - $150,000; Phase II - up to $1,000,000; STTR Phase I - $100,000, Phase II - $750,000.

Program Accomplishments (130):
Not Applicable.

Regulations, Guidelines, and Literature (140):
42 CFR 52; 42 CFR 66; 45 CFR 74; "NIH Guide for Grants and Contracts, and Supplements"; Grants will be available under the authority of and administered in accordance with the PHS Grants Policy Statement and Federal regulations at 42 CFR 52 and 42 USC 241; Omnibus Solicitation of the Public Health Service for Small Business Innovation Research (SBIR) Grant and Cooperative Agreement Applications; Omnibus Solicitation of the National Institutes of Health for Small Business Technology Transfer (STTR) Grant Applications.

Information Contacts (150)

Regional or Local Office (151) :
None.

Headquarters Office (152):
Dana A. Phares 6701 Rockledge Drive, Room 7176, Bethesda. Maryland 20892 Email: pharesda@nhlbi.nih.gov Phone: 301-435-0314

Website Address (153):
http://www.nhlbi.nih.gov/about/dcvs/

Related Programs (160):
Not Applicable.

Examples of Funded Projects (170):
Not Applicable.

Criteria for Selecting Proposals (180):

(continued)

EXHIBIT 13.6
(Continued)

The major elements in evaluating proposals include assessments of: (1) The scientific merit and general significance of the proposed study and its objectives; (2)the technical adequacy of the experimental design and approach; (3) the competency of the proposed investigator or group to successfully pursue the project; (4) the adequacy of the available and proposed facilities and resources; (5) the necessity of the budget components requested in relation to the proposed project; and (6) the relevance and importance to announced program objectives. The following criteria will be used in considering the scientific and technical merit of SBIR/STTR Phase I grant applications: (1) The soundness and technical merit of the proposed approach; (2) the importance of the problem the proposed research will address; (3) the qualifications of the proposed principal investigator, supporting staff, and consultants; (4) the technological innovation of the proposed research; (5) the potential of the proposed research for commercial application; (6) the appropriateness of the budget requested; (7) the adequacy and suitability of the facilities and research environment; and (8) where applicable, the adequacy of assurances detailing the proposed means for (a) safeguarding human or animal subjects, and/or (b) protecting against or minimizing any adverse effect on the environment. Phase II grant applications will be reviewed based upon the following criteria: (1) The degree to which the Phase I objectives were met and feasibility demonstrated; (2) the scientific and technical merit of the proposed approach for achieving the Phase II objectives; (3) the qualifications of the proposed principal investigator, supporting staff, and consultants; (4) the technological innovation, originality, or societal importance of the proposed research; (5) the potential of the proposed research for commercial application; (6) the reasonableness of the budget requested for the work proposed; (7) the adequacy and suitability of the facilities and research environment; and (8) where applicable, the adequacy of assurances detailing the proposed means for (a) safeguarding human or animal subjects, and/or (b) protecting against or minimizing any adverse effect on the environment.

- *Examples of Funded Projects:* Compare your project with those listed and ask yourself how your project fits in.
- *Criteria for Selecting Proposals:* Review and store the information here. Criteria are frequently listed with no regard to their order of importance and lack any reference to the point values they will be given in the review. Therefore, you should also obtain the rules from the *Federal Register,* agency publications, or a past reviewer.

After you've reviewed the CFDA entries, select the best government funding program for your project. Contact the federal agency by using the information listed under "Information Contacts." Once you have found an assistance program you wish to apply for, follow the direction contained within that program. Each program is unique and has its own requirements and procedures. Unlike Grants.gov, you cannot apply for an assistance program on the *CFDA* website.

When researching federal grant opportunities it is necessary to search via both Grants.gov and the CFDA. These valuable resources sometimes use different key words (search terms). In addition, they sometimes categorize granting opportunities differently.

It is also necessary to look at both Grants.gov and the CFDA when searching for funding in the scientific fields. Again, funding opportunities are often categorized under different search terms. For example, when looking for grants in geophysics, one tool may list opportunities under the search term *geophysics,* while the other may list geophysics opportunities under the search term *physics* and show no results under *geophysics.*

Federal Register

The *Federal Register* is the official daily publication for rules, proposed rules, and notices of federal agencies and organizations, as well as exclusive orders and other presidential documents. Frequently requested materials from the *Federal Register* include grant information. However, not all funding agencies use the *Federal Register* as their public information vehicle. For instance, the National Science Foundation (NSF) and the NIH use their own agency publications to announce grant opportunities, program rules, and notices.

As Table 13.1 indicates, the *Register* can be accessed for free at www.federal register.gov. A hardcopy of this government publication is provided for free public use in federal depository libraries throughout the United States. Locate your nearest library by visiting www.gpo.gov/libraries.

After you have used Grants.gov or the CFDA to select a potential government funding program for your project, phone, fax, or e-mail the contact listed in the synopsis or entry to find out what vehicle the funding agency uses to post legal notices regarding its grant programs. If it is the *Federal Register,* find out the days the *Federal Register* publishes notices, proposed rules, or final rules and regulations regarding the program you are interested in. Ask for the volumes, the numbers, the issue dates, and the pages. The more information you have, the easier it will be for you to locate the information for which you are looking via a *Federal Register* advanced search. However, you may also be able to secure all the information you need by conducting a *Federal Register* document search using the program's CFDA number or title.

For example, say you wanted to access the *Federal Register* through the Internet to look for notices by the DOE on a teacher quality partnership grant program that you found while searching Grants.gov or the CFDA for funding opportunities related to "teacher quality." You would click "search" on the *Federal Register's* home page and then click "document search" from the pull-down menu. When the search documents page comes up, you would enter the funding opportunity's title under "find." When the search results come up, you would then have the opportunity to select whether you wanted them listed by "relevant," "newest," or "oldest." By clicking "newest," the DOE's May 28, 2014, notice for your program of interest would come up as the first entry. Clicking on the entry would then bring you to the Teacher Quality Partnership Grant Program Notice inviting applications for new awards for fiscal year (FY) 2014. This particular notice in its entirety provides a full text of the announcement, including a funding opportunity description, award information, eligibility information, application and submission information, application review information, award administration information, agency contact information, and other miscellaneous information. However, contents of notices do vary.

Be aware that "Notices" is not the only section of the *Federal Register* that can be searched. Grantseekers can also look for rules, proposed rules, and presidential documents.

FedBizOpps

FedBizOpps (FBO) lists notices of proposed government procurement actions, contract awards, sales of government property, and other procurement information over $25,000—all updated daily. Thousands of separate contracting offices and numerous grant programs advertise billions in government contracts each year through FBO. These contracts may total hundreds of billions and are in addition to the $500 billion cited in Grants.gov. Currently you can search more than 28,500 active federal opportunities on FBO. Vendors can search FBO for opportunities based on the following elements: keyword or solicitation number, opportunity and procurement type, posted date, response deadline, last-modified date, contract award date, place of performance state, place of performance zip code, set-aside code, classification code, North American Industry Classification System code, agency or office locations, and ARRA Action.

Many successful nonprofit organizations have used the list of successful bidders to develop subcontracts and form consortia that work with the successful bidder to perform some aspect of the contract cost effectively. In the process, they develop a track record of successful performance that will provide the basis for their own successful bid in the future. Through subcontracts and consortia, these organizations are able to build a track record and gain familiarity with both the contracts process and federal contract offices. The FBO also advertises notices of meetings that assist bidders in developing insight into upcoming contracts.

Several training programs are available at the FBO website to teach the mechanics of using the system. Registration is free and although you do not need to register to use FBO, if you do register you can:

- Sign up for e-mail notifications based on keywords or other criteria.
- Monitor pending federal contracts.

- Add federal contract opportunities to your own "watch list" so you are notified of important events.

FBO is available online, free of charge at www.fbo.gov.

GrantSelect

GrantSelect is an online grants database that provides information on more than fourteen thousand funding opportunities available from state and federal governments, corporations, foundations, and other nonprofit organizations. Subscriptions to the GrantSelect database allows unlimited access to funding opportunities ranging from pure research grants to operating grants for nonprofit organizations and grants for the arts, humanities, biomedical and health care research, community services, children and youth, K–12 education, international programs, scholarships, fellowships, technology, economic development, higher education, environmental studies, alternative energy sources, and agriculture. Subscriptions include an e-mail alert service that will immediately notify subscribers of new and changed records in the database. Pricing for institutions, organizations, and individuals is available online at grantselect.com. You can order online via GrantSelect's web form or off-line by downloading the appropriate forms and sending or faxing the subscription order to the contact information provided in Table 13.1.

Sponsored Programs Information Network

Sponsored Programs Information Network (SPIN) is a widely used funding opportunity database produced by InfoEd Global. Originally developed by the Research Foundation of the State University of New York, the database tracks the funding opportunities of over forty thousand government, private, and nonprofit funding sources worldwide. SPIN's search engine allows users to query the database with either basic key word or advanced Boolean searches. InfoEd also offers the SPIN Global Suite, which includes the following:

- SPIN funding opportunities database
- GENIUS, a curriculum vitae–biosketch database
- SPIN Matching and Research Transmittal Service, an automated alerts system that notifies investigators of new programs that match their research interests

InfoEd Global has also come out with an electronic research administration software system that helps manage the administrative work involved in research from pre-award to post-award to financial tracking.

You can find more information about all of InfoEd's products and SPIN membership by calling (800) 727-6427 or visiting www.infoedglobal.com. More InfoEd contact information can be found in Table 13.1.

GrantForward

Illinois Researcher Information Service (IRIS) has been replaced by the grants database service GrantForward. GrantFoward is a subscription-based service that contains more than nineteen thousand funding opportunities, including eight thousand federal and foundation opportunities each. The grantseeker can search for funding opportunities spread across thirty-nine subject areas and 2,009 categories. The funding opportunity search also comes with automatic e-mail alerts.

GrantForward has two other components: researcher profiles and administration console. With researcher profiles each funding opportunity is matched to researchers based on research interests and career stages. The administration console coordinates limited submissions by specifying contact information, internal submission deadline, and other instructions. It also annotates opportunities with institution-specific information and disseminates the opportunities to appropriate faculty or researchers. Contact Cazoolde, Inc., for subscription pricing and plans (see List of Resources). Fourteen-day free trials are available.

Pivot

Pivot is a Community of Science (COS) grant-search engine that provides information on funding opportunities worth an estimated $33 billion and identifies researcher expertise from within or outside of your organization from leading organizations worldwide. It maintains a database of three million scholar profiles (drawing from Community of Scholars and COS profiles) and has the ability to compile prepopulated researcher profiles unique to your organization (and others) and match those to current funding opportunities. Once your university buys a subscription, you can perform searches using your descriptors and also review faculty profiles to identify people who have interests similar to yours. To learn more about Pivot and to request a free trial, contact sales@refworks-cos.com. Free live and recorded training webinars are also available.

GrantSearch

GrantSearch is a funding database designed exclusively for members of the Grant Resource Center (GRC), a not-for-profit service of the American Association of State Colleges and Universities. The database provides information on federal and private funding sources and allows the user to search for funding opportunities using five criteria: academic subject, activity, funding sponsor, deadline month, and text. GRC membership is open to public and private higher education institutions that offer four-year and graduate degrees. See Table 13.1 for contact information on GRC membership and GrantSearch.

Other Grants Databases and How to Take Advantage of Them

While there are numerous other grants databases which are also good, I have only mentioned those that my clients subscribe to or those that I have had the opportunity to use in my career. If your organization does not already subscribe to a fee-based grants database, check with your consortia partners before you invest your funds or those of your organization. In my last position as a director of research, I made it a point to meet with other colleges and nonprofit organizations my institution wanted to partner with and worked with them to coordinate our database purchases to give us a better, more complete system. At the time, one partner institution used IRIS and my university used SPIN. Although we used the same key word search terms with both databases, our results were different, which expanded our universe of potential funding sources. As it turned out, our partner's database had more foundation and corporate grants than our database contained. Request that your partners run your combined search terms on their database to ensure that you do not overlook an important grant prospect.

Federal Agency Internet Mailing Lists

Several federal agencies have established Internet mailing lists to electronically disseminate news about their activities and services. Subscribing to these will help you keep up to date on federal funding opportunities. The following is a list of some of the federal agencies that provide this type of service:

- NSF: National Science Foundation Update, formerly MyNSF, allows you to receive e-mail notifications about new content posted on the

NSF website, including new content categories such as images and videos, events, and upcoming due dates for funding opportunities. You can subscribe at service.govdelivery.com/service/multi_subscribe. html?code=USNSF&custom_id=823.

- NIH: The NIH Office of Communications and Public Liaison offers a free e-mail subscription service that allows you to receive e-mail when new information is available. With a subscription profile, you can get the updated information on the items of interest to you automatically without having to return to the website and check for changes. For instructions on how to subscribe to these free NIH e-mail updates and to select from NIH's subscription topics, visit www.nih.gov/email.htm.
- Centers for Disease Control and Prevention (CDC): At the CDC, you can subscribe to receive e-mail alerts about new information related to your topics of interest. For a list of available topics, and to subscribe, go to www.cdc.gov/other/emailupdates/.
- U.S. Department of Justice: *JustInfo,* sponsored by the U.S. Department of Justice National Criminal Justice Reference Service (NCJRS), is a biweekly newsletter containing information about new publications, funding and training opportunities, events, and web-based resources available from NCJRS federal sponsors. View previous issues and subscribe at https://puborders.ncjrs.gov/listservs/subscribe_justinfo.asp.
- U.S. DOE: The DOE offers subscriptions to electronic mailing lists for several of its newsletters, including the following:
  - *ED Review:* biweekly update on DOE activities
  - *ED RSS:* daily feed of DOE news, funding, and teaching resources
  - *OVAE Connection:* research, evaluation, and technical assistance on career and technical education, adult education, and community colleges
  - *PreventionED:* updates on substance abuse and violence prevention education issues, legislation, and funding opportunities
  - *Education Research News:* education research, evaluation, and statistics
  - *Research e-News:* newsletter of the Institute of Education Sciences
  - *School Turnaround Newsletter:* resources for turning around low-performing schools
  - *Superintendent Monthly:* updates on policy, research, grants, and more
  - *Teaching Matters:* ED's bi-weekly newsletter celebrating teachers and teaching
  - *Touching Base:* newsletter for the military community

For links to these newsletters and instructions on how to subscribe to their electronic mailing lists, visit www2.ed.gov/news/newsletters/index .html.

- National Institute for Standards and Technology (NIST) provides NIST news releases and the *NIST Tech Beat* newsletter containing recent research results and other NIST news and is published biweekly. For links to NIST news releases and *NIST Tech Beat,* visit www.nist.gov/public_affairs.

Assessing the information you need to locate available government funding is not difficult or expensive. Whether you use the Internet, a commercial database, or hardcopies of government publications, the key to locating federal grant funds and to commanding the respect of the bureaucrats you will interact with in your quest for grants is to do your homework and learn all you can about each program you are thinking about approaching.

For example, you should take into consideration whether the federal granting program you uncover uses "special" mechanisms to award their funding. For instance, a specific categorical program may have reserved a portion of their budget for one or more of the following:

- new or young grantseekers
- multiyear awards to initiate researchers' careers (e.g., NSF Career Development Awards)
- grants to special classes of grantees such as women, minorities, etc.
- Small Business Innovative Research grants intended to stimulate technological innovation in the private sector by supporting research or research and development on behalf of for-profit institutions to develop ideas that have potential for commercialization
- Small Business Technology Transfer grants aimed at stimulating scientific and technological innovation through cooperative research or research and development carried out between small business concerns and research institutions
- NIH research grant programs ranging from R01s used to support a discrete, specified, circumscribed research project, to R21s encouraging new, exploratory, and developmental research projects by providing support for the early stages of project development like pilot and feasibility studies, to R34s designed to support the development of the essential elements of a clinical trial

As you perform your first rough cut of grantors, you should look at whether you qualify for any of these "special" funding mechanisms. If you do, the competition may be less and your chances of success greater.

Now you must find the time to complete your search for federal grant opportunities. Review your action steps chart to see where and when you can fit this task into your busy schedule. Review Figure 13.1 and commit to a deadline.

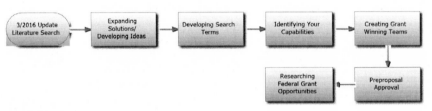

FIGURE 13.1
Action Steps Chart: Researching Federal Opportunities

14

Contacting Government Grantors, Past Grantees, and Past Reviewers

AT THIS POINT YOU HAVE RESEARCHED several government grant programs and you can almost smell the grant money. But hold on for the most important step of all: contacting the federal program officer or state grants staff. Because federal government grants are based on tax revenues, freedom of information laws require transparency and public disclosure related to grant programs. However, information on state and local grantors may be difficult to obtain. You are now aware of the resources the Internet provides and the advantages that federal grantseeking has over state and local grantseeking with respect to locating grant opportunities. These same disparities will be encountered as you seek to apply the preproposal contact strategies that follow. This is not to say that the information you are encouraged to obtain is any less important or useful on state and local proposals. It just may not be possible to get. Try to follow the suggested strategies with *all* government grantors. Even if a state grant program does not have the information you need available, it will usually respect you for asking the right questions.

The following preproposal contact strategies are not intended to provide you with an unfair advantage over your competition. The information is available to everyone. For example, it is imperative to have access to the grantor's priorities and the scoring rubric that the reviewers will use in evaluating and recommending proposals for funding. But I know from experience that some state grant programs develop their scoring system after the submittal deadline.

Do not be put off by my suggestion to contact grantors to augment your grants research even though many of my grant fellows have trouble with preproposal contact. They are awarded travel money and in some of my programs they are required to visit Washington, D.C., to meet with a program officer. Still, most hesitate and some even refuse to go. So I am not surprised that you may not be convinced of the importance of preproposal contact with a federal program officer, especially if you have bookmarked the program's website, registered, and already have its application form and guidelines. Like many other prospective grantseekers, you probably do not see the need to talk to government bureaucrats to complete your understanding of their programs. However, you should remember that your goal is not to *apply* for a grant; it is to be *awarded* a grant. Therein lies the reason for making preproposal contact. In fact, after forty-five years in the grants field, I can assure you that the principal investigators and project directors who are consistently funded across the board, from health research to humanities, actually contact government grantors several times a year, and not just during the preproposal period.

Several years before the first edition of this book was created, a study of ten thousand federal grant applications documented that those grantseekers who had made contact with federal program staff before submitting their applications experience a threefold increase in success over those who simply submitted the application. The key to their success was the opportunity to ask questions that may not have been covered in the *Catalog of Federal Domestic Assistance* (CFDA) program descriptions or agency publications.

When the successful grantees were asked what they discussed with the federal program officers, many said they asked questions that helped them to more closely meet the program guidelines. While this was the most frequent response, I believe they really asked questions aimed at uncovering what the program was actually interested in funding.

You can meet with program officers at conferences and professional meetings, as well as in their offices. Ask them what conferences are on their calendars and if they are speaking on any panels. Go to their presentations and ask if you could have a few minutes alone with them to ask questions. Some agencies have regional meetings that may be less expensive for you to attend. No harm can come from asking, only good!

When contacting a program officer, make no mistake about your intention. It is to confirm your grantor research and provide a more complete picture of what the grant program seeks to create and fund in your field. Your contact is professional, not personal. Even if you have very limited resources and no money for travel, do not be frustrated. While the study of ten thousand federal grantees was done years before e-mail was possible, it revealed no differences between telephone and face-to-face contact. The crucial point is that while you have done your homework, you need to make preproposal contact to confirm what you know and to find out more about the projects funded, and how the submitted proposals will be evaluated and by whom to prepare a winning proposal. My forty-five years of making contact with federal program officers have convinced me that when preproposal contact is done correctly, grantseekers can gain valuable insights. My contact has also proven to me that program officers actually value preproposal contact when done professionally; they respect grantseekers who research their programs.

When to Make Preproposal Contact

The timing of contact is critical. Each of the thousand-plus federal programs has a similar sequence of events related to its granting cycle. Review the diagram of the federal grants clock to help you determine where each of your prospective federal agency programs is in the grants process (Figure 14.1). Many grantseekers tell me that they only have six weeks to prepare a proposal after getting the application package. This is not true. All federal programs must comply with the steps outline in the grants clock shown in Figure 14.1. Also, most federal programs have similar deadlines and cycles each year. So don't wait!

1. The first step involves the dissemination of information regarding the agency's grant opportunity and a request to the public to help the agency develop the rules that will govern the grant program. In subsequent program cycles, the request is made to comment on last year's rules. This process may entail developing proposed rules, interim rules, and final rules. With each request, interested prospective grantees are usually given thirty days to submit their comments on the rules. The comments are published, the final rules are printed, and the announce-

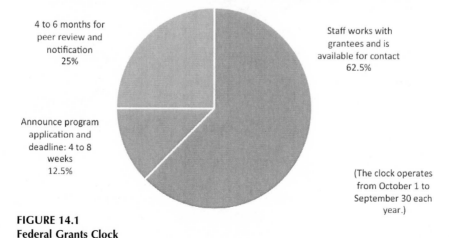

FIGURE 14.1
Federal Grants Clock

ments of deadlines are made in such publications as the *Federal Register,* the *NIH Guide,* and the National Science Foundation's (NSF) e-bulletin.

2. The federal program officer then develops the actual application package and places it on the agency's website for public access. This package is referred to as the *request for proposal* or the *request for application.*

3. The deadline for submissions is published.

4. Once proposals have been submitted through Grants.gov, they are forwarded to selected peer reviewers for evaluation. In some cases, the reviewers are required to go to a specified site to receive and review the proposals. In other cases, they may review them at home or in their offices. The reviewers must follow the agency's evaluation system and score each proposal according to the published guidelines. A staff review usually follows the peer review. In all cases, the staff reviewers provide the head of the agency with a list of proposals recommended for funding. The actual decision to fund is made by the director of the agency (or staff) and usually reflects the peer-review score but changes may be made for other reasons. For example, I was once told by a granting staff person that if the top scorers were all in one state, the agency might fund a high-ranking proposal from another state to provide a more equitable geographic distribution. (However, this information was presented during a casual conversation and therefore the actual process or variable used by the agency cannot be confirmed.)

5. The notices of award and rejection are made and the cycle starts again. Some federal programs with multiple deadlines repeat the process in four- and six-month cycles. If the program has more than one deadline each federal fiscal year, there may be several grants clocks running simultaneously.

Federal Grants Research Form

The key to providing you and your organization with federal funding is a combination of determination, hard work, and homework. The homework consists of systematic research, record keeping, and follow-up. The Federal Grants Research Form (Exhibit 14.1) will allow you to keep track of each of the grant programs you investigate (that is, those that seem like your most logical grant sources after your rough cut). Use Exhibit 14.1 to keep a record of your research and to help you select the best funding source for your proposal. In addition, the information you gather to complete this form will help you develop a successful proposal. (Later in this chapter you will receive more tips on making the preproposal contact needed to fully complete Exhibit 14.1.)

EXHIBIT 14.1
Federal Grants Research Form

Section 1
For (Your Project Reference or Title): _____
CFDA No. _____
Grants.gov Funding No. _____
Government Agency: _____
Deadline Date(s): _____

Create a file for each program you are researching and place all information you gather on this program in the file. Use this Federal Grants Research Form to:

- Keep a record of the information you have gathered.
- Maintain a log of all contact made with the federal program.

Agency Address: _____

Agency Director: _____ Program Director: _____
Name/Title of Contact Person: _____
Telephone Number: _____ Fax Number: _____
Email: _____ Web Site: _____

To prepare a professional proposal you need to gather the following information. Place a check mark next to the information you have gathered and placed in the file.

___ Program description from CFDA
___ Synopsis from Grants.gov
___ Subscription for automatic e-mail alert/notification for up-to-date program info
___ Copy of full announcement (link on Grants.gov)

Section 2: Checklist of Steps to Grants Success

1. Analyze past grantees (attach completed Exhibit 13.2 to this form)
   ___ Obtain list of past grantees.
   ___ Contact past grantees.

2. ___ Obtain evaluation/scoring rubric to be used on your proposal (attach copy to this form).

3. Analyze proposal review process.
   ___ Gather information on the reviewers and the proposal review process.
   ___ Contact past reviewer.

4. ___ Procure samples of successful pre-proposals and full proposals.

5. Confirm prospect research through contact with grantor.
   ___ Contact public funding source official via phone or e-mail.
   ___ Make appointment with a public funding source official.
   ___ Visit a public funding source official.

6. Make your decision to develop a proposal and to apply to a specific federal grant program.
   ___ Evaluate each potential grantor and tailor your approach and funding request.

The first section of Exhibit 14.1 deals with recording the program and contact information and securing the program description from the CFDA, the synopsis from Grants.gov, and a copy of the full announcement. There is also a reminder to subscribe to automatic e-mail alerts and notification for up-to-date program information. The second half of Exhibit 14.1 is composed of a checklist of six items you will need to procure to help you further analyze your prospective funding source. By knowing what information you are looking for, you will be ready to record it as you search the grantors and their websites.

Checklist 1: Analysis of Past Grantees

1. List of past grantees

You will find it beneficial to discover who has previously received funding by the program that interests you. In many case you can locate a list of past grantees on the agency's website. You can use the sample e-mail in Exhibit 14.2 to request a list of past grantees as well as guidelines and other relevant information. E-mail the contact person identified in your research or the pro-

EXHIBIT 14.2
Sample E-mail to a Federal Agency Requesting List of Past Grantees, Guidelines, and Other Relevant Information

From: <grantseeker@proactive.edu>
To: <contactperson@feds.gov>
Cc:
Sent: Date, Time
Subject: Information Request

Dear [Contact Person]:

I am interested in receiving information on [CFDA#, Program Title]. Please e-mail relevant website information and Internet addresses for application forms, guidelines, etc.

To increase my understanding of your program, I would also appreciate a list of last year's grant recipients. If this list is available on the Internet please provide the address. If it is not, please e-mail the list to me as an attachment.

Thank you for your assistance.

Name
Title
Organization/Institution
Address
Phone Number
Fax Number

EXHIBIT 14.3
Past Grantee Analysis Worksheet

1. Applications
   • How many applications were received? _____
   • How many applications were funded? _____

2. Award Size
   • What was the largest award granted? _____
   For what type of project? _____
   For how many years? _____
   • What was the smallest award granted? _____
   For what type of project? _____
   For how many years? _____

3. Grantor Type
   • What characteristics or similarities can be drawn from last year's list of grant recipients?
   • What is the size and type of grantee organization (i.e., public, private, college)?
   • What are the geographic preferences or concentrations?

4. Project Director/Principal Investigator
   • What title or degrees appear most frequently on the list of last year's recipients?
   • Does there seem to be a relationship between award size and project director degree?

5. From the list of last year's grantees, select two to contact for more information. Select grantees that you may have a link with and organizations that you are familiar with.

6. Based on the information gathered in questions 1–4, rate how well your proposal idea matches the prospective grantor's profile.
   _____ very well   _____ good   _____ fair   _____ not well

7. What programs can you now ask the program officer/contact person about as a result of your analysis?

gram announcement. You may have to request a list of past grantees by phoning the contact person. If you get his or her phone mail, leave a message about what you want and leave your phone number and e-mail address. Access to this list and the valuable information it provides is your right. If you do not receive a response to your initial request, request the list again, making sure to let the funding source know why you want it and that you are aware that you are entitled to this list under the Freedom of Information Act. If all else fails, you may be able to get this information from the public information officer of the agency, or you can ask your congressperson to get the list for you. By law, federal bureaucrats have to respond to a congressperson's request. He or she *will* get the list. Be aware, though, that bureaucrats may react negatively to the intervention of elected officials. Therefore, you should ask the elected official not to reveal for whom he or she is getting the list.

Several databases provide grantee information. For example, the NSF's Award Search allows you to search not only the title and abstract but the names, institutions, programs, and other information associated with an award. The FastLane server offers a list of recent awards, and the Budget Internet Information System provides summaries of award amounts by state, awardee institution, and the NSF Directorate.

With your past grantee list in hand, you are now ready to begin the analysis of your chances for success. Place the information you have obtained on the Past Grantee Analysis Worksheet (Exhibit 14.3) and analyze the information contained in the list of grantees. When this worksheet is completed, you will be able to get data on the number of applications. When you request information on the number of applications, let the program officer know you already have information on the number of awards. What you are trying to do is evaluate your chances of success by determining the overall success rate (number of applications versus number of awards).

2. Contacting a past grantee

Successful grant recipients can be approached and, while they are not required to, will generally share helpful information with you. Grantees will generally feel flattered that you called. By and large, they are not competing with you for funds because you will be seeking first-year funding and they will be seeking a continuation grant. Select a past grantee to contact. Choose one outside of your geographic area and one who is less likely to view you as a competitor. If you have a colleague at that grantee institution, contact him or her to help you connect with the principal investigator or project director. Tell the grantee how you got his or her name, congratulate him or her on the award, and then ask to speak to the person who worked on the proposal.

Ask the principal investigator or project director for a copy of his or her funded proposal. Be sure to request a copy of any preproposal or preapplication they submitted to obtain permission to submit their formal proposal. Assure them that you are just looking for a successful model to follow. You are interested in style, format, how they articulated the literature search, and how they developed the budget. For example, many proposal formats use their own vocabulary and seeing how a successful grantee arranged his or her winning proposal will be of great benefit to you. An example of a winning hypothesis and successful specific aims, primary objectives, methods, and protocols is much more useful to you than trying to interpret the guidelines and read between the lines.

I suggest you obtain at least two or three copies of funded proposals before you create yours. You are probably thinking that no one will share one, right? Well, you will be pleasantly surprised. I challenge my grant fellows on this matter all the time and I have never been proven wrong yet. One fellow sent an e-mail request for copies of funded proposals to five grant recipients as I instructed. He handpicked the five icons in his field to prove me wrong. To his amazement, three of the five responded within one week without even a follow-up request. One sent it in forty-eight hours and asked if the grantseeker would also like a copy of the reviewers' comments to increase the grantseeker's insights into what the reviewers liked and disliked. Even though the proposal was funded, some elements cost the grantee points and the reviewers wanted him to be aware of them so he would not make the same mistakes again.

I learned something from my fellow's experience. Now I always ask for a copy of the reviewers' comments in addition to a copy of the funded proposal.

You can also check with your organization's grants office to see if there have been any proposals submitted in the past to the agency or program you are interested in. If there are any, you should contact the principal investigator or project director to see if he or she would be willing to share a copy of the proposal and the reviewers' comments with you. It does not matter whether the proposal was accepted or rejected. You can learn from either scenario.

Remember, awarded federal and state proposals are public property. Rejected proposals are not public property and ownership is retained by the rejected grantee. Reviewing rejected proposals is of value because you can compare them to the awarded ones and focus on the differences. However, when asking for copies of rejected proposals and reviewers' comments you should be extra polite and diplomatic and explain exactly why you are asking to see them.

Select a few questions from the following list to ask the person who worked on the proposal, or ask any other questions that will help you learn more about the funding source.

- Did you call or go to see the funding source before writing the proposal?
- Whom did you find most helpful on the funding source's staff?
- Did you use your advocates or congressperson?
- Did the funding source review your idea or proposal before submission?
- Did you use consultants to help you on the proposal?
- Was there a hidden agenda to the program's guidelines?

- When did you begin the process of developing your application?
- When did you first contact the funding source?
- What materials did you find most helpful in developing your proposal?
- Did the funding source come to see you (site visit) before or after the proposal was awarded? Who came? What did they wear? How old were they? Would you characterize them as conservative, moderate, or liberal? Did anything surprise you during their visit?
- How close was your initial budget to the awarded amount?
- Who on the funding source's staff negotiated the budget?
- How did you handle matching or in-kind contributions?
- What would you do differently next time?

Checklist 2: Evaluation/Scoring Rubric

To prepare your grant-winning proposal you need to know as much as you can about the evaluation or scoring rubric. This information is crucial in preparing your proposal. The grants program may have specific criteria that they weigh more than other criteria. This information can also be used to assist you in allocating your time and even the space you allocate in the proposal toward what the grantor and the reviewers will concentrate on.

In past proposals, I have allocated too much of the limited space to the criteria I think are critically important and are areas of my expertise, only to get rejected and read reviewers' comments that were focused on areas I did not concentrate on.

To complete checklist item 2, attach a copy of the guidelines or scoring rubric that the reviewers will use to evaluate your proposal. It may be provided in the application deadlines or in another publication from the grantor. It is very important that you obtain it. There are usually several criteria. Some may be bulleted. You should label the criteria 1, 2, 3, and so on, and their required components 1.1, 1.2, 1.3, and so on. Make sure your completed proposal addresses all of the criteria. You will need this criteria to perform a quality circle or mock review before submittal (see chapter 16).

Checklist 3: Analysis of the Proposal Review Process

1. Gathering information on the reviewers and the proposal review process

To prepare the best possible proposal, you must know the background of the people who will be reviewing it and how it will be reviewed. Do not assume that your idea of who is a peer and thus appropriate to read and understand your proposal is accurate. You must tailor your writing to the real reviewer and write it toward the actual audience and their vocabulary, not yours. Request information on the review process from the federal program officer. This can be done in writing, by phone, by e-mail, or in person. I suggest sending an e-mail and then following up with the other methods if necessary. Exhibit 14.4 provides a sample e-mail you may use.

You want a profile of last year's reviewers or criteria related to what the grantor looks for in a reviewer so you can write a proposal based on the reviewers' expertise, educational degrees, publications, and so forth.

There is no harm in asking the program officer if you could observe a peer-review session as a learning experience. If you have the correct credentials and background to be a reviewer but lack the grant award experience, you could volunteer your services. Ask if you can submit your credentials and be of service to the program officer if there is ever a last-minute need for a reviewer. In addition, many program websites have instructions on how to submit your vita to become a reviewer.

EXHIBIT 14.4
Sample E-mail to a Federal Agency for Information on Reviewers and the Review Process

From: <grantseeker@proactive.edu>
To: <contactperson@feds.gov>
Cc:
Sent: Date, Time
Subject: Request for List of Reviewers

Dear [Contact Person]:

I am presently developing a proposal under your _____ program. I would like information on the areas of expertise represented on the peer-review committee. This information will help me prepare a quality proposal based on the level of expertise and diversity of the reviewers.

Information on the scoring rubric and process would also be helpful in that it would help me perform a quality circle or mock review of my proposal before submittal.

The information you provide will be appreciated and will help me produce a quality proposal worthy of the time you and the peer-reviewers invest in evaluating proposals.

Name
Title
Organization/Institution
Address
Phone Number
Fax Number

You could also ask the program officer if he or she could recommend a past reviewer you could talk with to increase your understanding of the process and avoid errors resulting in a rejected proposal. Inform the program officer that the information you gather from this contact will help you use a quality circle to perform a mock review (see chapter 16) of your proposal before submission and that you would like to mirror the actual review process as closely as possible. Remember, program officers like receiving quality proposals and working with grantseekers who are proactive. Therefore, the idea of conducting a presubmittal mock review will appeal to them. Also remember, this will not work if the deadline is only days away!

Some federal programs use the same reviewers each year and may be reluctant to give you any names. If this is the case, tell the federal bureaucrat that you would like to know at least the background and credentials of the reviewers so that you can prepare the best possible proposal by writing toward their level. You would ultimately like to know the types of organizations the reviewers come from, their titles, and whether the reviewers meet in Washington, D.C., or review proposals at home, at work, or on the Internet. Also request a copy of their reviewer training materials. Finally, if the system that the reviewers must adhere to has been published in the *Federal Register* or an agency publication, request a copy or the date of the publication so you can look it up.

You may also ask colleagues or your grants office if they have the name, e-mail address, or phone number of a past reviewer. You can also ask your grants office for any contact information they may have on a staff or faculty member at your institution or organization who has been a reviewer for the program. If you know any of the awarded grantees, contact them since programs frequently use past grantees as reviewers.

2. Contacting a past reviewer

Before you contact a past reviewer you should consider the fact that once contacted by you, he or she may be ineligible to read your proposal. Some programs request that you submit names of potential qualified reviewers. Just remember, you will not be able to include names of any that you have contacted.

When contacting a past reviewer, explain that you understand he or she was a reviewer for the program you are interested in and that you would like to ask a few questions about his or her experience as a reviewer of the program. Select a few questions about his or her experience as a reviewer for the program. Select a few questions to ask from the following list, or make up your own:

- How did you get to be a reviewer?
- Did you review proposals at a funding source location or at home?

- What training or instruction did the funding source give you?
- Did you follow a point system? What system? How did you follow it? What were you told to look for?
- How would you write a proposal differently now that you have been a reviewer?
- What were the most common mistakes you saw?
- Did you meet other reviewers?
- How many proposals were you given to read?
- How much time did you have to read them?
- How did the funding source handle discrepancies in point assignments?
- What did the staff members of the funding source wear, say, and do during the review process?
- Did a staff review follow your review?

Checklist 4: Samples of Successful Preproposals and Full Proposals

One of the steps in checklist item 1 suggested that you request a copy of a successful proposal when you contact a past grantee. This step is so critical in composing a winning grant that it deserves its own checklist number. Knowing how a funded grantee dealt with the design of the proposal; how he or she constructed and wrote the specific aims, the hypothesis, the protocol, objectives, methods, and evaluation design; and how he or she used consultants as well as any donated or in-kind contributions are essential to your success.

Assure these grantees that you are not after their exact ideas or approaches and that they can omit any sensitive data, formulas, and so on. You are looking at this as a model for success, and would consider fulfillment of this request as a collegial, courteous gesture.

Exhibit 14.5 provides a sample e-mail to send to a past grantee requesting a copy of his or her preproposal (if applicable) and full proposal. Tailor this e-mail to your field and personal style. If possible, it's a good idea to procure more than one sample preproposal as well as more than one full proposal. Remember to also request the reviewers' comments so you have an accurate picture of what the reviewers thought.

Checklist 5: Confirming Your Prospect Research through Contact with the Program Officer

1. Contact public funding source official via phone or e-mail.

Contacting public funding sources is an experience in itself. Your initial research should yield a contact name, e-mail address, phone number, and fax

EXHIBIT 14.5
Sample E-mail to a Past Grantee Requesting a Copy of a Successful Proposal

From: \<grantseeker@proactive.edu\>
To: \<successful past grantee\>
Cc:
Sent: Date, Time
Subject: Request for Copy of Funded Proposal

Dear [Successful Grantee]:

I obtained your name from the list of grantees under the _____
program. I am sure you are very pleased over your success and your award. I
am working on a proposal for the same program in a related, but different, area.
[You could add more about your area here.]

Since you are funded and we are not in competition, I am hoping you will
share of copy of your winning proposal with me. [If there was a preproposal
application, also ask for it.] I would like to review it for style, format, and the
best way to address the criteria components. Naturally, I expect you to withhold
any specific information you feel is proprietary.

It would also be very helpful if you could include your reviewers' comments to
help me focus on what they are looking for.

I look forward to receiving your materials and also to learning about your results
and possible presentation at a shared convention.

Name
Title
Organization/Institution
Address
Phone Number
Fax Number

number. Because of personnel changes and reassignments, the contact listed
may not be the best person to assist you. However, he or she should be able to
tell you who at the agency or program could best answer your questions. You
can also check the agency's website to make sure your contact information is
current. If your research does not yield the information you need, you could
use the *United States Government Manual* (www.usgovernmentmanual.gov)
to track down the phone number or e-mail address of the office likely to
handle the funds you are seeking.

After you have identified the appropriate program officer, my first choice is
to go see him or her in person. However, if this is not possible, I recommend
a combination of phone and e-mail contact. The purpose of this contact is
twofold:

- You want to confirm the validity of the program information you have and ask intelligent questions that demonstrate your understanding of the program's grant system. You also need to complete your Past Grantee Analysis Worksheet (see Exhibit 14.3).
- You want to position yourself and your institution or organization as thorough and capable.

Demonstrate that you have done your homework (research) and know about the program, and then ask a question or make a request to further your knowledge of the grant opportunity. For example, if you are requesting information on matching funds, state what you know from your research, and then ask your question. Do not ask what the matching requirements are when you already uncovered this information in Grants.gov, the CFDA, or a program announcement. Instead, let the program officer know, for example, that you are aware that a match is not *required* (if this is the case), and then ask if past applicants that ultimately became grantees volunteered to provide one anyway and, if so, what was the average size or range.

What really bothers federal program officers is when they get calls or e-mails from grantseekers asking what kind of projects they are funding this year or what they are looking for this year. These are what I call "flavor of the month" questions and are indicative of the types of questions asked by lazy, unsophisticated grantseekers.

In addition, several federal and staff program officers have told me that they are overwhelmed with questions and requests from grantseekers for information that is readily available from other sources such as the CFDA, *Federal Register,* Grants.gov, program guidelines, and so on. One way they deal with these lazy grantseekers is to ignore their e-mail and telephone requests. One federal program officer told me that his simple solution is to never respond to a first request for information unless it is an intelligent question that demonstrates that the grantseeker has done his or her home-work (research). He then went on to say that 80 percent of the prospective grantseekers he does not respond to initially do not call or e-mail a second time. On the upside, he stated that he always responds to a second request. So the moral of the story is to select intelligent questions that demonstrate your knowledge of the program, be persistent, phone first, and then follow up with an e-mail or vice versa.

Be careful not to ask too many questions or to make several requests at one time. Determine which of your possible questions will be the most critical in helping you determine your proposal approach, and ask one or two. If you do not get a response the first time, try again. In your follow-up contact, refor-mat the questions, note the date of your initial request, and ask again. Let the program officer know that you respect his or her time and understand how busy he or she is, but you need to know the answers to your questions and that you will recontact him or her another time if necessary.

Once contact is made with the program officer (whether it is by phone or e-mail) you should gather the same information as you would face-to-face. Since it may be difficult for the funding official to discuss your idea and approaches without seeing a written description of the project, ask whether you could mail, fax, or e-mail him or her a one-page concept paper and then recontact him or her for the purpose of discussion.

Although it may be difficult for you to "read" what the funding source is really saying through phone or e-mail contact, you must at least try to uncover any hidden agenda so that you can meet the grantor's needs and increase your chances of success. Review the list of questions in the questions to ask a program officer section of this chapter.

2. Make an appointment with a public funding source official.

The objective of seeking an appointment is to get an interview with an administrator of the program. Start by sending or e-mailing a letter requesting an appointment. Exhibit 14.6 provides a sample e-mail you may use. You may not get a response to this e-mail/letter. Its intent is to show that you mean business. Then follow the next few steps:

- Call and ask for the program officer or information contact.
- Record the name of whomever you speak to and ask if he or she is the correct person to contact. If he or she is not, ask who is, and how and when that person can be reached.
- Call back. Ask whether anyone else can answer technical questions about the program. You may get an appointment with an individual whose job is to screen you, but this is still better than talking to yourself. As an alternative, try to get an advocate to help you set up an appointment for later in the week. Do not be surprised if this results in an immediate appointment. Staff members may decide they would prefer to deal with you on the spot rather than later. Be careful using elected officials to make appointments for you or to accompany you on an appointment. Bureaucrats and politicians often do not get along well and you may appear as a candidate for future earmarking.
- When you get the program person on the phone, introduce yourself and give a brief (ten-word) description of your project. Explain that:
  - The need to deal with the specific problem your project addresses is extreme.

EXHIBIT 14.6
Sample E-mail to a Federal Agency Requesting an Appointment

From: <grantseeker@proactive.edu>
To: <contactperson@feds.gov>
Cc:
Sent: Date, Time
Subject: Request for an Appointment

Dear [Contact Person]:

My research on your funding program indicates that a project we are developing would be appropriate for consideration by your agency for funding under

_____.

I would appreciate five to ten minutes of your time to discuss the project and how it matches your program. The development of the project has created questions that I would like to discuss with you. Your insights and knowledge will help us in our focus.

My travel plans call for me to be in your area on _____. I will phone to confirm the possibility of a brief meeting during that time to discuss this important proposal

Name
Title
Organization/Institution
Address
Phone Number
Fax Number

- Your organization is uniquely suited to deal with this problem.
- You understand that the grantor's program deals with this need.
- You would like to make an appointment to talk about program priorities and your approach.

When you get an appointment, stop and hang up. If an appointment is not possible, tell the program representative that you have some questions and ask about the possibility of asking them now or arranging a ten-minute phone call in the future. Fill in any information you get (names, phone numbers, and so on) on the Federal Grants Research Form (see Exhibit 14.1).

3. Visit a public funding source official

A meeting is vital to getting the input you need to prepare a proposal that is tailored to the funding source. A visit also will provide you with the opportunity to update any information you have gathered on the funding source through your research.

The objective of this preproposal visit is to find out as much as possible about the funding source and how it perceives its role in the awarding of grants. Then you can use the newly acquired information to produce a proposal that reflects sensitivity to the funding source's needs and perception of its mission. According to the theory of cognitive dissonance, the more the funding source perceives a grantseeker as different from what the funding source expects, the greater the problems with communication, agreement, and acceptance. We want the funder to love us, so we need to produce as little dissonance as possible by looking and talking as the funder thinks we should. Just remember, Washington, D.C., is one of the most conservative areas in the country for dress. By dressing accordingly, you can avoid not getting heard because your attire creates dissonance. Asking a past grantee how the program officer dresses and how his or her office is laid out will give you insight into what the program officer likes.

When planning a personal visit, remember that it is better to send two people than one and that an advocate, advisory committee member, or graduate of your program has more credibility than a paid staff member. In deciding who to send, try to match the age, interests, and other characteristics of your people with any information you have on the funding official. Before the visit, role-play your presentation with your team members and decide who will take responsibility for various parts of the presentation and what questions each will ask.

It may be helpful to bring the following items with you on the visit:

- Materials that help demonstrate the need for your project
- Your Swiss cheese book
- A short DVD shown on your laptop, complete with sound, that documents the problem and the unique attributes that make you a logical choice as a grantee (The DVD could also summarize your approach to solving the problem, but the entire presentations should be short (no longer than three minutes) and simple. You do not need a projection system and a PowerPoint presentation unless you will be meeting with five or more grantor staff members.)
- Information of your organization that you can leave with the funding official. (However, never leave a proposal. Remember, at this point you are there to gather information to produce a better proposal.)

Your research will reveal gaps in your knowledge of the federal program. Wherever you are confused, write down your questions. Review the following list of possible questions I have developed during my career. Ask your questions and some of mine that are critical to your understanding of the program and the success of your proposal.

- I have located the program application on your website and found references to [*rules, announcements, and so on*]. Are there any other sources of information I should review?
- The [*CFDA, Grants.gov, or agency publication*] lists the program funding level at [*$$$$$*]. Do you expect that to change?
- My research shows that there are several different types of awards that fall under your program and this area of interest. What are the differences in the success rates (applications versus awards) in the granting mechanisms your program uses? [In addition to research and demonstration grants, many programs have special awards for young or new researchers or career awards to initiate and shape a career. The rules for qualifying for each type of granting mechanism vary, as does the funding. All these variables must be taken into consideration when deciding to apply to a program or a specific type of grant award.]
- How will successful grantees from last year affect the chances for new or first applicants? Will last year's grantees compete with new grantees, or have their funds been set aside? If their funds have been set aside, how much is left for new awards?
- Are there any unannounced programs or unsolicited proposal funds in your agency to support an important project like ours?
- The required matching portion is [*X*] percent. Would it improve our chances for funding if we provide a greater portion than this?
- The program announcement states that matching funds are suggested but not mandatory. I need to give my institution an idea of how much match is needed to meet the "suggested" amount. Could you provide me with a figure, or select three past grantees at random, and tell me how much match the grantees provided?
- If no match is required, would it help our proposal if we volunteered to cost share?
- What is the most common mistake or flaw in the proposals you receive?
- We have developed several approaches to this needs area. From your vantage point, you may know whether one of our approaches has been funded but not yet published. Could you review our concept paper and give us any guidance?
- Would you review or critique our proposal if we get it to you early?
- Would you recommend a previously funded proposal for us to read for format and style? [Remember, you are entitled to see funded proposals, but be cool.]

- What changes do you expect in type or number of awards this year (for example, fewer new awards versus continuing awards)?
- We will conduct a quality circle (mock review) to improve our proposal before we submit it. Could we get more information on the review process your office will conduct? Can we get a reviewers' package including instructions, scoring information, weighing of criteria, and so on? What is the background of the reviewers? How are the reviewers selected? Could one of our team members be a reviewer? How many proposals do reviewers read? How much time do they take to read and score each proposal?
- How are multiple applications to different programs in your agency that use the same basic proposal viewed?
- How is the project director's or principal investigator's commitment to other proposals viewed by your staff and the peer reviewers? [For example, a fellow of mine was included in a pending proposal for 5 percent of his time. He was told by his institution's research office that this commitment precluded him from applying to this particular federal program as the project director for his own proposal. I instructed him to contact the program officer and he learned he could apply if he agreed to drop the 5 percent commitment if he was awarded his grant that called for 50 percent of his time.]

EXHIBIT 14.7
Funding Source Staff Profile

Before each visit to a funding source, review this sheet to be sure you are taking the correct materials, advocates, and staff.

Agency Director: _____   E-mail: _____
Program Director: _____   E-mail: _____
Contact Person: _____   E-mail: _____

Education: College _____
　　　　　　　Postgraduate: _____

Work Experience: _____
Military Experience: _____
Service Clubs: _____
Interests/Hobbies: _____
Publications: _____

Comments:

Note: Do not ask the staff person direct questions related to these areas. Instead, record information that has been volunteered or gathered from comments or observations made in the office.

EXHIBIT 14.8
Public Funding Source Contact Summary Sheet

Project Title: _____

Complete a public funding source contact summary sheet each time you contact
a public funding source.

Agency Name: _____

Program Officer: _____

Contacted On (Date): _____

By Whom: _____

Contacted By: _____ Letter _____ Phone _____ E-mail _____ Personal Visit

Staff or Advocate Present: _____

Discussed:

Results:

Immediately after your visit, record any information you have gathered about
the funder on the Funding Source Staff Profile (Exhibit 14.7). Record the
results of your visit on the Public Funding Source Contact Summary Sheet
(Exhibit 14.8).

Checklist 6: Making Your Decision to Develop a Proposal and Apply to a Specific Federal Grant Program

So far you have not invested a tremendous amount of time writing your proposal. You have taken time to gather data and contact potential grantors. Now
you must decide which federal grant program you will apply to.

Your best project is the grant program that provides the closest match
between the project you want to implement and the profile you have developed of the grantor. Seldom is there a perfect fit between your project and
the grantor's program, and some tailoring and changes in your program will
likely add to your chances of success. Use the tailoring worksheet (Exhibit
14.9) to analyze each grant or program you are interested in and to select
the closest match. After reviewing your answers on the worksheet, rate your
prospect.

Remember that the competition (alluded to in question 1) and the award
rejection ration (alluded to in question 2) are critical to calculating your

EXHIBIT 14.9
Tailoring Worksheet

CFDA # _____   Prospect Rating   A. Excellent
Program Title _____   B. Good
Amount Requested _____   C. Fair
Percent Match/In-Kind _____

                                                 Estimated Success   A. 75%
                                                                     B. 50%
                                                                     C. 25%

1. How does your grant request match with the average award size to your
   type of organization? _____
   size of organization? _____
   location of organization? _____
   proposal focus? _____

2. What was the number of applications received versus the number of grants
   awarded in your area of interest?
   applications received _____
   grants awarded _____

3. How does your organization compare to the previous grantees relative to
   expertise of key individuals _____
   publications and previously funded proposals _____
   access to special equipment, space, etc. _____
   access to subjects _____

4. How would you rate the funding staff's interest in your concept?
   _____ very interested
   _____ interested
   _____ not interested
   _____ unknown

5. From the information you obtained on the reviewers and the review process,
   what should your writing strategy include? _____
   _____

6. Based on the information you obtained on the review process, how will
   points be distributed in the funding source's evaluation process?

                          Area   Point Value

   _____   _____
   _____   _____
   _____   _____

chances of success. After careful analysis, what chance do you think you have of attracting a grant from this prospect? A 25 percent chance? A 50 percent chance? A 75 percent chance?

Once you are fairly sure you are going to apply to a specific federal grant program, review its advertised procedures carefully. Many federal programs request that prospective applicants submit a letter of intent to alert them of your plan to submit a full proposal. This letter has no legal implications. In other words, you could change your mind and not apply. Its purpose is to help the granting agency estimate how many proposals it will receive and thus how many reviewers may be required for the peer-review process that will follow submittal. The letter needs to state that you are considering developing a proposal for their competition and should include the exact title of the program as stated in the announcement, its CFDA number, and its deadlines.

The letter of intent is considered a courtesy, and I always side with being courteous with those who control money! Those who submit the letter of intent may also be those who perform quality circles or mock reviews and submit early. I do not know whether any agencies keep track of the grantors who try to make their jobs easier. But if some do, I want to be on the courteous list.

Now that you have read about the importance of preproposal contact, how will you integrate it into your action steps chart (Figure 14.2)?

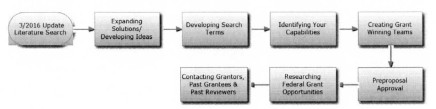

FIGURE 14.2
Action Steps Chart: Contacting Grantors/Grantees/Reviewers

15

Planning the Successful Federal Proposal

T HE PURPOSE OF THIS CHAPTER is to help the serious government grantseeker prepare a credible proposal in a proactive manner. To take advantage of the strategies and insights contained in this chapter, you must obtain
the application package for the most appropriate government granting agency.
Read the agency's guidelines and review this chapter to ensure that you have
integrated the best techniques into your proposal. This material is designed to
assist you with all federal grants, and as such, it is to be of general use.

Each federal agency has its own proposal format to which applicants must
adhere. If you have been successful in obtaining a copy of a previously funded
proposal, you have a quality example of what the funding source expects.
After reading exemplary proposals for forty-five years, I have learned that really excellent proposals do stand out. One does not have to be an expert in a
proposal's particular area of interest to determine whether the proposal is of
high quality. The required components or sections of each type of proposal—
a research proposal or a proposal for a demonstration or model project—are
remarkably similar. In general, federal applications include the following
sections:

- statement of the problem to be addressed
- search of relevant literature and documentation of the problem or need
  to demonstrate that you have a command of the relevant studies and
  knowledge in the field
- what you propose to study, change, or test (for a research project, the hypothesis and specific aims; for a model project, the measurable objectives)

- proposed intervention: the activities, methods, or protocol that state what you will do and why you have selected these methods or activities
- budget: the cost of the project broken down by category of expenditure
- evaluation: how you will establish the levels of change that constitute success and demonstrate that your intervention worked
- grantee credibility: unique qualities and capabilities that you possess and believe are relevant to support and complete the project
- reference to the criteria or scoring rubric of the grantor

Most federal grantors also require a summary or abstract, a title, an agreement to comply with federal assurances, and the attachment of pertinent materials that the reviewer may want to refer to while evaluating the proposal. Sections on future funding and dissemination of the research finding or model may also be included.

While the inclusion of these general components seems logical, the differences in terminology, space restrictions, and order or sequence from one federal application to another can be very perplexing. The novice grantseeker frequently asks why there is not a standard federal grant application form for all programs. It seems that this would make sense, but due to the variety of federal programs and the deep-seated conviction that each area of interest is distinct, this type of standardization will probably never happen. The point is that you must follow each agency's format exactly, make no changes and no omissions, and give each agency what it calls for, not just what you want to give. Even when you think you have already addressed an issue or question and that the agency's guidelines are redundant, repeat what the agency asks for and remember the golden rule of grantseeking: he or she who has the gold makes the rules! So follow those rules exactly.

Each federal agency has its own preferences concerning the components and order. What is similar from agency to agency is that in one way or another, the grantseeker's proposal must establish that he or she has a project that needs to be carried out to advance the field of research, knowledge, or service. Chapter 16 on conducting a quality circle or proposal improvement exercise discusses in more detail the federal agencies' systems for evaluating and scoring proposals, including how the different sections of the proposal compare in terms of importance in the final decision. When applying to a specific agency, it is expected that you will procure a copy of its desired proposal format and develop specific insights into the agency's scoring system and an idea of what an outstanding proposal looks like by obtaining a copy of a funded proposal.

Work through this chapter and collect the materials suggested. Then develop or rearrange your proposal in the format and order required by the grantor.

Documentation of Need

Most grantseekers begin their proposal with what they propose or want to do. Government grantors want to know why there is a need to do anything at all. To gain the reviewer's respect you must show that you are knowledgeable about the need in a particular area. Your goal in this section of the proposal is to use articles, studies, and statistics to demonstrate a compelling reason or motivation to deal with the problem now.

The grantor invariably must choose which proposals to fund this year and which to reject or put on hold; therefore, you must demonstrate the urgency to close the gap between what exists now and what ought to be in your special field (see Figure 15.1). Your proposed project will seek to close or reduce this gap.

THE GAP		
What exists now. What is real. What the present situation is.		What could be. The goal. The desired state of affairs, level of achievement.

FIGURE 15.1
The Gap Diagram

In a research proposal, need documentation involves a search of relevant literature in the field. The point of the literature search is to document that there is a gap in knowledge in a particular area. Currently in the scientific community it is necessary to enhance the motivation of the reviewer to fund your research project by suggesting the value of closing the gap, in monetary terms or in terms of increased knowledge, and by proposing what this new knowledge can lead to.

In proposals for model projects and demonstration grants, this section is referred to as the *needs statement* or *need documentation*. To be successful in grantseeking, you must produce a clear, compelling picture of the current situation and the desired state. Grantors are buying an altered or better state of affairs.

Creating a sense of urgency depends on how well you document the needs. Since not all proposals can be funded, you must make the funding source believe that movement toward the desired state cannot wait any longer. Those proposals that do not get funded did not do a good job of:

- documenting a real need (perceived as important)
- demonstrating what ought to be (for clients) or the field of interest

- creating the urgent need to close the gap by demonstrating that each day the need is not addressed, the problems grows worse or that there is unnecessary suffering, confusion, or wasted efforts

Documenting What Is

Use the following steps to document a need in a model or demonstration grant:

1. Review the section on performing a needs survey (chapter 5) to assess whether any of the methods described could help document the need.
2. Use statistics from articles and research (for example, "Approximately ___ women in the United States were murdered by their husbands or boyfriends last year").
3. Use quotes from leaders or experts in the field (for example, "Dr. Flockmeister said children who are raised in a family with spouse abuse have a ___ percent chance of being abused or of abusing their partners").
4. Use case statements (for example, "John Quek, a typical client of the Family Outreach Center, was abused as a child and witnessed his mother and aunt being abused").
5. Describe a national need and reduce it to a local number that is more understandable (for example, "It is estimated that ___ percent of teenagers are abused by their boyfriend or girlfriend by the time they reach age seventeen; this means that at West Side High School, ___ seniors in the graduating class may have already experienced abuse").
6. State the need in terms of one person (for example, "The abused spouse generally has ...").
7. Use statements from community people such as police, politicians, and clergy.
8. Make note in your literature search of any data you or your organization has generated, any articles published, and any quotes made that have appeared in newspapers. This will build your credibility as a qualified grantee. Refer to your work in a factual citation (for example, "Research carried out by ___ at ___ documented that ___ percent of the local population experienced a need for these services and programs").

When documenting what exists in a research grant, include the following:

1. The latest studies, research articles, and presentations to demonstrate your currency in the field.

2. Studies that demonstrate the scope and sequence of work in the field and its current state, and the necessity to answer your proposed research question before the field can move ahead.

3. A thorough literature search that does not focus only on a few researchers or data that reinforce your research position. Show how the diversity or conflict in the field reinforces the need to search for an answer to your question.

4. A logical flow of reference to the literature. The flow may consist of a chronological and conceptual demonstration that builds to the decision to fund your work. Remember, the literature search should not be a comprehensive treatise in the field that includes references to every contributor but, rather, a convincing documentation of significant works.

5. Citations to your own work in the field that build the case for the problem or need and your credibility. For example, the National Science Foundation (NSF) requires that you write in the third person. Therefore, you are not allowed to say, "I discovered this in my preliminary research." However, it is allowable to reference your previous work (for example, "A study done by (your name) demonstrated x, y, and z").

A study commissioned by *The Chronicle of Higher Education* suggests that female researchers do not cite their own work in scholarly papers as often as their male colleagues do.[1] My experience tells me that this gap may also exist in writing a grant proposal. Personal citation in a proposal counts, especially since many proposal reviewers are men who probably expect self-citation. Therefore, female proposal writers should take this into consideration when trying to secure grant funding.

Demonstrating What Ought to Be

To establish what ought to be, proven statistics may be difficult or impossible to find. Using experts' statements and quotes to document what ought to be is much more credible than using your opinion. Do not put your opinion in the needs statement. In this section you are demonstrating your knowledge of the field and showing that you have surveyed the literature. When establishing the gap, a quote from a leader in the field expressing the need to move on the issue and how movement could advance the field would be a great value.

Avoid terms that point to a poorly documented needs statement. They include the words many and most and expressions like a *great number* and *everyone knows the need for*. Make sure your needs statement does not include any of these types of words or expressions.

It is relatively easy to say what ought to be when discussing areas such as family violence or drug abuse but more difficult when dealing with bench or pure research. However, it is still important to demonstrate the possible uses your research could be related to even if you are working in the hard sciences. Documenting the other side of the gap is a necessity if you want to close the gap of ignorance in your field.

Creating a Sense of Urgency

The needs section should motivate the prospective funding source to help close the gap and move toward the desired state of affairs. One way to do this is to use the funding source's own studies, surveys, or statistics. The same basic proposal can be tailored to two different funding sources by quoting different studies that appeal to each source's own view of the need. By appealing to the views of individual sources, you will appear to be the logical choice to close the gap and move toward reducing the problem. (Review chapter 5 to remind you of what will happen if the gap is not addressed.)

Capabilities of the Project Investigator/Project Director and the Unique Contributions that the Applicant/Consortia will Provide

Most government grant programs will ask the applicant to substantiate the credibility of the applicant's key personnel who will deal with solving the established problem. This can be accomplished by referring to previous work of the project director and co-directors, or by referring to studies, research, or publications citing the work of the director and co-directors and consultants' contributions to the field.

Review chapter 8, "Capitalizing on Your Capabilities," to refresh your memory about the credibility builders of your personnel that you can work into your proposal. In the same way, review the assets that your organization and your partners' organizations bring to bear on your ability to compete with other applicants to carry out the methods and activities that you will be describing to close the gap you have identified.

If the proposal format required by the funding source does not have a section that deals with your capabilities, the end of the needs statement is the best place to put your credentials. To make a smooth transition from the need to your capabilities, do the following:

- Reference that it is the mission of your organization to deal with this problem.

- Summarize the unique qualities of your organization that make it best suited for the job. For example, your organization has the staff or facilities to make the project work.
- Capitalize on the similarities you share with other organizations. For instance, make a statement such as, "Our project will serve as a model to the other agencies that face this dilemma each day." Such statements will help the prospective grantor realize that the results of your project could affect many.
- Emphasize that the needs are urgent and that each day they go unmet the problem grows.
- Point out the unique capabilities of your consortia partners and the experience of your co-principal investigators.

What You Propose to Study or Change

Objectives provide the basis for the steps you propose to take to narrow or close the gap described in the needs statement. Objectives follow the needs statement because they cannot be written until the need has been documented and a gap created.

Since the accomplishment or attainment of each objective will help to close the gap, you must write objectives that are measurable and can be evaluated. It is critical to be able to determine the degree to which the objectives have been attained and, thus, demonstrate the amount of the gap that has been closed. Grantseekers preparing research proposals should note that the objective of a research proposal is to close the gap of ignorance or lack of understanding in their field or to expose poor treatments and suggest or prove new theories. The purpose of performing research or creating model or demonstration projects is to further knowledge. The proposed change can be referred to as an *objective, hypothesis,* or *specific aim.*

Government grantors have been putting increasing pressure on researchers to explain how their research can be used on a very practical level. This is not meant to demean basic research that may not relate to dramatic broader impacts or to minimize a humanist creating a book on ancient history. But be aware that grantors want to see their support make a contribution to the field. They are motivated by what the grantseeker will do and how it will impact the gap. Grantors want a component of every grant to deal with such issues as dissemination of results and how findings or books can be used to benefit the general public.

Objectives versus Methods

Objectives tell the grantseeker and the funding source what will be accomplished by this expenditure of funds and how the change will be measured. *Methods* state the means to the end or change. They tell how you will accomplish the desired change. Naturally, the ability to accomplish an objective depends on the methods or activities chosen.

When in doubt as to whether you have written an objective or method, ask yourself whether there is only one way to accomplish what you have written. If your answer is yes, you have probably written a method. For example, once a participant at one of my seminars told me that his objective was to build a visitors center for his organization's museum. When asked why he wanted to build a visitors center, he responded, "To help visitors understand the relationship between the museum buildings so that they can more effectively use the museum." Once he stated this out loud, he realized that his objective was really the effective utilization of the museums and that building a visitors center was just one method for accomplishing this objective. In other words, building the visitors center was a means to an end, just one way that my seminar participant could attempt to accomplish his objective. In fact, the reason a funding source might give money to support his project would be to help people use and appreciate the museum, not to build the visitors center. The bricks and mortar that make up the visitors center simply do not lend themselves to the same kind of measurement as the issue of effective utilization.

The following is a technique for writing objectives:

1. Determine result areas. Result areas are the key places you will look for improvement or change in the client population. Examples include the health of people over sixty-five years of age in St. Louis, better educated minority students, and more efficient use of a museum.
2. Determine measurement indicators. Measurement indicators are the quantifiable parts of your result areas. By measuring your performance with these indicators, you will be able to determine how well you are doing. Examples include the number of hospital readmissions of people over sixty-five years of age, scores on standardized tests, and the number of people who understand the relationship between museum buildings. Brainstorm a number of measurement indicators for each of your result areas, and then select the ones that reflect your intent and are the least difficult to use.
3. Determine performance standards. Performance standards answer the question, "How much (or how little) change do we need to consider ourselves successful?" Using the previous examples, we might

determine the following performance standards: a 10 percent drop in hospital readmissions, scores rising from the eightieth to the ninetieth percentile for freshman on the Flockman reading scale, or a 50 percent reduction in requests by visitors for directions from museum staff.

4. Determine the time frame. The time frame is the amount of time in which you want to reach your performance standards. It is your deadline. You might decide you want to see a 10 percent drop in hospital readmissions within six or eighteen months. Usually, this time frame is determined for you by the funding source. Most grants are for twelve months. In setting your deadlines, use months 1 through 12 instead of January, February, and so on because you seldom will start the grants when you expect, and seldom do they start in January.

5. Determine the cost frame. This is the cost of the methods or activities you have selected to meet your objectives. (This cost estimate can be obtained retrospectively from the project planner, the document you will fill out next.)

6. Write the objective. This step combines the data you have generated in the previous five steps. The standard format for an objective is as follows: "To [action verb and statement reflecting your measurement indicator] by [performance standard] by [deadline] at a cost of no more than [cost frame]." For example, "To increase the reading scores of freshmen from the eightieth to the ninetieth percentile on Flockman's reading scale in twelve months at a cost of $50,000."

7. Evaluate the objective. Review your objective and answer the question: "Does this objective reflect the amount of change we want in the result area?" If your answer is yes, you probably have a workable objective. If your answer is no, chances are that your measurement indicator is wrong or your performance standards are too low. Go back to steps 2 and 3 and repeat the process.

When writing program objectives, you should follow the same seven steps. Again, remember to emphasize results, not tasks or methods. Do not describe how you are going to do something; instead, emphasize what you will accomplish and the ultimate benefit of your program's work.

Hypothesis, Research Question, and Specific Aims

In a research proposal, the section on what the researcher proposes to study or change is referred to as the *research question* and *hypothesis to be tested* or the *specific aims*. The development of research proposals follows an analogous route to model and demonstration grants. There must be a clearly defined problem, question, or gap to be addressed.

Researchers are inoculated with the same virus that all grantseekers share: the "why" virus. (Why does this happen? What can we do to change it?) The researcher asks a question and then must search the literature in the field to determine what is already known and who would care if the question was answered. (What is the value or benefit? Who would value the closing of the gap?) For example, the question of whether treatment X or Y influences the healing time of a pressure sore (bedsore) is subject to a search of the literature to see what work has already been done in this area and to determine the importance of the question. (What exists now? What is the incidence or extent of the problem, and what is the future impact of not addressing the question?) If there is no compelling or motivating reason to use grant moneys to answer the question, the researcher is not likely to be successful.

The research question must be specific and focused. Many researchers are overly optimistic and select questions that are too broad or too many questions to investigate. This sets them up for failure because they cannot control the situation. In other words, they have too many forces or variables to deal with that can influence the outcome.

Researchers usually develop their questions into either a null hypothesis or an alternative hypothesis. In a *null hypothesis*, the researcher:

- Predicts that there is no basic difference between the two selected areas. For example, "There is no difference between pressure sores treated with X or Y."
- Sets up the study to measure the outcome, or the *dependent variable* (increased healing of pressure sores).
- Manipulates or changes the intervention, or the *independent variable* (use of treatment X or Y), to observe the effects of the two treatments on the dependent variable.
- Selects a statistical evaluation model before data are collected, which will be used to evaluate the differences in the intervention.

When there are significant differences between two treatments, the null hypothesis is disproved and the results are based on differences in treatment rather than on chance.

The alternative hypothesis predicts that there is indeed a difference between two treatments and suggests the direction of the difference. For example, "Treatment X will result in a healing rate that is 50 percent faster than treatment Y." The research protocol then seeks to prove that there is a difference at the level that is substantiated by the evaluation design to be used.

Looking at successful proposals to see how the research question was described is very insightful. Some researchers clarify the research question or the hypothesis in the proposal's specific aims.

The methods, activities, or protocol section is the detailed description of the steps you will take to meet the objectives, conduct your project, and prove or disprove your hypothesis. Methods identify:

- what will be done
- who will do it
- how long it will take
- the materials and equipment needed
- how the results will be measured

The protocol of a research proposal details how each experiment or trial will be carried out. The methods or protocols are all a function of what you set out to accomplish. The best order to follow is to write your objectives first and then develop your methods to meet them. In making up a realistic estimate of your project costs, avoid inflating the budget. Instead, consider adding several more methods to this section to ensure that your objectives are met. When you negotiate the final award, you will gain much more credibility with the funding source by eliminating methods instead of lowering the price for the same amount of work. The basic idea is that eliminating methods or steps impacts the ability to prove or create the desired change in the level of certainty wanted by both you and the grantor.

Historically, final awards for research proposals and model project proposals were followed by a letter that included a dollar amount significantly less than what was applied for. Criticism of this practice led many major grantors to announce that the methods for research and model or demonstration proposals should be cost analyzed and negotiated. Now both demonstration and research proposals must include a detailed cost estimate for each method or activity and must show each activity's effect on the outcome.

Your methods section or protocol plan must:

- Describe your program activities in detail and demonstrate how they will fulfill your objectives or research study.
- Describe the sequence, flow, and interrelationship of the activities.
- Describe the planned staffing for your program and designate who is responsible for which activities.
- Describe your client population and method for determining client selection.
- State a specific time frame.

- Present a reasonable scope of activities that can be accomplished within the stated time frame with your organization's resources.
- Refer to the cost-benefit ratio of your project.
- Include a discussion of risk (why success is probable).
- Describe the uniquenesses of your methods and overall project design.

The Project Planner (Exhibit 15.1) provides you with a format to ensure that your methods section reflects a well-conceived and well-designed plan for the accomplishment of your objectives. A copy of the project planner programmed to work with Microsoft Excel can be downloaded free of charge at www.dgbauer.com.

The Project Planner

An outcome of my forty-five years of work in grant and contract preparation, the project planner is a spreadsheet planning tool designed to assist you in several important ways. It will help you:

- Create a budget narrative that describes expenditures.
- Develop your budget by having you clearly define which project personnel will perform each activity for a given time frame, with the corresponding consultant services, supplies, materials, and equipment.
- Defend your budget on a activity-by-activity basis so that you can successfully negotiate your final award.
- Project a monthly and quarterly cash forecast for year 1, year 2, and year 3 of your proposed project.
- Identify matching or in-kind contributions.

Any spreadsheet function that provides you with the above information is fine. The goal is to get you to cost analyze your project so you can use this information to complete the budget section of your federal proposal. If your organization provides budget assistance, completing the spreadsheet will be of great help to those assisting you with this task.

The project planner will also help you develop job descriptions for each individual involved in your project and a budget narrative or written explanation documenting your planned expenses. Several federal granting agencies have been criticized for not negotiating final awards with grantees. Their practice has been to provide grantees with a statement of the final award with no reference or discussion of how the award differs from the amount budgeted in the application or how the reduction will affect the

EXHIBIT 15.1
The Project Planner

PROJECT TITLE: _____

A. List project objectives or outcomes A. B. B. List methods to accomplish each objective as A-1, A-2, ... B-1, B-2 ...	MONTH		TIME	PROJECT PERSONNEL	PERSONNEL COSTS		
	Begin	End			Salaries & Wages	Fringe Benefits	Total
	C/D		E	F	G	H	I
					$		-
					$		-
					$		-
					$		-
					$		-
					$		-
					$		-
					$		-
					$		-
					$		-
					$		-
					$		-
					$		-
					$		-
					$		-
					$		-
					$		-
					$		-
					$		-
					$		-
					$		-
					$		-
					$		-
					$		-

Total Direct Costs or Costs Requested From Funder	0
Matching Funds, In-Kind Contributions, or Donated Costs	
Total Costs	0

EXHIBIT 15.1
(Continued)
Proposal Developed for

Project Director: _____   Proposed Start Date _____   Proposal Year _____

CONSULTANTS CONTRACT SERVICES			NON-PERSONNEL RESOURCES NEEDED SUPPLIES - EQUIPMENT - MATERIALS				SUB-TOT ACTIVITY COST	MILESTONES PROGRESS INDICATORS	
Time	Cost/Week	Total	Item	Cost/Item	Quantity	Tot cost	Total J,L,P	Item	Date
J	K	L	M	N	O	P	Q	R	S
	$	-				$ -	$ -		
	$	-				$ -	$ -		
	$	-				$ -	$ -		
	$	-				$ -	$ -		
	$	-				$ -	$ -		
	$	-				$ -	$ -		
	$	-				$ -	$ -		
	$	-				$ -	$ -		
	$	-				$ -	$ -		
	$	-				$ -	$ -		
	$	-				$ -	$ -		
	$	-				$ -	$ -		
	$	-				$ -	$ -		
	$	-				$ -	$ -		
	$	-				$ -	$ -		
	$	-				$ -	$ -		
	$	-				$ -	$ -		
	$	-				$ -	$ -		
	$	-				$ -	$ -		
	$	-				$ -	$ -		
	$	-				$ -	$ -		
		0				0	0		% of Total
		0				0	0		

EXHIBIT 15.2
Sample Project Planner

PROJECT TITLE: __A Contract for Educational Cooperation - Parents, Teachers, and Students Charting AS Course for Involve A Course for Involvement__

A. List project objectives or outcomes A. B. B. List methods to accomplish each objective as A-1, A-2, … B-1, B-2 …	MONTH Begin	End (C/D)	TIME (E)	PROJECT PERSONNEL (F)	Salaries & Wages (G)	Fringe Benefits (H)	Total (I)
Objective A: Increase educational cooperation of parents, teachers, and students as measured on the responsible educational practices survey in 12 months at a cost of $64,705.00							$ -
A-1 . Develop the responsible educational practices survey with the advisory committee.							$ -
a. Write questions and develop a scale of responsibility for parents, teachers, and students.	January	Fevruary	4 weeks	PD Smith & 2 Graduate Students (GS)	West State University		$ -
A-2 Administer the survey to the target population.	February	March	4 weeks	2 GS	West State University		$ -
a. Develop procedure			4 weeks	PD Smith &	West State University		$ -
b. Get human subjects approval thru West State University							$ -
c. Graduate students to administer survey			4 weeks	2 GS	West State University		$ -
d. Input survey data			4 weeks*	Sec'y	$800	$160	$960*
e. Develop results			1 week	PD Smith	West State University		$ -
A-3 Develop curriculum	March	June					$ -
a. Review results of pre-test given to parents, teachers, and students			1 week	PD Smith	West State University		$ -
b. Develop a curriculum on responsibility concepts in education for each group			5 weeks	PD Smith	West State University		$ -
(includes workbook and DVD on each area of curriculum :			8 weeks*	Sec'y	$1,600	$320	$1920*
responsible use of time			8 weeks	Senior High Film Club	Jones Corporation Facility		$ -
homework responsibility							$ -
communication skills							$ -
A-4 Promote and carry out program	June	December					$ -
a. Use advisory group to announce program			24 Weeks	PD Smith	West State University		$ -
b. Public service spots on radio and television			24 Weeks	Sec'y	$4,800	$960	$5760*
c. Develop and send home a program							$ -
d. Schedule meetings with parent							$ -
e. Develop a student DVD							$ -
							$ -
							$ -
							$ -
							$ -
							$ -
							$ -
							$ -
							$ -
							$ -

Total Direct Costs or Costs Requested From Funder	0
Matching Funds, In-Kind Contributions, or Donated Costs	8,640
Total Costs	8,640

EXHIBIT 15.2
(Continued)

PROJECT TITLE: A Contract for Educational Cooperation - Parents, Teachers, and Students Charting AS Course for Involve: A Course for Involvement

A. List project objectives or outcomes A. B. B. List methods to accomplish each objective as A-1, A-2, … B-1, B-2 …	MONTH Begin	MONTH End	TIME	PROJECT PERSONNEL	Salaries & Wages	Fringe Benefits	Total
	C/D		E	F	G	H	I
Objective A: Increase educational cooperation of parents, teachers, and students as measured on the responsible educational practices survey in 12 months at a cost of $64,705.00						$	-
						$	-
A-1. Develop the responsible educational practices survey with the advisory committee.	January	Fevruary	4 weeks	PD Smith &	West State University	$	-
a. Write questions and develop a scale of responsibility for parents, teachers, and students.				2 Graduate Students (GS)		$	-
A-2 Administer the survey to the target population.	February	March	4 weeks	PD Smith &	West State University	$	-
a. Develop procedure			4 weeks	2 GS	West State University	$	-
b. Get human subjects approval thru West State University						$	-
c. Graduate students to administer survey			4 weeks*	Sec'y	$800	$160	$960*
d. Input survey data			4 weeks*		West State University	$	-
e. Develop results			1 week	PD Smith	West State University	$	-
A-3 Develop curriculum	March	June				$	-
a. Review results of pre-test given to parents, teachers, and students			1 week	PD Smith	West State University	$	-
b. Develop a curriculm on responsibility concepts in education for each group			5 weeks	PD Smith	West State University	$	-
(includes workbook and DVD on each area of curriculum :			8 weeks*	Sec'y	$1,600	$320	$1920*
responsible use of time			8 weeks	Senior High Film Club	Jones Corporation Facility	$	-
homework responsibility						$	-
communication skills						$	-
A-4 Promote and carry out program	June	December	24 Weeks	PD Smith	West State University	$	-
a. Use advisory group to announce program			24 Weeks	Sec'y	$4,800	$960	$5760*
b. Public service spots on radio and television						$	-
c. Develop and send home a program						$	-
d. Schedule meetings with parent						$	-
e. Develop a student DVD						$	-
						$	-
						$	-
						$	-
						$	-
						$	-
						$	-
						$	-
Total Direct Costs or Costs Requested From Funder							0
Matching Funds, In-Kind Contributions, or Donated Costs							8,640
Total Costs							8,640

methods and outcome. As more importance is placed on the budget negotiation and the planning of project years, the more valuable the project
planner will become.

You will find the following explanation of each project planner column
helpful as you review the blank project planner in Exhibit 15.1 and the sample
project planner in Exhibit 15.2.

1. Project objectives or outcomes (column A/B): List your objectives or
   outcomes as A, B, C, and so on. Use the terms the prospective grantor
   wants. For example, grantors may refer to the objectives as *major tasks*,
   enabling objectives, or *specific aims*.
2. Methods (column A/B): Also in the first column, list the methods or
   protocol necessary to meet the objectives or outcomes as A-1, A-2, B-1,
   B-2, C-1, C-2, and so on. These are the tasks you have decided on as
   your approach to meeting the need.
3. Month (column C/D): Record the dates you will begin and end each
   activity in this column.
4. Time (column E): Designate the number of person-weeks (you can use
   hours or months) needed to accomplish each task.
5. Project personnel (column F): List the key personnel who will spend
   measurable or significant amounts of time on this activity and the accomplishment of this objective or specific aim. The designation of key
   personnel is critical for developing a job description for each individual.
   If you list the activities for which the key personnel are responsible, and
   the minimum qualifications or background required, you will have a
   rough job description. Call a placement agency to get an estimate of
   the salary needed to fill the position. The number of weeks or months
   will determine full- or part-time classification. This column gives you
   the opportunity to look at how many hours of work you are providing
   in a given time span. If you have your key personnel working more
   than 160 hours per month, it may be necessary to adjust the number of
   weeks in column E to fit a more reasonable time frame. For example,
   you may have to reschedule activities or shift responsibility to another
   staff member.
6. Personnel costs (columns G, H, I): List the salaries, wages, and fringe
   benefits for all personnel. Special care should be taken in analyzing staff
   donated from your organization. The donation of personnel may be a
   requirement of your grant or a gesture you make to show your good
   faith and appear as a better investment to the funding source. If you
   do make matching or in-kind contributions, place an asterisk by the
   name of each person you donate to the project. Be sure to include your

donation of fringes as well as wages. As you complete the remaining columns, put an asterisk by anything else that will be donated to the project. All costs with an asterisk will be automatically totaled to the donated or matching box for each area.

7. Consultants and contract services (columns J, K, L): These three columns are for the services that are most cost-efficiently supplied by individuals who are not in your normal employ. They may be experts at a skill you need that does not warrant your training a staff member or hiring an additional staff person (you may need someone skilled in evaluation, computers, commercial art, and so forth). There are no fringes paid to consultants or contract service providers.

8. Nonpersonnel resources needed (columns M, N, O, P): List the components that are necessary to complete each activity and achieve your objective, including supplies, equipment, and materials. Many a grantseeker has gone wrong by underestimating the nonpersonnel resources needed to complete a project. Most grantseekers lose out on many donated or matching items because they do not ask themselves what they really need to complete each activity. Travel, supplies, and telephone communications are some of the more commonly donated items.

   Equipment requests can be handled in many ways. One approach is to place total equipment items as they are called for under your plan under column M (item) and to complete the corresponding columns appropriately—cost per item (column N), quantity (column O), and total cost (column P). However, this approach may cause problems in the negotiation of your final award. The grantor may suggest lowering the grant money by the elimination of an equipment item that appears as though it is related to the accomplishment of only one activity, when in actuality you plan to use it in several subsequent activities. Therefore, I suggest that if you plan to list the total cost of equipment needed in your work plan next to one particular activity, designate a percentage of usage to that activity and reference the other activities that will require the equipment. This way you will show 100 percent usage and be able to defend the inclusion of the equipment in your budget request.

   In some cases, you may choose to allocate the percentage of the cost of the equipment to each activity. If you allocate cost of equipment to each activity, remember that if you drop an activity in negotiation, you may not have all the funds you need to purchase the equipment.

9. Subtotal cost for each activity (column Q): This column can be completed in two ways. Each activity can be subtotaled, or you can subtotal several activities under each objective or specific aim.

10. Milestones, progress indicators (columns R, S): Column R should be used to record what the funding source will receive as indicators that you are working toward the accomplishment of your objectives. Use column S to list the date on which the funding source will receive the milestone or progress indicator. Refer to the sample project planner (see Exhibit 15.2) to see how these columns justify the expenditure.

Please note that you might want to develop a computer-generated spreadsheet version of the project planner so that your objectives or other information can be easily added, deleted, or changed. This would be especially useful when the grant amount awarded is less than the amount requested, because you could experiment with possible changes without too much trouble. Remember, a downloadable Microsoft Excel version is available free of charge at www.dgbauer.com.

Indirect Costs

An aspect of federal grants that is critically important yet poorly understood by many grantseekers and other individuals connected with grants is the concept of indirect costs. Indirect costs involve repaying the recipient of a federal grant for costs that are difficult to break down individually but are indirectly attributable to performing the federal grant. These costs include such things as:

- heat and lights
- building maintenance
- payroll personnel
- purchasing

Indirect costs are calculated by using a formula that is provided by the Federal Regional Controller's Office and are expressed as a percentage of the total amount requested from the funding source (total from column Q of your project planner), or as a percentage of the personnel costs (total from column I of your project planner).

Recent developments in the area of indirect costs have led the federal government to strictly enforce the definition of costs eligible for reimbursement under a grant's direct expenditures versus those eligible under its indirect expenditures. Under the Office of Management and Budget's guidelines, costs related to the handling of increased grant-supported payroll, increased purchasing, or grant-related travel reimbursement are already covered under indirect costs. Therefore, any added personnel that fall under the category of secretarial support are not eligible to be added to your grant. All personnel in your grant should have a special designation and job description showing that their duties are not secretarial but rather extraordinary and thus eligible to be funded under the grant.

Budget

While preparing the budget may be traumatic for unorganized grantseekers, you can see that the project planner contains all the information you need to forecast your financial needs accurately. No matter what budget format you use, the information you need to construct your budget is contained in your project planner. The project planner, however, is not the budget; it is the analysis of what will have to be done and the estimated costs and time frame for each activity.

In most government proposal formats, the budget section is not located near the methods section. Government funders do not understand why you want to talk about your methods when you talk about money. As you know, the budget is a result of what you plan to do. If the money you request is reduced, you know you must cut your project's methods. Draw the public funding source back into your project planner during any budget negotiations so that they too can see what will be missing as a result of a budget cut. If you must cut so many methods that you can no longer be sure of accomplishing your objectives, consider refusing the funds or reducing the funds or reducing the amount of change (reduction of the need) outlined in your objectives when negotiating the amount of your award. The sample budget in Exhibit 15.3 is provided for your review. In a research proposal, show how limiting your intervention or protocol will affect the reliability and validity of your research.

If you are required to provide a quarterly cash forecast, use the grants office timeline in Exhibit 15.4. The project activities or methods (A-1, A-2, B-1, B-2) from your project planner should be listed in the first column. The numbered columns across the top of the timeline indicate the months of the duration of the project. Use a line bar to indicate when each activity or method begins and ends. Place the estimated cost per method in the far-right column. Use a triangle to indicate where milestones and progress indicators are to occur (taken from columns R and S of your project planner). By totaling costs by quarter, you can develop a quarterly forecast of expenditures. Complete a separate grants office timeline and project planner for each year of a continuation grant or multiyear award.

EXHIBIT 15.3
A Sample Project Budget

PROJECT NAME: Nutrition Education for Disadvantaged Mothers through Teleconferencing	Expenditure Total	Donated/ In-Kind	Requested from This Source
	$148,551	$85,122	$63,429
I. PERSONNEL			
A. Salaries, Wages			
Project Director @ $2,200/mo 10 mos. x 400 hours	13,200	13,200	
Administrative Assistant @ $1,600/mo. x 12 mos. x 100% time	19,200		19,200
Data Input Specialist @ $1,300/mo x 12 mos. x 100% time	15,600		15,600
Volunteer time @ 9.00 x 10 mos. x 400 hours	36,000	36,000	
B. Fringe Benefits			
Unemployment Insurance (3% of first $18,600)	1,400	450	990
FICA (6.2% of first $87,000 of each employee salary)	2,976	953	2,023
Health Insurance ($150/mo. per employee x 12 mos.)	5,400	1,800	3,600
Workmen's Compensation (1% salaries paid: $48,000)	480	144	336
C. Consultants/Contracted Services			
Copy Editor ($200/day x 5)	1,000		1,000
PR Advisor ($200/day x 10)	2,000		2,000
Accounting Serv. ($250/day x 12)	3,000	3,000	
Legal Services ($500/day x 6)	3,000	3,000	
Personnel Subtotal	**103,296**	**58,547**	**44,749**
II. NONPERSONNEL			
A. Space Costs			
Rent (1.50/sq. ft. x 400 sq. ft. x 12 mos.)	7,200	7,200	
Utilities ($75/mo. x 12 mos.)	900	900	

(continued)

EXHIBIT 15.3
(Continued)

B. Equipment			
Desk ($275 x 1)	275		275
Computer, Printer, Copy Machine, Rental ($300/mo x 12 mos.)	3,600		3,600
Office Chairs ($50 x 3)	150		150
File Cabinets ($125 x 3)	375	375	
Electronic Blackboard & Misc. Equip. for Teleconferencing	7,200		7,200
C. Supplies (Consumables)			
(3 employees x $200/yr.)	600	600	
D. Travel			
Local			
Project Director ($.40/mile x 500 miles/mo x 12 mos.	2,400		2,400
Administrative Assistant ($.40/mile x 750 miles/mo. x 12 mos.)	3,600		3,600
Out-of-Town			
Project Director to Nutrition Conference in St. Louis Airfare Per Diem ($75/day x 3) Hotel ($100/nt. x 3)	450 225 300		450 225 300
E. Telephone			
Installation ($100/line x 3)	300	300	
Monthly Charges ($25/line x 3 lines x 12 mos.)	900	900	
Long Distance ($40/mo x 12 mos.)	480		480
F. Other Nonpersonnel Costs			
Printing ($.30 x 25,000 brochures)	7,500	7,500	
Postage ($.34 x 25,000)	8,500	8,500	
Insurance ($25/mo. x 12 mos.)	300	300	
Nonpersonnel Subtotal	$45, 255	$26,575	$18,680
Personnel Subtotal	$103,296	$58,547	$44,749
Project Total	$148,551	$85,122	$63,429
Percentage	100%	57%	43%

EXHIBIT 15.4
Grants Office Time Line

Activity Number	1	2	3	4	5	6	7	8	9	10	11	12	Total Cost of Activity

	1st Quarter	2nd Quarter	3rd Quarter	4th Quarter	Total
Quarterly Forecast of Expenditures					

EXHIBIT 15.5
Standard Form (SF) 424A

BUDGET INFORMATION – Non-Construction Programs OMB Approval No. 0348-0044

SECTION A – BUDGET SUMMARY

Grant Program Function or Activity (a)	Catalog of Federal Domestic Assistance Number (b)	Estimated Unobligated Funds		New or Revised Budget		
		Federal I	Non-Federal (d)	Federal I	Non-Federal (f)	Total (g)
1.		$	$	$	$	$
2.						
3.						
4.						
5. Totals		$	$	$	$	$

SECTION B – BUDGET CATEGORIES

6. Object Class Categories	GRANT PROGRAM, FUNCTION OR ACTIVITY				Total
	(1)	(2)	(3)		(5)
a. Personnel	$	$	$	$	$
b. Fringe Benefits					
c. Travel					
d. Equipment					
e. Supplies					
f. Contractual					
g. Construction					
h. Other					
i. Total Direct Charges *(sum of 6a-6h)*					
j. Indirect Charges					
k. TOTALS *(sum of 6i and 6j)*	$	$	$	$	$
7. Program Income	$	$	$	$	$

Authorized for Local Reproduction

Standard Form 424A (Rev. 7-97)
Prescribed by OMB Circular A-102

SECTION C - NON-FEDERAL RESOURCES

(a) Grant Program	(b) Applicant	(c) State	(d) Other Sources	(e) TOTALS
8.	$	$	$	$
9.				
10.				
11.				
12. TOTAL *(sum of lines 8-11)*	$	$	$	$

SECTION D - FORECASTED CASH NEEDS

	Total for 1st Year	1st Quarter	2nd Quarter	3rd Quarter	4th Quarter
13. Federal	$	$	$	$	$
14. Non-Federal					
15. TOTAL *(sum of lines 13 and 14)*	$	$	$	$	$

SECTION E - BUDGET ESTIMATES OF FEDERAL FUNDS NEEDED FOR BALANCE OF THE PROJECT

(a) Grant Program	FUTURE FUNDING PERIODS (Years)			
	(b) First	(c) Second	(d) Third	(e) Fourth
16.	$	$	$	$
17.				
18.				
19.				
20. TOTAL *(sum of lines 16-19)*	$	$	$	$

SECTION F - OTHER BUDGET INFORMATION

21. Direct Charges:	22. Indirect Charges:
23. Remarks:	

Authorized for Local Reproduction Standard Form 424A (Rev. 7-97)

EXHIBIT 15.6
Instructions for Standard Form (SF) 424A

Public reporting burden for this collection of information is estimated to average 180 minutes per response, including time for reviewing instructions, searching existing data sources, gathering and maintaining the data needed, and completing and reviewing the collection of information. Send comments regarding the burden estimate or any other aspect of this collection of information, including suggestions for reducing this burden, to the Office of Management and Budget, Paperwork Reduction Project (0348-0044), Washington, DC 20503.

PLEASE DO NOT RETURN YOUR COMPLETED FORM TO THE OFFICE OF MANAGEMENT AND BUDGET. SEND IT TO THE ADDRESS PROVIDED BY THE SPONSORING AGENCY.

General Instructions

This form is designed so that application can be made for funds from one or more grant programs. In preparing the budget, adhere to any existing Federal grantor agency guidelines which prescribe how and whether budgeted amounts should be separately shown for different functions or activities within the program. For some programs, grantor agencies may require budgets to be separately shown by function or activity. For other programs, grantor agencies may require a breakdown by function or activity. Sections A, B, C, and D should include budget estimates for the whole project except when applying for assistance which requires Federal authorization in annual or other funding period increments. In the latter case, Sections A, B, C, and D should provide the budget for the first budget period (usually a year) and Section E should present the need for Federal assistance in the subsequent budget periods. All applications should contain a breakdown by the object class categories shown in Lines a-k of Section B.

Section A. Budget Summary Lines 1-4 Columns (a) and (b)

For applications pertaining to a *single* Federal grant program (Federal Domestic Assistance Catalog number) and *not requiring* a functional or activity breakdown, enter on Line 1 under Column (a) the Catalog program title and the Catalog number in Column (b).

For applications pertaining to a *single* program *requiring* budget amounts by multiple functions or activities, enter the name of each activity or function on each line in Column (a), and enter the Catalog number in Column (b). For applications pertaining to multiple programs where none of the programs require a breakdown by function or activity, enter the Catalog program title on each line in *Column* (a) and the respective Catalog number on each line in Column (b).

For applications pertaining to *multiple* programs where one or more programs *require* a breakdown by function or activity, prepare a separate sheet for each program requiring the breakdown. Additional sheets should be used when one form does not provide adequate space for all breakdown of data required. However, when more than one sheet is used, the first page should provide the summary totals by programs.

Lines 1-4, Columns (c) through (g)

For new applications, leave Column (c) and (d) blank. For each line entry in Columns (a) and (b), enter in Columns (e), (f), and (g) the appropriate amounts of funds needed to support the project for the first funding period (usually a year).

For continuing grant program applications, submit these forms before the end of each funding period as required by the grantor agency. Enter in Columns (c) and (d) the estimated amounts of funds which will remain unobligated at the end of the grant funding period only if the Federal grantor agency instructions provide for this. Otherwise, leave these columns blank. Enter in columns (e) and (f) the amounts of funds needed for the upcoming period. The amount(s) in Column (g) should be the sum of amounts in Columns (e) and (f).

For supplemental grants and changes to existing grants, do not use Columns (c) and (d). Enter in Column (e) the amount of the increase or decrease of Federal funds and enter in Column (f) the amount of the increase or decrease of non-Federal funds. In Column (g) enter the new total budgeted amount (Federal and non-Federal) which includes the total previous authorized budgeted amounts plus or minus, as appropriate, the amounts shown in Columns (e) and (f). The amount(s) in Column (g) should not equal the sum of amounts in Columns (e) and (f).

Line 5 - Show the totals for all columns used.

Section B Budget Categories

In the column headings (1) through (4), enter the titles of the same programs, functions, and activities shown on Lines 1-4, Column (a), Section A. When additional sheets are prepared for Section A, provide similar column headings on each sheet. For each program, function or activity, fill in the total requirements for funds (both Federal and non-Federal) by object class categories.

Line 6a-i - Show the totals of Lines 6a to 6h in each column.

Line 6j - Show the amount of indirect cost.

Line 6k - Enter the total of amounts on Lines 6i and 6j. For all applications for new grants and continuation grants the total amount in column (5), Line 6k, should be the same as the total amount shown in Section A, Column (g), Line 5. For supplemental grants and changes to grants, the total amount of the increase or decrease as shown in Columns (1)-(4), Line 6k should be the same as the sum of the amounts in Section A, Columns (e) and (f) on Line 5.

Line 7 - Enter the estimated amount of income, if any, expected to be generated from this project. Do not add or subtract this amount from the total project amount, Show under the program

(continued)

EXHIBIT 15.6
(Continued)

narrative statement the nature and source of income. The estimated amount of program income may be considered by the Federal grantor agency in determining the total amount of the grant.

Section C. Non-Federal Resources

Lines 8-11 Enter amounts of non-Federal resources that will be used on the grant. If in-kind contributions are included, provide a brief explanation on a separate sheet.

> **Column (a)** - Enter the program titles identical to Column (a), Section A. A breakdown by function or activity is not necessary.

> **Column (b)** - Enter the contribution to be made by the applicant.

> **Column (c)** - Enter the amount of the State's cash and in-kind contribution if the applicant is not a State or State agency. Applicants which are a State or State agencies should leave this column blank.

> **Column (d)** - Enter the amount of cash and in-kind contributions to be made from all other sources.

> **Column (e)** - Enter totals of Columns (b), (c), and (d).

Line 12 - Enter the total for each of Columns (b)-(e). The amount in Column (e) should be equal to the amount on Line 5, Column (f), Section A.

Section D. Forecasted Cash Needs

Line 13 - Enter the amount of cash needed by quarter from the grantor agency during the first year.

Line 14 - Enter the amount of cash from all other sources needed by quarter during the first year.

Line 15 - Enter the totals of amounts on Lines 13 and 14.

Section E. Budget Estimates of Federal Funds Needed for Balance of the Project

Lines 16-19 - Enter in Column (a) the same grant program titles shown in Column (a), Section A. A breakdown by function or activity is not necessary. For new applications and continuation grant applications, enter in the proper columns amounts of Federal funds which will be needed to complete the program or project over the succeeding funding periods (usually in years). This section need not be completed for revisions (amendments, changes, or supplements) to funds for the current year of existing grants.

If more than four lines are needed to list the program titles, submit additional schedules as necessary.

Line 20 - Enter the total for each of the Columns (b)-(e). When additional schedules are prepared for this Section, annotate accordingly and show the overall totals on this line.

Section F. Other Budget Information

Line 21 - Use this space to explain amounts for individual direct object class cost categories that may appear to be out of the ordinary or to explain the details as required by the Federal grantor agency.

Line 22 - Enter the type of indirect rate (provisional, predetermined, final or fixed) that will be in effect during the funding period, the estimated amount of the base to which the rate is applied, and the total indirect expense.

Line 23 - Provide any other explanations or comments deemed necessary.

One of the more common federal budget forms for nonconstruction projects is Standard Form (SF)-424A (Exhibit 15.5). The instructions for completing SF-424A are shown in Exhibit 15.6. As with other budget forms, if you have completed a project planner, you already have all the information you need to complete SF-424A.

Many grantors also require that you submit a narrative statement of your budget, explaining the basis for your inclusion of personnel, consultants, supplies, and equipment. This is known as a *budget narrative*. Again, your completed project planner will help you construct the budget narrative and explain the sequence of steps. The budget narrative gives you the opportunity to present the rationale for each step, piece of equipment, and key person that your proposal calls for.

Keep foremost in your mind that these federal funds are the result of taxes paid by individuals like you, as well as corporations. It is your responsibility to make the plan for how you propose to spend these moneys as precise and as clearly related to the project outcome as possible. The tendency to "round up" numbers and pad budgets is a threat to your credibility and could affect your ability to gain the peer reviewers' and federal staff's confidence.

Remember, do not leave anything to chance. All required forms must be completely precise.

Evaluation

Federal and state funding sources generally place a much heavier emphasis on evaluation than do most private sources. While there are many books written on evaluation, the best advice is to have an expert handle it. I suggest enlisting the services of a professional at a college or university who has experience in evaluation. Professors generally enjoy the involvement and the extra pay and can lead you to a storehouse of inexpensive labor: undergraduate and graduate students. A graduate student in statistics can help you deal with the problem of quantifying your results inexpensively, while he or she gathers valuable insight, experience, and some much-needed money.

Irrespective of who designs your evaluation, writing your objectives properly or designing your protocol carefully will the make the process much simpler. Most grantseekers have little problem developing objectives that deal with cognitive areas or areas that provide for results that can be easily quantified. The problems start when they move into the affective domain, because values, feelings, and appreciation can be difficult to measure. Use consultants to assist you. You will gain credibility by using an independent third party to carry out your evaluation analysis.

If you use the techniques presented in this chapter for writing objectives and ask yourself what your client population will do differently after the grant, you should be able to keep yourself on track and develop an evaluation design that will pass even the most critical federal and state standards. For example, a grant to increase appreciation of opera could be measured by seeing how many of the subjects pay to attend an inexpensive performance after the free ones are completed.

The Summary or Abstract

The summary or abstract is usually written after the proposal is completed. After the title, the summary or abstract is the second most often read, and therefore most important, part of a proposal. The summary or abstract must be succinct, clear, and motivating so the reader (reviewer) does not lose interest. It is important to determine whether the grantor uses summaries or abstracts. The terms are not interchangeable and, therefore, require different consideration.

In a sense, the summary or abstract has a dual purpose. Its first purpose is to provide the peer reviewer with a clear idea of what the proposed research or project will result in. After it is funded, it provides prospective grantseekers with an example of the type of research or project the federal agency funds. The summary or abstract becomes public information when it is placed on the funding source's website and in databases.

Unfortunately, some applicants do not devote enough time to preparing their summary or abstract and the description that is made public does not do the funding agency or the grantee's project or research justice. To get grant-seekers to pay more attention to this section of their proposals, some federal agencies score the summary or abstract in the overall proposal evaluation. Whether this area is scored or not, it plays a critical role in setting up the expectations of the reviewer before he or she gets into the body of your proposal.

In general terms, the summary or abstract is a much-abbreviated version of your proposal and should contain a concise description of the need for your project, your project's goal or hypothesis, objectives or specific aims, approach or protocol, and evaluation design. Use your summary or abstract to show readers that they will find what they want in your proposal (since you have the scoring system), and try to follow the same order in the summary or abstract as you do in your proposal. You can determine which components to emphasize in your summary or abstract by reviewing the point or evaluation system the funding source will apply. Place more emphasis by devoting more space in the abstract or summary to the components that will be weighted more heavily in the scoring or review process. In addition, you may want to include the key words or criteria that the grantor is looking for. Make sure your abstract or summary is arranged so that it is easy to read. Do not crowd the contents by using every inch of space designated for this area. Instead, highlight important parts with bullets, bold print, or underlining, as long as these visual aides are allowed.

Many funding sources have explicit requirements concerning the summary or abstract. Some designate the space and number of words or characters that can be used, while others require potential grantees to underline a certain number of key words or phrases. Exhibit 15.7 defines what the NSF expects in a project summary and provides very specific instructions in terms of what person the summary should be written in and what it should include. The NSF's guidelines even go so far as to state that the project summary should not be an abstract of the proposal. Be sure to verify your funding source's rules before constructing this critical part of your proposal.

EXHIBIT 15.7
National Science Foundation Profile Summary

From the National Science Foundation Grant Proposal Guide
NSF 14-1 February 2014

2. Sections of the Proposal

b. Project Summary

Each proposal must contain a summary of the proposed project not more than one page in length. The Project Summary consists of an overview, a statement on the intellectual merit of the proposed activity, and a statement on the broader impacts of the proposed activity.

The overview includes a description of the activity that would result if the proposal were funded and a statement of objectives and methods to be employed. The statement on intellectual merit should describe the potential of the proposed activity to advance knowledge. The statement on broader impacts should describe the potential of the proposed activity to benefit society and contribute to the achievement of specific, desired societal outcomes.

The Project Summary should be written in the third person, informative to other persons working in the same or related fields, and, insofar as possible, understandable to a scientifically or technically literate lay reader. It should not be an abstract of the proposal.

Proposals that do not contain the Project Summary, including an overview and separate statements on intellectual merit and boarder impacts, will not be accepted by FastLane or will be returned without review.

If the Project Summary contains special characters it may be uploaded as a Supplementary Document. Project Summaries submitted as a PDF must be formatted with separate headings for the overview, statement on the intellectual merit of the proposed activity, and statement on the broader impacts of the proposed activity. Failure to include these headings may result in the proposal being returned without review.

Additional instructions for the preparation of the Project Summary are available in FastLane.

Title Page

Federal granting programs have a required face sheet or title page that must be included in your federal grant applications or proposals. The most common is SF424 (Exhibit 15.8; instructions for completing this form are included in Exhibit 15.9). Remember, you are dealing with a bureaucracy and, therefore, should double-check all requirements and make sure all necessary forms are completed per instructions.

EXHIBIT 15.8
OMB Number: 4040-00C
Standard Form (SF) 424

OMB Number: 4040-0004
Expiration Date: 8/31/2016

Application for Federal Assistance SF-424

* 1. Type of Submission:	* 2. Type of Application:	* If Revision, select appropriate letter(s):
☐ Preapplication	☐ New	
☐ Application	☐ Continuation	* Other (Specify):
☐ Changed/Corrected Application	☐ Revision	

* 3. Date Received:	4. Applicant Identifier:

5a. Federal Entity Identifier:	5b. Federal Award Identifier:

State Use Only:

6. Date Received by State:	7. State Application Identifier:

8. APPLICANT INFORMATION:

* a. Legal Name:

* b. Employer/Taxpayer Identification Number (EIN/TIN):	* c. Organizational DUNS:

d. Address:

* Street1:
Street2:
* City:
County/Parish:
* State:
Province:
* Country:	USA: UNITED STATES
* Zip / Postal Code:

e. Organizational Unit:

Department Name:	Division Name:

f. Name and contact information of person to be contacted on matters involving this application:

Prefix:	* First Name:
Middle Name:	
* Last Name:	
Suffix:	

Title:

Organizational Affiliation:

* Telephone Number:	Fax Number:

* Email:

(continued)

EXHIBIT 15.8
(Continued)

Application for Federal Assistance SF-424

* 9. Type of Applicant 1: Select Applicant Type:

Type of Applicant 2: Select Applicant Type:

Type of Applicant 3: Select Applicant Type:

* Other (specify):

* 10. Name of Federal Agency:

11. Catalog of Federal Domestic Assistance Number:

CFDA Title:

* 12. Funding Opportunity Number:

* Title:

13. Competition Identification Number:

Title:

14. Areas Affected by Project (Cities, Counties, States, etc.):

| | Add Attachment | Delete Attachment | View Attachment |

* 15. Descriptive Title of Applicant's Project:

Attach supporting documents as specified in agency instructions.

| Add Attachments | Delete Attachments | View Attachments |

(continued)

EXHIBIT 15.8
(Continued)

Application for Federal Assistance SF-424

16. Congressional Districts Of:

* a. Applicant [　　　　　]　　　　　　　　　　* b. Program/Project [　　　　　]

Attach an additional list of Program/Project Congressional Districts if needed.

[　　　　　　　　　　　　　]　[Add Attachment]　[Delete Attachment]　[View Attachment]

17. Proposed Project:

* a. Start Date: [　　　　　]　　　　　　　　　　* b. End Date: [　　　　　]

18. Estimated Funding ($):

* a. Federal [　　　　　]

* b. Applicant [　　　　　]

* c. State [　　　　　]

* d. Local [　　　　　]

* e. Other [　　　　　]

* f. Program Income [　　　　　]

* g. TOTAL [　　　　　]

* 19. Is Application Subject to Review By State Under Executive Order 12372 Process?

☐ a. This application was made available to the State under the Executive Order 12372 Process for review on [　　　　　].

☐ b. Program is subject to E.O. 12372 but has not been selected by the State for review.

☐ c. Program is not covered by E.O. 12372.

* 20. Is the Applicant Delinquent On Any Federal Debt? (If "Yes," provide explanation in attachment.)

☐ Yes　　☐ No

If "Yes", provide explanation and attach

[　　　　　　　　　　　]　[Add Attachment]　[Delete Attachment]　[View Attachment]

21. ***By signing this application, I certify (1) to the statements contained in the list of certifications** and (2) that the statements herein are true, complete and accurate to the best of my knowledge. I also provide the required assurances** and agree to comply with any resulting terms if I accept an award. I am aware that any false, fictitious, or fraudulent statements or claims may subject me to criminal, civil, or administrative penalties. (U.S. Code, Title 218, Section 1001)**

☐ ** I AGREE

** The list of certifications and assurances, or an internet site where you may obtain this list, is contained in the announcement or agency specific instructions.

Authorized Representative:

Prefix: [　　　　　]　　　　　* First Name: [　　　　　]

Middle Name: [　　　　　]

* Last Name: [　　　　　]

Suffix: [　　　　　]

* Title: [　　　　　]

* Telephone Number: [　　　　　]　　　　Fax Number: [　　　　　]

* Email: [　　　　　]

* Signature of Authorized Representative: [　　　　　]　　　* Date Signed: [　　　　　]

EXHIBIT 15.9
Instructions for SF 424

Public reporting burden for this collection of information is estimated to average 60 minutes per response, including time for reviewing instructions, searching existing data sources, gathering and maintaining the data needed, and completing and reviewing the collection of information. Send comments regarding the burden estimate or any other aspect of this collection of information, including suggestions for reducing this burden, to the Office of Management and Budget, Paperwork Reduction Project (0348-0043), Washington, DC 20503.

PLEASE DO NOT RETURN YOUR COMPLETED FORM TO THE OFFICE OF MANAGEMENT AND BUDGET. SEND IT TO THE ADDRESS PROVIDED BY THE SPONSORING AGENCY.

This is a standard form (including the continuation sheet) required for use as a cover sheet for submission of preapplications and applications and related information under discretionary programs. Some of the items are required and some are optional at the discretion of the applicant or the Federal agency (agency). Required items are identified with an asterisk on the form and are specified in the instructions below. In addition to the instructions provided below, applicants must consult agency instructions to determine specific requirements.

Item	Entry
1.	**Type of Submission:** (Required) Select one type of submission in accordance with agency instructions. • Preapplication • Application • Changed/Corrected Application – If requested by the agency, check if this submission is to change or correct a previously submitted application. Unless requested by the agency, applicants may not use this to submit changes after the closing date.
2.	**Type of Application:** (Required) Select one type of application in accordance with agency instructions. • New – An application that is being submitted to an agency for the first time. • Continuation - An extension for an additional funding/budget period for a project with a projected completion date. This can include renewals. • Revision - Any change in the Federal Government's financial obligation or contingent liability from an existing obligation. If a revision, enter the appropriate letter(s). More than one may be selected. If "Other" is selected, please specify in text box provided. A. Increase Award B. Decrease Award C. Increase Duration D. Decrease Duration E. Other (specify)
3.	**Date Received:** Leave this field blank. This date will be assigned by the Federal agency.
4.	**Applicant Identifier:** Enter the entity identifier assigned by the Federal agency, if any, or applicant's control number, if applicable.
5a.	**Federal Entity Identifier:** Enter the number assigned to your organization by the Federal Agency, if any.
5b.	**Federal Award Identifier:** For new applications leave blank. For a continuation or revision to an existing award, enter the previously assigned Federal award identifier number. If a changed/corrected application, enter the Federal Identifier in accordance with agency instructions.
6.	**Date Received by State:** Leave this field blank. This date will be assigned by the State, if applicable.
7.	**State Application Identifier:** Leave this field blank. This identifier will be assigned by the State, if applicable.
8.	**Applicant Information:** Enter the following in accordance with agency instructions: a. **Legal Name:** (Required) Enter the legal name of applicant that will undertake the assistance activity. This is the name that the organization has registered with the Central Contractor Registry. Information on registering with CCR may be obtained by visiting the Grants.gov website. b. **Employer/Taxpayer Number (EIN/TIN):** (Required): Enter the Employer or Taxpayer Identification Number (EIN or TIN) as assigned by the Internal Revenue Service. If your organization is not in the US, enter 44-4444444. c. **Organizational DUNS:** (Required) Enter the organization's DUNS or DUNS+4 number received from Dun and Bradstreet. Information on obtaining a DUNS number may be obtained by visiting the Grants.gov website. d. **Address:** Enter the complete address as follows: Street address (Line 1 required), City (Required), County, State (Required, if country is US), Province, Country (Required), Zip/Postal Code (Required, if country is US). e. **Organizational Unit:** Enter the name of the primary organizational unit (and department or division, if applicable) that will undertake the assistance activity, if applicable. f. **Name and contact information of person to be contacted on matters involving this application:** Enter the name (First and last name required), organizational affiliation (if affiliated with an organization other than the applicant organization), telephone number (Required), fax number, and email address (Required) of the person to contact on matters related to this application.
9	**Type of Applicant:** (Required) Select up to three applicant type(s) in accordance with agency instructions: A. State Government B. County Government C. City or Township Government D. Special District Government E. Regional Organization F. U.S. Territory or Possession G. Independent School District H. Public/State Controlled Institution of Higher Education I. Indian/Native American Tribal Government (Federally Recognized) J. Indian/Native American Tribal Government (Other than Federally Recognized) K. Indian/Native American Tribally Designated Organization L. Public/Indian Housing Authority M. Nonprofit with 501C3 IRS Status (Other than Institution of Higher Education) N. Nonprofit without 501C3 IRS Status (Other than Institution of Higher Education) O. Private Institution of Higher Education P. Individual Q. For-Profit Organization (Other than Small Business) R. Small Business S. Hispanic-serving Institution

(continued)

EXHIBIT 15.9
(Continued)

Item	Entry
	T. Historically Black Colleges and Universities (HBCUs) U. Tribally Controlled Colleges and Universities (TCCUs) V. Alaska Native and Native Hawaiian Serving Institutions W. Non-domestic (non-US) Entity X. Other (specify)
10.	**Name Of Federal Agency:** (Required) Enter the name of the Federal agency from which assistance is being requested with this application.
11.	**Catalog Of Federal Domestic Assistance Number/Title:** Enter the Catalog of Federal Domestic Assistance number and title of the program under which assistance is requested, as found in the program announcement, if applicable.
12.	**Funding Opportunity Number/Title:** Enter the Funding Opportunity Number and title of the opportunity under which assistance is requested, as found in the program announcement.
13.	**Competition Identification Number/Title:** Enter the Competition Identification Number and title of the competition under which assistance is requested, if applicable.
14.	**Areas Affected By Project:** List the areas or entities using the categories (e.g., cities, counties, states, etc.) specified in agency instructions. Use the continuation sheet to enter additional areas, if needed.
15.	**Descriptive Title of Applicant's Project:** (Required) Enter a brief descriptive title of the project. If appropriate, attach a map showing project location (e.g., construction or real property projects). For preapplications, attach a summary description of the project.
16.	**Congressional Districts Of:** (Required) **16a.** Enter the applicant's Congressional District, and **16b.** Enter all District(s) affected by the program or project. Enter in the format: 2 characters State Abbreviation – 3 characters District Number, e.g., CA-005 for California 5th district, CA-012 for California 12th district, and NC-103 for North Carolina's 103rd district. • If all congressional districts in a state are affected, enter "all" for the district number, e.g., MD-all for all congressional districts in Maryland. • If nationwide, i.e. all districts within all states are affected, enter US-all. • If the program/project is outside the US, enter 00-000.
17.	**Proposed Project Start and End Dates:** (Required) Enter the proposed start date and end date of the project.
18.	**Estimated Funding:** (Required) Enter the amount requested or to be contributed during the first funding/budget period by each contributor. Value of in-kind contributions should be included on appropriate lines, as applicable. If the action will result in a dollar change to an existing award, indicate only the amount of the change. For decreases, enclose the amounts in parentheses.
19.	**Is Application Subject to Review by State Under Executive Order 12372 Process?** Applicants should contact the State Single Point of Contact (SPOC) for Federal Executive Order 12372 to determine whether the application is subject to the State intergovernmental review process. Select the appropriate box. If "a." is selected, enter the date the application was submitted to the State.
20.	**Is the Applicant Delinquent on any Federal Debt?** (Required) Select the appropriate box. This question applies to the applicant organization, not the person who signs as the authorized representative. Categories of debt include delinquent audit disallowances, loans and taxes. If yes, include an explanation on the continuation sheet.
21.	**Authorized Representative:** (Required) To be signed and dated by the authorized representative of the applicant organization. Enter the name (First and last name required), title (Required), telephone number (Required), fax number, and email address (Required) of the person authorized to sign for the applicant. A copy of the governing body's authorization for you to sign this application as the official representative must be on file in the applicant's office. (Certain Federal agencies may require that this authorization be submitted as part of the application.)

The title of a proposal is very important. It is the first part of your proposal to be read by reviewers, and, if unclear or misleading, it may be the only part read! Take time to develop a title that ensures your proposal will get attention.

The title of your proposal should:

- Describe your project.
- Express your project's results, not methods.
- Describe your project's benefits to clients.
- Be short and easy to remember.

The best titles are like newspaper headlines, descriptive and to the point. Titles that try to entice the reader by giving only part of the story or creating a mystery seldom work. Do not use jargon, buzzwords, biblical characters, or Greek gods in your proposal since you cannot be sure that the funding source will be familiar with your reference. For example, calling your solar energy project "Apollo's Flame" could work to your disadvantage if the reviewer does not know who Apollo is or fails to make the connection.

Acronyms should be used only if the funding source has a preference for them. Trying to develop a title that describes the benefits of your project is difficult enough without trying to use specific words that will result in a catchy acronym.

Since you have written the proposal, it is easy for you to develop tunnel vision and attribute more meaning to the words in the title than a person reading it for the first time would. To make sure this does not happen, read your title to other people who know little or nothing about your proposal, and then ask them what they think the proposal is about based on the title. Have friends read the proposal and ask them for title suggestions.

Titles can vary in length and can be up to ten or thirteen words. Some federal programs have rules on the number of characters or spaces used in a title. Check the rules.

The key to writing a good title is to ask funding officials what they prefer and to examine a list of titles used by past grantees. This will give you a more accurate idea of what the funding source really likes.

Future Funding

Most funding sources are buying a piece of the future. It is in their best interest to see any project they fund continue even though their guidelines may prohibit them from supporting continuation. If the project continues they are able to take credit for it and its benefits over a great length of time. Unfortunately, many grantseekers ignore the funding source's interest in keeping the investment alive and neglect to mention a future financing plan in their proposals. If you cannot think of ways to finance your project after your federal grant funds run out, try brainstorming with your advisory committee. Perhaps you could continue your project through:

- service fees
- membership fees
- support from agencies like the United Way
- big gift campaigns aimed at wealthy individuals
- an endowment program
- foundation and corporate grants
- a direct-mail campaign
- other fund-raising mechanisms

Include the cost of one or more of these activities in your expenses and budget them in the grant. You are not automatically considered an ingrate for doing this; rather, you may come across as a good executor of the funding source's estate. You are planning for continuation.

Dissemination

In addition to the good that will come from meeting the objectives and closing the gap established in your needs statement, much good can come from letting others know what you and the funding source have accomplished. Others in your field will come to know your name and ask you to enter into consortia with them. In addition, other funding sources will have knowledge of your application and possibly look at ways to extrapolate it to their program. The idea is to get more PR and mileage out of your work in addition to that which you will derive from having an article published in a journal in your field.

Explore how you could disseminate the results of your grant by:

- mailing a final report, quarterly journal, or a newsletter to others in field
- sponsoring a seminar or conference on the topic
- attending a national or international conference to deliver the results of the project (many government funding officials cannot travel to conferences, but they can fund you to go and disseminate the results)
- providing a satellite downlink to others in your field
- producing a DVD of the project
- creating a website and allowing others to download parts of your work

Activities aimed at disseminating project results are viewed positively by most funding sources. In general, they want their agency and program name up in lights and are willing to pay for it. So build the costs related to dissemination in your budget. Remember, you can always negotiate down the cost for dissemination in your budget, but you may be surprised at how much the grantor will want to keep in.

Attachments (Appendix)

The attachments can provide the winning edge when your proposal is compared to a competitor's. Throughout the proposal development process, you should be gathering materials that could be used in the attachment section of your proposal. Your final task is to select which materials to include. Naturally, you want to choose those that will best support your proposal and build credibility. Whether the funding source skims over them or examines them in detail, attachments may include:

- studies or research, tables, charts, and graphs
- vitae of key personnel

- minutes of advisory committee meetings
- a list of board members
- an auditor's report or statement
- letters of recommendation or endorsement
- a copy of your IRS tax-exempt designation
- pictures or architect's drawings
- copies of your agency's publications
- a list of other funding sources you will approach for support

Check funding source rules to determine what is required and the regulations regarding how long your attachments section can be. Guidelines usually state the maximum number of pages it can have. Many funding sources will not want you to include the full vitae of key staff and will specify that you attach abbreviated resumes or biosketches instead.

Also check funding source rules for the appropriate appendix format. Provide a separate table of contents for your appendix, and number the pages for easy reference.

Writing Your Federal or State Proposal

Your proposal must reflect what the funding source wants and what the reviewers will be looking for. To create a winning proposal:

- Follow the guidelines exactly (even when they seem senseless, or when you think you are repeating yourself).
- Fill in all the blanks (if not applicable mark NA).
- Double-check all computations.
- Include anything the funding source asks for, even if you think you already provided the information under another section of your proposal.

When writing your proposal, keep in mind that it must be readable and easy to skim. Place special emphases on vocabulary, style, and visual attractiveness and, above all, consider the intended audience (the reviewer).

Vocabulary

Your research on the probable reviewer will have given you an idea of the reviewer's level of expertise and their depth of knowledge in your subject areas. Be sure your proposal uses language appropriate to the reviewers. Shorter words are generally better than long, complex words; avoid buzzwords unless you are sure the reviewer expects them. Define all acronyms, or avoid them completely. You want to avoid using language that is under or over the reviewer's level. In most cases I have had to simplify proposals because the reviewers were technically literate lay readers rather than experts in the field.

Writing Style

By now you should have some idea of the background of the typical reviewer selected by the grantor agency and how much time the reviewers spend reading each proposal. These peer reviewers are under pressure to use their time efficiently, so you must produce a proposal that is poignant, yet organized and easy to read. Your best aid here is to review two or three successful proposals. After all, they followed the golden rule—they got the gold! When you analyze them, I bet you will find that they adhere to the following grant winner techniques:

- Use simple sentences (no more than two commas) and short paragraphs (five to seven lines).
- Begin each section with a strong motivating lead sentence.
- Make sure your writing style cannot be construed as cute or offensive to the reader.
- Avoid stating the obvious and talking down to the reviewer.
- Develop a user-friendly proposal. One of the peer reviewers may be chosen to defend your proposal to the rest of the review panel. In this case, you want to be certain to make the reviewer your friend by organizing and referencing attachments in such a way that they can be used to mount a good defense and to answer the other panelists' questions.

Visual Attractiveness

Due to the formats required under electronic submission, your creativity is severely limited in terms of visual attractiveness. However, the need still exists to make your proposal stand out from the rest of the pile. Depending on submission rules, the application of allowable techniques is designed to make your proposal more interesting, draw reviewers to the salient points, and make the areas that are part of the scoring rubric stand out. While space is always a problem, you are better off to edit your proposal to keep it from looking crowded and to make it more readable and reviewer friendly.

Reviewers usually must struggle thorough several proposals. In addition, their reading is frequently interrupted and they often have to return to a proposal in the middle of a section. Tired reviewers need all the help you can give them to locate and score the important sections of your proposal. For example if you use "1, 2, and 3" to explain the order of your methods or protocols, it is easier to see the numbers if they are justified to the left margin rather than burying them in a paragraph. Also, it has been noted by funding sources that there are often more "firsts" than "seconds" and "thirds." Reviewers get frustrated when there is a "first" with no following points. Reviewers may also take you to task for using an ordinal approach (1, 2, and 3) when there is no reason for "3" to follow "2" and could, in fact, be presented first. You will understand how important readability, writing style, and visual attractiveness are after you read several samples of funded proposals followed by your own.

Even scientific research need not look boring to the reviewer. Again, review any electronic submittal rules and then look to enhance the "readability" of your proposal by making your points stand out through

- underlining
- bullets
- different fonts
- various margins and s p a c i n g
- **bold headings**
- pictures and graphics
- charts and tables

While you must follow the grantor's rules regarding type font, number of characters per inch, line spacing, and so on, your computer and laser printer can provide you with a wealth of creative ways to make your proposal more readable. Avoid creativity for its own sake, but think of the reviewer and your goal to hit those review criteria as you write your proposal.

Online Proposal Preparation

The advent of Grants.gov has hastened compliance with Congress's paperless environment. While there are variations in applications between agencies and even programs within the same federal agency, the Grants.gov portal governs all proposal submissions. Proposal creation is governed by this system as well. Not only are you required to transmit your proposal electronically, the creation or writing of your proposal is also accomplished on the agency's website. Electronic submission then moves the proposal from the creation or writing status to submission, and then to a pending or under review status.

Grants.gov not only supplies the grantseeker with the ability to search for grantors in twenty-six federal agencies and over one thousand grant programs, but also allows you to procure an application online once you have located the best program.

While you do not have to log on to search, you do have to get registered to apply for and submit a grant request. You or your organization must complete the Grants.gov registration process. Once registered, it is possible for you and your co-principal investigators and project directors to work on separate sections of your proposal simultaneously. However, you must retain the access code given to you through the registration process to retrieve your proposal.

Discuss the proposal development online process with a successful grantee if at all possible. You can gain valuable insights by asking successful grantees about the online application problems they encountered and how they overcame them. For example, you could discover through conversation with a successful grantee that the federal agencies are not licensed to provide software programs with spell or grammar check and that to perform these functions you must download the proposal, clean it up, and upload it back into the agency's application program. Even this relatively simple process can become fraught with difficulties, especially if you are doing it at the last minute. When the deadline is looming and hundreds, if not thousands, of proposal creators and writers are changing and transmitting tens of thousands of documents, problems occur. So the more you know early on in the process, the better.

If you are fortunate enough to have an institutional grants office, you can check with it for its recommended submittal procedures. Most colleges, universities, and major nonprofit organizations have a central office to deal with proposal development. In fact, it is even common for universities to have colleges, departments, or centers with their own policies and procedures dealing with federal electronic submission.

Starting out by contacting the offices in your organization that are involved with the submittal process is smart and polite. In addition, keep in mind that you will ultimately need these people for submission. If your organization has obtained federal grant funds recently, they probably already have designated a person who is the only one allowed to move a proposal from the creation or writing part of proposal development to the actual submittal state (more about that later). Find out how your institution's system is set up so you do not hit any snags later.

The Grants.gov website states that the registration process can take between three to five business days, but if all the steps are not completed in a timely manner, the process could take as long as four weeks. So I suggest you or your organization register early, submit early, and verify that your submissions are received on time and validated successfully.

When will you create your actual proposal using the strategies in this chapter? Review your action steps chart to determine when you will set aside the time to write your federal proposal. Use Figure 15.2 to place this action step in your plan.

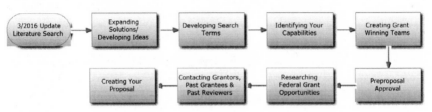

FIGURE 15.2
Action Steps Chart: Creating Your Proposal

Note

1. Rina Shaikh-Lesko, "Lowered Cities," *The Chronicle of Higher Education,* March 21, 2014, Vol. LX, No. 27.

16

Improving Your Federal Proposal: The Grants Quality Circle

SINCE THE SEVENTH EDITION I have had the opportunity to work with several hundred Bauer grants fellows. This has afforded me additional opportunities to observe the efforts of putting proposals through mock reviews and quality circles before submittal. This continued experience has validated my initial findings on the incredible success rates that come from the use of this technique. One of my fellows was rejected on all eight proposals he submitted in the year prior to his participation in my program and the quality circle process. In the next one and one half years, he was awarded eight of nine proposals for a total of $1 million. While it is impossible to ascribe all that success to quality circles since he used other proactive grantseeking techniques outlined in *The "How To" Grants Manual,* he believes that the insights he gathered from the quality circle reviews were instrumental in his success.

At the College of Arts and Sciences at the University of Alabama, it is mandatory that my grants fellows take part in the quality circle process and subsequently they have consistently recorded over 50 percent success rates. One fellow's National Science Foundation (NSF) Career Award proposal was reviewed in my quality circle training seminar in June. Based on the comments, suggestions and feedback she derived from the quality circle, she revised her proposal for the July deadline and was ultimately awarded the grant. The areas where she made significant changes suggested by the quality circle team turned out to be areas the reviewers acclaimed. She was even told by the program officers that it was the best proposal they received that year and one of the best ever. To top it off, it was her first NSF proposal!

One of the most exciting and gratifying experiences of my forty-five-year grant career has been the way quality circles have reduced failure and increased the success of my grantseekers. In the seventh edition of *The "How To" Grants Manual,* I was honored to include the following quote from Dr. William Wiener, professor and former vice provost for research at Marquette University, that attests to the positive impact the quality circle concept has when implemented and reinforced from an institution's grants/research office.

> Marquette University has more than doubled its external funding since Bauer and Associates have assisted us with our Research Development Program. This is due in part to the growing use of quality circle reviews where faculty provide a small group of interested people with a draft of their proposal for critical analysis. Quality circles have greatly enhanced the quality of the proposals that we submit to funding agencies. Quality circle reviews provide the faculty with feedback on their draft proposals, which results in stronger applications.

Dr. Weiner has since moved to the University of North Carolina, Greensboro, where he is the Dean of the Graduate School. He has incorporated the proactive grantseeking strategies in this book into a unique fellows program for graduate students. The program is a condensed version of my regular program using the fall semester to equip the participants with the skills necessary to apply for grants to continue their graduate studies the following academic year.

The program has a strong focus on the use of the quality circle concept to help the fellows approach their spring deadlines. Their mentors are encouraged to attend the quality circle training and to use the concept with their students. As of this writing, two cohort groups have completed the program and many have successfully obtained grants to further their education.

Many funded grantees have traditionally taken advantage of a presubmission review of their proposals by a colleague or two. While this technique is positive, its value depends on how knowledgeable those reviewing your proposal are of the field and how much they know about the actual peer review system that will be used by the reviewers. For example, while a four-hour review of your proposal by one of your colleagues will be quite detailed, it may actually be counterproductive in its suggestions if the real reviewer is to spend just one hour reviewing it. The secret to improving your federal proposal is to conduct a mock review that emulates the actual review system as closely as possible. Of course, the *first* step is to be proactive and to make sure you have enough time to take advantage of this most valuable technique. The *second* step is to get the relevant information on the reviewers and the scoring process.

Proactive grantseekers initiate proposal development early in the federal grant cycle and therefore have sufficient time to have their proposals reviewed by their peers before submission. You will improve your proposal and significantly increase your chances for success by asking several colleagues or members of your grant advisory committee to voluntarily role-play being the review team that will ultimately pass judgment on your proposal. This pre-submission review process is really a test run or mock review, and the group conducting it acts as your quality circle, as described in William Edward Deming's work on total quality management (TQM).[1]

If you follow the TQM model, you will not pay your quality circle participants to take part in the activity. They should be motivated by their desire to help you improve your proposal, increase its probability of excellence, and, thus, enhance the image of your organization. It is to everyone's advantage to position your institution in the most favorable manner. In many institutions, the grants office will help you set up this improvement exercise and, when necessary, may even pay for refreshments or lunch. In some instances, course release time is also offered as an incentive for leading mock reviews.

The following quote from Dr. Amy Henderson-Harr, assistant vice president of research and sponsored programs at SUNY Cortland, further bears out the impact that quality circle reviews can have on an entire institution.

> At SUNY Cortland, we are able to use the quality circle concept of peer review and the skills acquired to not only improve our grant success rates, but apply the teachings to improving other aspects of academic work, including curriculum proposals, program assessments and interdisciplinary collaborations to improve what we do. The quality circle process has brought seasoned faculty together with novice grant seekers to jointly enrich and advance scholarship. Most importantly, the quality circle seminars have changed the way we see ourselves, in that we have higher standards and know that we can do better by changing the way that we approach grants through the application of quality circles. We're much more apt to think strategically in pre-planning, developing thematic connections throughout the text, relying upon each other for areas we need help on, and accept[ing] feedback. Most of all, we're learning from each other and respecting what we all bring to the process as members of our institution. It's enlightening and transformative. Perhaps the best of all!

As previously mentioned, the most significant factor in the success of this improvement exercise is how closely each aspect of the mock review resembles the actual federal or state review. The benefits you can derive from this technique are directly related to your ability to create the scenario in which the actual reviewers will find themselves.

To arrange a quality circle that is similar to what the actual review will be like, secure pertinent information on the background of last year's reviewers, a copy of the scoring system that will be used, and an outline of the actual process. Through preproposal contact (see chapter 14), you should have already collected information about the setting in which your proposal will be reviewed.

To make this exercise as valuable as possible, provide your mock review group or grants quality circle with data on the following:

- the training each reviewer receives
- the setting in which proposals are reviewed (the federal agency, the reviewer's home, both sites, and so on)
- the review process: Does one reviewer defend the proposal while others try to locate flaws or weaknesses?
- the scoring system: Are scores averaged? Are the highest and lowest scores eliminated and the remainder averaged?
- the amount of time spent reviewing each proposal

Your quality circle participants should also be provided with a copy of the *Catalog of Federal Domestic Assistance* or the program application guidelines, as well as information on past grantees and results of preproposal contact with grantor staff. Providing copies of funded proposals as references is valuable. However, they need not be considered required reading.

It is essential that you instruct the members of your grants quality circle to spend only the same amount of time reviewing your proposal as the actual reviewers. Some of your mock reviewers may mistakenly think they will be helping you by taking an inordinate amount of time to read your proposal carefully. However, if actual reviewers will skim parts of the proposal, then our mock reviewers should do the same. Remind your quality circle participants that they should be trying to *mirror* the actual reviews, not do a better job! If the actual reviewers will invest over sixty minutes reviewing and scoring each proposal, consider distributing your draft proposal to the members of your grants quality circle before they come together. Ask them to bring the proposal to the meeting with the positive areas highlighted. They should also bring their scores for each section and suggestions on the areas to be improved.

The proposal sequence to be followed should emulate that which the actual review will undergo. One exception is the evaluation of the title and abstract or summary. The participants should read and score the title and the abstract or summary, and discuss the impact those elements had on their expectations of what the project was about. They should also discuss the impression the title and the abstract or summary gave them concerning the organization of the proposal.

Four or five reviewers or participants should be selected to participate in the mock review or quality circle. The Sample Letter/E-Mail Inviting and Individual to Participate in a Grants Quality Circle (Exhibit 16.1) and the Federal/State Grants Quality Circle Worksheet (Exhibit 16.2) will help you carry out this valuable exercise.

Exhibit 16.3 outlines the roles that each person on the quality circle will play. The greatest difficulty in conducting the quality circle falls on the facilitator. The facilitator's main job is to keep the process of review, evaluation, and discussion positive. The purpose is to role play how the reviewer will see this proposal and to put the most positive and productive foot forward. The instructions are quite clear. Ask each quality circle participant for the positive comments before moving to the areas to improve. To avoid quality circle participants giving their own opinions, the facilitator will use the actual scoring system and the criteria that the actual reviewers will employ to evaluate, rank, and score the proposal.

EXHIBIT 16.1
Sample Letter/E-mail Inviting an Individual to Participate in a Grants Quality Circle

---

Date

Name
Address

Dear   :

I would like to take this opportunity to request your input in helping our [organization, group, team] submit the very best grant proposal possible. We are asking that you review the enclosed proposal from the point of view of the federal reviewer. The attached materials will help you role-play the actual manner in which the proposal will be evaluated.

Please read the information on the reviewers' backgrounds and the scoring system, and limit the time you spend reading the proposal to the time constraints that the real reviewers will observe. A grants quality circle worksheet has been provided to assist you in recording your scores and comments.

A meeting of all mock reviewers composing our quality circle has been scheduled for [date]. Please bring your grants quality circle worksheet with you to this meeting. The meeting will last less than one hour. Its purpose is to analyze the scores and brainstorm suggestions to improve this proposal.

Sincerely,

Name
Phone Number

EXHIBIT 16.2
Federal/State Grants Quality Circle Worksheet

The following information is designed to help you develop the proper focus for the review of the attached proposal.

1. The Review Panelists
   Proposals are read by review panelists with the following degrees and backgrounds:
   Degrees: _____
   Backgrounds (Age, Viewpoints, Biases, and So On): _____
   _____
   _____

2. The Time Element and Setting
   Number of proposals read by each reviewer: _____
   Average length of time spent reading each proposal: _____
   Proposals are read at the:
   ___ reviewer's home ___ reviewer's work ___funder's location ___ other site

3. The Scoring System
   a. The scoring system that will be employed is based on a scale of: _____
   b. The areas to be scored are (list or include attachment):
      Area   Total Possible Points   Your Score
      _____
      _____
      _____

   c. According to the total points per area, how many points represent an outstanding, superior, adequate, weak, or poor score? For example, if the total points possible for one area are 25, 0–8 = poor, 9–12 = weak, 13–19 = adequate, 20–23 = superior, and 24–25 = outstanding.
      _____
      _____

   d. After recording your scores, list the positive points of the proposal that may appeal to the actual reviewer. Also list those areas that seem weak and may cost valuable points. List suggestions for improvement
      _____
      _____
      _____

EXHIBIT 16.3
Conducting a Quality Circle Review/Roles

Group Facilitator

The group leader or facilitator is responsible for keeping the group on task, having the group focus on the proposal's positive aspects before moving on to its negative ones, and reinforcing a constructive learning atmosphere. The facilitator may engage in reading and scoring the sections as well, but should reserve his or her comments and scores till last. The group leader may decide to facilitate discussion only if that is his or her desire.

The facilitator will request the scores for each section or part of the proposal before asking for the positive areas and areas to be improved. The facilitator is advised to rotate the request for comments to start each section among the participants, and to encourage everyone to participate. The facilitator will set a constructive tone and learning focus by asking each participant for his or her positive comments first, and will interrupt any participant who moves to the areas to be improved before each participant has presented his or her comments. After all positive comments have been presented the focus will turn to the areas that need to be improved to raise the score for each section.

Proposal Initiators/Writers

The creators of the proposal under review may choose to either attend the quality circle meeting, or not be present and just receive the results. If present, they should not be allowed to interrupt the process, defend the proposal, or provide any additional information. However, they may ask questions to clarify points at the conclusion of the discussion on each of the sections to be reviewed. A short introduction including information learned through preproposal contact or from successful grantees or past reviewers may be included to help prepare the participants.

Quality Circle Participants

The exercise participants are expected to adhere to the suggestions on reading time frames, development of helpful comments, and the scoring of each section. They are allowed to raise questions, but asking questions of the proposal initiators should be kept to a minimum and allowed only when necessary to promote a realistic review.

This is not a critique, nor a defense of a dissertation. To succeed and be-come a practice that proposal developers want to be involved in, it must be a positive experience. Learning what may be missing or could be improved is beneficial and constructive for the proposal developer if the experience is handled correctly.

In some cases it is not feasible to assemble a group of volunteers for a qual-ity circle. There may be too few colleagues in your organization to conduct a role-playing activity such as this, confidentiality may be an issue, personality problems may exist, or competitions in the field could rule out the possibility of such an activity occurring. One option in these instances is to ask one or two individuals whom you trust from outside your organization or off cam-pus to review your proposal. Provide them with the same data and worksheets discussed previously, and, if absolutely necessary, offer them an honorarium for their efforts ($200 is common). You could request that they sign a nondis-closure agreement. Most university grant offices have these agreement forms and will be happy to share a copy with you. This way you can tailor the agree-ment to your project with minimal effort. Seldom are these extraordinary security measures necessary with colleagues, but this is an option you may want to consider to ensure that no one steals your idea.

A look at a few selected scoring systems and criteria reveals the importance of knowing how your proposal will be reviewed and how important it is to share this information with your mock reviewers. Please note that by the time this edition of this book is published, the scoring rubrics and criteria presented here may have changed. Therefore it is very important that you validate the evaluation system to be used on your proposal and procure in-formation on the most current one.

As an example, the Department of Education may select one or more of the following factors in determining the selection criteria to evaluate applications submitted in a grant competition:

- need for project
- significance
- quality of the project design
- quality of project services
- quality of project personnel
- adequacy of resources
- quality of the management plan
- quality of the project evaluation
- strategy to scale

Then the different offices within the Department, like the Office of Educational Research and Improvement, may apply a specific point system based on a total of 100 points to each selected criteria. Often the point system is heavily weighted toward one or two criteria like significance and project design.

The NSF and the National Institutes of Health (NIH) do not use evaluation systems based on a total of 100 points. They use a rating system more than a point system. In situations like these, the grantseeker must ask more questions of the grantor so that he or she can ascertain what looks "good" under each criterion. After all, to play the game you need to know *all* the rules.

All NSF proposals are evaluated through the use of two National Science Board–approved merit review criteria.

- Criterion 1: What is the intellectual merit of the proposed activity?
- Criterion 2: What are the broader impacts of the proposed activity?

In some instances, the NSF employs additional criteria as required to highlight the specific objectives of certain programs and activities.

The NSF's rating scale includes:

- Excellent—Outstanding proposal in all respects, deserves highest priority for support
- Very Good—High quality proposal in nearly all respects, should be supported if at all possible
- Good—A quality proposal, worthy of support
- Fair—Proposal lacking in one or more critical aspects, key issues need to be addressed
- Poor—proposal has serious deficiencies

Some of the criteria considered within specific institutes in NIH, like the National Institute on Aging, include:

- scientific, technical, or medical significance
- appropriateness and adequacy of research
- qualifications of principal investigator/staff
- availability of resources
- appropriateness of budget
- adequacy of plans to include both genders and minorities
- protection of human subjects

Exhibit 16.4 shows NIH's grant application scoring system. The scoring system uses a 9-point rating scale from 1, which equals exceptional, to 9 which

EXHIBIT 16.4
The NIH Grant Application Scoring System

Impact	Score	Descriptor	Additional Guidance on Strengths/Weaknesses
High	1	Exceptional	Exceptionally strong with essentially no weaknesses
High	2	Outstanding	Extremely strong with negligible weaknesses
High	3	Excellent	Very strong with only some minor weaknesses
Medium	4	Very Good	Strong but with numerous minor weaknesses
Medium	5	Good	Strong but with a least one moderate weakness
Medium	6	Satisfactory	Some strengths but also some moderate weaknesses
Low	7	Fair	Some strengths but with at least one major weakness
Low	8	Marginal	A few strengths and a few major weaknesses
Low	9	Poor	Very few strengths and numerous major weaknesses

Minor Weakness: An easily addressable weakness that does not substantially lessen impact
Moderate Weakness: A weakness that lessens impact
Major Weakness: A weakness that severely limits impact

Non-numeric score options: NR = Not Recommended for Further Consideration, DF = Deferred, AB = Abstention, CF = Conflict of Interest, NP = Not Present, ND = Not Discussed equals poor, for the overall impact/priority score as well as the individual review criteria (e.g., significance, investigator, innovation, approach, environment). Ratings are provided only in whole numbers, not decimals.

Few techniques suggested in this book will have a more dramatic effect on the quality of your proposals than the grants quality circle. Support for this activity will be rewarded through the promotion of a better image with reviewers and federal staff, as well as an increase in quality proposals from staff members participating in this activity. After the suggestions from your quality circle have been incorporated into your final proposal, you are ready to move on to submission.

Use the action steps chart shown in Figure 16.1 to plan ahead for incorporating the use of a quality circle review into your plan.

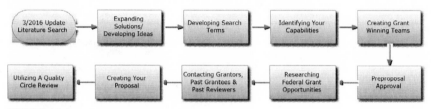

FIGURE 16.1
Action Steps Chart: Utilizing a Quality Circle Review

Note

1. Gary Fellers, *The Deming Vision: SPC/TQM for Administrators* (Milwaukee: ASQC Quality Press, 1992).

17

Submission:
What to Do and What Not to Do

A LTHOUGH THIS CHAPTER ADDRESSES the federal grants system, much of the information it contains can also be applied to other government funding sources such as state, county, and city. Irrespective of which type of public funding source you are submitting your proposal to, you do not want to do anything at this late stage that may have a negative impact on your submitted proposal's outcome.

What to Do

Submit your proposal a day or two before the deadline. A week before is even better. Do not position yourself as a last-minute applicant who beats the deadline by a few minutes. After all of your hard work, you do not want to position yourself as a loser. Grantors have told me that they worry about funding last-minute Herculean proposal developers because they are likely to experience problems with their expenditure rates (that is, having leftover money that ends up as a grant continuation or extension), late or missing reports and evaluations, and a host of other maladies that could make the grantor's program look bad to Congress.

Follow all instructions and every rule. Do not wait until your proposal has been written, has undergone a mock review, and is ready to be sent out before you read the submission guidelines prescribed by Grants.gov. Review the submittal requirements early to make sure you have enough time to comply with them. Do not jeopardize your chances for success by failing to show funders that you have read and complied with their rules for submission.

Unfortunately, many grantseekers read the requirements too late and find that they cannot meet the grantor's deadlines. They then include a note with their proposal saying that they will forward the necessary documents at a later date. This is a red flag to grantors and alerts them that this applicant may be a problem. This may even get your proposal automatically rejected.

Even with extensive application guidelines and instructions, grantseekers make mistakes in obtaining appropriate or authorized signatures and following specific requirements regarding page length, number of pages, assurances, and so on. In fact, it would be too time consuming to list all of the problems federal grantors have in gaining compliance with their rules. Review and follow the submittal procedures contained in your application package carefully.

Grants.gov is the primary means for applying for federal grants, and its submittal procedures must be followed precisely. If you wish to apply for a grant through Grants.gov, you and your organization must complete the Grants.gov registration process. To register, your organization will need to provide its Data Universal Number System (DUNS) number. If your organization does not have one, go to the Dun & Bradstreet website at http://fedgov. dnb.com/webform to obtain the number. You should receive your DUNS number information online the same day you register.

Your organization must also be registered with the System for Award Management (SAM). If your organization is not registered with SAM, an authorizing official of your organization must register online at www.sam.gov. If you already have a taxpayer identification number (TIN) or an employment identification number (EIN), your SAM registration will take three to five business days to process. If your organization does not have a TIN or EIN, allow two weeks for obtaining the information from the Internal Revenue Service. Note that if your organization had an active record in the Central Contractor Registration, it has an active record in SAM and does not need to do anything in SAM at this time, unless a change in your business circumstances requires updates to your entity records.

Staff members from your organization designated to submit applications are called authorized organization representatives (AORs). Before you can submit proposals online via Grants.gov, your e-business point of contact (E-Biz POC) has to approve AORs to submit applications on behalf of your organization, and the AORS must have completed profiles with Grants.gov to create their username and password. There can be more than one AOR for your organization and in some cases the E-Biz POC is also the AOR for an organization. Check with your grants office to see who your AOR is.

All of the registration steps should be completed fairly quickly. However, registration problems can arise at one stage or another. Therefore, start early so you do not miss any deadlines due to nonregistration.

The date and time of submittal will be recorded with your proposal. Keep this in mind when submitting your proposal, especially since a program officer once confided in me that her office used the data and time record as one way to break ties when proposals were scored equally. Indeed, the early bird may get the worm (grant).

Many colleges, universities, and large nonprofit organizations have agreements with software contractors to manage the pre- and post-award handling of their proposals, including submission. For example, some use the InfoEd eRA Portal for Electronic Grants Administration (https://unrprod.infoed global.com). This InfoEd suite, which is compatible with SPINPlus, the company's funding opportunities and CV database service, includes:

- proposal development
- proposal tracking
- project management
- compliance systems
- clinical trials management
- technology transfer modules

No matter what administrative system you use, alert the group or office early that you will require their services to submit your federal proposal and that your organization has already received all the necessary clearances. You can now see how helpful it would be if you employed the sign-on process outlined in chapter 10 (see Exhibit 10.2). By employing this process, the people involved in sign off will have advanced knowledge of your project.

Many new sign-off systems use electronic copies of proposals. Check to see what your proposal looks like when received by electronic submission. What happens to graphics and to the layout and design? A little care may pay off dramatically.

Some systems also use electronic signatures. While this process is efficient, it can still grind to a halt if an administrator is unavailable. Again, starting early can avoid problems.

However, depending on your grants administration system, getting your proposal in early does not always pay off. In general, I recommend grantseekers to complete their quality circles and proposal revisions early and to get their proposals to their institution's research office weeks before the deadline. However, in some cases grants and research offices do not handle proposals on a first-in, first-out basis. Instead, they use deadline dates. Essentially, they reward last-minute proposal developers and put them ahead of the early birds. This is just one reason why it is so important to double-check with your institution's grants office in advance to see when it needs your proposal to do its job and to confirm the sign-off and submittal process.

What Not to Do

It is recommended that you limit the use of elected representatives in the grants process, especially at submittal time. Your institution may have rules governing who can contact elected officials. Due to politics and the controversy over the earmarking of federal grant funds, I recommend you avoid earmarking, congresspeople, and senators. Federal bureaucrats view the use of congresspeople and their aides as potentially unethical and possibly illegal. Elected officials want to be viewed by you, the voter and grant applicant, as ready to help in any way, but their assistance should be enlisted only when your own efforts have failed in preproposal contact and information gathering about past grants and federal program priorities.

Do not ask program officers for extra time or a later submittal date, and do not ask to send in any parts of the proposal after the deadline. Do not contact program officers after submission. This is viewed as an attempt to influence the grantor's review process and decision. On a rare occasion, advancements in the field could dramatically affect a proposal you have already submitted. In this instance, you should alert the program officer of the ramifications of the advancements and how they will affect your proposal's protocol or budget. Send the program officer an e-mail explaining the situation and ask him or her to pass the information on to the reviewers if he or she feels it is appropriate to do so. For example, a piece of equipment or software that could reduce the length of your grant period or result in significant savings could impact your selection as a grantee. Therefore, it would be optimum if the program officer passed this information on to the review group. However, it is solely at the discretion of the program officer to send the new information to the reviewers.

Now that you are aware of the ins and outs of proposal submission, place the submittal date for your federal application on your action steps chart (Figure 17.1).

Chapter 17

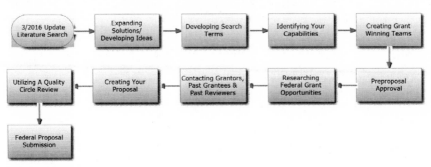

FIGURE 17.1
Action Steps Chart: Federal Proposal Submission

18

Federal Grant Requirements

M ANY NONPROFIT ORGANIZATIONS and even small colleges exhibit great fear and trepidation over the many rules regarding federal grant moneys. These fears are basically unwarranted and should be of concern only to nonprofit organizations that do not have adequate fiscal rules and regulations. The restrictions governing usage of federal funds are understandable and in many cases reasonable. Yes, there are instances of disallowed expenditures two or three years after a grant has been completed, but they are avoidable. Most people remember the exception rather than the rule. Over $500 billion in federal grant funds were awarded last year and only a small fraction of grantees will have their expenditures disallowed or experience a problem with an audit. In most cases, your existing personnel, accounting, and purchasing procedures will be adequate. If you must make changes in your system to ensure the adequate handling of federal funds, however, do so. Such changes will increase the credibility of your system.

With the increase in consortia grants and grants with several co-principal investigators who may be with different nonprofit organizations, you will be required to list one partner as the official fiscal agent for the funds. All partners must comply with relevant Office of Management and Budget (OMB) circulars that govern how federal funds can be expended by each organization. If your nonprofit is not experienced in federal grants management, include a college or university partner in your consortia and ask it to be the fiscal agent. Colleges and universities have experience in this area and have the software systems in place to comply with the guidelines.

The Federal Grants Requirement Worksheet (Exhibit 18.1) will help you comply with most federal grant requirements. If your institution has a grants administration office, this worksheet may not be necessary, but you, the project director, still need to know the facts so that you can help in the overall administration of your grant.

Federal Grants Requirement Worksheet

The Federal Grants Requirement Worksheet will help you familiarize yourself with and keep abreast of the basic obligations your nonprofit organization agrees to fulfill by accepting federal grant funds.

1. Complete the first section of the worksheet when you receive notice of funding. Include the federal account identification number and all other information you can supply. It is critical that you record the actual start date or date funded so that you do not charge any grant expenditures before the grant's official award date. Review your project planner and record the dates on which you must supply progress indicators, milestones, or progress reports.
2. List the OMB circulars that will govern your grant expenditures (see Exhibit 18.3 at the end of this chapter) and where the circulars are located.
3. Record any information about the number of years of funding that can be applied for.
4. Indicate the percentage and dollar total of the cost-sharing or matching fund requirements, where the records will be kept, and who will be responsible for keeping them.
5. Acceptance of federal funds requires that your organization have a policy regarding drug use and counseling of employees.
6. If your grant calls for the creation of unique materials, make note of the rules regarding copyrights, patents, ownership, and use. Noting these in advance reduces problems later.
7. The fair and equal employment rules are reasonable and should pose no problems for most nonprofit organizations.
8. List the office or person responsible for approval of projects that involve copyrights or patents, or the use of human and animal subjects, recombinant DNA, or radioactive material. If you work for an organization that already has institutional review boards, be sure to check with those groups. If your organization does not have institutional review boards or committees, do not initiate them. Instead, involve a university- or college-related individual on your grants advisory committee, and ask him or her to use his or her institution's review board.

EXHIBIT 18.1
Federal Grants Requirement Worksheet

Project Title: _____

Project Director: _____

Federal Account Identification Number: _____

Agency Staff: _____

Agency Phone Number: _____ Agency Fax Number: _____

Agency Email: _____

Notification of Award Received on (Date): _____

Start Date of Project: _____ End Date of Project: _____

Dates Reports are Due: _____

Final Report Due On (Date): _____

Number of Years Funding Can Be Applied For: _____

Matching or In-Kind Requirements: _____% $ _____

Where Matching or In-Kind Records Will Be Kept: _____

Who Will Be Responsible for Keeping Them: _____

Federal Rules Governing This Grant

OMB Circulars/Guidelines Governing Grant Expenditures:

_____

_____

Location of OMB Circulars/Guidelines Governing Grant Expenditures:

_____

_____

Special Rules and Federal Management Circulars (List from Assurances Section of Proposal):

_____

_____

Location of Special Rules and Federal Management Circulars:

_____

_____

Federal Rules and Your Organization's Policy On
Copyrights: _____

_____

Patents: _____

_____

Drug Usage and Counseling: _____

Fair and Equal Employment: _____

_____

(continued)

EXHIBIT 18.1
(Continued)

Institutional Review Boards (Include Person Responsible for Compliance and Approval)

Human Subjects:

_____

_____

Animal Subjects:

_____

_____

Recombinant DNA:

_____

_____

Radioactive Material:

_____

_____

Research Misconduct:

_____

_____

Other:

_____

_____

Even though your proposal may not call for the performance of hard-core research, the federal government is very broad in its interpretation of what activities pose a potential danger to humans. In fact, federal officials require human subjects' approval for most needs assessment surveys, model projects, and demonstration grants.

Raising and Documenting Matching Funds

One of the more confusing areas of federal grants is the requirement of matching funds or in-kind contributions (also known as *cost sharing*). An organization can be asked to supply cash, services, or facilities to match a percentage of the grant. This requirement may change over the years that federal funds support the project. For example, year 1 may require a 20 percent match, year 2 a 40 percent match, and year 3 a 50 percent match.

EXHIBIT 18.2
Worksheet on Sources of Matching Funds

Project Title: _____

Total Project Cost: $ _____

Match Required: _____% $ _____

Review each of the following sources of matching funds. Check with federal
officials to ensure that your match is in compliance with their rules and will be
accepted. Make sure that nothing listed under your match has been provided
from federal funds.

1. Personnel—List the percentage of time and effort of each individual who will
   be contributing to the match. Include salaries, wages, and fringe benefits.

   Options:

   Include the time and effort of volunteers, consultants, and corporate sponsors
   if allowable by the grantor.

   If the project calls for staff training or development, will your organization be
   required to increase salaries? If so, check with the grantor to see whether this
   can be listed as a match.

2. Equipment—List any equipment that will be purchased primarily to carry out
   this project. Include the cost of each piece and the total equipment cost.

3. Facilities—List the location, square footage, and cost per foot for each facility
   and the total facilities (space) cost.

4. Foundation/Corporate Grantors—What other grantors could you approach for
   a grant to match this grant?

   Foundations:

   Corporations:

5. Fundraising Activities—In some cases you may have to resort to fundraising
   activities to develop your matching portion. List the activities and the net
   return expected from each.

   Special Events (Dance, Raffle, etc.):

   Sales of Products:

   Other:

In some cases, the federal instructions state that a match is not required but
encouraged. If you have inquired into this matter, discovered that a match
will help you get funded, and have designated a specific amount in your
budget for a match or in-kind contribution, be aware that this match must be
documented and will be subject to an audit to verify the amount. It is always
wise to document and list the efforts and costs that will be provided by your

organization and partners. Review your project planner for any personnel, consultants, contract services, supplies, equipment, or materials that will be contributed to your project. Remember not to list anything that is being supplied to this grant that was provided under any other federal program.

The Worksheet on Sources of Matching Funds (Exhibit 18.2) can help you plan a successful matching funds campaign before you approach federal agencies. The worksheet contains several standard methods for cost sharing and provides an evaluation system for each method. (This worksheet can also be useful when working with foundations and corporations that request matching support.)

Federal Grants Management Circulars

The highly regulated, detailed rules about grants management are probably the most imposing characteristics of federal grants. These rules may specify allowable costs, indirect cost rates, accounting requirements, and the like. Before getting involved in government grants, you and your accounting department should review the appropriate grants management circulars. Such a review usually diminishes fears about your organization's ability to comply with federal grant requirements. In most cases you will find that your organization, from purchasing to personnel, has safeguards in effect that meet the requirements. If there are areas that look as if they may pose a problem, they can be addressed in a general manner for all federal grants, or handled separately case by case to avoid any difficulties.

The OMB produces circulars outlining uniform standards for financial dealings with government granting agencies. These circulars can be accessed online at www.whitehouse.gov/omb/circulars. To obtain circulars that are not available online, call the OMB's information line at (202) 395-3080.

The following section is a broad description of OMB Circular A-110.

OMB Circular A-110

OMB Circular A-110 is titled "Uniform Administrative Requirements for Grants and Agreements with Institutions of Higher Education, Hospitals, and Other Non-Profit Organizations." This circular sets forth standards for obtaining consistency and uniformity among federal agencies in the administration of grants and agreements with institutions of higher education, hospitals, and other nonprofit organizations. The circular is divided into the following four subparts:

- Subpart A—General
- Subpart B—Pre-Award Requirements
- Subpart C—Post-Award Requirements
  - Financial and Program Management
  - Property Standards
  - Procurement Standards
  - Reports and Records
  - Termination and Enforcement
- Subpart D—After-the-Award Requirements

OMB Circular A-110 also includes an appendix that addresses contract provisions.

Other Grants Management OMB Circulars

Colleges and universities will also be interested in OMB Circular A-21, which defines cost principles for federal research and development grants to educational institutions. All nonprofit organizations should familiarize themselves with OMB Circular A-122, "Cost Principles for Non-Profit Organizations," and state and local governments must also review OMB Circular A-102, "Grants and Cooperative Agreements with State and Local Governments." Please be advised that you should always refer to the most current circular of the specific rules and regulations in your area.

Exhibit 18.3 lists all of the grants management OMB circulars in numerical sequence. Be sure to request the appropriate OMB circulars for your type of organization and review the rules with your fiscal staff.

EXHIBIT 18.3
Grants Management OMB Circulars

Cost Principles

A-21, Educational Institutions
A-87, State, Local and Indian Tribal Governments
A-122, Non-Profit Organizations

Administrative Requirements

A-102, State and Local Governments
A-110, Institutions of Higher Education, Hospitals, and Other Non-Profit Organizations

Audit Requirements

A-133, States, Local Governments, and Non-Profit Organizations

---

19

Dealing with the Decision of Public Funding Sources

THE FEDERAL GOVERNMENT has continued to make improvements in the entire grants process. This includes making award determinations that are understandable and consistent across all of its agencies and one thousand granting programs. Instead of making determinations that left grantseekers confused (such as "supportable but not fundable") most federal granting agencies now use the following determinations:

- Accepted as written and at the requested amount of funding
- Accepted with modifications (usually budget modifications that will affect some activities)
- Rejected with reviewers' comments (the proposal did not reach the level or score required for funding, but comments have been included, possibly to encourage resubmittal)
- Rejected without reviewers' comments (the proposal did not reach the level required to invest the time necessary to respond to the proposal in detail, no comments were included, and thus the grantseeker has no idea whether to resubmit)

Accepted

If your proposal is accepted as constructed and at the requested amount, consider taking the following steps:

1. Thank the grantor. Whether you are notified by phone, letter, or e-mail, send the program or project officer a thank-you letter expressing your appreciation for the time and effort staff and reviewers expended on your proposal.
2. Request the reviewers' comments, and include your e-mail address.
3. Ask the federal officer for insight into what you could have done better. Yes, you can even improve a funded proposal. Learn how.
4. Invite the program or project officer for a site visit.
5. Ask the official what mistakes other grantees often make in carrying out their funded grant so you can be sure to avoid those errors.
6. Review the reporting requirements. What does the grantor require (milestones, progress indicators, budget documentation, changes in budget categories, and so on) and when?

Accepted with Budget Modifications

Should your proposal be accepted with budget modifications, do the following:

1. Send the funding source a thank-you letter.
2. E-mail or call the funding source and suggest that the program officer refer to your project planner to negotiate the budget terms.
3. Discuss the option of reducing some of the project's methods or activities to arrive at the amount the funding source has in mind or was recommended by the reviewers.
4. If several activities must be eliminated, consider dropping the accomplishment of an objective or reducing the expected degree of change.
5. If you are forced to negotiate away the supporting structure necessary to achieve your objectives or prove or disapprove your hypothesis, be prepared to turn down the funds. After all, you do not want to enter into an agreement that will cause you to lose credibility later.
6. If your project planner or other spreadsheet program was not allowed to be submitted with your proposal or as an attachment, ask to send it to them now to assist in evaluating the impact of any budget changes or reductions.

Rejected with Comments

If your proposal is rejected but reviewer suggestions and comments are provided, review them. Are there comments or suggestions common to several of the reviewers? Do the comments point to a basic problem with the approach or protocol or with the importance of dealing with the problem in general? Do the reviewers suggest changes that you entertain in a resubmittal without dramatically altering your grants approach? Do the comments suggest resubmittal?

If you get the sense from the reviewers' comments that resubmittal with the suggested changes is a good idea, consider the following:

1. Send the funding official a thank-you letter or e-mail in appreciation for his or her time and effort as well as that of the reviewers and staff. Let the funding official know that although you were aware of the risk of failure before you invested your time in applying, you would appreciate assistance in changing your proposal and reapplying.
2. Ask the funding official for more suggestions.
3. Find out whether your proposal could possibly be funded as a pilot project, as a needs assessment, or in some other way.
4. Ask whether there are any ways the funding source could assist you in getting ready for the next submission cycle, such as conducting a preliminary review.
5. Ask whether it would be wise for you to reapply. What are your chances and what would you have to change? (Reapply if the program officer is even the slightest bit optimistic.)
6. Ask whether you could become a reviewer to learn more about the review process and how to improve your proposal.

By examining the reviewers' comments you may find that some reviewers scored a section of your proposal outstanding, while others gave the same section a low score. This situation can create a dilemma. Changing your proposal to reflect one reviewer's comments may negate another reviewer's comments, and your changes could result in resubmission scores that are just average. Ask the grantor what you can do about this situation. Also, ask an outside expert to review your proposal; even if you must pay someone to review the proposal, you need insight into what is causing the discrepancy.

Your resubmittal application should take the reviewers' comments to heart and the changes you make in your proposal should reflect them. You may even mention that the changes made in your resubmittal were suggested by the original reviewers. Sending the same proposal in hopes of different reviewers and a better outcome is not viewed positively. Some reapplications will require you to address the changes between the revised proposal and your initial attempt in a separate section of the proposal.

Rejected without Comments

Agency reviewing procedures call for a process that eliminates proposals with a low likelihood of funding from a thorough review. Some grantors even require that 25 to 50 percent of the applications they receive are given this brief and expedited review, and then returned to the applicants without reviewer comments. Many of the rejected applications that are not read thoroughly or evaluated and scored are believed to be of low quality and not likely to produce the intended outcomes. Often they are also cited for errors in the application itself or for nonallowable costs or inappropriate ideas.

If your proposal is rejected outright and you do not receive comments, or if you receive a notice stating that there are many more credible proposals than funding available, it may be necessary to develop a different approach and not even consider resubmitting the same proposal. It does no good to defend your proposal or to write a nasty response. When rejected, I like to think that I may be ahead of my time and more visionary than the reviewers. Discuss options with your advisory group and brainstorm a different approach to solving the problem.

In addition, write or e-mail the program officer to thank him or her for the opportunity and ask if you could:

1. Be a reviewer to learn how to prepare a better proposal.
2. Meet with him or her to discuss a new approach.

No matter what the determination (accepted, accepted with modifications, rejected with comments, or rejected without comments), or the degree to which your proposal was reviewed, your response to your grant application's outcome must be positive. Whether you are jubilant or depressed, thank the grantor and demonstrate your willingness to learn from the experience and, if possible, the funding source's feedback.

Be sure to put a reminder to deal with the funder's decision on your action steps chart so you do not forget to send a thank-you (see Figure 19.1).

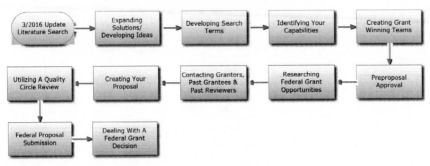

FIGURE 19.1
Action Steps Chart: Dealing with a Federal Grant Decision

20

Follow-Up with Government Funding Sources

THE OBJECTIVE OF FOLLOW-UP is to position yourself as an asset to funding sources while avoiding being a pest. You want to develop professional relationships and maintain contact with funding sources throughout the whole grants process, not just at submittal and award time. In addition to advising funders of your willingness to serve as a reviewer, consider:

- sending them copies of your accepted articles
- forwarding notes on special articles or books in your area to them
- inviting them to visit your organization
- asking whether they would like to speak at your professional group or association's conference, or at a special grants conference
- asking them what meeting or conferences they will be attending so that you can look them up
- requesting information about what you can do to have an impact on legislation affecting their funding levels or allocations

By remaining on a grantor's internet mailing list (like the *National Science Foundation Update*) or reviewing the *Federal Register,* you will get news of their activities, services, and next funding opportunities. Do not wait until next year's deadline to begin thinking about your ensuing application. Start to plan for next year right after funding decisions are made for the current year.

The best way to learn what is going on is to visit the funding source personally. Keep in touch. Watch for meeting announcements in the *Federal Register.* Testify at committee hearings that will affect the agency and its funding level. Send the agency blind copies of your efforts to have an impact on legislation and increased appropriations for the program. By doing so, you are helping to ensure that its program receives continued funding. It ensures that they have a job, and that you continue to have a funding source. Use your association memberships and legislative committees to push for changes that benefit the particular agency, and write to Senate and House appropriations committees to request increased funding. Attend professional meetings and sessions where program officers are speaking, and ask questions.

Developing Continued Grant Support

Although federal officials may change jobs and positions, they seem to re-appear again and again. A systematic approach to recording research on funding sources and officials will prove useful as you come across old friends and make new ones. By maintaining your relationships, whether you have received funding or not, you demonstrate to funding sources that you plan to be around for a while and that you will not forget them as soon as you receive their checks. Unfortunately, changes in staffing at government agencies make maintaining contacts more difficult. Just when things are going great, the program officers you have been working with will move on. But take heart; they may appear again somewhere down the grants road, so keep on their good side!

If you have used the concepts presented in this manual to develop a proactive grants process, you have a system that alerts you to changes in program rules, deadlines, and the like through the *Federal Register,* mailing lists, personal contacts, and established links. The key to continued success is to repeat these steps that have brought you to this point.

Part 3
PRIVATE/FOUNDATION FUNDING OPPORTUNITIES

21

Understanding the Foundation Grants Marketplace

I F YOU DID NOT TAKE THE MARKETPLACE QUIZ in chapter 11, you may be about to make a frequent, but deadly, mistake that 75 percent of my seminar participants make as they approach foundation grant opportunities. They overestimate the amount of foundation grant funding. When asked to estimate the percentage foundation grants accounted for in 2013's $335 billion of private philanthropy, they guessed that it was 35 to 40 percent. In reality it was only 15 percent, or $48.96 billion. This actuality must be taken into consideration when planning your foundation grants strategy.

The foundation grants marketplace can be very rewarding in terms of the types of projects funded and the relatively high rate of success (50 percent or better) that is achievable when the correct strategies are implemented. Chapter 22 will build on the knowledge you need to succeed in this marketplace and show you how to do the research necessary to determine the best foundation for your proposal. Incorporating the following marketplace data in your pursuit of foundation grants should dictate your approach and ultimately increase your success rate.

The Foundation Center through its Foundation Stats (http://foundation center.org) collects and publishes data on the size, scope, and giving priorities of U.S. foundations. Their most recent data indicate that there were 86,192 foundations in 2012. I project that the number of foundations has and will increase as the baby boomer population ages and seeks ways to shield some of their wealth from taxes and provide a legacy for their values.

It is important to understand that foundations are established by individuals, families, or organizations to further their areas of interest and support what *they* want, and not to support what you and your organization want. You are an instrument through which the foundation grantors can reinforce their values and accomplish what they want to do. Your task is to match your projects with their values so they can meet their needs through you at a price they can afford. Do not waste your time or the grantor's time trying to convince them to change their values to match yours.

The Internal Revenue Service (IRS) requires foundations to grant at least 5 percent of the value of their assets each year. Most foundations are heavily invested in stocks, bonds, and certificates of deposit. These investments took a tremendous hit in the recession. According to the *Chronicle of Philanthropy,* foundations are seeing surges in the current economic recovery, although most have still not recovered from the loss of assets seen during the recession. In 2013, assets for eighty-three of the largest foundations saw an estimated increase of 7.5 percent over 2012. However, sixty-six of the eighty-three foundations were still 16.5 percent below their 2007 asset levels and 6.4 percent below their 2007 level of giving (grant making).[1] In short, be conservative in your foundation grant requests!

As you know, government grant programs provide online assistance, allow personal contact, and make data readily available regarding guidelines, scoring rubrics, and review systems. This is all possible because the federal government has thousands of employees. Contrast this to foundation staff levels, which are very low. For example, in 2009 the Foundation Center surveyed 11,617 foundations. Of the foundations surveyed, only 27.4 percent, or 3,178, reported having *any* staff and the median number of staff for foundations reporting staff was 2.0 (foundationcenter.org/findfunders/statistics). The same survey indicated that only 26.1 percent of the foundations surveyed, or 3,035 of the 11,617, maintained a website. With these facts in mind, it is not surprising that only a few of the largest foundations provide any assistance or allow for personal contact. Most will only state that you need to send them a one- or two-page letter proposal or letter of inquiry.

Besides having few or no staff members, the vast majority of foundations do not have expert reviewers to review your proposals, nor do they publish review criteria. In addition, little is known about their decision-making strategy. These factors make it difficult for the rejected grantee to improve a proposal for resubmittal.

Nonprofit organizations have been publically expressing concern regarding transparency in the foundation grants process. They want information on the review process, similar to that available in the federal grants marketplace. This includes information on best practices and how foundations measure grantee performance. While this information would certainly help grantseekers, it would require foundation grantors to hire staff. At this point, most foundations only contact the awarded grantees because they have no staff to send rejection notices to the unsuccessful, let alone reviewers' comments on how to improve and resubmit.

In addition, just a handful of foundations use electronic submission. Why would they want more proposals when it is doubtful that they can (or do) read all that they currently receive? If foundations were more transparent and let grantseekers know what they were truly interested in supporting, they might receive fewer but more focused proposals. If they developed websites that included sample winning proposals, scoring rubrics, breakdowns of support by organization, and a range of awards, they might get proposals they are willing to read and fund.

But remember this is not your money or taxpayers' money. It is the money of the individuals who used their wealth to create the foundation and thus we must follow the golden rule of grantseeking, "Those who have the gold make the rules." However, since these wealthy individuals were provided an IRS tax break, they must provide the grantseeker with a copy of their 990 IRS foundation tax return. This provides you with the ability to figure out what the foundation has supported. You will learn more about how to use this in your research in the following chapter.

Most novice grantseekers get a computer printout of foundations interested in their general area and create a generic proposal (sort of a one-size-fits-all approach). They then send this self-focused proposal on what they want to all the foundations they can. This approach is almost guaranteed to fail. Some grantseekers may look at the average size of grants from a foundation but forget that average can provide you with a faulty conclusion. Some foundations may choose to fund millions to one nonprofit organization and the rest of their funded proposals average only a few thousand. The median size for foundation grants (one-half above and one-half below) is only $30,000. We read about the big awards and assume that they are common. Good research will provide you with the data to develop a tailored proposal, which is the focus of chapter 24.

To fully understand private foundations you need to think like the wealthy individuals who create them and serve on their boards. Let us assume you have created a foundation to move vast sums of your wealth into a tax-deductible entity that will allow you, your family, and friends to fund projects and organizations that further your values, beliefs, and life's work. As you already know, according to IRS rules, you must give away at least 5 percent of the market value of your foundation's assets each year to nonprofit groups your bylaws designate as recipients or the IRS will penalize your foundation and levy a tax. However, the costs related to the administration of your foundation (that is, staffing, office space, equipment, travel, board salaries, and so

TABLE 21.1
Grantseekers' Private Foundation Decision Matrix

Type of Foundation	Geographic Need	Type of Project	Grant Award Size for Field of Interest	Image	Credentials of P.I./P.D.	Preproposal Contact	Application	Review System	Grants Admin. (Rules)
National General Purpose	National need-local regional population	Model, Innovative	Large, medium	National image	National	Write, phone, email	Short concept paper—longer form if interested	Staff and some peer review	Few audits and rules
Special Purpose	Need in area of interest	Model, Innovative, Research	Large to small	Image not as critical as solution	Strong image in field of interest	Write, phone, email	Short concept paper—longer form if interested	Board review (some staff)	Few audits and rules
Community	Local need	Operation, Replication, Building/Equipment	Small	Local image	Respected locally	Write, phone, email, go see	Short letter proposal	Board review	Few audits and rules
Family	Varies—but geographic concern for need	Innovative, Replication, Building/Equipment, Some Research	Medium, Small	Regional image	Local, Regional	Write, phone, email	Short letter proposal	Board review	Very few audits and rules
Nonprofits, Service Clubs, etc.	Local	Replication, Building/Equipment, Scholarship	Small	Local image and member involvement	Local	Write, phone, email, present to committee or member	Short letter proposal	Committee review and/or member vote	Few audits and rules

forth) are included in this 5 percent. For instance, if the market value of your foundation's assets is $10 million, and you decide to disburse the minimum required amount of 5 percent or $500,000, you can subtract from this the cost of your director, support staff, office, and overhead, which could easily reach $250,000, leaving you only $250,000 to give away in the form of grants. So what can you do to reduce your administrative costs and increase the portion of the 5 percent you can distribute through the grants process? You can decide not to hire a director, create an office, or have a staff. After all, you do not need a staff or reviewers. You know what you want to fund; thus, you want to make as much money as possible available for grants. In addition, to avoid receiving lots of proposals from well-intended nonprofits, you stipulate that applicants are preselected and that application is by invitation only. Now you are thinking like the creator of a foundation.

To be a successful foundation grantseeker, you must discover what your prospective foundation funding source values, seek to understand how it looks at the world, and present your project in such a way that to reject it would actually conflict with the foundation's values, stated beliefs, and past giving patterns. Review chapter 3 and the concept of values-based grantseeking to increase your understanding of private foundations and what motivates the individuals who create them. To further assist you in the research process, read the following description of the basic types of foundations and then review the Grantseekers' Private Foundation Decision Matrix (Table 21.1) to help you select which of the four basic types of private foundations is right for your project: national general purpose, special purpose, community, or family. Please note that there is not an established criterion for these classifications and the information provided here is to help you develop a rough idea of the types of foundations that compose the total number of foundations.

National General Purpose Foundations

To be designated as a national general purpose foundation, a foundation does not need to fit a hard-and-fast definition. *National general purpose* refers to the foundation's scope and type of granting patterns. Foundations in this group have a philanthropic interest in several subject areas and make grants for proposals that will have a broad-scale impact across the United States and the world. They prefer model, creative, innovative projects that other groups can replicate to solve the same or similar problems. Since national general purpose foundations like to promote change, they do not usually fund deficits, operating income, or the many necessary but not highly visible or creative functions of organizations. Recently a growing number have been funding operating costs because the nonprofit organizations they depend on to do the work they value may not be around to apply if the nonprofits cannot make payroll.

National general purpose foundations have staff and, in some instances, use professional consultants as reviewers. Their applications are usually longer than those of the other types of foundations, and they often have more rules and regulations. They expect those they fund to have major players and experts on staff and in consortia, and their grant size is larger than those of other foundations. In addition, they are likely to have websites.

Of the 86,192 foundations in 2012, there were probably less than 300 national general purpose foundations. Even though there are so few, most people have no trouble naming one, such as the Rockefeller or Ford Foundation. This is because they get a lot of attention for the size of the awards they make and the initiatives they launch. Unfortunately, the public image of these well-known foundations is what leads many grantseekers into thinking that the foundation marketplace in general makes more and bigger grants that it actually does.

Special Purpose Foundations

Often confused with national general purpose foundations because some are very large and financed by unusually large asset bases, special purpose foundations are different in that they define their area of concern quite specifically. For example, the Robert Wood Johnson Foundation is a special purpose foundation in the health field, and the Exxon Education Foundation and the Carnegie Foundation for the Advancement of Teaching are special purpose foundations focusing on education. While grant sizes can be considerable, special purpose foundations put the applicant's likelihood of making a contribution or a breakthrough in their area of concern foremost and *may* put less importance on staff prestige, publishing, and so forth.

There are probably only a few hundred of these dedicated special purpose foundations, and the key to success in this marketplace is to match your project with the foundation's specific area of interest and to demonstrate how your project will impact it.

Community Foundations

According to the Foundation Center, there were 750 community foundations in the United States in 2011. Although they use a variety of geographic parameters to define *community*, community foundations are easy to identify because their name denotes the area the serve (for example, San Diego Foundation, Cleveland Foundation, North Dakota Foundation, and Oregon Foundation). They may even cite the zip codes of the areas they fund within.

Some think that community foundations are family foundations that restrict their granting to a particular state, city, or zip code. This is not the case. There is a trend, however, that small family foundations place their assets in the community foundation and let them do all the IRS compliances. In many cases, family foundations use proposal submissions to community foundations to screen their proposals and recommend funding. Community foundations develop their own asset bases and fund projects and programs that no other type of foundation would consider supporting. Their donors are community members (or past members), many of whom put a bequest in their will to provide the foundation with funds that will provide benefits to the community they loved. Some may place restrictions on who and what is eligible. Community foundations exist to deal with local needs. They fund areas from program deficits, to operating funds, to seed money for a needs assessment that might lead to a larger state or federal grant. They do not care if prospective grantees have national stature in their field. They just want to make sure that the funds they grant will be used to make a difference in the communities they serve. In general, community foundations are concerned with what works and are more interested in supporting the replication of successful projects than in taking chances with experimental approaches or research.

Many community foundations have special programs that help smaller family foundations by administering their investments and assisting them in soliciting applications, selecting grantees, and meeting their IRS reporting requirements. The community foundations may sponsor a grants forum or focus meeting for these smaller, local foundations, but most of these grantors actually fall under the family foundation category.

Family Foundations

There were approximately 38,671 grant-making family foundations in 2010. These foundations represented more than half of all independent foundations and accounted for $20.6 billion in grants. Because their granting patterns represent the value of the family members whose interests have been memorialized by the creation of the foundations, granting patterns of family foundations vary widely from foundation to foundation and change frequently. Therefore, you must research them thoroughly to keep abreast of changes in interests and commitment.

According to the Foundation Center, larger family foundations included in their 2010 grants sample favored health and education, directed the biggest share of their giving for programs, and prioritized giving for the economically disadvantaged.

Sixty-two percent of family foundations reported less than $1 million in assets in 2010, and most funded locally in small amounts. In fact, 49 percent gave less than $50,000 in 2010. However, if they value what you propose, and you are in the right locale, you should consider them when developing your grants plan.

Nonprofit Organizations, Membership Groups, Professional Societies, and Service Clubs

In addition to the four basic types of private foundations, many nonprofit organizations, membership groups, professional societies, and service clubs award grants, and many even have foundations attached to them. The awards made through these groups are usually small and limited to a special field of interest. For example, a Kiwanis group may choose to provide support only for the purpose of improving business education in local schools.

The application forms used by these groups are typically short and easy to complete, and they will often provide funding for things that the four basic types of foundations would not consider supporting. While they have been known to provide matching funds for government grants, support for travel to conferences and meetings, and honorariums for experts and guest lecturers, they are particularly interested in funding things that will improve their image and the image of their members in the community.

Types of Grants Made by Private Foundations

The major vehicle of support by private foundations is a cash grant or award. The majority of foundations do not make grants to individuals except in the form of scholarships, and even those may be made through educational institutions. Most private foundations prefer the third-party 501(c)(3) tax-exempt organization affiliated with the grantee handle and disburse the award.

Program-related investments (PRIs) and mission-related investments (MRIs) are alternatives to cash grants and awards, and foundations that make them do so as a supplement to their existing grant programs.

In the PRI vehicle, your organization applies to a foundation for a low-interest loan, venture capital, or an investment in a charitable-use property.

PRIs are often made to organizations with an established relationship with the grant maker. A large portion of PRI dollars support affordable housing and community development. PRI support has also been provided for a variety of capital projects such as preserving historical buildings, repairing churches, emergency loans to social service agencies, and protecting and preserving open space and wildlife habitats. For private foundations, PRIs are eligible to count against the 5 percent payout that foundations are required to make each year to retain their tax-exempt status.

MRIs are market-rate investments that support the mission of the foundation by generating a positive social or environmental impact, while generating reasonably competitive rates of financial return. They use foundation assets—as distinct from grants budgets—to achieve a public benefit. They broadly support foundations' missions and programmatic goals and do not count toward a foundation's charitable distribution requirements.

Known as *mission investing,* only 14 percent of the 1,200 foundations surveyed by the Foundation Center in 2011 engaged in PRIs and MRIs. While this form of investing accounted for only a small percentage of the billions in total foundation giving, it should be considered as a potential component of your grants plan. However, if you are interested in seeking PRIs and MRIs, you must do careful research on the foundation first to ensure that it is interested in this type of work.

Another type of foundation that is a financial force in many local communities is the private grant-making health foundation created from the conversion of nonprofit hospitals and health maintenance organization to for-profit status. Federal law requires that proceeds from the sale of assets of tax-exempt entities go to charity. One way this requirement can be met is to establish a foundation to benefit the community previously served by the nonprofit. Most of the private grants-making health foundations are dedicated to funding health-related projects, although some define health broadly and do provide funding for a variety of community purposes.

Grantseekers' Private Foundation Decision Matrix

The Grantseekers' Private Foundation Decision Matrix (see Table 21.1) summarizes the principal types of private foundation funding sources, their major funding characteristics and preferences, and their similarities and differences. Familiarizing yourself with this information will help you create a prioritized list of the best foundations to approach and to determine the appropriate amount of funding to request from each.

Keep in mind that the size of the majority of foundation grant awards is smaller than grantseekers think. Instead of making the mistake of asking for an inappropriate amount of funding from one foundation, consider breaking your proposal into fundable parts with each part appealing to the values and grant award sizes of a different type of foundation funder.

Column 1 of the matrix lists the major foundation funding source types. Columns 2 through 10 provide information on variables such as geographic area, need, type of project, and award size. Please note that the matrix is meant to point you in the right direction only. Follow-up research will allow the proactive grantseeker to further estimate the funder's interest, the appropriateness of the project, and the proper grant size to request before proposal preparation and submission.

To achieve grants success you must be vigilant in attempting to consider all aspects of your proposal from the grantor's point of view. It should be increasingly evident that the "one proposal fits all" method of grantseeking will not meet with a positive response from such a diverse group of private grantors.

Who and What Private Foundations Fund

Most foundations award the majority of their funding in the states where they are located, and unfortunately, there is a great disparity in the number of foundations from state to state. In fact in 2011, 46 percent of the fifty largest foundations by total giving were located in just two of the fifty states (California and New York).

If you are located in one of the other forty-eight states, remember that even nonprofit organizations in states with none of the fifty largest foundations, still attract some grants from foundations located in other states. For example, North Dakota is a state with none of the largest foundations. Yet in a 2011 national sample of grants awarded by one thousand of the largest foundations, North Dakota was still able to attract 242 grants totaling $27,719,524.

Instead of spending time rationalizing that your project fits into a grantor's funding priorities, spend your time considering the areas in which foundations concentrate their support and how you can redefine your project to fit into those areas with the greatest percentage of foundation grants. Table 21.2 illustrates foundation grants by recipient category. A quick review of this table demonstrates that human services receives the greatest percentage of foundation grants at 27.7 percent, with education second at 19 percent.

TABLE 21.2
Foundation Grants by Recipient Category

Recipient Category	Percentage of Foundation Grants
Human Services	27
Education	19
Health	13
Arts/Culture	13
Public Affairs/Society Benefit	12
Environment and Animals	7
Religion	3
International Affairs, Development, Peace, and Human Rights	2
Science and Technology	2
Social Science	1
Other	<1

Source: Foundation Center, Distribution of Grants from FC 1000 Foundations by Subject Area, 2011, http://data.foundationcenter.org.

Unfortunately, the data on what subject areas receive what amount of foundation grant support is not always accurate, consistent, or up to date. For example, the Foundation Center's last report on the distribution of grants by subject area is from 2012 and is based on one thousand of the largest foundations. The percentages in Table 21.2 may or may not be applicable to *all* of the 2012 foundations or to *all* of today's foundations. However, they can begin to help you define your projects by categories and provide you with an estimate of your potential for foundation support in your subject area.

Within each recipient category, you should examine the subcategories to determine which gets the largest part of the money. Table 21.3 breaks education into several categories and shows that of the grants given to education, elementary and secondary received the greatest percentage, followed by higher education. With this in mind, if higher education is your project's original focus and you redefine it to include an elementary or secondary component by partnering with a school, you could substantially increase your chances of receiving a grant from a foundation. While I do not want you to become a sheep in wolf's clothing by making your project look like something it is not, review how you can redefine your project (chapter 7) and think how a consortium or a different lead partner would provide a much better match to foundation interests and granting patterns.

TABLE 21.3
Percent of Foundation Grants by Education Subcategory

Education Subcategories	Percent of Education Grants by Subcategory
Elementary and Secondary	39
Higher Education	31
Education Services	13
Graduate/Professional	7
Student Services	4
Library Science/Libraries	3
Adult and Continuing	1
Policy Management and Information	1
Vocational and Technical	1

Source: Foundation Center, Distributions of Grants from FC 1000 Foundations to U.S. Recipients, for Education, 2011, http://data.foundationcenter.org.

Also review the *type* of support you are searching for (that is, building or renovations, program development, research, and so on), and ask yourself if you could change your focus slightly (redefine it) to appeal to more grantors because of their preferences for certain types of support. Table 21.4 shows types of support by percentage of dollar value of grants. Based on this information, if you were seeking a grant to fund computer equipment and software, you would not expect to attract a foundation grant since computer technology accounts for only 0.5 percent of the total awarded by percentage of dollar value. Further research on the Foundation Center's website reveals, in a sample of over 1,122 larger foundations, that this area attracted only 809 grants of the 215,217 awarded.

By redefining how the computer equipment and software was going to be used and by whom, you could refocus on a type of support that would increase your chances for funding. For example, if you could demonstrate that it was to be used in conjunction with program development, you would dramatically increase your chances since program development received 55 percent of the total awarded by percentage of dollar value. When redefining your project you should also take into consideration the average dollar value of grants. For instance, the average dollar value for a computer technology grant is $150,327, while the average size for a program development grant is $200,829. (The average dollar value of grants for each type of support is available at *Giving USA 2012: The Annual Report on Philanthropy for Year 2011*.)

TABLE 21.4
Types of Support Awarded by Percentage of Dollar Value of Grants, 2011

Type of Support	Percentage of Dollar Value of Grants
General Support	28.6
Capital Support	21.2
Capital Campaigns	1.7
Building/Renovations	8.8
Computer Technology	0.5
Equipment	0.8
Land Acquisition	0.2
Endowments	4.9
Debt Reduction	0.1
Collections Acquisition	4.2
Program Support	55.0
Program Development	43.9
Conferences/Seminars	0.9
Faculty/Staff Development	0.8
Curriculum Development	1.3
Electronic Median/Online Services	1.8
Seed Money	3.9
All Other	2.4
Research	16.8
Student Aid Funds	3.1
Other	2.0
Not Specified	16.7

Source: *Giving USA 2012: The Annual Report on Philanthropy for Year 2011.*

The private foundation grants marketplace is misunderstood not only by individual grantseekers, but also by entire institutions that have added to the confusion by arbitrarily deciding that government grant applications and contracts should go through a university grants office and that foundation grant proposals should be handled by an institution's development office. One reason in support of this decision is that the development office in most universities is tied to a university foundation: the 501(c)(3) entity required to submit proposals. However, the problem lies in the fact that many development offices limit the access that faculty members have to private foundations so that the development office can use the foundation marketplace to attempt to fund administrative priorities, such as capital campaigns and endowments. This problem is compounded by the fact that only a small percentage of foundation dollars is actually awarded to fund these types of capital support projects (1.7 percent for capital campaigns and 4.9 percent for endowments). For example, a quick review of Table 21.4 (types of support) demonstrates clearly that foundations prefer to fund the types of projects that emanate from faculty, such as program and research grants (over 49 percent of the number of grants awarded and over 71 percent of the dollar value).

While some universities have dealt with this issue by developing two separate 501 (c)(3) tax-exempt entities, one for the university's overall grants effort and another for its development effort, one thing is critical for the grantseeker to understand. The quest for a private foundation grant needs to be coordinated within our institution or organization so that you can make sure you do not approach a foundation that is already being approached by several of your colleagues. Not only is this embarrassing, but it presents the prospective grantor with a negative image of you and your institution.

Many foundations allow only one proposal from one institution at one time and will immediately disallow all of the proposals submitted by the institution if they receive multiple applications. To avoid this type of problem, use one or more of the research tools presented in chapter 22 to locate the foundation most suited to fund your project, and then develop a profile of what it funds. Take this profile and Exhibit 10.1 to your grants or development office (or any other pertinent office) to gain approval to make preproposal contact. This will provide your institution with the heads-up it needs to ensure its integrity with prospective funding sources and to move you one step closer to grants success.

Note

1. Doug Donovan and Sarah Frostenson, "Foundation Assets Are Climbing, but Grants Are Still Competitive," *The Chronicle of Philanthropy*, March 23, 2014, http://philanthropy.com/article/Foundation-Assets-Reach/145407?cid=megamenu.

22

Researching Potential Private Foundation Grantors: How to Find the Foundation Best Suited to Fund Your Project

A KEY TO SUCCESSFUL GRANTSEEKING with foundations is to gather the most complete and accurate information possible on each foundation before you approach them. The whole point of your research effort is to focus on the sources most likely to fund your proposal. Even if you are a novice grantseeker, do not be tempted to send letter proposals to any and all foundations that are even remotely related to your project area. If preproposal contact is allowed or a proposed format is provided or suggested, take every opportunity to develop an individualized, tailored proposal for each of your best prospects.

The Foundation Research Form (Exhibit 22.1) will help you record valuable foundation data. Review Exhibit 22.1 carefully so you know what to look for and how to use this information. Complete one worksheet for each foundation you research. Seldom will you uncover all the data requested in Exhibit 22.1, but try to complete as much information on the form as possible, and remember that even a partially completed worksheet will help you make a more intelligent decision on whether you should solicit grant support from a particular foundation funding source.

For each foundation your research uncovers, look first at its areas of interest, activities funded, and geographic funding preferences. Do not even bother recording the foundation's name and address on the worksheet (see Exhibit 22.1) unless it funds your area of interest in your geographic area. You should think of yourself as a broker who is seeking to match the interests of each partner. If there is a match, move right to the money. Although foundations can grant more than the minimum 5 percent of their assets required

EXHIBIT 22.1
Foundation Research Form

The following form outlines the data you need to collect to make a decision
to seek funding from this grant source. Your attempts to collect as much of this
information as possible will prove rewarding. (When feasible, record the source
of the information and the date it was recorded.)

1. Name of Foundation: _____
   Address: _____
   Phone: _____ E-mail: _____
   Website _____

2. Contact Person: _____
   Title: _____
   Any Links from Our Organization to Contact Person: _____
   _____

3. Foundation's Areas of Interests: _____
   _____
   _____

4. Eligibility Requirements/Restrictions:
   a. Activities Funded/Restricted: _____
   _____
   _____

   b. Organizations Funded/Restricted: _____
   _____
   _____

   c. Geographic Funding Preferences/Restrictions: _____
   _____
   _____

   d. Other Requirements/Restrictions:
      Application Information _____
      Proposal Length/Restrictions _____
      Application Submittal _____
      Deadline Date(s) _____
      Submittal Rules _____

(continued)

EXHIBIT 22.1
(Continued)

5. *Information Available*   *In Possession Of*

   IRS 990-PF Tax Return (Year)   _____

   Guidelines   _____

   Newsletters   _____

   Annual Report   _____

   _____   _____

   _____   _____

6. a. Board Members:

   _____

   _____

   _____

   b. Staff   Full Time   Part Time

   _____   _____   _____

   _____   _____   _____

   _____   _____   _____

7. Deadline: _____

   Application Process/Requirements/Submission:

   _____

   _____

   _____

8. Financial Information

   Asset Base: $_____

   Are there current gifts to build the asset base?   Yes _____   No_____

   If yes, how much? $_____

   Total number of grants awarded in 20___: _____

   Total amount of grants awarded in 20___: $_____

   High Grant: $_____

   Low Grant: $_____

   Average Grant: $_____

   In our interest area there were _____ grants, totaling $_____

   High grant in our interest area: $_____

   Low grant in our interest area: $_____

   Average grant in our interest area: $_____

(continued)

EXHIBIT 22.1
(Continued)

---

9. Grant Requests versus Grants Funded

    Number of proposals received in 20___: _____

    Number of proposals funded in 20___: _____

10. Sample Grants in Our Area of Interest:

    Recipient Organization   Amount

---

by the Internal Revenue Service (IRS), many follow the 5 percent guideline. Therefore, uncovering financial information such as the amount of their asset bases can be very insightful.

Use the databases and research tools described in this chapter to complete the information required on Exhibit 22.1 for those foundations that appear to fund in your area of interest (see question 3). Compare the areas and activities funded, the types of organizations funded, and the geographic areas funded to your request.

You may have to access several references to gather the information requested on Exhibit 22.1. For example, you will be instructed in this chapter to rely on the only verifiable data: the prospective foundation's IRS 990-PF tax return. Many grantseekers jump at the first good match and do not even bother to complete Exhibit 22.1's question concerning financial information. But remember, one grant to your area of interest is not enough to warrant your preparation of a proposal. Research the number of awards and the average award size in your area of interest. And when looking into foundation finances, take into consideration that approximately 50 percent of foundation awards are for less than $10,000. If your total request is $10,000 or more, you may want to work a few smaller grants from several foundations into your funding strategy.

It is also very useful to try to determine the number of proposals received (grant requests) versus the number of proposals (grants) funded (see question 9, Exhibit 22.1). Unfortunately, however, most foundations do not report the number of proposals received. I have heard foundation directors report that their funding rate is between 5 and 8 percent. They have also reported that most applicants seem to do little research on the foundation's interests and doubt that more than 10 percent ever reviewed the foundation's IRS 990-PF tax return. One foundation director told me that approximately 50 percent of the proposals he receives go immediately into a shredder because they request exorbitant amounts of funding in areas in which the foundation has no interest.

In addition to the research you conduct on grant-making foundations, you should also uncover and record as much information as possible on the decision makers in those foundations. The Funding Executive Research Worksheet (Exhibit 22.2) is designed to help you do this.

EXHIBIT 22.2
Funding Executive Research Worksheet

---

1. Funding Source Name: _____

2. Name of Contact Person/Contributions Officer: _____

3. Title: _____

4. Business Address: _____

_____

5. Education
   College: _____
   Post Graduate: _____

6. Military Service: _____

7. Clubs/Affiliations: _____

_____

8. Corporate Board Memberships: _____

_____

9. Business History (Promotions, Other Firms, etc.): _____

10. Other Philanthropic Activities: _____

_____

11. Newspaper/Magazine Clipping(s) Attached: Yes _____   No _____

12. Contacts/Linkages in our Organizations: _____

_____

13. Recent Articles/Publications: _____

14. Awards/Honors: _____

Naturally, you do not have to have information on a foundation's executives (that is, directors, trustees, board members, contributions officers, and so forth) to consider submitting a proposal, but the more you know about the decision makers, the greater your chances of success. The information you collect and record on your Funding Executive Research Worksheet will help you in three major ways:

- It will allow you to determine, in advance, likely preferences and biases you will encounter if you are lucky enough to arrange an in-person meeting.
- It will make it easier to locate links between your organization and a funding source.
- It will help you tailor your proposal to the board members' interests and values and present the problem and solution in a way that will attract the attention of the decision makers.

Recording accurate research on foundation decision makers will raise your chances of success. In addition, your ability to attract future funding will increase as you develop a history and file on each of the grantors in which you are interested. Enlist volunteers to ferret out the information you need. Use the Internet to help you gather the data you desire. Talk to your public library's librarian or a college or university librarian after you read this chapter to see what additional resources and techniques they suggest. Let your research guide your solicitation strategy and proposal development process.

The Foundation Center

Established in 1956, The Foundation Center is a leading source of information about philanthropy with a special emphasis on foundation grant making. The center covers its operating expenses through grants from foundations, corporations, the sale of publications, and fee-based subscriber services. The center's headquarters is in New York City and it has field offices located in Atlanta, Cleveland, San Francisco, and Washington, D.C. These five library–learning centers are each staffed by foundation center employees and house all of the Foundation Center's publications, foundation tax returns, and many other supplementary materials and services useful to grantseekers.

The Foundation Center also provides free funding information through more than 470 Funding Information Network locations (formerly called *Cooperating Collections*). The network consists of libraries, community foundations, and other nonprofit resource centers that can be found across the United States and the world. Locate the network nearest you by visiting grantspace.org/Find-Us. In addition to having a core collection of the Foundation Center's publications, many network partners have IRS tax returns for their state and in some cases, neighboring states. Networks also have several other valuable grants resource materials, including:

- digital grant guides in popular subject areas
- state foundation directories
- searchable foundation grant-related databases

Foundation Funding Research Tools

Basic research tools for developing your list of potential foundation grantors can be accessed at little or no charge on the Internet and usually within a short distance from your workplace at one of the Foundation Center's network locations. The major resources for foundation research include foundation directories, databases, foundation websites, and IRS tax returns.

Directories

The Foundation Directory is the major source of information on the largest U.S. foundations. Available in hardcopy and through a variety of online subscription options, the 2014 edition provides information on the ten thousand largest U.S. foundations by total giving and information on nearly sixty thousand sample grants.

The contents found in the *Directory*'s entries varies based on the availability of information. The data elements found in most of the entries include contact information, foundation type, financial data, purpose and activities, fields of interest, types of support, limitations, publications, application information, officers and directors, number of staff, employer identification number, and selected grants.

In addition to foundation entries, there are several indexes to help you locate potential funding sources including:

- index to donors, officers, trustees
- geographic index
- international giving index
- types of support index
- subject index
- foundations new to the edition index
- foundation name index

The most productive approach to using the *Foundation Directory* is to first review chapter 7 on redefining your project idea. After identifying key words and fields of interest (for example, *environment, health education curriculum development,* or *folk arts for children*), you can use the *Directory*'s subject index to determine which foundations have an active interest in the area for which you are seeking grant support. Another approach is to use the types of support index to identify foundations interested in your type of project (for example, conferences or seminars, building or renovation, equipment, program development, and matching or challenge grants).

Before you rush into reviewing the actual foundation entries, remember that a significant portion of foundations possess a geographic homing device. In other words, they give only where they live. The *Directory*'s geographic index will point you in the direction of those foundations that may be interested in your project because of its location. Do not despair if the use of the geographic index produces limited prospects. Many foundations have a national and even an international interest in certain areas. While these foundations may not have granted funds in your state or community before, they may do so if approached properly.

Another technique that will add a whole new dimension to your foundation grants effort is to become adept at using the index to donors, officers, and trustees. When your organization's friends provide you with their links, pay special attention to those people who list board memberships or friends on foundation boards. In most cases, your friends will be willing to discuss your project with fellow board members or with friends who serve on other boards.

As you do your research, be sure to record the name of the foundation, the state, and the directory entry number for each foundation you are interested in. Recording this information will help you refer to the foundation quickly. The best match will be a foundation that funds your subject area, type of project, and geographic area.

The Foundation Directory Part 2 is also available for your use. The 2014 edition of this directory includes the next ten thousand largest foundations, by total giving and features over forty thousand sample grants.

You may also access *The Foundation Directory Supplement,* which provides the latest facts on thousands of foundations in *The Foundation Directory* and *Directory Part 2.* Changes in foundation status, officers and trustees, contact information, and giving interests are highlighted in new entries.

The directories described previously and the supplements are published by the Foundation Center, 79 Fifth Avenue, New York, NY, 10003-3076. To order one of these products call the Foundation Center's customer service line at (800) 424-9836 or visit the Foundation Center's website at www.foundationcenter.org/marketplace. You can also access and use these hardcover directories for free at your nearest network location.

Databases

The Foundation Center offers five subscriber-based online resources.

- *Foundation Directory Online Basic* is a database of the ten thousand largest private and community foundations in the United States based on their annual giving.
- *Foundation Directory Online Plus* is a database of the ten thousand largest private and community foundations in the United States based on their annual giving and over 2.4 million recently awarded grants.
- *Foundation Directory Online Premium* is a database of the twenty thousand largest private and community foundations in the United States based on their annual giving and over 2.7 million recently awarded grants.
- *Foundation Directory Online Platinum* is a database of over 108,000 foundations, corporate giving programs, and grant-making public charities in the United States and over three million recently awarded grants.
- *Foundation Directory Professional* is a database of over 108,000 foundations, corporate giving programs, and grant-making charities in the United States; a database of over four thousand sponsoring companies; a database of over three million recently awarded grants; and a keyword-searchable database of over one million recently filed IRS forms 990 and 990-PF. This feature is exclusive to the *Professional* database. There are seven search fields available on the search 990s screen. The first search field provides keyword searching capability across the text of every 990 and 990PF in the database simultaneously. The remaining six search fields are used to refine your search by various criteria.
- *Foundation Directory Professional* also provides subscribers with the ability to search across a funder's grants with customized search indexes; the ability to map a funder's grants for any given year by recipient type or primary subject and disbursements by county, city, ZIP code, or congressional district; the ability to chart a funder's grants for any given year by recipient type or primary subject and disbursements by secondary and tertiary category; and the ability to sign up to receive funder-specific e-mail alerts.

Subscription fees vary depending on which level you choose: basic, plus, premium, platinum, or professional. Visit https://secure3.foundationcenter.org/fdo/signup for more information and to view plan fees. However, please note that some public libraries, and libraries at institutions of higher education may be able to perform electronic searches for you for free. Many large nonprofits, colleges, and universities already subscribe to the *Foundation Directory Online* and other searchable databases containing foundation grants information and enlisting their services can save you money. Explore the possibility of computer search and retrieval by contacting an established grants office near you.

The least expensive method of performing your foundation research is to use the Foundation Center's Foundation Directory Online Free. Formerly Foundation Finder, this free search tool contains information on nearly ninety thousand grantmakers and over 250,000 IRS forms 990-PF. A few hours using this free tool will provide you with a rough idea about foundations that may be appropriate for your project. You can also search requests for proposals posted in *Philanthropy News Digest* at the same website: foundationcenter.org/findfunders.

NOZA is a private foundation database containing more than one million foundation grant records. It provides free foundation searching but has a monthly fee for accessing individual and corporate philanthropy data. For more information or to search foundation grant records, visit www.noza search.com.

There are several other electronic funding databases available that are accessible by subscription only but offer current and in-depth information and vary in price.

- *GrantSelect*, an online database compiled and edited by Schoolhouse Partners, contains funding opportunities ranging from pure research grants to arts programs, biomedical and health care research, community services programs, children and youth programs, K–12 education funding, international programs, and operating grants for nonprofit organizations. See www.grantselect.com.
- *The Chronicle of Philanthropy's Guide to Grants* database allows *Chronicle of Philanthropy* subscribers to search every grant from foundations and corporations published by the *Chronicle* since 2006. It allow allows subscribers to view listings of forthcoming grant deadlines. See www.philanthropy.com/grants.

Foundation Websites and the Internet

The use of the Internet to research private funding sources via foundation websites is growing. However, it is estimated that 90 percent of foundations are still without websites. There are a variety of reasons for this, including lack of staff and limited geographic giving interests. Many foundations give only locally and do not want the unsolicited worldwide proposals that having a website may bring. Therefore, for many grant makers you will still need to use alternative research methods.

One foundation out of the ordinary is the Community Foundation of Greater Des Moines. Not only does it have a website, it also allows prospective grantees to apply online. It has grant applications available for completion through an online web portal called Manage My Grants. However, here again, the number of private grantors that allow Internet submittal of proposals is surprisingly small.

Through portals such as the Foundation Center's *Foundation Directory Online Free* (foundationcenter.org/findfunders), grantseekers can find links to the websites of foundations, corporate grant makers, grant-making public charities, and community foundations. In addition, the Council on Foundations (www.cof.org) offers links to its members' websites.

Exhibit 22.3 is a sample of a foundation's website and the type of information you can sometimes gather online. In this example, you can obtain

EXHIBIT 22.3
Sample Foundation Website

Jean and Louise Dreyfus Foundation, Inc.
Mailing Address: 315 Madison Avenue, Suite 900, New York, NY 10017
Phone: (212)599-1931
FAX: (212)599-2956
Email: info@jldreyfus.org

Home
Grant Guidelines
Application Procedure
Recent Grants
Trustees & Staff
Contact Us

Note: Until further notice, the Foundation will be accepting letters of inquiry from organizations that have a prior relationship with the Foundation. We ask that all other grant seekers refrain from sending letters at this time.

Grant Guidelines & Eligibility

The Foundation is committed to funding direct service organizations and those projects which will produce systemic change. To this end the Foundation favors programs which can eventually be replicated or which have the potential to be funded by independent or government sources in the future. Occasionally organizations will be awarded grants to strengthen their infrastructure or for general operating support. The Foundation encourages matching funds from other charitable organizations, public financial drives, individuals and government bodies

Grants are made only to organizations whose tax-exempt status has been recognized by the I.R.S. The Foundation does not award grants to individuals.

(continued)

EXHIBIT 22.3
(Continued)

Jean and Louis Dreyfus Foundation, Inc.

Home
Grant Guidelines
Application Procedure
Recent Grants
Trustees & Staff
Contact Us

Application Procedure

The initial approach to the Foundation should consist of a two-page letter of inquiry describing the organization requesting support and outlining the project in question.

Letters should be addressed to:

Ms. Edmee de. M. Firth
Executive Director
Jean and Louis Dreyfus Foundation, Inc.
315 Madison Avenue, Suite 900
New York, NY 10017

Phone: (212)599-1931
FAX: (212)599-2956
Email: info@jldreyfus.org

Letters of inquiry for initial approach are <u>due postmarked no later than January 15th and July 15th for the Spring and Fall cycles respectively</u>. All such inquires will be acknowledged with a letter of receipt, and further communication will follow if further information is required or if a full proposal is being requested (the foundation uses its own application form). Letters received later than the established deadlines will be automatically held until the next review cycle. Any discussion or indication of interest concerning a grant inquiry or application should not be construed as a commitment by the Foundation.

(continued)

EXHIBIT 22.3
(Continued)

Jean and Louis Dreyfus Foundation
Grants List 2013

Total Grants 2013:   **$692,550**

Grants for Aging

Alzheimer's Association New York City Chapter
Dementia Training for Professional Caregivers $25,000

American Federation for Aging Research
Medical Student Training in Aging Research (MSTAR) Program $25,000

BronxWorks
Seniors Home Improvement Program $15,000

Educational Alliance
Center for Balanced Living $15,000

Jewish Community Council of Greater Coney Island
Home Relief Program At-Risk Elderly $10,000

Medicare Rights Center
Community Partners Program $20,000

Mount Sinai Medical Center
Mount Sinai Chelsea – Village House Call Program $15,000

Project Find
Homeless In-Reach Program $10,000

Sunnyside Community Services
Center for Active Older Adults $15,000

Visiting Neighbors
General Support/Health Advocacy Program $15,000

Weill-Cornell Medical College
Division of Geriatrics and Gerontology
Geriatric Mental Health Initiative $25,000

Total Grants for Aging 2013 $190,000

(continued)

EXHIBIT 22.3
(Continued)

Jean and Louis Dreyfus Foundation, Inc.

Home
Grant Guidelines
Application Procedure
Recent Grants
Trustees & Staff
Contact Us

Trustees & Staff

Nicholas L.D. Firth
President

Katie Firth Bank
Vice-President

Karen L. Rosa

Winthrop Rutherfurd, Jr.

Edmee de M. Firth
Vice President and Executive Director

Jessica Keuskamp
Program Director

---

the Jean and Louis Dreyfus Foundation's guidelines, application procedure, grants list, and roster of trustees and staff from its website. (Note that the Dreyfus Foundation is presently only accepting letters of inquiry from organizations that have a prior relationship with the foundation.)

Several nonprofit organizations have developed websites with grantor information. There are also bulletin boards and chat boxes that focus on foundation and corporate grantors. Check with your membership groups and your peers to see what is available, or perform your own Internet search.

Conducting research to locate your most likely foundation grantors need not be labor intensive or costly. Using electronic databases and websites in your search will save you time, but the actual information you will find is identical to that in the print form. The key is to locate the data that will enable you to estimate your chances for success before you invest any more time in seeking a foundation grant.

Internal Revenue Service Tax Returns

Once you have located the foundations that may be interested in your project, the next step is to go beyond the synthesized data you found in directories, databases, and websites and gather precise data from the foundations' IRS tax returns. Taking ten minutes to review a foundation's tax return is the key to finding the best funding source for your project.

Form 990-PF is the annual tax return that U.S. private foundations must file with the IRS. Federal law requires that all foundations provide their tax returns for public information purposes. While the Foundation Directories are useful reference tools, they are basically compilations of information from many sources, and there is no guarantee as to the accuracy of the information provided. The IRS, however, deals in specifics. By reviewing the returns of private foundations you believe to be your best funding prospects, you can find valuable information such as the actual amount of assets, a complete list of grants paid out including grants for less than $10,000, application guidelines, and the names of board members, officers, and trustees.

Larger foundations often issue annual reports or have websites that contain a listing of their grants. But the IRS form 990-PF may be the only source where you can find a complete grants list for smaller and midsized foundations.

Exhibit 22.4 is a sample of parts of form 990-PF. Taken off of the Foundation Center's website, this sample demonstrates that finding the information you need on a 990-PF is relatively easy.

- Page 1, top section and line 25 provide date, name, address, assets, and contributions, gifts and grants paid.
- Page 6, part VIII, line 1 provides the list of officers, directors, trustees, and foundation managers, and their compensation.
- Page 10, part XV, line 2 a, b, c, d provides application information.
- Page 11, part XV, line 3 provides grants and contributions paid during the year or approved for future payment (which gives you some indication of how involved the funding source is in awarding multiple-year grants).

Copies of tax returns for the past three years can be viewed for free at the Foundation Center's learning libraries in New York City and Washington, D.C. The Atlanta, Cleveland, and San Francisco offices of the Foundation Center contain IRS form 990-PF returns for the southeastern, Midwestern, and Western states respectively. You can also access foundation tax returns for free on the web at foundationcenter.org/findfunders/990finder/. In some cases it is also possible to access them on foundation websites. Guidestar

EXHIBIT 22.4
IRS Foundation Annual Return Form 990-PF

Form **990-PF**	**Return of Private Foundation**	OMB No. 1545-0052
Department of the Treasury Internal Revenue Service	or Section 4947(a)(1) Nonexempt Charitable Trust **Treated as a Private Foundation** Note. The foundation may be able to use a copy of this return to satisfy state reporting requirements.	2011

For calendar year 2011 or tax year beginning , 2011, and ending , 20

Name of foundation **NAME**	A Employer identification number
Number and street (or P.O. box number if mail is not delivered to street address) Room/suite **ADDRESS**	B Telephone number (see instructions)
City or town, state, and ZIP code	C If exemption application is pending, check here ▶ ☐

G Check all that apply: ☐ Initial return ☐ Initial return of a former public charity
☐ Final return ☐ Amended return
☐ Address change ☐ Name change

H Check type of organization: ☐ Section 501(c)(3) exempt private foundation
☐ Section 4947(a)(1) nonexempt charitable trust ☐ Other taxable private foundation

I Fair market value of all assets at end of year *(from Part II, col. (c),* line 16) ▶ $ **ASSETS**

J Accounting method: ☐ Cash ☐ Accrual
☐ Other (specify) _____
(Part I, column (d) must be on cash basis.)

D 1. Foreign organizations, check here . . . . ▶ ☐
2. Foreign organizations meeting the 85% test, check here and attach computation . . . ▶ ☐

E If private foundation status was terminated under section 507(b)(1)(A), check here . . . . ▶ ☐

F If the foundation is in a 60-month termination under section 507(b)(1)(B), check here . . ▶ ☐

	Part I Analysis of Revenue and Expenses *(The total of amounts in columns (b), (c), and (d) may not necessarily equal the amounts in column (a) (see instructions).)*	**(a)** Revenue and expenses per books	**(b)** Net investment income	**(c)** Adjusted net income	**(d)** Disbursements for charitable purposes (cash basis only)
	1 Contributions, gifts, grants, etc., received (attach schedule)				
	2 Check ▶ ☐ if the foundation is **not** required to attach Sch. B				
	3 Interest on savings and temporary cash investments				
	4 Dividends and interest from securities				
	5a Gross rents				
	b Net rental income or (loss)				
Revenue	6a Net gain or (loss) from sale of assets not on line 10				
	b Gross sales price for all assets on line 6a				
	7 Capital gain net income (from Part IV, line 2) . .				
	8 Net short-term capital gain				
	9 Income modifications				
	10a Gross sales less returns and allowances				
	b Less: Cost of goods sold . . .				
	c Gross profit or (loss) (attach schedule)				
	11 Other income (attach schedule)				
	12 **Total.** Add lines 1 through 11				
Operating and Administrative Expenses	13 Compensation of officers, directors, trustees, etc.				
	14 Other employee salaries and wages				
	15 Pension plans, employee benefits				
	16a Legal fees (attach schedule)				
	b Accounting fees (attach schedule)				
	c Other professional fees (attach schedule) . . .				
	17 Interest				
	18 Taxes (attach schedule) (see instructions) . . .				
	19 Depreciation (attach schedule) and depletion . .				
	20 Occupancy				
	21 Travel, conferences, and meetings				
	22 Printing and publications				
	23 Other expenses (attach schedule)				
	24 **Total operating and administrative expenses.** Add lines 13 through 23				
	25 Contributions, gifts, grants paid **GRANTS PAID**				
	26 **Total expenses and disbursements.** Add lines 24 and 25				
	27 Subtract line 26 from line 12:				
	a **Excess of revenue over expenses and disbursements**				
	b **Net investment income** (if negative, enter -0-) .				
	c **Adjusted net income** (if negative, enter -0-) . .				

For Paperwork Reduction Act Notice, see instructions.   Cat. No. 11289X   Form **990-PF** (2011)

(continued)

EXHIBIT 22.4
(Continued)

Form 990-PF (2011)   Page **6**

Part VII-B	Statements Regarding Activities for Which Form 4720 May Be Required *(continued)*

5a During the year did the foundation pay or incur any amount to:

   (1) Carry on propaganda, or otherwise attempt to influence legislation (section 4945(e))?   ☐ Yes ☐ No

   (2) Influence the outcome of any specific public election (see section 4955); or to carry on, directly or indirectly, any voter registration drive?   ☐ Yes ☐ No

   (3) Provide a grant to an individual for travel, study, or other similar purposes?   ☐ Yes ☐ No

   (4) Provide a grant to an organization other than a charitable, etc., organization described in section 509(a)(1), (2), or (3), or section 4940(d)(2)? (see instructions)   ☐ Yes ☐ No

   (5) Provide for any purpose other than religious, charitable, scientific, literary, or educational purposes, or for the prevention of cruelty to children or animals?   ☐ Yes ☐ No

  b If any answer is "Yes" to 5a(1)–(5), did **any** of the transactions fail to qualify under the exceptions described in Regulations section 53.4945 or in a current notice regarding disaster assistance (see instructions)?   **5b**

   Organizations relying on a current notice regarding disaster assistance check here   ▶ ☐

  c If the answer is "Yes" to question 5a(4), does the foundation claim exemption from the tax because it maintained expenditure responsibility for the grant?   ☐ Yes ☐ No

   If "Yes," attach the statement required by Regulations section 53.4945–5(d).

6a Did the foundation, during the year, receive any funds, directly or indirectly, to pay premiums on a personal benefit contract?   ☐ Yes ☐ No

  b Did the foundation, during the year, pay premiums, directly or indirectly, on a personal benefit contract?   **6b**

   If "Yes" to 6b, file Form 8870.

7a At any time during the tax year, was the foundation a party to a prohibited tax shelter transaction?   ☐ Yes ☐ No

  b If "Yes," did the foundation receive any proceeds or have any net income attributable to the transaction?   **7b**

Part VIII	Information About Officers, Directors, Trustees, Foundation Managers, Highly Paid Employees, and Contractors

1 List all officers, directors, trustees, foundation managers and their compensation (see instructions).

(a) Name and address	(b) Title, and average hours per week devoted to position	(c) Compensation (If not paid, enter -0-)	(d) Contributions to employee benefit plans and deferred compensation	(e) Expense account, other allowances
OFFICERS				

2 Compensation of five highest-paid employees (other than those included on line 1—see instructions). If none, enter "NONE."

(a) Name and address of each employee paid more than $50,000	(b) Title, and average hours per week devoted to position	(c) Compensation	(d) Contributions to employee benefit plans and deferred compensation	(e) Expense account, other allowances

Total number of other employees paid over $50,000   ▶

Form **990-PF** (2011)

(continued)

EXHIBIT 22.4
(Continued)

Form 990-PF (2011) Page **10**

Part XIV **Private Operating Foundations** (see instructions and Part VII-A, question 9)

1a If the foundation has received a ruling or determination letter that it is a private operating foundation, and the ruling is effective for 2011, enter the date of the ruling . . . . . . ▶

b Check box to indicate whether the foundation is a private operating foundation described in section ☐ 4942(j)(3) or ☐ 4942(j)(5)

	Tax year	Prior 3 years			
2a Enter the lesser of the adjusted net income from Part I or the minimum investment return from Part X for each year listed	**(a)** 2011	**(b)** 2010	**(c)** 2009	**(d)** 2008	**(e)** Total
b 85% of line 2a					
c Qualifying distributions from Part XII, line 4 for each year listed					
d Amounts included in line 2c not used directly for active conduct of exempt activities . .					
e Qualifying distributions made directly for active conduct of exempt activities. Subtract line 2d from line 2c . .					
3 Complete 3a, b, or c for the alternative test relied upon:					
a "Assets" alternative test—enter:					
(1) Value of all assets					
(2) Value of assets qualifying under section 4942(j)(3)(B)(i)					
b "Endowment" alternative test—enter ⅔ of minimum investment return shown in Part X, line 6 for each year listed . . .					
c "Support" alternative test—enter:					
(1) Total support other than gross investment income (interest, dividends, rents, payments on securities loans (section 512(a)(5)), or royalties)					
(2) Support from general public and 5 or more exempt organizations as provided in section 4942(j)(3)(B)(iii)					
(3) Largest amount of support from an exempt organization					
(4) Gross investment income . . .					

Part XV **Supplementary Information** (Complete this part only if the foundation had $5,000 or more in assets at any time during the year—see instructions.)

1 **Information Regarding Foundation Managers:**

a List any managers of the foundation who have contributed more than 2% of the total contributions received by the foundation before the close of any tax year (but only if they have contributed more than $5,000). (See section 507(d)(2).)

b List any managers of the foundation who own 10% or more of the stock of a corporation (or an equally large portion of the ownership of a partnership or other entity) of which the foundation has a 10% or greater interest.

2 **Information Regarding Contribution, Grant, Gift, Loan, Scholarship, etc., Programs:**

Check here ▶ ☐ if the foundation only makes contributions to preselected charitable organizations and does not accept unsolicited requests for funds. If the foundation makes gifts, grants, etc. (see instructions) to individuals or organizations under other conditions, complete items 2a, b, c, and d.

a The name, address, and telephone number of the person to whom applications should be addressed:

b The form in which applications should be submitted and information and materials they should include:

APPLICATION

c Any submission deadlines: **INFORMATION**

d Any restrictions or limitations on awards, such as by geographical areas, charitable fields, kinds of institutions, or other factors:

Form **990-PF** (2011)

(continued)

EXHIBIT 22.4
(Continued)

Form 990-PF (2011)				Page 11

Part XV   Supplementary Information (continued)

3   Grants and Contributions Paid During the Year or Approved for Future Payment

Recipient	If recipient is an individual, show any relationship to any foundation manager or substantial contributor	Foundation status of recipient	Purpose of grant or contribution	Amount
Name and address (home or business)				
a *Paid during the year*				
GRANTS PAID				
Total . . . . ▶			3a	
b *Approved for future payment*				
FUTURE GRANTS				
Total . . . . ▶			3b	

Form **990-PF** (2011)

(www.guidestar.org) and NOZA (www.nozasearch.com) are two other sources where you can obtain 990-PF tax returns.

Please note that the tax returns you will be able to access will typically be one to two years old. In addition, if you cannot find a particular organization's 990-PF, it may be because the organization you are looking for files a 990 instead. In general, churches, hospitals, schools, and publicly supported organizations file 990s.

Since you are already armed with knowledge on the foundation marketplace (see chapter 21) and now you know how to research potential private foundation grantors, when will you integrate this activity into your action steps chart? In some cases you may need to address the foundation grants process before your federal grant aspirations because you need preliminary data or because you need to finish a publication first. Refer to Figure 22.1 and configure your plan.

EXHIBIT 22.1
Action Steps Chart: Researching Foundation Grantors

23

Contacting a Private Foundation Before Submission

CONTACTING THE PRIVATE FOUNDATION before you write your proposal will help you validate your research and gather additional information about the grantor's priorities and interests. Most importantly, preproposal contact will allow you to tailor your proposal according to the particular approach or method that each private foundation will find interesting and provide you with the information needed to determine the appropriate amount to request. You can also use this contact to explore the grantor's feelings about funding only a portion of the total amount your project requires. The purpose of this contact is not to convince the grantor to fund your proposal but to ensure that your approach will meet the grantor's needs. By contacting the foundation funding source before you submit, you increase your chances of success over five times. Do not miss out on this tremendous opportunity if you have a contact person or you have a linkage to help you get in the door.

How to Contact Private Foundation Grantors

Now that you realize how important preproposal contact is, here is the bad news. Most private foundations are understaffed, and as many as eighty thousand have no staff. Therefore, making contact with them is very difficult. Many private foundation application instructions state "no contact except by letter," and your research will show that many addresses for private funding sources are actually addresses for trust departments of banks, accountants' offices, websites, or post office boxes.

Naturally, you do not want to talk to a trust officer at a bank, but speaking with a foundation board member would be a big help. With so few foundations occupying their own offices, the chances of talking to a foundation's director or staff are limited to the largest foundations. What is significant, however, is that each foundation usually has eight to ten board members. This means that there are approximately 861,920 board members serving the 86,192 (2012 figures) foundations and you may be surprised at how many your advocates know! These board members are the actual decision makers, and they can be contacted effectively through your webbing system.

One foundation director underscored the importance of using links to board members when she told me that:

- One-third of her foundation's grants will be awarded to her board members' favorite nonprofit organizations.
- One-third will go to her board members' friends' favorite nonprofits.
- One-third will be up for grabs to those who write creative, persuasive proposals that match the interests and values of her foundation.

At this point your research should already include the names of your best foundation prospects' decision makers and board members. Ask the leaders of your organization whether they know any of these people and, if so, whether they would help you by using this informal means of contact. Perhaps your link can set up lunch or a conference call. If you do not uncover a link, your plan should be to follow the grantor's guidelines as outlined in the various resource publications (see chapter 9 for more information on webbing and links).

If there is an office and contact is not ruled out or discouraged, you should:

- Write a letter requesting a visit.
- Telephone to set up a visit or phone interview.
- Make a personal visit to the grantor.

Contact by Letter

Be very selective when sending a letter requesting an appointment and information on a grantor's program. Since very few private foundations have the staff resources necessary to respond to written requests, do not be surprised if you receive a proposal rejection notice even though you asked only for application guidelines or an appointment.

EXHIBIT 23.1
Sample Letter/E-mail to a Private Foundation Requesting Information

Date
Name
Title
Address

Dear   :

I am developing a project that deals with   and provides
benefits to [or in]   . My research indicates that
this area is an important concern of the [name of foundation].

Please use the enclosed [e-mail address or self-addressed stamped envelope] to
send me information on your desired format for proposals or other guidelines. I
would also appreciate it if you could add us to your mailing list so that we could
receive your annual reports, newsletters, and any other materials you think might
be useful to us as we work on this and related projects that benefit our shared
area of concern.

Thank you for your cooperation.

Sincerely,

Name/Title
Organization
Address
E-mail Address

Exhibit 23.1 provides a sample letter to a foundation requesting information. (This letter could be sent as an e-mail, but not all foundations provide e-
mail addresses for correspondence purposes.) This letter may be the only way
to receive an application form from the hundreds of foundations that do not
have a website and state that you must send for their application. Please note
that this is not a letter proposal or letter of inquiry. These types of proposals
are described in chapter 24.

Contact by Telephone

Telephone contact with a private foundation may take the place of face-to-
face contact or may be used to set up a visit. When you are successful at telephoning a private foundation, you can be sure you have contacted one that
falls within the small percentage of those having an office and a paid staff.

Even if you are telephoning the grantor in hopes of setting up a visit, be ready to discuss your project. Many grantors use the telephone very effectively for quickly assessing projects and determining their interest in them before agreeing to discuss the project face-to-face or inviting you to make a written application. After all, it is much easier to tell a grantseeker that they are not really interested in a project over the telephone than it is in person, or to have to read about an idea that is not going to make it.

If the grantor wants to discuss your project before giving you an appointment, ask whether you could e-mail or mail a short concept paper and call back when he or she has your outline in hand and has had time to review it.

If he or she agrees to a visit, set the date. Do not offer any more information at this time, but do ask what he or she recommends that you bring. Also ask about:

- providing a short video clip on a DVD
- presenting a PowerPoint presentation or full-motion video
- the number of staff to be present so that you can bring the appropriate number of copies of information about your organization
- the possibility of him or her making a visit to your location
- his or her travel plans, whether he or she will be near you, or whether he or she will be attending any conferences or meetings you will attend or where you will be presenting

If a personal visit is not possible, you will be forced to discuss your project over the telephone. The questions you ask over the phone will actually be the same as those you would ask if you were to make a personal visit. Therefore, review the following section on the visit and designate the questions to ask a funding source.

The Visit

Visiting in person is the best way to get to know the foundation, but visits are difficult to arrange since most foundations have no office and are not heavily staffed. If you are fortunate enough to get a visit, use your time wisely.

Who Should Go

Your credibility will be higher if you take a nonstaff representative with you. An articulate, impressive volunteer, advocate, advisory committee member, or board member is an excellent choice. Two people are the maximum. You do not want to overpower the grantor by sending three or more people. Use the information you collected from your webbing and linkages to choose a partner that provides a close match to the funding source. Use age, education, club affiliation, and other personal characteristics as the basis of your choice.

On several occasions I have had a past grantee help me make preproposal contact. In one instance, the past grantee arranged lunch for all of us when the grantor made a site visit to her program.

Dress according to the information you have about the funding source. Dress in the foundation world is conservative, and usually it is better to be overdressed than underdressed. Dress codes differ in the East, the West, the South and the Midwest areas of the United States, so be aware of geographic influences. The best person to ask about the appropriate dress for a particular funding source may be a past grantee.

Materials to Bring

The materials you will need to bring are those you have already gathered and organized from your research. You may also want to bring sample audiovisual aids that document the need in a more interesting or vivid manner and help show the funding source how important it is to meet the need *now*. If you do use audiovisual aids, make sure they are in balance with your request. A three- to five-minute DVD that documents the problem and your organization's selected uniquenesses would be appropriate if you are making a large request ($250,000), but inappropriate for a smaller ($5,000) request. At this point it is still proper to have several possible approaches to meeting the need. Therefore, you should have the cost and benefits and pros and cons of each approach outlined and ready for presentation. You want to learn which approach the prospective funding source likes best; you are not trying to convince the grantor that you have "the one and only way to solve the problem." Your Cost-Benefit Analysis Worksheets from chapter 6 will usually elicit more than enough response to begin a conversation.

Questions to Ask a Foundation Funding Source

Review these questions to determine which would be the most appropriate to ask based on your current knowledge of the funding source. You may want to assign specific questions to each of the two individuals going to the meeting and prepare for the visit by role-playing various answers.

1. We have developed several feasible approaches. Would you please comment on which ones look the most interesting to you (or would look the most interesting to the board)?

2. Last year, your foundation awarded $_____ to our kind of project and the average size of the award was $_____. Will this remain consistent?
3. Our research indicates that your deadlines last year were _____ and _____. Will they be the same this year?
4. Does it help if proposals are submitted early? Do proposals that are submitted early receive more favorable treatment?
5. How are proposals reviewed by your foundation? Who performs the review? Outside experts? Board members? Staff? Is there a scoring system or checklist they use that you could share with us?
6. Are there more current granting priorities? (Give them a copy of your research sheet to determine whether your research accurately reflects their priorities.)
7. What do you think of submitting more than one proposal in a funding cycle?
8. Is the amount we are requesting realistic in light of your current goals?
9. Do you ever provide grant support jointly with another funding source and, if so, is that approach appropriate here?

The following two questions should be asked only when the grantor seems very encouraging.

10. Would you look over our proposal before our formal submission if we finished it early?
11. Would you recommend a proposal that you have funded that you think is well written? If so, I will contact the grantee to request a copy.

Ask question 12 only if the grantor is not very encouraging.

12. Can you suggest any other funders who may be appropriate for this project?

Private Foundation Report Form

Each time a member of your staff contacts a funder in person, over the phone, or through e-mail, he or she should complete and save a Private Foundation Report Form (Exhibit 23.2). This simple procedure has a number of important benefits. It will keep you from damaging your credibility by repeating the same questions or having the funder say, "I gave that information to _____ from your organization. Don't you people ever talk to each

EXHIBIT 23.2
Private Foundation Report Form

Complete one of these forms after each contact with a private foundation.

Funding Source: _____

Funding Source Address: _____

_____

Funding Source Contact Person: _____

Telephone Number: _____ Fax:_____ E-mail: _____

Contacted On (Date): _____

Contacted By (Name): _____

Type of Contact: Phone _____ Visit _____ Other (Explain) _____

Objective of Contact: _____

_____

_____

Results of Contact: _____

_____

_____

Follow-up: _____

_____

---

other?" Also, it will allow another person from your organization to pick up where you leave off when you take that next promotion.

Successful grantees recognize the importance of contacting the funding source before writing the proposal. The purpose of the contact is not to make small talk but to validate research and gather data needed to address the grantor's changing or hidden agenda. Using the techniques in this chapter to contact and record contact with private grantors will be an essential part of your grantseeking strategy.

While this action step is critical to your success, contacting a foundation before submission may not always be possible. However, if your research uncovers a way to contact the prospective grantor, go to Figure 23.1 and place this step in your plan.

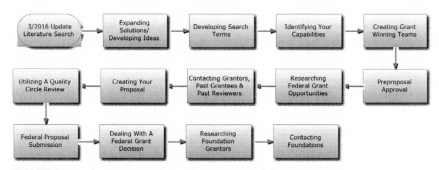

FIGURE 23.1
Action Steps Chart: Contacting Foundations

24

Applying for Private Foundation Funds: Letter of Inquiry and Letter Proposal

Creating a Winning Letter of Inquiry

WHILE THIS MAY SOUND LIKE AN EXERCISE IN SEMANTICS, a letter of inquiry (LOI) is really just a very condensed proposal. It is a one- to two-page mini proposal aimed at interesting the foundation enough to invite you to submit a full proposal. Basically, the LOI should describe the grantee organization and outline the project in question. It is qualitatively different from a letter proposal in that it lacks the specifics and details. However, it still must include and, indeed, highlight the components of your project or program that will motivate the grantor to request more information. You do not have to explain how you will do everything, but you must establish that you have a plan and that you will provide more information in the full proposal.

The natural tendency when faced with the challenge of writing a one-page LOI is to focus intently on what it is *you* want to accomplish and how you want to do it. In contrast, most prospective grantors are self-focused and intent on what *they* and *their* organization value and think is in their best interests.

If you look at this process from the grantors' point of view, they skim through hundreds to thousands of proposals in search for those that reflect and reinforce their values. They want to know how the goals and objectives of *your* program relate to *their* mission and how the results will satisfy *their* goals. They are generally adverse to risks (unless your research shows otherwise). They do not want to invest their grant funds in uncertain or unproven projects or research. They are understaffed, and few have experts in the field to refer to for scientific or programmatic evaluations. If they have staff members who perform initial screening and logging of proposals, these staff members may have little professional training and usually base their initial screenings on a general description of the areas in which the foundation board is interested. Therefore, it is imperative that your LOI immediately focuses on the grantor and provides a clear picture or summary within the first few sentences of what your project seeks to create. You will be able to do this if you have done a good job researching your foundation prospect and have reviewed its most recent 990-PF tax return (see chapter 22).

LOIs are more difficult to create than other types of proposals that allow more words. With an LOI you must weigh each word and spend hours, not minutes, on each paragraph. After all, you have only a few words to hook the reader. You must write from the foundation's vocabulary, values glasses, and point of view; and avoid terms, acronyms, and buzzwords that shift the focus to you.

Your LOI should be on your best stationery, preferably with a list of your board members' names in the left margin. Board members provide credibility. If you have formed a special advisory committee for your project, you might want to consider having their names in the margin, especially if some of them are nationally or even locally known.

Almost all proposals, whether they are letters of inquiry or letter proposals, should start with the name or title of the proposed project. The title is a necessary handle on which the grantor will rely to log your proposal into his or her database and to refer to your proposal when, and if, it comes up for discussion by the board. Your title should not be too lengthy, but like the rest of your proposal it should focus on what will be changed, how it will be changed, and who will benefit. Foundation grantors see their funds as impacting a problem, changing a target population, or furthering a favorite solution or protocol. Your LOI, and its title, should focus on the problem to be solved and the difference that will be made.

Foundation board members make assumptions based on titles. They assume they understand what the project proposes to accomplish based on the words used in the title. Unfortunately, there may be a disjuncture here, and the proposal may not deal with their expectations at all. To make sure this does not happen to you, read your title to several individuals who know nothing about your project, and ask them what they think the proposal that follows is all about. You will probably be amazed at the misconceptions and find yourself creating a new, clearer title aimed at steering the reader in the right direction.

Follow the title with a short paragraph (two to three sentences) summarizing the project. Use positive action words and a few well-chosen facts.

The next paragraph should focus on the issue that the project will seek to reduce or solve. Your research should provide some insight into other projects and approaches the foundation has funded. Yours should not be identical, but you can pick up a theme or preference by looking at what they have invested in the past. It is not, "We hope to change this situation." It is, "Together we *will* change this situation."

Follow this with a paragraph on how you will impact the problem or issue. Include a few sentences on how and why your organization or consortium is particularly well suited to bring about the change you suggest. Most foundations will require some idea of the budget and cost. Usually in an LOI the budget can be in paragraph form. But be sure to be clear on what the total cost will be and if there are any other funders (already committed or to be approached) and any in-kind or matching commitment from your organization or consortium.

The secret to a successful LOI is to follow the foundation's specifications and to create a miniproposal that is motivating and compelling. The goal is to have the funding source request a full proposal that meets its needs and interests. But many grantseekers have been surprised when their brief LOI resulted in a check without the need to submit a longer proposal!

Some foundations have specific guidelines for LOIs. For example, the Park Foundation requests that applicants submit (1) a cover letter that includes a summary of the project and (2) an inquiry cover sheet that is downloadable from its website. As is always the case, make sure you know the guidelines for the foundation you are interested in.

If you have submitted an LOI that has won you the opportunity to submit a full proposal, or the grantor's guidelines request that you submit a full or longer proposal, the following format will assist you. Remember, even a full proposal is usually thought of as a letter, not as a lengthy treatise on the topic. Many grantseekers have reported that they like to prepare the slightly longer letter proposal described in this chapter and then edit it to a shorter LOI making sure that they are keenly aware of what they must cut out and thus what they choose not to say.

The Letter Proposal

Historically, private foundations have used the letter proposal format as the primary component of their application process. Now federal and state granting programs are showing a shift in this direction, and some are requesting a short three- to five-page preproposal document that is similar to creating a letter proposal. Public funding sources may call the letter proposal a white paper, a preproposal paper, or a concept paper. Foundations may call it a letter proposal or just a brief proposal that, in most cases, is limited to two pages. In some cases grantors will not send a prospective grantee an application package unless they like the approach outlined in the letter proposal or concept paper. Although this preproposal screening may sound negative at first, it really is not such a bad idea because it prevents grantseekers from completing a more lengthy application for a project that the prospective grantor has little interest in funding or reviewing.

Foundations use the letter proposal format simply because they do not have the time or staff to read long, tedious proposals. They want short, concise letters and grant billions of dollars each year based on two to three pages of content. Some larger foundations may send out a request for proposals. They will specify details such as length, but most are less than five pages and many request that they be double-spaced.

Letter proposals are often read by board members during relatively brief meetings. A survey of foundations revealed that most foundations meet one to three times a year for an average of one to three hours each time. Within this short time frame, they must read an overwhelming number of letter proposals; therefore, it is imperative that your proposal attract and retain their interest.

In an effort to save time, some groups of grantmakers have adopted a common grant application (CGA) format to allow grant applicants to produce a single proposal for a specific community of funders. Exhibit 24.1 shows the checklist for Colorado's CGA. Go to http://foundationcenter.org/find-funders/cga.html for a list of participating groups. However, before applying to any funder that accepts a common application form, be sure to check that your project matches the funder's stated interests, and ascertain whether the funder would prefer an LOI in advance of receiving the application.

If your research provides you with an application format to follow, use it exactly as outlined. For instance, the Herbert B. Jones Foundation provides guidelines for the application format as well as the program budget and appendix, and unequivocally states that applicants must adhere strictly to the format presented. Some foundations provide a concept paper template to follow. Others, like the Sid W. Richardson Foundation, provide an interactive application form that is accessible by downloading it from the Foundation's website. However, keep in mind that many foundations do not provide interactive online application forms. Therefore, you usually cannot change the amount of space allotted to each section. Whatever the case may be, follow all guidelines exactly, but look for opportunities where you can incorporate all or any of the main components of the letter proposal suggested here into the prospective funding source's required format.

EXHIBIT 24.1
Colorado Common Grant Application

 Colorado Common Grant Application

CHECKLIST

The Colorado Common Grant Application (CGA) consists of the following components, which should be submitted in the order listed below. This checklist is provided to help ensure a complete proposal. It does not need to be submitted with the proposal.

Note: If your proposal is for a building project or land acquisition, check the Common Grant Forms website to see if the grantmaker accepts the CGA for Capital Campaigns or contact the grantmaker directly if they are not listed on the website.

☐ Check specific grantmakers' guidelines and verify that they accept the CGA and determine whether or not they have made modifications to their application requirements.

☐ Comply with any unique application requirements.

☐ **Section I: Cover Letter (one page)**
Include the purpose of the grant request and a brief description of how the request fits with the grantmaker's mission and grantmaking priorities.

☐ **Section II: Summary Sheet Form**
Use the 2-page template provided.

☐ **Section III: Narrative**

☐ *Formatting:* Use 12-point font with 1-inch margins and include the **HEADING** provided for each question. It is not necessary to repeat the text of the questions.

☐ *Page Limit:*
General Operating Requests: 4-page limit; answer questions 1-3; 5(a), 5(b), 5(c); and 6-11.
Program or Project Requests: 5-page limit; answer questions 1-4; 5(a), 5(b), 5(d); and 6-11.

Narrative Questions

☐   1. Organization Background
☐   2. Goals
☐   3. Current Programs
☐   4. Program or Project Requests Only
☐   5. Evaluation
☐   6. Collaboration
☐   7. Inclusiveness
☐   8. Board/Governance
☐   9. Volunteers
☐   10. Planning
☐   11. Optional

(continued)

EXHIBIT 24.1
(Continued)

Colorado Common Grant Application

☐ **Section IV: Attachments**
If you omit any of the required attachments, provide an explanation as to why.
Note: Some grantmakers will not accept an incomplete proposal, regardless of an explanation.

Financial Attachments

☐ 1(a). Organization budget
☐ 1(b). Program or project budget, if applicable
☐ 2. Current (year-to-date) financial statements
☐ 3. Year-end financial statements, audit, and Sources of Income Table
☐ 4. Major contributors
☐ 5. In-kind contributions
☐ Explanation of items in financial attachments, if applicable

Other Attachments

☐ 6. Board of directors list
☐ 7. Proof of IRS federal tax-exempt status, dated within the last five years
☐ 8. Anti-discrimination statement adopted by the board of directors
☐ 9. Key staff
☐ 10. Annual report, if available
☐ 11. Evaluation results (optional): Provide the organization's most recent evaluation results, relevant to this request.

Additional Attachments for Organizations Using a Fiscal Agent/Fiscal Sponsor

Note: Many grantmakers do not accept proposals from organizations using a fiscal agent/fiscal sponsor. Therefore, be sure to check each grantmaker's guidelines prior to submitting a proposal.

☐ 1. The memorandum of understanding or the contract between the organization and the fiscal agent/fiscal sponsor.
☐ 2. Financial attachments 1(a), 2, and 3 for the fiscal agent/fiscal sponsor.
☐ 3. Proof of IRS federal tax-exempt status for the fiscal agent/fiscal sponsor, dated within the last five years.
☐ 4. Board of directors list for the fiscal agent/fiscal sponsor.

Thank you for your time and effort in completing this application.

A User's Guide for the CGA is available at www.coloradocommongrantforms.org.

Constructing a Letter Proposal

In general, when writing a letter proposal, use more white spaces, bullets, and short inviting paragraphs. Never use small fonts in an effort to include more. Board members are usually older and small font will make your proposal less likely to be read. If font is not specified, use twelve to thirteen characters per inch. Double space when required, and read and heed all application guidelines. The main components of a letter proposal are as follows:

- an introductory paragraph stating the reason for writing
- a section explaining why this grantor was selected
- a needs section that presents the problem you will solve
- a solution section that states what you will do and how
- a uniqueness paragraph that shows why your organization is the best choice for implementing the solution
- a request for funds section that asks for money and summarizes your budget
- a closing paragraph that provides a contact for more information if needed
- signatures of your highest-ranking officials and partners
- attachments, if allowed

Introductory Paragraph

Begin by stating your reason for writing to the funding source, and mention who your link to the grantor is, when possible. In some cases your link may prefer to remain anonymous and endorse your proposal at a board meeting. In other instances your link may actually instruct you to refer to him or her in your proposal. If so, you could say something such as the following:

> Katie Macrino [your link, a past board member, trustee, or staff member of the foundation] and I have discussed the mutual concerns of the Kleineste Foundation [funding source] and [your organization] in meeting the nutritional needs of the elderly [subject area or problem].

If you cannot mention a link, begin your letter proposal with the next most important factor: why the grantor was selected for solicitation or how you knew the grantor would be interested in your proposal.

Why the Grantor was Selected

Foremost in the reader's mind is why he or she should be reading your proposal. This is your opportunity to position yourself and your organization as winners that do their homework. You want the prospective funding source to know you are not blanketing the foundation world with a "one proposal fits all" approach. What you need to make clear in this paragraph is that, based on what you have discovered through your research, you believe the funding source is very likely to find your proposal interesting. This means saying, for example, "Our research indicates that your foundation is committed to the support of health care for the indigent. In the last three years you have dedicated over $4 million to this important area." In this example, you would also refer to the percentage of the funding source's total grant dollars that went to supporting health care for the indigent or mention a major or significant accomplishment made in this area through a previously awarded grant.

This paragraph need not be long. You want to demonstrate that you have taken the time to research the funding source's interests and that your proposal will address an issue that has been a concern of the grantor. By doing so, your proposal will command the respect of the reader and warrant the investment of time he or she will take to review it. At this point, it is obvious that this proposal is tailored to this foundation.

Again, you are following Festinger's theory of cognitive dissonance. To keep the reader interested in your proposal, you are going to have to present a proposal that reinforces his or her values and feelings of worth and importance. Seek to align your organization with the values of the grantor by adding something such as, "It is with our mutual concern for (or commitment to) the welfare of the indigent that we come to you with this exciting proposal."

Needs Section

While this may be referred to as your *vision* or *statement of purpose,* there must be an underlying situation or problem that must be remedied or changed by your action and the foundation's support. You do the work, and the grantor supplies the necessary ingredient—the money.

If you have constructed a Swiss cheese book as suggested in chapter 4, you already have gathered statistics, case studies, quotes, and articles to document a compelling statement of need for action. The main difference between stating the need in a letter proposal to a foundation and stating it in a federal grant application is that you have the opportunity to incorporate the human element in your appeal to the private grantor. While your letter proposal must be based on fact, you can help the foundation board members motivate themselves by presenting the more human side of the problem. The challenge is to portray compelling needs without overusing either the facts (by quoting too many research articles) or the human-interest aspects of the problem.

Select the component of the need that will most likely convince the grantor that the gap between what is and what ought to be must be closed *immediately*. To accomplish this you must have done research on the values and perspective of the grantor. Use what you have learned to describe the gap in a manner that is tailored to each particular funding source. With today's technology you could even scan a picture into your needs paragraph that may be worth a thousand words.

In a few paragraphs, your letter proposal must:

- Include a few well-chosen statistics.
- Exhibit sensitivity to the geographic perspective of the grantor.
- Portray the human side of the problem.

Whether your proposal is for a model project, research, or a service model, your statement of need must be more compelling than your competitor's to keep the reader interested. Readers must want to read the rest of your proposal to discover what you are going to do about closing the gap you have so eloquently and succinctly documented. Many novice grantseekers overlook or underestimate the importance of the needs section of their letter proposal; they assume readers must already know about the need since they have granted funds to this area in the past. This assumption is a mistake. Grantors do know about the need, but they expect you to command their respect by proving *your* expertise in the field by documenting the problem as in the following example.

> The need for cancer prevention and treatment in the United States continues to grow—but not equally for all races. If you were diagnosed with cancer in 1950, you would have a slightly higher survival rate if you were black. Today, however, the statistics are dramatically reversed. In a study by Stotts, Glynn, and Baquet, African Americans were ranked first among U.S. ethnic groups with the lowest cancer survival rate and first with the highest age-adjusted rates of cancer incidence and mortality. What happened to reverse this rate of survival and what can be done about it?

The importance of documenting the gap between what exists now and what could be, should be, or will be with your foundation partner's investment is the basis for your accountability. If you can provide a visual and dramatic picture of the problem and document the incidence and severity of it and how it affects your target population, you can then tell the grantor how the situation will change and how the change will be measured in the solution section of your letter proposal. It is not a canceled check that the grantor wants; it is a changed situation, and the achievement of your project's objectives and goals.

Solution Section

What will you do to close the gap you have just documented? The solution section of your proposal calls for a brief description of the approach you propose to use to solve the problem. In most cases your approach will not totally eliminate the problem, but you must describe how much of the gap you will close (your objective). While describing how you will close the gap, include the measurement indicator you will use to evaluate the success of your approach. Foundations do not want elaborate evaluation designs here. However, you do need to give them an idea of how much will change as a result of your proposed solution. Review the section in chapter 15 on writing objectives.

Depending on the number of total pages allowed, one entire page of your proposal may be dedicated to this section, or you may have to limit this section to one or two paragraphs of five to seven lines each. While you need to have a legitimate plan, you must guard against making the methodology too elaborate. Since you are the content expert, you may have difficulty viewing your proposal from the reader's point of view. Ask yourself the following questions:

- How much does the reader really need to know about the proposed solution?
- Will the reader understand my plan?
- Will the words used in the description of my solution be familiar to the reader?
- Is all the information included critical to convincing the funder that I have a sound, worthwhile plan, or am I including some of it just for myself?

Remember, while you are concerned with how you will solve the problem, grantors are concerned with what will be different after their money is spent. If possible, use this section to summarize your approach and objectives and refer the funder to your project planner for more information, as in the following example:

What can we do in Smithville to promote the sharing of responsibility for education among schools, parents, and children? At Smithville Elementary School we have developed a program aimed at increasing responsible behavior and encouraging parental involvement in the classroom and at home. Teachers will actually work with parents and students to develop tailored, individual contracts to produce increases in all levels of education and the quality of course work. The attached project planner outlines each objective and the activities that will foster the changes we desire. Through the education and involvement of parents in their children's responsible use of out-of-school time, our program will provide the catalyst for decreasing time spent on computer games, texting friends, and television viewing by students. The goal is to increase the completion of homework assignments, improve test scores, and promote physical activities that will improve the health of our youth.

Uniqueness Section

This part of your letter proposal could also be called the "why we are capable and qualified" section. In the uniqueness section, you want to assure the grantor that your organization is the best choice for implementing the solution. Assuming you have held the reader's interest up to this point, he or she knows:

- why you have selected the funding source
- that there is a compelling need
- that you have a plan to address this need

The key question in the grantor's mind at this critical moment is whether your organization is the right one to address the problem

If you have completed the uniqueness exercise in chapter 8, you already have a list of your organization's strengths and positive qualities and, if appropriate, the unique advantages of your consortia members. Select items from the list to include in this section of your letter proposal. Choose credibility builders that will convince the grantor that you have the commitment, staff, skill, buildings, and equipment to do the job. For example, you could say something like:

Serving the elderly has been the sole mission of Rock of Ages Home for over 50 years. Since our inception we have continually received superior ratings from the state board. Our staff members represent over three hundred years of experience, and their commitment to doing more than their call of duty is exhibited by their willingness to *volunteer* time to develop this model approach for serving Alzheimer's patients.

Request for Funds Section

You must make a precise request for money. If you want to demonstrate that you have done your homework, refer to the fact that your request is (or is close to) the grantor's average-size award for your area of interest.

If your request from this grantor does not cover the entire cost of the project, reference those other sources that have already given support, list the others you will be approaching, or mention that such a list is available upon request.

You can summarize the budget categories that make up your total request, or you can provide prospective grantors with the portion of the budget that you would like them to fund. Since you are working under a severe space limitation, your budget summary should be arranged in paragraph form or in several short columns. If you submit your project planner with your proposal, you can refer to the column subtotals in your planner. For example, "The salary and wages, including fringe benefits, total $49,000. The work of the project director and other employees called for in this proposal is documented on page 3 in columns G, H, and I of the project planner."

To keep the focus on the value of the project and the results that you are seeking, you may want to divide the cost of the project by the number of people who will benefit from it. Consider the effect your project may have over several years, and calculate a cost per person served or affected by the project. For example, "In the next five years the equipment that you provide under this grant will touch the lives of approximately five thousand students by helping them to read on grade level for the first time, and at a cost of only $5.63 per person served."

This section should also make reference to how you expect to sustain the project or program after its creation. Foundations do not want to look bad because a program they started ultimately left its recipients in the lurch or out in the cold.

Before constructing this component of your letter proposal, review the foundation's guidelines once again. Some foundations have very specific budget guidelines that must be strictly adhered to.

Closing Paragraph

Many grantseekers close their letter proposals with a statement reflecting their willingness to meet with the prospective grantor to discuss their proposals. While a visit is highly unlikely unless the prospective grantor is a large foundation with a staff, I have had a foundation grantor make a visit to my organization before making the funding decision. However, references to such a meeting are usually futile. Instead, use the closing of your proposal to underscore your willingness to provide any further documentation or information the funding source may desire.

This brings up the question of who from your organization will be the best person to communicate with the prospective grantor. While you, the proposal developer, may have written the proposal, you probably will not be the individual to sign it. Therefore, in your closing paragraph request that your prospective grantor contact you (or the individual responsible for the project) for more information or to answer any questions. For example, "I encourage you to telephone me at my office or to call Ms. Connors directly at _____ to respond to technical questions or for additional information." Be sure to include a telephone number and extension, and test the line that will be used for this purpose to be certain that it is answered by a courteous and knowledgeable representative of your organization. You could also refer to your organization's website for more information or for answers to frequently asked questions. Your contact person's e-mail address should be included as well.

Signatures

Even though you are submitting what seems to be a letter, it is a grant application and constitutes an agreement between your organization and the grantor if it is accepted. Therefore, as is standard in agreements, the administrator or officer who holds the appropriate rank and responsibility to enter into these types of arrangements should sign it. If the link to the grantor is not your chief operating officer or chief executive officer, there is no reason why two individuals cannot sign the proposal—the link and the administrator or your consortia partner.

Because the board is legally responsible for the consequences of your organization's actions, including a board member's signature along with the chief executive officer's may impress the grantor. Just remember that the purpose of the signature is to provide the proposal with legal commitment and credibility.

Attachments

Most foundations require the inclusion of certain attachments such as a:

- list of current board of directors, trustees, and officers showing names and professional affiliations

EXHIBIT 24.2
Sample Letter Proposal to a Foundation

Nikhil Allen, Executive Director
A.O. Smith Foundation
1409 East Oxford Pkwy
Henderson, NV 89400

Dear Mr. Allen:

While working with creative programs to reduce drop-out rates in Nevada's K–12 schools, our staff provided pilot program training to your funded project in the Clark County School District. Dr. Jean Sanchez from *Drop In to Win* found our session and materials extremely helpful. He encouraged our nonprofit organization, *Nevada Read by 3*, to explore a grant opportunity with the A.O. Smith Foundation. Your record of supporting 26 innovative programs with over $3 million in grant funding, documents your concern and passion for young people and aligns perfectly with our case statement and mission.

Nevada's dropout rate continues to increase with every survey. Currently Clark County has the fifth worse graduation rate in the country at 44.5 percent. The current recession and Nevada's 15 percent unemployment rate has resulted in a 25 percent cut in education and a leading gubernatorial candidate who pledges to eliminate one in five current teaching positions.

K–12 teachers in Nevada are facing pay cuts, decreasing benefits, and increasing class sizes. To make matters worse, there are no funds for in-service education or materials to help the classroom leader who has already been struggling and is now faced with increasing numbers of educationally disadvantaged students.

Research by Dr. Timin Brown on evaluating model projects on dropout reduction in Virginia and Ohio has documented a direct correlation between reading skills in third grade and dropout rates. Dr. Brown has developed an intervention program entitled Read by 3 which has been designed to dramatically reduce drop-out rates and problematic classroom behavior. Essentially, students in the program are not promoted to fourth grade unless they reach the corresponding reading level. Dr. Brown's evaluation of similar programs in other states has documented success when the schools, teachers, and parents buy into the concept.

Once in the program, the K–3 classroom leader will receive training, materials, and mentoring to set up the reading success that the program relies on. Participating teachers will receive a "Read by 3 Tool Box" and support to put the program in place.

Over the next 10 years this proactive program will dramatically reduce dropout rates and increase high school completion. Of course there will still be a need for programs like Dr. Sanchez's *Drop In to Win* while these new readers work their way up the educational staircase. But ours is a solution that will change the situation in the long run.

(continued)

EXHIBIT 24.2
(Continued)

We have letters of commitment from 11 urban and rural school districts to join the program. A.O. Smith Foundation's support of $250,000 in year 1 will enable 5 of these districts to initiate the program. Our research indicates that the A.O. Smith Foundation understands the value of multi-year funding, and after evaluation we expect year 2 and year 3 of your Foundation's support to be matched by 10 and 20 percent respectively. Our goal is to have year 4 paid by state funding.

Your support is catalytic to making these changes in the face of what are difficult days for the classroom leader who is feeling abandoned and unappreciated. We stand ready to supply you and your board with any additional information you may need to make your decision. We also invite you to visit our office and to meet with our key personnel. Please direct all questions and correspondence to our project director, Dr. Brown at [telephone number] or [email address].

Sincerely,

Dr. Thomas Watkins, Director
Nevada Read by 3

- copy of 501(c)(3) Internal Revenue Service determination letter of tax exempt status
- audited financial statement for most recent fiscal year
- operating budget for the organization as a whole
- project budget
- collection of recent publications
- organizational background including history and mission
- curricula vitae for the project's senior staff

Most foundations do not encourage prospective grantees to submit any additional materials with their proposal. This includes other attachments as well as DVDs, CDs, videotapes, and so on. You could, however, consider including your project planner as a page in your proposal rather than as an attachment, and be sure to always refer to it by page number. In general, your proposal should give the impression that you have more information, which you are willing to give the prospective grantor if desired. Including too much with the proposal, however, may reduce the likelihood that it will be read and funded.

As you can now see, the letter proposal follows an orderly progression that focuses on the needs and interests of the funding source. As you gain insight into your prospective grantor, you will develop the ability to write grant-winning foundation proposals. A sample letter proposal to a foundation (Exhibit 24.2) is included for your review. Please note that this is an example, not a real proposal, and the facts are not up-to-date.

If you have made the decision to use the foundation grants marketplace, it is time to commit to writing the proposal. Be sure you know the foundation's deadline for submittal and then move to your action steps chart (Figure 24.1). Log the deadline dates and the name of the foundations you will write your proposal for in your plan.

FIGURE 24.1
Action Steps Chart: Applying For Foundation Funds

25

Quality Circles, Proposal Submission, the Decision, and Follow-Up: Private Foundation Funding Sources

Foundation Quality Circle/Proposal Review Committee

BEFORE SUBMISSION YOU WANT TO ENSURE that your proposal is of the highest quality. Just as with government grant proposals, you should put your foundation proposal through a quality circle or proposal review committee critique. This mock review process is much easier than it is with federal proposals since foundations seldom have a scoring system or peer review. But the lack of information on what foundation board members are looking for and how they evaluate proposals is disconcerting to the serious foundation grantseeker. The best suggestion I can provide is to invite a group of four to six people whose backgrounds most closely resemble those of the foundation board to come together for one hour to review your proposal and role play being the board members.

You can find a list of the foundation's board members on the foundation's tax return (990-PF), and then you could also look up each member in *Who's Who in America* (see list of resources), which can be accessed for free at your public library. (It can also be purchased and free trials of its online subscription database are available at marquiswhoswho.com/online-database.) However, you cannot go wrong if you assume they are educated and wealthy and want to carry out projects that reflect similar values as those of the past projects they have supported. Their values and interests change very slowly, if at all.

Provide quality circle participants with any background data on the foundation decision makers that you can uncover. To help your participants in their role playing, summarize your research on Exhibit 25.1, the Foundation

EXHIBIT 25.1
Foundation Profile Worksheet

FOUNDATION PROFILE WORKSHEET

Proposal Title:

Prospective Funding Source:

Areas of Interest of Funding Source:

Sample of Grants in Interest Areas:

General Funding Source Information:

Number of Proposals Received Last Year: _____
Number of Proposals Funded Last Year: _____
Amount of Money Distributed Last Year: _____
Anticipated Distribution of Money This Year: _____

Application Process and Guidelines:

Proposals Reviewed: ___ Monthly   ___Quarterly   ___ Annually
                ___ As Needed   ___ Other

Proposal Format and Length:

Attachments Allowed:

Proposal Review Procedure: (Attach scoring rubric or criteria)

Proposals Are Read By:	Time	Educational Background	Socio/Econ Background	Known Biases/ Viewpoints	Other
Funding Official					
Funding Staff					
Review Committee					
Board Members					
Other					

Profile Worksheet, and provide each one with a copy. Make available as much information as possible but accept the fact that some of the fields may be blank due to the lack of transparency in foundation grant funding.

Ask the group members to read your proposal rapidly and designate those areas they think the foundation's board would like with a plus symbol (+) and those areas they think could be improved with a minus symbol (–). Ask them for their suggestions on improvement and how they think you can incorporate the revisions into your final proposal.

One method that will provide you with a prioritized list of what the group sees as the most positive and the most negative is values voting. Provide your mock reviewers with the instructions on the Quality Circle Proposal Improvement Worksheet (Exhibit 25.2). After they read the proposal, ask them to focus on the positive areas that would appeal to the grantor and combine responses to identify up to ten major areas. List the areas on the Quality Circle Proposal Improvement Scoring Worksheet (Exhibit 25.3). Each participant must allocate a total of ten points to the areas listed and place their points in

EXHIBIT 25.2
Quality Circle Proposal Improvement Worksheet

QUALITY CIRCLE PROPOSAL IMPROVEMENT WORKSHEET

Thank you for assisting us in our efforts to produce quality proposals that are a credit to our organization. You are being asked to review the attached proposal from the viewpoint of the funding source. The following information has been obtained to assist you in developing a perspective that most closely matches that of the real decision makers. Your prejudices and experience will be valued and encouraged. However, they should be kept apart from your thoughts on how the actual funding source would view this proposal.

- Please read the funding source description from the attached foundation profile.
- Role play how you would see our proposal from their eyes.
- Read the proposal and indicate the elements you feel may be appealing to this funding source with a plus (+).
- Read the proposal and indicate with a minus (–) the elements you feel might be viewed negatively by the funding source.
- Use the quality circle proposal improvement scoring worksheets (one for positive areas, one for negative areas) to score the proposal, applying points to each area. A total of ten points can be allocated.

Since we are simulating the way in which the proposal will be read by this funding source, follow the time constraints that our research has uncovered (see the Foundation Profile Worksheet). Remember, funders don't always pour over every word. Many skim the proposal in a few minutes, while some spend several hours.

EXHIBIT 25.3
Quality Circle Proposal Improvement Scoring Worksheet

Circle One: Positive Points/Areas to Improve										
List Areas Identified	Initials								Total Points Per Area	Rank
-------------------------									------	------
Individual Total	10	10	10	10	10	10	10	10		

List Methods to Improve Areas:

the column on the scoring sheet under their initials. A total of ten points must be allocated. The more points out of the ten that are allocated to an area, the stronger the participants feels about it.

The same process is followed on a separate list of areas that are negative and detract from the proposal's fundability. This list of areas needing improvement or problem areas will be circulated to each participant with instructions to allocate ten minus points over the areas in their column. For example, if the quality circle participants feels the proposal did a weak job of showing a need for the project he or she might allocate –3 points to this area. If the budget request section was even weaker, he or she might allocate –4 and so on.

Each list is then added left to right and scores placed in the total point per area column. The areas can then be ranked from highest to lowest. This will provide the proposal developers with the most positive areas that they must work to keep in the rewrite, as well as the areas that they must improve.

This technique is of critical importance as the proposal developer tries to fix the problems within the page and space limitations. Many times after the problem areas are fixed, the positives disappear or are severely reduced. A balance must be sought to ensure that the best areas are retained as the problem areas are remedied.

Rewrite your proposal accordingly. Thank your mock review or quality circle participants and tell them you will let them know the outcome. Send them an e-mail or handwritten thank-you note a week after the exercise. In some cases, I have attached a copy of the improved proposal, highlighting the improvement made due to the feedback given by the quality circle participant.

Submittal

The submittal deadlines set by private foundation funding sources must be taken just as seriously as those set by the government. If you cannot meet a deadline, you will appear to be a poor steward of funds, so try to be prompt, or, better yet, early. Private foundations, unlike the government, have been known to give a few extra days' "grace" period when the prospective grantee has a good explanation for the delay and the benefit of personal contact. However, it still does not look good when you need extra time, especially when the deadline has usually been published for a year or more, or worse yet, has been the same date for many years.

When you are submitting your request to a large foundation, you can:

- Deliver it in person.
- Have an advocate or board member deliver it for you.
- Send it in by the United States Postal Service or private carrier.
- Submit it electronically via the Internet if available.

When sending in your proposal, always request a return receipt. Obtain delivery confirmation whether you use the United States Postal Service, the United Parcel Service, or FedEx. This way you will have proof that your proposal arrived on time, along with a signature that could prove useful in follow-up.

It is expected that an increasing number of foundations will develop websites and offer online proposal submittal. If your prospective funding source has a website, be sure to check if this method of submittal is available to you. Even if you submit your proposal electronically, print it off and make sure that electronic submittal did not somehow affect its visual attractiveness. In several of my online submittals I have asked the grantors if I could supply a duplicate print copy. Note on each copy that a duplicate has been provided, and be sure to get both copies (the electronic and print version) in before the deadline. As a courtesy, you can also offer to provide the grantor with a copy of the proposal for each of its board members.

Make note of the following:

- Send the contacts or links you discovered through the webbing and linkage process a copy of your letter proposal.
- Ask these friends to push for your proposal at the board meeting or to contact their friends or other board members to encourage a favorable decision.
- Minimize personal contact once you have submitted your proposal to avoid appearing pushy.

The Decision and Follow-Up

Private foundation grantors are generally more prompt than government funders at letting you know their decision about your proposal. They will give you a simple yes shortly after the board's scheduled meeting. If the answer is yes, you should do the following immediately:

- Send both a handwritten and e-mail thank-you letter to the funding source. One foundation trustee told me that one of the only records that her foundation keeps on grantees is whether or not they thank the foundation. She said, "If an organization that receives a grant doesn't thank us, they do not receive another grant from us."
- Find out the payment procedures. Usually the acceptance letter comes with a check. If a check is not enclosed, the letter will at least inform you of when you will receive payment. Due to staff shortages, small foundations will usually grant the entire amount requested in one lump sum. Large foundations with staff may make partial or quarterly payments based on your cash forecast.
- Check on any reporting procedures that the funding source may have. Most small foundations consider the canceled check a completion report. However, I suggest you send the funding source a more formal completion report as a courtesy.
- Ask the funding source when you might visit to report on the grant, and invite funders to visit you when traveling in your area.

- Ask, or have your link ask, the funding source what was best about your proposal and what could have been better. Although most grantors will not comment on your proposal, it cannot hurt to ask.

Most funding sources feel neglected once they have given away their money. You can get on their list of good grantees by following up. Your follow-up checklist should include:

- putting funding sources on your public relations mailing list so that they will receive news or press releases
- keeping your funding source files updated and having a volunteer maintain current lists of grants funded by each of your grantors
- writing to funding sources two years after they have funded you to let them know how successful you are and to thank them again for their farsightedness in dealing with the problem

Since you are now aware of the critical staff shortage in foundations, you should not be surprised that most foundations do not even send out rejection notices. Hopefully, this will be less the case as more foundations use e-mail. A woman in one of my seminars remarked that she was still waiting to hear about a foundation proposal she submitted two years prior. I assured her that it was rejected. With foundation grants, no news is bad news. In either case, rejection or no news, I suggest you do the following:

- Send a thank-you letter to the funding source. Express your appreciation for the time and effort spent on reviewing your proposal.
- Remind the funder what an important source of funds it is.
- Ask for helpful comments on your proposal and whether the funding source would look favorably on resubmission with certain changes.
- Ask whether the funder could suggest any other funding sources that may be interested in your project.

If the foundation has no staff and you have no links, you may not find answers to your questions. Try again. Successful grantseekers are persistent! However, you should also be aware that you may not hear *anything* from the funding source.

The steps suggested in part 3 of this book follow the book's unifying principle: that is, look at everything you do from the perspective of the grantor. From preproposal contact, to writing your thank-you letter, to follow-up, consider how you would want to be appreciated and recognized for your contribution now and in the future.

Part 4

PRIVATE/CORPORATE FUNDING OPPORTUNITIES

26

Understanding the Corporate Grants Marketplace

ACCORDING TO *Giving USA, 2014* corporate investments with nonprofit organizations in 2013 accounted for five percent of the $335 billion in philanthropy, or $17.88 billion.[1] You may ask why corporations make *any* commitment at all to nonprofit philanthropy, especially when their shareholders and corporate boards are primarily interested in the bottom line. By learning the answer to this question, you will gain the understanding you need to make the most of this very lucrative marketplace. Yes, lucrative, because corporations fund projects that the federal government would never fund. In fact, corporate funds can provide a catalyst to your project and organization and allow you to gather the preliminary data need to get larger, government grant support. Even though corporate contributions decreased by 1.9 percent in 2013 from 2012 (adjusted for inflation the actual decline was more like 3.2 percent), we are still talking about $17.88 billion that you can acquire based on a one- to three-page proposal.

To understand this marketplace you must put on the values glasses of corporate decision makers (see chapter 3). What would encourage them to motivate themselves to support your project? Think quid-pro-quo, this for that, and what is in it for them. In general, corporations calculate exactly what their investment will garner them in returns.

This reminds me of something a corporate executive who attended one of my grants seminars once said to me. When I began my lecture section on corporate giving, he stood up and objected bitterly to my language. He stated that corporations never *give away* anything, including money. They *invest* in nonprofit organizations and expect a *return* on their investments. When I asked him what the guiding principal was in his company's grants program his response was "enlightened corporate self-interest."

The concept of corporate self-interest as the guiding principle of corporate philanthropy actually has its basis in law. The Internal Revenue Act of 1935 made it legal for corporations to deduct 5 percent of their pretax revenues for charitable donations. The general consensus was that these gifts (which many still view as the purview of the stockholders and not the corporation) were to be used for purposes that directly benefited the corporation's business or interests. It took eighteen years for this concept to be challenged.

In 1953 in *A.P. Smith Manufacturing Co. v. Barlow et al.*, the New Jersey Supreme Court ruled that corporate contributions for purposes other than a direct benefit to the business were indeed legal. The case involved a contested gift of $1,500 made by the A.P. Smith Manufacturing Company's board of directors to Princeton University for general maintenance. Until that time, the company's corporate practice had been to sponsor only educational research projects that related to the company's business. The stockholders charged that the gift was a misappropriation of corporate funds, but the Supreme Court ruled otherwise. This ruling has been referred to as the "Magna Carta" of corporate philanthropy, and it ultimately changed the ground rules for corporate contributions forever.

The year 2014 marked the sixty-second anniversary of this ruling, which made it legal for a corporation to award gifts and grants that do not directly benefit its business. Still, corporate giving is primarily motivated by corporate self-interest. Corporate giving is usually a "this-for-that" exchange. Even when the grant may not be directly related to the corporation's business or products, the corporation still receives public relations value in the community or marketplace.

A 2013 study conducted by the Indiana University Lilly Family School of Philanthropy, *Giving Beyond Borders: A Study of Global Giving by U.S. Corporations,* found that the majority of the surveyed Fortune 500 companies reported *corporate mission and value* as the goals for their giving (sponsored by Global Impact, October 13, 2013, www.philanthropy.iupui.edu). The study also indicated that the surveyed corporations gave or invested in the communities they lived in to build and enhance their business reputation. They listed K–12 education and libraries, disaster relief, human services, public-society benefit, and higher education as their primary areas of support.

These areas of support are similar to those cited in *Giving USA, 2014* and taken from the Conference Board's *Giving in Numbers* survey on 2013 contributions, with education (K–12 and higher) ranked as number 1, followed by health and human services, community and economic development, civic and public affairs, culture and arts, disaster relief, environment, and others.

According to the *National Directory of Corporate Giving,* nineteenth edition (see chapter 27), companies often favor causes in the public eye like education with an emphasis on math, science, minority education, and school reform. They also like to invest in environmental issues, low-income housing, and preventive health maintenance.

Historically, education has received the largest portion of the corporate philanthropic dollar. As you ponder your ability to attract corporate support for your college, university, school, or educationally related nonprofit group, you need to consider the following. Traditionally, higher education has been the industry's subcategory of choice. Corporations figured out long ago that without the raw ingredient of a trained workforce they could not produce competitive products or services. Today, they realize that they need higher education graduates to maintain a competitive place in an increasingly global marketplace. However, higher education cannot assume that it will always receive the largest share of the corporate education dollar. A considerable challenge has been successfully mounted by secondary education, elementary education, and even preschool education.

While education has historically attracted the most *cash* share of corporate philanthropy, the health category receives a greater percentage of total corporate contributions when you consider all forms of support (cash and noncash). One reason for this may be the escalating costs of health care and the fact that health and human services programs, projects, and research may provide direct benefits to employees, which decreases the need for services and, hence, lowers the corporation's employee health costs.

While one could argue that support for education, human services, civic and community affairs, and health make a company look good and enhances the general community, how would you explain a corporation's interest in arts and culture? As a past board member and grantseeker for a museum, I once asked a corporate contributions committee member how I could make my museum proposal more attractive to the committee. I was told I should document certain overriding factors, such as:

- the use of the museum by current corporate employees, their families, and their friends
- the number of corporate employees and their family members who volunteer at the museum
- how the museum interfaces with the local chamber of commerce and how its presence promotes tourism and visitor to the area
- the existence of programs designed to provide family tours and so forth to those whom the corporation is seeking to recruit

As a result of our conversation, we developed a community introduction program that matched our board members with prospective employees that the corporation was seeking to hire and relocate to our area. This moved us from a grant to support the museum to a contract to provide an introduction service, but it was undesignated cash that we could use as we saw fit.

Irrespective of what a corporation supports, you can be sure that its expenditures, be they philanthropic dollars or noncash gifts, are related to its enlightened corporate self-interests. The bottom line is that as you develop your corporate grants strategy, you must view your institution's or organization's ability to provide corporations with what they value.

Now that you have a better understanding of what corporations are interested in and why they invest in nonprofits, it is time to consider the varied mechanisms that companies employ to make their corporate investments. Since corporations are concerned with how their support will provide returns, they may employ more than one mechanism to garner the public relations, product sales, and positioning they value. Companies provide support to nonprofits through four avenues: corporate contribution program gifts and grants, corporate foundations, corporate marketing noncash support, and corporate research program contributions and grants.

Corporate Contributions Program Gifts and Grants

Corporate contributions programs are the mechanism of choice in corporate philanthropy. Usually high-ranking corporate officials decide what portion of the corporation's net earnings before taxes (NEBT; the bottom line of profits after manufacturing, sales, and marketing costs have been deducted) will be made available as gifts and grants. This money is then deducted from the corporate taxes due the government and directed to a corporate contributions committee made up of corporate executives and representatives of employee groups or unions. The committee then disperses the funds to colleges, universities, and other nonprofit organizations that the corporation values. Since many existing corporations are relatively small, with only a few employees, it can be surmised that the larger the company, the more likely it is to have a corporate contributions program and to engage in this mechanism of corporate philanthropy.

Current Internal Revenue Service (IRS) rules allow corporations to donate up to 10 percent of their pretax income (NEBT) in gifts and grants to nonprofit organizations as a tax deduction. However, the practice of donating a *set* percentage annually is not widespread. A good indicator of a company's dedication to social responsibility is the percentage of their NEBT that they donate. The Committee Encouraging Corporate Philanthropy (CECP) reports that corporate giving as a percentage of corporate pretax profits went from a high of 2.1 percent in 1986 to a low of 0.8 percent in 2013. This percentage has been steadily eroding as companies question the return on their investment for their philanthropic expenditures and slow growth in corporate pretax profits.

As with other corporate data, like the exact number of corporations in the United States, statistics on corporate contribution giving are difficult to verify. Companies are not required to publicize direct corporate giving programs or sustain prescribed funding levels. It is interesting to note that corporate philanthropic contributions are not even required to be reported to stockholders in an itemized format. Stockholders are not entitled to a list of recipient organizations and the associated amounts of grants support. Only the IRS receives such a list with the corporate tax return and it is not at liberty to share it with anyone.

Because corporate tax returns are not publically available, it is difficult to ascertain the funding priorities of corporate contributions programs. Interests vary from company to company but historically, education, health and human services, and international support have been the biggest recipients of corporate contributions programs. It is no surprise that international support is one of the recipients of corporate contributions programs. Contributions made by corporations usually benefit the corporation, its employees, or the community in which it operates, and since we are rapidly becoming a global economy, the "community" is changing to an international one. However, *overall* giving to international affairs slowed in 2013 due, in part, to fewer disaster relief contributions compared with prior years, the general decline in giving by corporations, and changes in donor giving preferences.

Corporate Foundation Grants

In this grants mechanism, companies designate a portion of their entitled write-off of pretax profits to be transferred to a foundation (usually named after the corporation) from which grants are paid. The main reason for initiating a corporate foundation is to stabilize a corporation's philanthropy program. Corporate foundations lead to a more uniform and stable approach to corporate philanthropy than giving programs that rely solely on a percentage of company profits each year. Programs tied to company profits are subject to the seesaw effect, because profits can vary widely from year to year. Funds from the corporate foundation corpus can be moved to grants in lean profit years.

Many corporations maintain both a corporate contributions program and a corporate foundation. This allows the company some flexibility in making grants. For example, if profits are down one year, the corporate contributions program can be supported by expending some of the assets that have built up in the foundation. The corporation can level out the highs and lows of its corporate contributions over periods of high, low, and no profits and still maintain some level of support for its favorite nonprofit organizations. While all foundations are required to pay out a minimum of 5 percent of their assets, the CECP reports that many corporate foundations pay out a much higher percentage.

Like the other types of foundations discussed in chapter 21, corporate foundations must list the benefactors of their grants, file a yearly IRS Form 990, and make these tax returns available for public viewing. This requirement can become a problem for corporations when their stockholders object to the types of organizations or specific projects that the corporate foundation supports. In addition, the public scrutiny to which the corporate foundation is subject allows for social activists and leaders of particular causes to research the foundation's giving pattern and arrange for demonstrations at stockholder meetings that could result in negative public relations. To avoid such problems, many corporations only make noncontroversial grants (for example, a grant to the United Way) through their foundation; they make all other grants through their corporate contributions program that does not require public disclosure.

The number of corporate foundations is approximately 2,700 and giving by these grant-making foundations grew to an estimated $5.73 billion in 2013. Since corporate foundations are an extension of a profit-making company, they tend to view the world and your proposal as any corporation would. They must see a benefit in all of the projects they fund. Many of these corporate foundations fund grants only in communities where their parent corporations have employees or a special interest. Historically, human services and education are the top priorities of corporate foundations, and while international support is generally one of the top priorities for corporate contributions programs, it takes a much lower place in corporate foundation support.

Corporate Marketing Noncash Support

While it is estimated that 25 percent of corporate support to nonprofits comes in the form of noncash support such as donated products, this figure is probably deceptively low. Corporate support in the form of products is likely to be far greater than the reported levels, but data on this mechanism are difficult to collect and analyze. Much is simply not reported and thus is impossible to track.

Many corporate contributions of products may not be recorded as gifts because they are being used to position the products in the user's marketplace to gain future sales. In essence, these product gifts could be questioned by the IRS because they may not qualify as true gifts; some quid pro quo (or this-for-that) is involved in the transaction, but the company writes off the associated costs before net earnings are ever calculated to avoid any problems.

For example, I once worked with an organization that approached a specific corporation for equipment needed for a research project. The request was granted and we got our $100,000 piece of equipment. However, the corporate executive did not want a letter from us acknowledging the contribution. He just wanted a signed invoice that we received the equipment and to have his company and the equipment cited in all references and project results. The company also wanted us to provide them with feedback on their equipment's performance, which they would then use in future product development. When asked how he was going to write off this $100,000 donation, the corporate executive remarked that it was considered a sales or marketing expense and as such, was subtracted from the company's NEBT.

If your project involves equipment, software, furniture, supplies, and so on, approaching corporations that build or import these items may be productive.

Corporate Research Program Contributions and Grants

Corporations have traditionally supported colleges, universities, and nonprofit organizations' attempts to apply science to further the development of new technologies, patents, and breakthroughs in their fields of interest. Some corporations also contribute to nonprofit organizations based on the nonprofit's ability to contribute to the testing, improvement, or creation of a new product. The litmus test as to whether the support provided is really a grant is whether the nonprofit that is the recipient of the corporate support is acting as a free agent or is a captive contractor for the corporate sponsor of the proposed work.

To be considered a true corporate grant, the results of the research must be published and shared for the "greater good" of the field. The more specific the benefits are to just one company's product or research, the less likely it will fulfill IRS's requirements to qualify for a deduction. If the work is to be prescribed by the corporation, or the freedom to publish the resulting data is restricted, and any patents derived are the sole ownership of the corporation, the corporation's support will be not be viewed by the IRS as a grant but rather as a fee for services rendered or a corporate contract. If the support is viewed as a corporate contract, it is not allowed to be written off as a charitable contribution. However, it could be considered as a research or marketing cost and as such could be deducted before the company arrives at its NEBT.

While you do not need to be concerned with how the company deducts these costs from its balance sheet, it is crucial to both you and your institution or organization to clarify the intellectual property rights (copyrights, patents, and so forth) before entering into any research-related agreement.

Some corporations may prefer to contract with you and your organization to perform prescribed research that would not qualify as a donation or gift. On the other hand, several competing corporations may decide to fund a combined research project that benefits their whole field. In fact, trade organizations frequently create research grants programs that address industry issues that benefit all of their members.

Review your proposed project and consider how it provides your prospective corporate grantor with what it values. Then, based on these variables, determine which corporate grant-making mechanism best fits your project (Exhibit 26.1). Compare the corporate self-interest variables in the column on the left of the exhibit to the four basic mechanisms for corporate support presented in the top row of the exhibit.

Corporate Funding and Ethical Issues

Most researchers are aware of the traditional hierarchy of grant support. By tradition, government, peer-reviewed grants have been viewed as the most prestigious, followed by foundation grants (not always peer reviewed and subject to foundation board bias), and finally, corporate grants support (reviewed by a biased corporate grants committee looking for a return on its investment). However, the traditional ways of looking at corporate grants have changed dramatically over the last decade. One reason for this change has to do with the government's cuts in research. The cuts have encouraged, if not forced, universities to partner with the corporate world to collaborate, transfer technology, and develop intellectual property. Sheldon Krimsky, in his book *Science in the Private Interest: Has the Lure of Profits Corrupted the Virtue of Biomedical Research,*[2] questions whether universities should be turned into instruments of wealth rather than protected enclaves whose primary roles are as sources of enlightenment. The traditional assumption that research findings that come from the ivory tower of higher education are true and not biased or corrupt has been challenged by science selling findings to the highest bidder.

EXHIBIT 26.1
Corporate Grants Support Worksheet

Corporate Self Interest	Corporate Contributions Program Gifts and Grants	Corporate Foundation Grants	Corporate Marketing Noncash Support	Corporate Research Program Contributions and Grants
Ability to Attract High-Quality Personnel				
Benefits Workers or Their Families				
Benefits Overall Community Where Parent Corporation Has Factory or Special Interests				
Positions Product in such a Way that It Results in Future Sales				
Product Development—Tests, Improves, or Creates a New Product				
Research—Furthers Knowledge in Corporation's Field of Interest				
Other:				

There exists a tremendous pressure to trade off the values of higher education as the costs for supporting research soar and the government cuts its funding for peer-reviewed research and continues to support earmarked noncompetitive grants. Not only has Congress pushed the bounds of ethical standards related to research but it has also left the university and the researcher little choice but to surround themselves with corporations that have never been the bastion of ethical standards.

The big question now is how much financial gain the researcher will get by proving what the company wants. In fact, the incentives given by companies in stock and whether the company is owned by the researcher have now become the operant questions from which to judge the research findings.

Corporate support for research presents problems all across the nonprofit sector because the profits from potential products are so high. How far can this corporate interest in research take us? Several universities have auctioned off exclusive rights to their intellectual resources and their reputations to corporate bidders as a result of budget cuts. They pledge to maintain scientific ethics, but would they really do research that questioned their corporate partners' products? The lines are so blurred that some universities have actually warned their researchers that they could be sued if their research costs their corporate sponsors to lose profits.

The bottom line is that researchers must be very careful when dealing with corporate grantors. They come at a price. Being forewarned is being forearmed.

Notes

1. *Giving USA: The Annual Report on Philanthropy for the year 2013* (Chicago: Giving USA Foundation, 2014).

2. Sheldon Krimsky, *Science in the Private Interest: Has the Lure of Profits Corrupted the Virtue of Biomedical Research?* (Lanham, MD: Rowman & Littlefield, 2004), 2.

27

Researching Corporate Grantors: How to Find the Corporate Funding Source Best Suited to Fund Your Project

To be a successful corporate grantseeker, you will need to gather accurate information on your prospective corporate grantors before you approach them. The Corporate Research Form (Exhibit 27.1) outlines what information you will need to collect. The biggest mistake you can make with this marketplace is to send the same proposal to all the companies in your field. Your research will result in your ability to create targeted, tailored, winning proposals.

How you research the corporate marketplace depends on many factors, including the type of corporate grants mechanism you are pursuing. You must ask why a corporation would value your proposal. If your project is related to products, product positioning, product development, or research, you can cast a wide corporate net. In fact, you can move beyond local boundaries and look across the country for the corporations best suited to fund your project.

To do so, you must first determine which major corporations could possibly be affected by your project. Develop a list of the products and services (the key words) that could be related to your project, and then use your Internet browser to find companies that deal in these goods and services.

You will also want to find out if there are major industry-specific associations or membership groups that fund research or projects in your field. For instance, the Society of Manufacturing Engineers funds beneficial research in its field, and there are many more like it.

While you should look outside of your local area for corporate grantors when your project is related to research and product development, remember that most corporations give where they live. Therefore, you may find that

EXHIBIT 27.1
Corporate Research Form

The following form outlines the data you need to collect to make a decision
to seek funding from this grant source. Your attempts to collect as much of this
information as possible will prove rewarding. (When feasible, record the source
of the information and the date it was recorded.)

Name of Corporation: _____

Name of Corporate Foundation: _____

Name of Corporate Contributions Program: _____

Address: _____

Phone: _____ Fax: _____ E-mail: _____

Web site: _____

Contact Person: _____

Title: _____

Any Links from Our Organization to Contact Person: _____

_____

_____

Corporation's Areas of Interests: _____

_____

_____

Eligibility Requirements/Restrictions:
a. Activities Funded/Restricted: _____

_____

_____

b. Organizations Funded/Restricted: _____

_____

_____

c. Geographic Funding Preferences/Restrictions: _____

_____

_____

d. Other Requirements/Restrictions: _____

_____

_____

_____

_____

_____

_____

(continued)

EXHIBIT 27.1
(Continued)

Information Available   In Possession Of

IRS 990-PF Tax Return (Year)   _____ (Corporate Foundation Only)
Guidelines   _____
Newsletters   _____
Annual Report   _____
Previously Funded Proposals   _____
Reviewer Information   _____
Evaluation Criteria   _____

Contributions Committee Members/Board of Directors/ Foundation Officers:

_____
_____
_____
_____

Deadline(s): _____

Application Process/Requirements:

_____
_____
_____

Financial Information

Fiscal Year: _____
Corporate Sales: $_____
Parent Company: _____
Corporate Sites: _____
# of Employees: _____
Credit Rating: _____ Source: _____
Private or Publicly Held: _____
If Publicly Held: Stock Price $_____ Dividend: $_____
Products Produced/Distributed: _____
_____
_____
_____

(continued)

EXHIBIT 27.1
(Continued)

For Corporate Foundations:

Asset Base: $_____

Are there current gifts to build the asset base?   Yes _____   No_____

If yes, how much? $_____

Total number of grants awarded in _____: _____

Total amount of grants awarded in _____: $_____

High Grant: $_____
Low Grant: $_____
Average Grant: $_____

In our interest area there were: _____ grants, totaling $_____

High grant in our interest area: $ _____

Low grant in our interest area: $ _____

Average grant in our interest area: $ _____

Grants Received versus Grants Funded

Number of proposals received in _____: _____

Number of proposals funded in   _____: _____

Sample Grants in Our Area of Interest:

Recipient Organization	Amount
_____	_____
_____	_____
_____	_____
_____	_____

targeting corporations that are hundreds or thousands of miles away is not productive unless they have a vested interest in your project or research.

Checking with your grant office and development office is always recommended when dealing with corporations, and it is absolutely essential when contacting companies close to home. Corporate people assume that anyone who submits a proposal or contacts the has the approval of the institution or organization he or she represents, and you risk negative positioning if the right hand does not know what the left is doing. This does not mean that you should not consider local corporations, but do your research and make a case to your organization as to why you and your project should be allowed to proceed to submittal with each target corporation.

Doing your homework on corporate grantors can be more frustrating than researching federal or foundation sources. You will find much less information available on corporate grants awarded by companies that do not use a foundation to make their grants, and the information you do find will be much less reliable. The reason for the lack of sound data on corporate giving is that there are no laws allowing public review of corporate contributions programs. Companies must record their corporate charitable contributions on their Internal Revenue Service (IRS) tax return, but no one, not even a stockholder, has the right to see the return.

Except for the portion of corporate grants that is awarded through corporate foundations, corporate data are not subject to validation, and hence the reporting is not always accurate. The data on corporate giving are derived from self-reported, voluntary responses to surveys and questionnaires. Even the corporate contributions data reported to *Giving USA* are based on a voluntary survey conducted by the Conference Board, a nonprofit organization with a reputation for keeping corporate responses confidential.

Irrespective of the difficulties in obtaining accurate corporate granting information, there are still several good resources of information on corporate support. The Foundation Center, in particular, is a good source of information on corporate foundation grants. Its publication, *The National Directory of Corporate Giving*, nineteenth edition, provides information on 3,212 foundations and grant-making public charities identified by the Foundation Center as established and funded primarily by companies and 1,769 direct corporate giving programs. Entries include program descriptions and information on fields of interest, annual giving amounts, average size of grants awarded, giving limitations, key contact names including officers, donors, and trustees, and application procedures. Grantseekers interested in researching corporate donors can also use the Foundation Center's database, Foundation Directory Online (FDO) Professional, which includes, among other things, information on over four thousand companies. *The Corporate Giving Directory*, thirty-fifth edition, published by Information Today, Inc., is another good source. It provides profiles on one thousand of the largest corporate foundations and corporate direct giving programs in the United States and has fourteen indexes—eight devoted to corporations and foundations and six biographical. Entries include contact information, giving philosophy, application procedures, restrictions, and specific grants given. The *Directory* also provides information on direct giving programs that are not included on IRS Forms 990 or corporate annual reports. (See the list of resources for ordering information.) In addition, the annual 990-PF tax returns for corporate foundations can be accessed through the Foundation Center's website, its learning and library centers, and its funding information networks (see chapter 22).

Corporate funders can also be found through the Internet, especially since many companies now maintain a presence on the web. There are several helpful portal sites available, including:

- www.foundationcenter.org/findfunders/ (the Foundation Center's website)
- www.fundsnetservices.com/ (Fundsnet Services Online)
- www.manta.com (a free online business directory that allows you to search for companies in your area by products and services)

While it makes sense to check out these websites and the corporate grant resource books available in your public library and at the Foundation Center's regional collections, another important source for data is your local chamber of commerce. Your chamber of commerce may be able to provide you with a list of local corporations and information on number of employees, total values of payroll, and products and services provided. You can obtain this list by visiting or phoning your chamber, and in some instances the information is available on its website.

If you cannot access this information through your chamber of commerce, you can get it by doing a search on the web for your city's top employers by number of employees. If your institution or organization is not in a large metropolitan area, and there is no chamber of commerce, contact your nearest economic development agency, industrial park headquarters, or business incubator. One of these groups should have the data you need to uncover the corporations in your geographic area.

A list of top employers by number of employees is most valuable as you begin to target your local grantors and develop your strategy on why they should be interested in your proposal. For example, when I was an associate professor at the University of Alabama, Birmingham, I asked for and received a list of the area's largest employers from the local chamber of commerce (Exhibit 27.2). While this list is now dated, at the time I discovered the following facts after reviewing the information:

- The university I was employed by was the area's largest employer (and still is).
- Of the top ten largest employers, only three were profit-making corporate prospects.
- Seventy percent of the ten largest employers were nonprofit organizations and in competition with me for corporate support.
- Seventy percent of the next group (ten to twenty largest employers) were profit making but had only 19,890 employees in total compared to the nonprofits' 87,556 employees.

EXHIBIT 27.2
Chamber of Commerce List: Top Employers – Birmingham/Hoover Metropolitan Area

Company	Employees
1. University of Alabama at Birmingham	18,750
2. BellSouth	5,485
3. Baptist Health System, Inc.	5,000+
4. Birmingham Board of Education	5,000
5. City of Birmingham	4,989
6. Jefferson County Board of Education	4,800
7. Jefferson County Commission	3,875
8. AmSouth Bancorporation	3,785
9. Bruno's Supermarkets, Inc.	3,477
10. Children's Health System	3,200
11. Wachovia	3,094
12. Alabama Power Company	3,000
13. Blue Cross-Blue Shield of Alabama	3,000
14. Drummond Company, Inc.	2,900
15. Brasfield & Gorrie, L.L.C.	2,800
16. St. Vincent's Hospital	2,800
17. United States Postal Service	2,800
18. Compass Bancshares	2,696
19. Brookwood Medical Center	2,600
20. American Cast Iron Pipe Company	2,400

In addition to having to deal with the harsh reality of these facts, I also had to come to terms with the fact that hundreds of local nonprofits were targeting this corporate group, that the rest of my university had designs on the same local corporations that I did, and that I would have to plead my case for approval to submit a proposal to a development team comprising representatives from colleges and departments other than mine.

Once you have identified your distant and nearby potential corporate funding sources, you will need to gather basic information about your corporate prospects such as areas of company operations, products and services, corporate officers, and fiscal data. The following websites are a good place to start researching corporate information:

- www.sec.gov/edgar/searchedgar/webusers.htm (EDGAR database that contains information on companies whose stocks are traded publically)
- www.hoovers.com (a comprehensive subscription-based site that provides information on public and private companies in the United States and abroad)
- www.forbes.com (free online information on the five hundred largest private companies in the United States)

Several of the Dun & Bradstreet or Standard & Poor's products and publications will provide the basic information you will need on profitability, board members, and so on.

The *D&B Million Dollar Directory (MDDI)* provides information on privately held and public companies and their executives, and covers thirty-four million businesses worldwide and over seventy-five million executives. The series is published in five volumes. The first three volumes contain alphabetical listings, while the fourth and fifth are cross-referenced volumes grouped geographically by state and by standard industrial classification (SIC). A typical *MDDI* entry includes the following:

- complete North America family tree (hierarchy of related businesses)
- SIC codes
- North American industry classification system (NAICS) codes
- user profiles
- D-U-N-S number
- company name, address, telephone number
- state of incorporation
- parent company name
- founded or ownership date
- annual sales and total employment
- stock exchange ticker symbol
- banking or accounting relationship
- up to six industry classifications and business descriptions
- company officers and directors

The D&B Million Dollar Directory Database is the online equivalent to the *MDDI*. It is a subscription-based database that provides data on businesses such as addresses, ticker symbols, key officers, number of employees, sales, and so on. It provides downloading into various outputs, search capabilities using a combination of up to thirty different search criteria, and the ability to create and save searches based on individual user profile. (See the list of resources for ordering information for both D&B products.)

Standard and Poor's NetAdvantage is an online business reference tool for academic libraries, public libraries, and corporate libraries and information centers. It provides industry surveys and detailed descriptions of companies, industries, and mutual funds. It contains private company information on over eighty-five thousand companies that are not publicly traded and allows NAICS code searching. It also has biographies of thousands of corporate executives and directors. (This biographical information is very valuable in that it can be used with your grants advisory committee to uncover links and expand corporate relationships.) To find company information, the subscriber starts with either the *simple search* box on the homepage or the *companies* tab in the navigation bar, types in a company name or ticker, and then clicks on the arrow. An overview of the company will be displayed, which includes a summary of the company's business and a brief fact sheet. The menu to the left of this overview provides access to more detailed information and vital statistics including financials, competitors, stock report, corporate records, industry surveys, and company news. Check with your university or public library to see if they have access to this corporate resource.

In addition to the D&B and Standard & Poor's resources, your library should also have *Who's Who in America* and other books on outstanding individuals in your geographic area. The more you know about the people you will be approaching for a grant, the more prepared you will be to create a powerful appeal that motivates the grantor to award you funds. Corporate leaders have much more written about them than federal bureaucrats, and your local librarian can show you how to use free resource tools to learn more about corporate grant prospects. Check the list of resources in the back of this book for commercially available materials that you will find helpful in your search for corporate funding sources.

Profits are the bottom line in corporate philanthropy. It there are no profits there is little incentive to donate money to reduce taxes. Since corporate contributions depend on a company's profitability, your corporate research should include information on revenue. There are several ways to obtain accurate data on profitability. You can:

- Access a corporation's website to learn about its new products and plans.
- Track a corporation's stock prices on the DOW, NASDAQ, or AMEX.
- Include a stockholder on your advisory group to help you monitor corporate profits.
- Involve a corporate executive on your advisory group who subscribes to Dun & Bradstreet's financial services and ask him or her to request a Dun & Bradstreet report on your prospective corporate grantor. This report will rate the fiscal stability of the company and give you a sense of

the company's ability to support your proposal. (A corporate person will understand the values of corporations and may have linkages to companies you are interested in pursuing for grant support.)

- Purchase a few shares of stock in each publicly held company in your area. If you receive a dividend check, you will also receive corporate reports, proxy statements, and up-to-date information on top corporate administrators and board member changes. You might even make some money, and if you get rejected by a corporation you can always sell its stock for revenge!

The corporate research strategies recommended in this chapter will at least provide you with the ability to gather the name, address, e-mail address, and phone number of the corporate contact person; information you will find necessary to take the next step in your grant-winning strategy step—contacting a grantor before submission.

Before you do so, it is important to decide whether you will incorporate researching corporate grantors in your action steps chart. Figure 27.1 shows this step in the "ideal plan." However, you may decide to bypass the corporate marketplace as a result of the knowledge you gathered in chapters 26 and 27. But if this marketplace does hold some potential for you, be it in funding or products, review your action steps chart to determine where researching corporate grantors will fit and when you will have the time to do it.

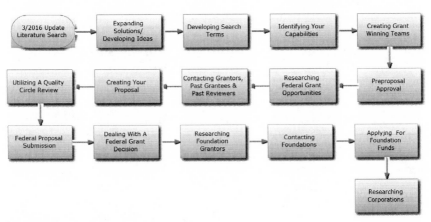

FIGURE 27.1
Action Steps Chart: Researching Corporations

28

Preproposal Contact with Corporate Grantors

J UST AS WITH PRIVATE FOUNDATION GRANTSEEKERS, corporate grantseekers who discuss their projects with the appropriate corporate funding officials before submitting their proposals increase their success rates. Experience
leads me to believe that the impact of preproposal contact on success rates is
much higher in the corporate marketplace than the foundation, and could
approach a tenfold factor.

With such a dramatic positive effect on success rates, one would wonder
why some grantseekers do not take advantage of contacting a grantor before
writing their proposal. Chapter 21 on the foundation marketplace reveals
that only a few thousand of the 86,192 foundations occupy an office and
could actually carry out contact with prospective grantees. Many novice
grantseekers assume that since corporations have employees, they must have
individuals they can contact regarding grants. By now, you should know to
apply your corporate grants values to this area of your grantseeking. As you
know, corporations do not like to "give away" money and their executives are
dedicated to making profits. Taking time with a grantseeker is not high on
their list of things to do. Even when a corporation has a corporate contributions program, the corporation views it as a cost center and usually has only a
few paid staff dedicated to the program. Remember that even if the company
uses a corporate foundation as its granting vehicle, any staff are written off as
part of its charitable contribution.

How to Contact Corporate Grantors

Corporate webbing and linkages become critical here (see chapter 9). It pays to figure out who may know whom, and who would be willing to make an appointment or open a door for you. If you do not have a linkage to any of your prospective corporate grantors, consider creating one by inviting selected corporate representatives to take part in your advisory group, or by hosting an open house or public forum for them.

Your initial point of contact may not always be the individual listed in your research as the corporate foundation contact or the chair of the corporate contributions committee. Your initial contact person may be a salesperson for the corporation, clients of your organization who work for the company, and so on. Many corporations pay special attention to proposals that can be linked to employees that are volunteers of the prospective

EXHIBIT 28.1
Sample Inquiry Letter/E-mail to a Corporation

Name
Title
Address

Dear _____:

We at (<u>nonprofit organization</u>) are developing a project which deals with (problem) and provides benefit to [or in] (<u>target population</u>). Our research indicates that this area is an important concern of the (<u>name of corporation or corporate foundation</u>).

[Choose from the following paragraphs]

(<u>Name and title</u>) from our organization is planning a trip to (<u>corporation's geographic location</u>) and would appreciate being able to talk with you regarding an exciting project that we feel would be of mutual benefit. I will be contacting you soon to discuss this further.

[Or]

We would like to explain our innovative solution in a full proposal, and request that you send or e-mail us a request to apply or your application guidelines or form.

Thank you for your cooperation.

Name/Title
Organization
Address
E-mail

---

grantee's organization. Most will state that they do not accommodate any preproposal contact. Therefore, it is imperative that you follow the formal instructions your research uncovers. If you uncover a name, an e-mail address, or a phone number, assume that you can contact the person listed. If your research states no contact except by letter or application, then follow those instructions. However, informal contact through an advisory committee member, advocate, or linkage is still advised. In these instances, the important thing is that *you* are the one making the contact. If your advisory committee member, advocate, or linkage can orchestrate a conference call or preferably a face-to-face meeting, go with him or her. If you are instructed to request current guidelines or an application package, you can use the sample inquiry letter or e-mail shown in Exhibit 28.1. If the instructions call for a letter of inquiry or a letter proposal and do not allow for formal preproposal contact, use the foundation outline in chapter 29.

Contact by Telephone

If contact by telephone is allowed or encouraged, call to discuss how your project relates to the corporation's interest. Let the person to whom you are speaking know that you have done your homework. If it is a corporate foundation, use the information you obtained from its tax return (IRS form 990-PF) to show your knowledge of it past granting interests. If the corporate grantor seems interested in your project, do not be afraid to inquire about the possibility of a face-to-face meeting. If a visit is out of the question, then discuss the same issues over the phone as you would in person.

The Visit

While often the most anxiety producing, a face-to-face visit is usually the best way to discuss your project and to gauge the interest of the corporate grantor.

Who Should Go

It is advisable for you to take either an advocate, linkage, or an advisory committee member with you. A good listener who can summarize and reflect back what you believe is the grantor's position is a good choice. Successful corporate people are skilled at making sales calls, and they will expect you to be skilled when asking for their money. You do not want to appear as a fast-talking used-car salesperson, but your approach should be well rehearsed and professional, and your appearance should be conservative, reflecting that of the corporate official's as closely as possible. Remember, corporate people do dress for success but there may be vast differences between industry types.

Materials to Bring

A hardcopy or electronic version of your proposal development workbook with the appropriate exhibits and worksheets will be a great confidence builder. Also bring a short video clip or DVD that you can play on your laptop to document the need and the unique qualities you and your institution bring to the solution. Use your battery to power your short two- to three-minute presentation. If the corporate representative asks you to join his or her colleagues in a conference room, ask if you could set up a PowerPoint or video presentation on the corporation's equipment. Make sure you are familiar with and ready to use the corporation's data projection system and have wires to fit anything you may encounter.

What to Discuss with a Corporate Grantor

Review the following topics of discussion and tailor them to your particular situation and prospective corporate funding source. Remember that the purpose of these discussions is to verify the information you gathered through your research and to gain more insight into how to produce a proposal that the prospective grantor will find impossible not to fund.

1. Discuss the need for your project or research and then introduce your solutions. Briefly explain the various approaches you are considering to solve the problem, and then ask if any one approach is preferred over the others. Asking for the corporation's input is often a good way to start.
2. Verify all information you have on the corporation's granting programs and patterns. Show the corporation's representatives that you have looked at their annual reports, or corporate foundation tax returns, by the comments you make and the questions you ask. For example, "I can see from my research that this area is important to your corporation because it represents 50 percent of all your granted projects. My research indicates that your board is very educated and sophisticated in this field. Will they be the group that reads and selects the proposals for approval?"

Corporate Grantor Report Form

Whether you, your advocate, linkage, advisory member, or staff person makes contact with the prospective grantor, make sure that *who* was contacted and *what* was discussed is documented. Complete a Corporate Grantor Report Form (Exhibit 28.2) after each contact with a corporate funding source whether the contact was made in person, over the phone, or through an e-mail.

EXHIBIT 28.2
Corporate Grantor Report Form

Complete one of these forms after each contact with a corporate grantor.

Funding Source: _____

Funding Source Address: _____

_____

Funding Source Contact Person: _____

Telephone Number: _____ Fax: _____

E-mail: _____

Contacted On (Date): _____

Contacted By (Name): _____

Type of Contact: Phone _____ Visit _____

Other (Explain) _____

Objective of Contact: _____

_____

_____

_____

Results of Contact: _____

_____

_____

_____

Follow-up: _____

_____

_____

_____

It is a good habit to place your intentions to contact corporate grantors on your action steps chart (Figure 28.1). Adding this step to your chart will keep you out of trouble with your administration by serving as a visual reminder to obtain permission from your grants office to pursue these corporate opportunities prior to contacting them.

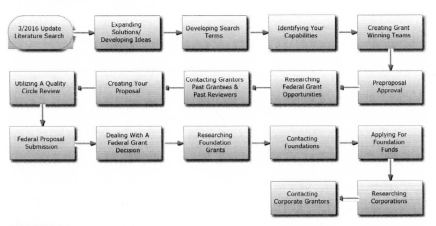

FIGURE 28.1
Action Steps Chart: Contacting Corporate Grantors

29

Applying for Corporate Funds

MANY OF THE CORPORATE GRANTORS you will approach for funding have had experience developing applications for use with government grants and contract procurement programs as bidders and contractors. They have professional teams that put together succinct and well-written proposals, sales and marketing materials, and presentations for their sales prospects. They value e-mail and correspondence that is effectively written. They know that nonprofit organizations and educational institutions do not possess the resources to compete with them. Yet they expect professional approaches. Of all the grantor types, they are probably the most critical and demanding audience you will encounter in your grants quest.

Construct your corporate proposal as outlined in this section, and have a quality circle or mock review of your proposal performed by corporate individuals from your advisory group. While you have chosen to make the nonprofit world your base of operation, you must recognize that your value glasses are different from those who have chosen the for-profit world as their primary frame of reference and that you must adjust your proposal writing style accordingly.

Remember from chapter 26, corporations do not like the "g" word and do not respond well when proposal writers ask them to *give* them funding. Grantseekers targeting corporate funds must use the "i" word for "invest" instead. Considering what you have already learned about corporate self-interest, this should make sense to you. To be successful in the corporate grants marketplace, you must be able to convince the prospective grantor that the company will get a *return on its investment* if it funds your project.

The fact that only a few of the larger corporations have staff members dedicated to contributions or community relations, and that most do not rely on outside readers or peer reviewers to evaluate submitted proposals, means your proposal will probably be read by individuals on the corporate foundation board, the corporate board, research and development types, salespeople, or marketing representatives. Corporate contributions committees are often composed of a mix of these types of individuals.

As with the private foundation marketplace, you will fail miserably if you take the "one size fits all" approach and blanket the corporate community with the same proposal that starts with, "We want _____. Please send money." To make matters worse, the corporations you approach with this method are likely to never forget the poorly developed, mass-produced proposal you submitted to them.

The successful corporate letter proposal follows the same basic order as the proposal to a private foundation. The main components are as follows:

- an introductory paragraph stating the reason for writing
- a paragraph explaining why this grantor was selected
- a needs paragraph
- a solution paragraph
- a uniqueness paragraph
- a request for funds paragraph
- a closing paragraph
- signatures
- attachments, if allowed

Some corporations specify a proposal format and rules on such things as number of pages on their websites. If they specify a short, one-page letter proposal or letter of intent, but provide little in the form of guidance, use the proposal format suggested previously. However, instead of addressing each component in a full paragraph, use just a sentence or two. The key is to identify the problem and how you will close the gap between what is and what should be.

Introductory Paragraph

If you have a linkage to the corporation, use it here. For example:

When this exciting project to increase the technology skills of educators was discussed with Karl Meister, the vice president of your corporate board, he suggested we ask the McGuiness Corporation to consider a role in increasing teacher competencies.

You could also mention a volunteer connection in your opening paragraph. This is a particularly good idea since many corporations will not invest in a local nonprofit organization unless their employees are voluntarily involved with it. Consider using your introductory paragraph to refer to the commitment of their employees to your cause. For instance:

> Ellie Mung, your Region Four supervisor, and I have discussed Karson Computer's role in increasing the performance of our students through the use of applied technology. As chairperson of our school technology advisory committee, Ms. Mung has donated over one hundred hours of time and has been instrumental in making our computer laboratory a reality.

In the case of a research-related project, you might refer to an employee linkage who has served on your advisory committee, given a talk or lecture to your staff or students, served as a mentor, or allowed students to shadow workers to gain insight into the corporate marketplace.

Always check with your linkages before submitting your letter proposal, and provide them with a draft copy of the section that refers to them to be sure that they are agreeable. If you do not have a linkage to which you can refer in the opening paragraph, start your letter proposal by focusing on the grantor.

Why the Grantor Was Selected

This paragraph presents you with another opportunity to express your knowledge about the grantor. The purpose of this section of your letter proposal is to establish that the similarities between what the grantor values and what you and your organization value are why you selected this grantor. Align your organization with the values of the grantor by saying something such as the following:

> As the McGuiness Corporation has become an international leader in innovative technology related to energy conservation, the Hudson Laboratory has dedicated its research to the same field of study.

If it is a corporate foundation, you have access to its Internal Revenue Service (IRS) return (990-PF) and should use it. For instance, if you know that in the past three years the corporate foundation has funded eight projects for over $1 million to assist nonprofits in conserving energy and lowering operating costs, mention it. Unfortunately, corporate contribution grants cannot be tracked. Therefore, you will have little, if any, research from which to work.

Needs Paragraph

This section of your corporate proposal must establish that you have a command of the current knowledge in your field. You must convince the reader–reviewer that you know what exists now in your field of expertise and that you know what needs to happen to close the gap between what is and what should be. The gap provides the reason why your proposal cannot be rejected. If the corporate grantor is truly interested in the area and in contributing toward solving the problem, then that corporate grantor must keep reading your proposal and ultimately fund your project.

The following example illustrates the proposal writer's expertise in the field and identifies the gap.

> The problem is simple. The solution is not. Current accepted theory used to explain the energy expended in the X reaction does not account for Y. The inability to predict Y costs our energy conservation effort billions of dollars in the United States alone.

Make sure that you do not mention your proposed solution or your organization in the needs section of your letter proposal except if you need to make reference to your own studies or findings. One way to ensure that you do not make this mistake is to include a transition sentence or two that enables you to move smoothly from the problem to your solution. For example, "What must be done to address and close this gap? We have developed an innovative solution that provides your corporation with an exciting opportunity."

Solution Paragraph

The purpose of this paragraph is to provide a short summary of the methodology that will be employed to solve the problem. Corporate executives are accustomed to using spreadsheets to analyze the steps and costs involved in planning and evaluating just about everything they do in the corporate world. Therefore, if space allows (you need to be able to submit at least three pages) it is a good idea to include a one-page project planner or spreadsheet (see chapter 15) as page two of your corporate proposal. Refer to this project planning aid as a one-page summary of your more detailed plan. Make mention that you have several more pages of project planners that detail the methods summarized on the page included in your letter proposal and that you would be happy to provide them upon request. Remember that corporate people are likely to ask for more detail, might visit you, and could ask you to come to them. While they may not designate a specific amount of time to grants, they do have an office and a travel budget.

Uniqueness Paragraph

The corporate grantor wants to be assured that you, your organization or institution, and your project are the right investment choice. Most non-profits reflect on their organizations' missions and history when creating this section. While this may work with private foundations to demonstrate commitment to the field of interest, corporate grantors want facts, data, statistics, and examples of winning characteristics. They want to know that you have been a grant winner before. What really matters to them is the breakthroughs your institution, program, or lab have made in the field, and the competency and productivity of your staff. While you may have written the proposal, you will probably not be the individual to sign it. Therefore, it is okay to refer to yourself in this paragraph as the qualified leader to carry out the plan.

Think of this paragraph as part of a corporate marketing brochure. For example, what convinces you to buy a particular product from one company over another? It is probably that company's credibility, the proof that it stands behind its product, and its commitment to quality. These are the same attributes that corporate funding sources want to see in their grantees.

Request for Funds Paragraph

As in all proposals, you must ask for the money. While you may think this is obvious, many corporations have reported that grantseekers sometimes refer to the total cost of the project without ever asking for the specific amount they want from them. If you are targeting a corporate foundation, you have access to its 990-PF IRS tax return and can use the data provided on that form to decide how much to request. However, it is difficult to know how much to request from a corporation that awards grants through a contributions program due to the lack of available public information. If you are unable to decipher an appropriate amount through preproposal contact, you will have to guess. As you learned in chapter 11, most grantseekers think that corporate grants account for 30 to 35 percent of the $335 billion donated per year, when it is actually 5 percent. With this in mind, you might want to scale down your request. Anything over $100,000 is a very large corporate commitment.

If you are forced to divide your project into several fundable pieces, explain that in this paragraph. Also name-drop any of the grantors who have already granted you funds. You and your project are a junk bond until someone else with a good reputation buys in. Then you become a blue-chip stock.

Your project planner should help the corporate decision maker evaluate the appropriateness of your request. If you must present a budget, avoid dedicating a whole page to this purpose. Use a paragraph form budget instead and refer to the column totals on your project planner.

Refer to the return for its investment by dividing the total cost by the number of people the project will serve. In a research proposal, compare the requested amount to the benefits that may occur as a result of answering the research question and closing the gap in the field or knowledge, and suggest what this may lead to in the future. Both of these approaches are quite successful with corporate grantors.

Corporate grantors want to know how you intend to continue a program or project that you will use their grant to initiate. How much will it take to continue this project, and how do you intend to procure that money? For example, the Boeing Company has stated on its corporate website that Boeing's philanthropic strategy is to contribute toward sustainable, measurable growth and self-sufficiency for the organizations with which it partners. This principle has guided its charitable grant contributions.

Closing Paragraph

Do not start this paragraph by stating that you would like to meet with the grantor; the grantor already knows you would. Instead, invite the grantor to meet with you and your key personnel and to visit your institution, organization, laboratory, and so on. Be sure to express your desire to provide any additional information and request that the prospective grantor contact you (or the individual responsible for the project) to provide that information or to answer any questions.

Signatures

Corporate people expect your proposal to be signed by an administrator or officer who holds rank and responsibility within your organization or institution. This is viewed by the corporate grantor as an institutional commitment and endorsement. It is best to have more than one signature. Therefore if possible, include the signature from your consortia partners, which can be impressive to them.

Attachments, if Allowed

While most corporations do not *encourage* attachments, they may be allowed in proposals for research grants. In these instances, project planner spreadsheets detailing your protocol are recommended over text.

Corporate application instructions for other types of grants (nonresearch) will usually restrict the use of any attachments. For example, when applying for a $300,000 grant from the BellSouth Foundation, the application instructions received by my institution specifically stated that letter proposals were restricted to five double-spaced pages of twelve to thirteen characters per inch and that no attachments were allowed. The guidelines also stated that the Foundation would request further information from a select group of applicants from which one-half would be funded. We eventually received a letter stating that our proposal had made the first cut and that of the total two hundred applicants, we were one of the twenty under consideration. Along with that letter came a list of ten questions that the reviewers had regarding our proposal. We were required to answer these questions, limiting our responses to a total of three double-spaced pages. Our $300,000 successful grant consisted of eight double-spaced pages (four single-spaced pages).

Review the fictitious sample corporate proposal in Exhibit 29.1. This sample includes the main components of a letter proposal outlined in this chapter. You are encouraged to develop your own style, but include these integral parts in any letter proposal you submit. Even when provided with an online application or specific guidelines like those in Exhibit 29.2, try to incorporate the concepts suggested in this chapter into your proposal. For instance, in the needs section work in the fact that through your research you are aware of the company's strong commitment to resolving this problem. And, after the section outlining your solution, slip in a few sentences explaining to the prospective corporate funding source why you are a unique grantee, and the best choice to implement the solution.

Just as with foundations, you may want to try this marketplace before you go after federal or state grant funding. If you are able to interest a corporation in supplying your program with equipment or software, you increase your fundability with these other funding sources. Once you have decided that preparing a corporate grant request is going into your plan, place "applying

EXHIBIT 29.1
Sample Letter Proposal to a Corporation

Nancy Owens, Executive Director
Nevada Power Foundation
1374 Chichester Highway
Spurks, NV 87999

Dear Ms. Owen:

Your corporation's support for the Nevada Student Success Fair and your $1 million contribution to the Power Our Students campaign speak louder than words of your concern and commitment to Nevada's students and their success. The board, staff, and volunteers at Nevada Read by 3 share your values for education and tomorrow's workforce.

The latest surveys show Nevada leading the nation in unemployment (nearly 15 percent). In addition, our dropout rate before the current recession placed us in the lowest 20 percent of the United States. With our recent 25 percent cut in education, our dropout rate has gotten worse. In a recent Las Vegas Sun article, Clark County reported the fifth worst graduation rate in the U.S. at 44.5 percent. Experts agree that for recovery to take place in our state we need to access affordable power (your job) and an educated, qualified workforce (our job).

An Alliance for Excellent Education study (funded by the MetLife Foundation) estimated that if Nevada's 15,998 dropouts for the class of 2015 graduated with their class in 2014–2015, their estimated additional lifetime income would have been $4,159,568,400.

Cutting the nation's dropout rate in half would yield $45 billion annually in new federal tax revenue (Columbia University Report). When you compare the cost of dropouts to that of the government bail out of banks, financial institutions, the auto industry, and AIG, you find that all of this is still less than the economic cost of just five years of dropouts in the United States.

How can we break this chain and support both economic and educational change that results in high school completion? *The Nevada Read by 3* program has an answer. We cannot impact all grades in all Nevada schools in three years. But we can implement a program that that has proven effective in K through 3.

Basically, the program:
- Provides teachers with the training and materials they need to help students in K through 3 improve their reading scores.
- Only promotes those third grade early learners who read at the appropriate level.

Many studies on dropouts cite inferior reading skills as one of the main causal factors. The program proposed by *Nevada Read by 3* will provide Nevada teachers at four pilot schools, two urban and two rural, with instruction, materials,

(continued)

EXHIBIT 29.1
(Continued)

mentors, and volunteers to get all of their students to the appropriate reading level. Students who take part in this program will have less disciplinary action, truancies, and problems with the law as they advance to grades 4 through 12.

We are uniquely suited to carry out this model project because we will be working under the guidance of a nationally recognized expert in the field, Dr. Tim Martin of the University of Nevada's College of Education. Dr. Martin will lead our team as the Nevada Power Foundation provides the initial catalyst to demonstrate the change we need. Your phase one funding of $100,000 will provide the start up costs. In years two and three the participating schools will provide a match of 10 percent and 20 percent respectively. Our goal is to eventually have a self-sustaining program that is totally paid for by the schools.

Your name will appear on all materials and on the "Read by 3 Tool Box," as well as on software and all dissemination pamphlets. We have project cost analysis spreadsheets and full budget documentation available on your request. We encourage you and your staff to contact Dr. Martin for any additional material or questions, or to arrange a site visit to our office. Dr. Martin can be reached at [telephone number] or [email address].

Sincerely,

Dr. Thomas Watkins, Executive Director

Nevada Read by 3

EXHIBIT 29.2
J.P. Morgan Chase Philanthropic Grant Programs: Guidelines

How to Apply—U.S.

U.S. Domestic Applicants

To be considered for support, a potential grantee must first submit an online Letter of Inquiry. You will receive an automatic electronic notification after the Letter of Inquiry has been successfully submitted. We will notify your whether or not we are able to consider your proposal for funding at this time.

Questions on the letter of inquiry will include:

A brief description of your organization's
- Mission
- Program/projects
- Program/project budget
- Geography to be served
- Your contact information

If your proposal qualifies for further consideration, you will be asked to complete a full grant application.

Grant applications may be submitted throughout the year. If you received funding in the previous year(s), you will be asked to submit an impact report on use of funds prior to applying for new funding.

The grant application will be evaluated based on the following guidelines:
- Alignment with our pillars of philanthropic giving
- Demonstration of effective organizational, programmatic and financial objective setting and management
- Evidence of broad-based support, with an accounting of funds received from public and private sources
- Description of target population to be served
- Evidence that the service is a response to a valid need, is superior to other competing services and/or encourages collaboration with other organizations for maximum leverage
- Documentation of previous program success or substantial reasons to expect such success in the future.

Required Documents

Your organization's IRS 501 (c) 3 determination letter
Your organization's IRS W9 Form
The organization's most recent audited financial statements
A list of your organization's board members and their affiliations

List of Contact Information by State

for corporate funds" on your action steps chart (Figure 29.1). Where does this step fit in your overall plan?

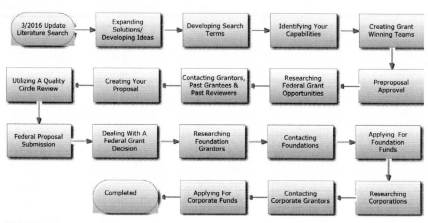

FIGURE 29.1
Action Steps Chart: Applying for Corporate Funds

30

Corporate Proposal Submission, the Decision, and Follow-Up

B EFORE SUBMITTING YOUR PROPOSAL to a corporate grantor, put it through a quality circle (see chapters 16 and 25) that resembles the actual review process as closely as possible. The purpose of this exercise is to get an unbiased first impression of your proposal from individuals who view it from the perspective of enlightened, corporate self-interest.

Ask two or three of your colleagues and two of your advisory committee members from the corporate world, or a professor from your local college's business school to participate. Encourage everyone to role-play being corporate executives. Unless you have information otherwise, inform all participants that the real reviewers will be corporate executives who read your proposal in less than five minutes. They should also be made aware that the real reviewers (the corporate executives) will most likely not follow any specific scoring or rating system and will not provide any comments to the applicants. Therefore, you, the applicant, really need their feedback. Ask your quality circle participants to designate those areas of the proposal they think a corporate executive would like with a plus sign (+) and those areas they think the corporate executives would dislike with a minus (–) sign. Discuss suggestions for improving or highlighting the positive sections and for rewriting the negative sections.

If you are using noncorporate volunteers to perform your quality circle or mock review you will need to remind them that they are role-playing and should not point out what they themselves like or don't like about the proposal. They should critique the proposal from the viewpoint of the corporate executive. The real corporate decision makers may have MBAs or be CPAs and will be concerned about the positioning or public relations value of the grant. (Review chapter 25 and complete Exhibits 25.1, 25.2, and 25.3.)

What makes this review prior to submittal so difficult is the lack of corporate grantor scoring rubrics. Therefore, first inform your mock reviewers what your research has uncovered (see Exhibit 25.1) relative to who and what the corporation has supported and how much those grant awards were. Then apply the foundation values voting technique discussed in chapter 25 to your corporate quality circle or mock review.

It works well to conduct the quality circle in conjunction with an early breakfast or over lunch. The whole exercise should take less than one hour.

Submission

Many of the larger corporate grantors now allow online application and submittal. For the medium and smaller corporations you will likely be sending a print copy of your proposal to the contact person listed in your research. Even when you apply and submit online, print your proposal out to be certain that the font and graphics are not altered. In addition, send a hard copy of your proposal to the funding source just in case it does not receive the electronic version. Submit the proposal a few days before the deadline. When mailing your proposal, require a proof of receipt, and be sure to send it via a carrier that can guarantee delivery like the United States Postal Service, United Parcel Service, or FedEx. As with foundation grant submittals, you could offer to forward a copy of your proposal for each corporate board member.

Also, send copies of your final proposal to your corporate linkages so that they know you finally submitted your proposal and are aware of exactly what you requested. Thank them for the assistance they provided up to this point and for the assistance they may provide in the future to help get your submitted proposal funded.

The Decision

Corporate grantors may communicate only to those to whom they will award a grant. They may not take the time and effort to notify those they reject. In any case, your research will provide you with the dates that the corporate board meets, and from these dates you can approximate when you should hear from the grantor.

Rejected

If you do not hear by six months after the deadline date, your proposal was probably rejected. If you do not receive a rejection letter, you may also receive little to nothing in the way of constructive criticism, redirection of your efforts, or reapplication rules. Some corporate grantors do not allow you to resubmit immediately. For example, I was once told by a corporate foundation that I could not resubmit for three years. Other grantors may advise you never to resubmit due to new restrictions or changes in their priorities and philosophy. Learn what you can from the grantor, your advocates, and your linkages and reapply when it is allowable and advisable.

Even if rejected, send a thank-you letter that acknowledges the time the funding source invested in the selection process, and express your gratitude for its foresight in dedicating profits to impacting these problems and areas of interest. Credit them for their commitment and do not be a sore loser.

Awarded

If your proposal is funded, send a thank-you letter as outlined previously, but include an invitation to visit your institution or organization to see the important work you are conducting and the unique qualities you mentioned in your proposal. You should also request any comments the grantor may have that would help you improve on a future proposal to it or another corporation. However, do not expect a response.

Follow-Up

Whether you are successful or not in your corporate grants quest, try to maintain professional contact. Like you, corporate decision makers are trying to keep up on the advances in your mutual field of interest. Send them an interesting article that your research uncovers, or even an article of yours that is scheduled for publication. Let them know you are alive between the deadline dates. Seek them out at conferences and meetings, and ask them questions about their next grant opportunities.

Persistence and the maintaining of a professional interest in their area of concern will pay off. You will improve your relationship with them and have chances to learn of their upcoming grant priorities. Remember that being persistent is different from being a pest! Keep your relationship focused on the need for your projects and research, and their opportunities for involvement.

The best approach to grantseeking is to develop a long-term and mutually beneficial relationship between you, your organization, and the grantor. This relationship should be based on honesty and a sincere concern for the grantor's needs. Saying thank you is a crucial element in building such a relationship.

31

Putting It All Together to Work for You

E ACH GRANTSEEKER IS UNIQUE in his or her organization and in his or her desire to attract grant funding. Because of this, it is a challenge to create one book that will work for all of you. However, I am confident that you *all* will be rewarded if you practice the strategies outlined in this book. Even when I had a proposal rejected, the grantor confided in me that the board used my proposal before their next meeting to show the members what a well-constructed proposal looked like. He also told me that the board had changed its priorities at that meeting and that there was no way I could have known this in advance.

The proactive grant strategies presented in this book need to be consciously and consistently applied to your grants effort to be effective and efficient. Follow the steps outlined in each chapter and review the figures found at the end of the chapters that diagram the step-by-step process and illustrate the sequence and progression of the steps. Skip any of the steps and your probability of success will be reduced. My grant fellows consistently achieve a 70 percent success rate by sticking to this method.

A major challenge for you is how to integrate grantseeking into your already busy professional life. Like it or not, the realities of life impact your grantseeking. Not only do you have to find the time to accomplish the steps to grants success, but you must also deal with the demands of your jobs. Some of you have administrative and program responsibilities. Others are busy teaching, preparing labs, counseling students, and so on. And what about the personal life you are tying to carry on in between all of this? No wonder self-help books on time management are so popular.

The good news is that the time management techniques outlined in chapter 4 can be applied to *all* areas of your life, and not just to your grantseeking activities. I suggest you apply the time management and organizational techniques you have learned to at least your professional life, so that you can integrate your grantseeking into your job-related, real-world scenario. Put those job tasks that are directly related to your grantseeking into your monthly plan or timeline along with your proactive grants steps. For example, you may be working on a publication that you will need to use as a citation in your problem or needs section of your search of relevant literature. This work can be done simultaneously with your other grantseeking steps during the same month, and you do not necessarily have to finish the publication before you accomplish a step in your proactive grants system. It may not be a publication. It could be a survey that you want to administer, meeting with your advisory group, speaking at a conference, and so on.

One way of keeping track of your grantseeking-related professional tasks and incorporating them with the proactive grants steps outlined in this book is to visualize them on an action steps chart (see chapter 4). Figure 31.1 shows the tasks in the boxes that are occurring simultaneously. Those that are prerequisites or must be completed before others are placed in such a manner that the proper sequencing is readily seen.

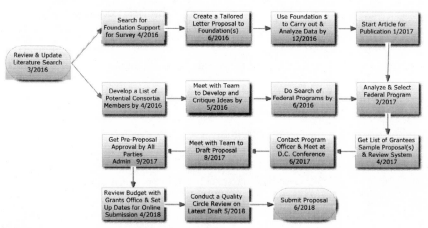

FIGURE 31.1
Action Steps Chart: Sample Plan for Putting It All Together

There is no wrong way to construct or utilize a monthly action steps chart. The process should evolve and be tailored in a way that works best for you. One of my grant fellows made her monthly action steps chart into her screensaver. This way, she is reminded each day of the month of the steps she has planned to take to achieve grants and professional success. It has been my experience that, irrespective of the adaptation of the conceptual framework you apply, you are bound to receive extraordinary benefits by charting the proactive steps to your success.

Take a few minutes to plot out your one- and five-year plans as discussed in chapters 2 and 4. Place grantseeking steps, publications, grants deadlines, conferences, trips to see program officers, and so forth on your proactive grants chart. Success doesn't just occur from random acts. It results from working your plan and to do that you must first have a plan.

The ability to develop grant funding for projects, programs, and research has been critical to my reaching my personal and professional goals. Sharing my formula for success in this book is a great honor and privilege. Plan well, do well, and thank you for purchasing this book.

List of Resources

Y OU MAY WISH TO LOOK AT COPIES of these recommended grant tools before you purchase them. Many of the resources listed include locations where you can find the materials and get assistance from helpful staff. Many institutions have developed joint or cooperative grants libraries to reduce costs and encourage consortium projects.

The list of resources is divided into the following sections:

- Government Grant Research Aids
- Foundation Grant Research Aids
- Corporate Grant Research Aids
- Government, Foundation, and Corporate Grant Resources
- Electronic Resources

GOVERNMENT GRANT RESEARCH AIDS

Tips

1. There are over one thousand federal depository libraries throughout the United States and its territories. All the government publications listed here are available in print copy at these libraries. To locate a federal depository library near you, visit http://www.gpoaccess.gov/libraries.html.

2. Many federal agencies have newsletters or agency publications. You can ask to be placed on their mailing lists to receive these publications. Some are available online.

3. Contact federal programs to get the most up-to-date information.

4. All of the government grant publications listed here are also available through your congressperson's office.

Government Publications

Catalog of Federal Domestic Assistance (CFDA)

The Catalog is the government's listing of federal programs, with details on eligibility, application procedures, and deadlines, including the location of state plans. It is published at the beginning of each fiscal year, with supplementary updates during the year. Indexes are by agency program, function, popular name, applicant eligibility, and subject. Access is free online at http://www.cfda.gov. A hard copy is also at federal depository libraries.

Code of Federal Regulations (CFR)

This is the codification of the general and permanent rules published in the *Federal Register* by the executive departments and agencies of the federal government. Access is free online at http://www.gpoaccess.gov/cfr/.

Congressional Record

The *Congressional Record* covers proceedings and debates of the United States Congress. Access is free online at www.gpo.gov/fdsys. A hard copy is also at federal depository libraries, or for purchase at the Government Printing Office's (GPO) online bookstore at http://bookstore.gpo.gov.

FedBizOpps (Federal Business Opportunities)

A database of federal government contracting opportunities including notices of proposed government procurement actions, contract awards, sales of government property, and other procurement information. Available free online at http://www.fbo.gov.

Federal Register

Published five times a week (Monday through Friday), the *Federal Register* supplies up-to-date information on federal assistance and supplements the

Catalog of Federal Domestic Assistance (CFDA). The *Federal Register* includes public regulations and legal notices issued by all federal agencies and presidential proclamations. Of particular importance are the proposed rules, final rules, and program deadlines. An index is published monthly. It is available for free at www.federalregister.gov. A hard copy is also at federal depository libraries.

Grants.gov

This is the central storehouse for information on over one thousand federal grant programs and access to approximately $500 billion in annual awards. Access is free online at http://www.grants.gov.

United States Government Manual

This is the official handbook of the federal government and provides comprehensive information on the agencies of the legislative, judicial, and executive branches. It is available online for free at http://www.gpo.gov/fdsys. A print copy can be purchased from the U.S. Government Online Bookstore at http://bookstore.gpo.gov. It can also be located in federal depository libraries.

Other Popular Government Websites

Department of Education: www.ed.gov
Department of Housing and Urban Development: www.hud.gov
National Endowment for the Humanities: www.neh.gov
National Institutes of Health: www.nih.gov
National Science Foundation: www.nsf.gov

Commercially Produced Publications

Federal Yellow Book

This directory contains over one thousand pages of federal government listings, including federal government phone numbers, e-mails, addresses and biographical information.
Price: $615.00
Order from:
Leadership Directories, Inc.
1407 Broadway, Suite 318

New York, NY 10018
Phone: (800)627-0311
Fax: (212) 645-0931
Or order online at http://www.leadershipdirectories.com

The Grant Application Writer's Workbook: National Institutes of Health, 2010

This is a guide on how to succeed with new changes at NIH.
Price: $75.00
Order online from:
Grant Writers' Seminars & Workshops LLC
http://www.grantcentral.com/workbooks.html

The Grant Application Writer's Workbook: National Science Foundation FastLane

This workbook deals with how to prepare for FastLane submission of grant proposals.
Price: $75.00
Order online from:
Grant Writers' Seminars & Workshops LLC
http://www.grantcentral.com/workbooks.html

The Grant Application Writer's Workbook: Successful Proposals to Any Agency

This workbook provides information on preparing successful application submittals to agencies other than NIH or NSF.
Price: $70.00
Order online from:
Grant Writers' Seminars & Workshops LLC
http://www.grantcentral.com/workbooks.html

Washington Information Directory, 2014/2015

With more than ten thousand listings, this directory contains contact information for:

- Congress and federal agencies
- nongovernmental organizations

- policy groups, foundations and institutions
- governors and other state officials
- U.S. ambassadors and foreign diplomats

Print edition $175.00; also available in online version
Order hardcover online or request price for electronic version at http://
  cqpress.com
Sage Customer Service
2455 Teller Rd.
Thousand Oaks, CA 91320
Fax: (805)375-5291

FOUNDATION GRANT RESEARCH AIDS

Many of the following research aids can be found through the Foundation Center's Library/Learning Centers and Funding Information Network
partners. If you wish to purchase any of the following Foundation Center
publications, order online at http://www.foundationcenter.org/marketplace
or contact:
  The Foundation Center
  Customer Service
  79 Fifth Avenue
  New York, NY 10003-3076
  Phone: (800) 424-9836
  Fax: (212) 807-3691

The Foundation Directory, March 2014, 2,698 pages

The most important single reference work available on grant-making foundations in the United States, this directory includes information on the ten
thousand largest foundations. Each entry includes a description of giving interests, along with address, telephone numbers, current financial data, names
of donors, contact person, and IRS identification number. Several indexes are
included to help you locate your best leads.
  Price: $215.00
  Order from: The Foundation Center

The Foundation Directory, Part 2, March 2014, 2,234 pages

This directory provides information on ten thousand mid-size foundations.

Price: $185.00
Order from: The Foundation Center

The Foundation Directory Supplement, September 2013

The *Supplement* updates the *Directory* so that users will have the latest addresses, contacts, policy statements, application guidelines, and financial data.
Price: $125.00
Order from: The Foundation Center

Foundation Grants to Individuals, twenty-third edition, July, 2014, 1,752 pages

This directory provides a comprehensive listing of over 9,600 independent and corporate foundations that provide financial assistance to individuals.
Price: $75.00
Order from: The Foundation Center

Private Foundation IRS Tax Returns

The Internal Revenue Service requires private foundations to file income tax returns each year. Form 990-PF provides fiscal details on receipts and expenditures, compensation of officers, capital gains or losses, and other financial matters. These may be viewed online for free at

- foundationcenter.org/findfunders/990finder/
- www.guidestar.org
- www.nozasearch.com

Directories of State and Local Grant Makers

Visit the Funding Information Network closest to you to determine what directories are available for your state and surrounding region. You can also go to http://foundationcenter.org/getstarted/topical/sl_dir.html to obtain a bibliography of state and local foundation directories.

Other Popular Foundation-Related Web Sites:

The Council on Foundations: www.cof.org
The Foundation Center's homepage: www.foundationcenter.org

CORPORATE GRANT RESEARCH AIDS

Corporations interested in corporate giving often establish foundations to handle their contributions. Once foundations are established, their Internal Revenue Service returns become public information, and data are compiled into the directories previously mentioned under Foundation Grant Research Aids.

Corporate contributions that do not go through a foundation are not public information, and research sources consist of :

- information volunteered by the corporation
- product information
- profitability information

The 2011 Corporate Contributions Report

The results of this annual survey include a detailed analysis of beneficiaries of corporate support, but do not list individual firms and specific recipients. The report is based on the 2011 edition of The Conference Board Corporate Contributions Survey.

    Price: Free for members; $395.00 for nonmembers
    Order online from: http://www.conference-board.org/publications
    The Conference Board
    845 Third Avenue
    New York, NY 10022-6600
    Phone: (212) 339-0345, customer service

Dun & Bradstreet's (D & B) Million Dollar Database (MDDI)

This is a subscription-based database available on the Internet. It provides basic data on U.S. companies, such as addresses, ticker symbols, key officers, number of employees, and sales. It also provides brief, searchable executive biographies and titles, listings of international office of U.S. companies, and the ability to download to spreadsheet or print out lists of companies. Also available online from Dun & Bradstreet is the D & B North American Million Dollar Database that provides information on U.S. and Canadian public and private businesses, and the D & B International Million Dollar that provides information on international companies. Call company for pricing.

    The D & B Corporation
    103 JFK Parkway

Short Hills, NJ 07078
(800) 526-9018, customer service

The National Directory of Corporate Giving, nineteenth edition, September 2013, 1,878 pages

This directory provides profiles of 4,160 companies making contributions to nonprofit organizations. It includes 3,212 foundation and grant-making public charities identified by the Foundation Center as established and funded primarily by companies and 1,769 direct corporate giving programs.

Price: $195.00
Order from:
The Foundation Center
79 Fifth Avenue
New York, NY 10003-3076
Phone: (800) 424-9836
Fax: (212) 807-3691
http://www.foundationcenter.org/marketplace

North American Industry Classification System Manual, 2012

Developed for use in the classification of establishments by type of activity in which they are engaged.

Price: printed version $62.00; CD-ROM version with search and retrieval software $79.00
Order online from http://www.ntis.gov/products/naics.aspx
National Technical Information Service (NTIS)
5301 Shawnee Rd.
Alexandria, VA 22312
Phone: (800) 553-6847 or (703) 605-6000
Fax: (703) 605-6900

Who's Who in America, 2015, sixty-ninth edition

This publication is known for its life and career data on noteworthy individuals. The 2015 edition chronicles American leadership with information on approximately ninety-one thousand individuals. It is available in hard copy and on the Internet.

Price: $789.00 for print version; call Kelli MacKinnon at (908) 673-1160 for online pricing

Order print version from:
  Marquis Who's Who
  430 Mountain Ave., Suite 400
  New Providence, NJ 07974-1218
Or online at
  http://www.marquiswhoswho.com

Other corporate-related web sites:
  Business Journal's Book of Lists: www.bizjournals.com
  Corporate Information: http://corporateinformation.com
  Hoovers: www.hoovers.com
  Prospect Research Online: www.iwave.com
  Securities and Exchange Commission (SEC): www.sec.gov

GOVERNMENT, FOUNDATION, AND CORPORATE GRANT RESOURCES

The following newsletters can be purchased from CD Publications. Order by phone at (855)237-1396 or online at www.cdpublications.com.

- *Children and Youth Funding Report:* Coverage of federal, foundation, and private grant opportunities for programs in areas such as public assistance, child welfare, youth crime, juvenile justice, education, mental health, substance abuse, job training, disability services, health care, and other children, youth, and family related areas, $419.00
- *Community Health Funding Report:* Highlights funding sources for a wide range of healthcare concerns, including substance abuse, teen pregnancy, minority healthcare, maternal/child health, chronic illness, mental health and HIV/AIDS programs, $419.00
- *Federal and Foundation Assistance Monitor:* Features a comprehensive review of federal funding announcements, private grants and legislative actions affecting community programs including education, economic development, housing, children and youth services, substance abuse, and health care, $419.00
- *Native American Report:* Contains the latest news from Congress, the courts and federal agencies as well as updates from around the country on developments that could affect tribal interests, $359.00
- *Private Grants Alert:* Provides sources of new private grant opportunities in an online format, $329.00

- *Community Development Digest:* Provides authoritative reports on the community development block grant program (CBDG) as well as covering Congressional legislation, agency regulations, and federal funding/ opportunities for community and economic development, $559.00
- *Housing Affairs Letter:* Contains news affecting public and private housing interests such as federal budget developments, affordable housing concerns, issues surrounding toxic mold, tax credits for builders, and more, $559.00
- *Aging News Alert:* Reports on successful senior programs, funding opportunities, and federal actions affecting the elderly and highlights corporate and foundation grants, $329.00

Schoolhouse Directories and Books

The following directories and books can be purchased from Schoolhouse Partners. Order by phone, by downloading a printable order form, or from Schoolhouse Partners online bookstore at http://shop.schoolhousepartners.net.
Schoolhouse Partners LLC
1281 Win Hentschel Blvd.
West Lafayette, IN 47906
Phone: (765)237-3390

> *Directory of Biomedical and Health Care Grants,* April, 2014, $109.95, 1,098 pages
> *Directory of Grants in the Humanities,* February, 2014, $149.95, 1,192 pages
> *Directory of Research Grants,* August, 2013, $149.95, 1,134 pages
> *Funding Sources for K–12 Education,* September, 2012, $79.95, 768 pages
> *Funding Sources for Children and Youth Programs,* July, 2014, 776 pages
> *Operating Grants for Nonprofit Organizations,* April, 2013, $79.95, 558 pages
> *Funding Sources for Community and Economic Development,* August, 2013, $109.95, 1,192 pages
> *Education Department General Administrative Regulations (EDGAR),* March, 2012, $49.95, 180 pages

Giving USA, 2014

The annual report of philanthropy for the year 2013
Price: $75.00
Order online at www.givingusareports.org

The PRI Directory, July, 2010, 430 pages

This directory deals with the funding of nonprofits via program-related investments (PRIs) and loans by foundations. Often used to support community revitalization, low-income housing, microenterprise development, historic preservation, and human services, this directory lists leading funders, recipients, project descriptions, and includes tips on how to secure and manage a PRI. Published in partnership with PRI Makers Network, the price is $95.00.
Order from:
The Foundation Center
79 Fifth Ave.
New York, NY 10003-3076
Phone: (800) 424-9836
Fax: (212) 807-3691
http://marketplace.foundationcenter.org/publications/directories

ELECTRONIC RESOURCES

There is a wealth of information available through free and subscription online databases and guides. Check with your librarian and your grants office to locate those electronic resources to which you may already have access.

BIG Online America

This is a membership-based keyword and field searchable database with detailed information and profiles on 25,000 foundations, corporate donors, matching gifts programs, in-kind donations, and government grant makers. For information visit http:bigdatabase.com, call BIG Online at (888) 638-2763, or email info@bigdatabase.com.

The Celebrity Foundation Directory, November 2013, 531 pages

This digital publication available in a downloadable PDF format includes descriptions of more than 1,880 foundations started by VIPs in the fields of business, entertainment, politics, and sports.
Price: $59.95
Order from:
The Foundation Center
79 Fifth Avenue
New York, NY 10003-3076

Phone: (800)424-9836
Fax: (212) 807-3691
http://marketplace.foundationcenter.org/publications/directories

Director Connections (beta)

Director Connections (beta) is a mapping product designed to show the user the diverse network connections between foundations and the various boards they sit on. The newest feature in *Director Connections (beta)* is called *Connection Finder*, which allows users to view relationship network maps, starting with the organizations they already know, and lets them explore possible connections with those organizations they want to know. For more information visit http://bigdatabase.com, call (888) 638-2763, or email info@ bigdatabase.com

Foundation Center Digital Grant Guides

The 2014 edition of the digital grants guide series covers fifteen popular subject areas. Each guide includes grant listings and subject, geographic, and recipient indexes as well as keyword—searching tools and links to Foundation Directory Online Free, the Center's free web resource for even more details on profiled funders. The single digital edition version for each guide is available for $39.95. Library wide versions are $99.95. Order from http://marketplace.foundationcenter.org/Publications/Digital-Grant-Guides

- *Grants for the Aging,* 2014 Digital Edition
- *Grants for Capacity Building, Management & Technical Assistance,* 2014 Digital Edition
- *Grants for Community and Economic Development,* 2014 Digital Edition
- *Grants for Environmental Protection & Animal Welfare,* 2014 Digital Edition
- *Grants for Higher Education,* 2014 Digital Edition
- *Grants for Mental Health, Addictions & Crisis Services,* 2014 Digital Edition
- *Grants for Arts, Culture & The Humanities,* 2014 Digital Edition
- *Grants for Children & Youth,* 2014 Digital Edition
- *Grants for Elementary & Secondary Education,* 2014 Digital Edition
- *Grants for Foreign & International Programs,* 2014 Digital Edition
- *Grants for Hospitals & Health Organizations,* 2014 Digital Edition
- *Grants for People with Disabilities,* 2014 Digital Edition

- *Grants for Religion, Religious Welfare & Religious Education,* 2014 Digital Edition
- *Grants for Women & Girls,* 2014 Digital Edition
- *Grants for Services for the Homeless,* 2014 Digital Edition

Foundation Directory Online Plans

The Foundation Directory Online Free is the Foundation Center's only free research tool to find basic information on nearly 90,000 grantmakers. All other online databases are subscription plans and include *The Foundation Directory Online Professional, The Foundation Directory Online Platinum, The Foundation Directory Online Premium, The Foundation Directory Online Plus,* and *The Foundation Online Directory Basic.* The basic subscription allows you to search the nation's largest ten thousand foundations and provides detailed grant maker profiles including trustees, officers, donors, and recent IRS form 990s for $19.95 per month or $195.00 per year. Contact the foundation center at (800) 424-9836 for information and pricing for the other plans or visit https://subscribe2.foundationcenter.org/fdo/signup.

Foundation Grants to Individuals Online

This database includes descriptions of nearly ten thousand foundations and public charity programs that fund individuals for scholarships and fellowships, writer residencies, composing, film, visual and performing arts, academic research and professional support, and emergency medical and financial needs.

Price: One month, $19.95; three months, $36.95; six months, $59.95; one year, $99.95
Order from:
The Foundation Center
79 Fifth Ave.
New York, NY 10003-3076
Phone: (800)424-9836
Fax: (212)807-3691
http://www.foundationcenter.org/marketplace

GrantSelect

GrantSelect is a searchable database of funding opportunities for nonprofits, universities, research organizations and public entities.

To learn more and for pricing information, visit http://grantselect.com or http://schoolhousepartners.net.

Subscribe online or offline by printing out and faxing or mailing the completed subscription form to:

Schoolhouse Partners LLC
1281 Win Hentschel Blvd.
West Lafayette, INC 47906
Phone: (765) 237-3390
Fax: (812) 988-647

GrantsWire

GrantsWire is a subscription-based service that provides subscribers with fifty-two weekly e-mails. Weekly e-mails include summaries of federal, private, and corporate grant opportunities; who's eligible; how funds can be used; and hard-to-find contact information. Each weekly e-mail also includes just announced rules that affect how you operate your grant-funded programs. You can review this product for 30 days.

Subscription Price: $249.00
Order online at www.thompson.com
Thompson Subscription Center
P.O. Box 41868
Austin, TX 78704
Tel. (800)677-3789

Grant Forward

Grant Forward is a subscription based database of funding opportunities containing records on over nineteen thousand federal and private funding opportunities in the sciences, social sciences, arts, and humanities. Users can search for funding opportunities spread across thirty-nine subject areas and 2009 categories. For more information and subscription pricing visit www .grantforward.com.

Cazoodle, Inc.
1800 S. Oak, Suite 204 B
Champaign, IL 61802
(217)864-8378

The Sponsored Programs Information Network (SPIN)

SPIN is a database of federal and private funding sources. The price depends on the institution's level of research and development expenditures. For pricing, more information, or to order, contact:
InfoEd Global
5 Washington Square, Suite 2
Albany, NY 12205-5512
Phone: (800) 727-6427
Fax: (518)713-4201
www.infoedglobal.com

PIVOT

PIVOT is a *Community of Science (COS)* comprehensive database of funding information available on the web. To learn more or to request a free trial visit http://pivot.cos.com/about_pivot

USA.gov

Visit www.usa.gov for links to phone numbers and e-mail addresses for U.S. government agencies and officials

Other Electronic Grant Resources:

The Chronicle of Philanthropy's Guide to Grants, http://www.philanthropy.com/grants

Index

About the Author

David G. Bauer has been a successful grantseeker for forty-five years. His experience in applying winning grants strategies has provided for a successful career as a K–12 educator, college professor, director of development and grants management, and consultant to major nonprofit organizations. Over his career he has trained more than forty thousand individuals seeking grants from a variety of target populations and for many causes. This breadth of experience has enabled him to develop materials that are clear, simple, and easy to apply. He has authored ten books on winning grants and administering grants programs, some having appeared in several editions. He has also developed several videotape series and two software programs in the field.

As president of David G. Bauer Associates, Inc., Bauer is continually developing new techniques, products, and programs to increase grants success. One such program is his highly successful research fellows program that he has conducted at several universities, including the University of Alabama, Wake Forest University, Marquette University, and Western Michigan University. Faculty members in these programs spend a year in intensive grants training and Bauer coaching based on Bauer's tried and proven techniques. A significant increase in grants success has been attributed to these programs, which are based on the techniques presented in *The "How To" Grants Manual*.